The Post-Reform Guide to Derivatives and Futures

Founded in 1807, John Wiley & Sons is the oldest independent publishing company in the United States. With offices in North America, Europe, Australia and Asia, Wiley is globally committed to developing and marketing print and electronic products and services for our customers' professional and personal knowledge and understanding.

The Wiley Finance series contains books written specifically for finance and investment professionals as well as sophisticated individual investors and their financial advisors. Book topics range from portfolio management to e-commerce, risk management, financial engineering, valuation and financial instrument analysis, as well as much more.

For a list of available titles, visit our Web site at www.WileyFinance.com.

The Post-Reform Guide to Derivatives and Futures

GORDON F. PEERY

WILEY

John Wiley & Sons, Inc.

Published by John Wiley & Sons, Inc., Hoboken, New Jersey.
Published simultaneously in Canada.

For general information on our other products and services or for technical support, please
contact our Customer Care Department within the United States at (800) 762-2974, outside
the United States at (317) 572-3993 or fax (317) 572-4002.

Wiley also publishes its books in a variety of electronic formats. Some content that appears in
print may not be available in electronic books. For more information about Wiley products,
visit our web site at www.wiley.com.

ISBN 978-0470-55371-8 (cloth); ISBN 978-1118-20540-2 (ebk);
ISBN 978-1118-20541-9 (ebk); ISBN 978-1118-20542-6 (ebk)

Printed in the United States of America.

10 9 8 7 6 5 4 3 2 1

To Pamela and Andrew, Allison, David,
and the rest of the Peery family:
For their love and support each day.
Also to David Perry, Jonathan Yarowski, Andrew Petersen,
Anthony Nolan, Michael Caccese, Donald Moorehead,
Richard Bendit, Richard Jones, Mac Dorris, John Vogel,
Thomas Phelps, Bill Quicksilver, Ted Latty, Steve Molitor,
and finally Susan Ervin: For professional opportunities
in large law firms for over 15 years
in finance, in general,
and futures and derivatives, in particular.

Contents

Preface

There is nothing more difficult to carry out, nor more doubtful of success, nor more dangerous to handle, than to initiate a new order of things.

—Machiavelli

The derivatives market is the largest and most important financial market in the world and has been for some time. Regardless of whether we realize it, many of us use derivatives and we benefit from their use. Yet these financial instruments are frequently misunderstood and over the years have been the target of widespread criticism.

Following the 2008 market crises, derivatives were the subject of historic reform. Although certain aspects of that reform were necessary, others appear to be based on a firmly-held belief by a few influential policymakers that derivatives were public enemy number one. Judging from their reform initiatives in the derivatives area, they must have believed that derivatives were bad for society. This belief is far from reality.

An absurd reality, actually, is the fact that, even though derivatives are critically important to our local and world economies and therefore to our society, relatively few people have a clear understanding of these financial instruments, their surprisingly widespread use and the exceedingly limited role which the vast majority of derivatives played in the 2008 market crises. This reality served as an important catalyst for this book and www.DerivativesGuide.com.

Another catalyst for this book was a sudden, dramatic sea change in global markets that took place just as I submitted this book for publication.

Market participants appeared to have abandoned ship in many respects when it came to investing in traditional stock markets. In summer and early fall of 2011, we saw a historic development as investors worldwide withdrew well over $90 billion from traditional equity investments according to EPFR Global.[1] This startling development not only reflects a loss of faith in traditional markets and investments, but it also suggests the need for investors to use derivatives to take advantage of market volatility, which I believe caused the widespread flight from traditional investments in the first place. Where there is volatility, the practice of derivatives absolutely *thrives*.

Derivatives offer creative, flexible, and even ingenious ways to profit in markets fraught with volatility, and contrary to some investors' perceptions, many have taken advantage of these powerful financial tools to do exactly that. Even as U.S. and other regulators dramatically expand derivative regulation, derivative use has *increased*, according to a report by the U.S. Comptroller of Currency[2] during the global investor flight from equity markets.

However, without proper public and private controls and monitoring, and, of course, without at least a baseline understanding of derivatives by the market and the new law that governs derivatives, investors will understandably be reluctant to fully utilize these powerful tools. Many must first overcome fear, and then develop a foundation for understanding derivatives and the new derivative marketplace, and this book is designed to facilitate that development.

Derivatives should not be intimidating, but they are to many; yet they are all around us, an indelible part of our everyday decision making and economies at all levels. They are impossible to remove and therefore will remain in our everyday life until the end of time, just as they existed in the beginning of time, as we shall see in the history of derivatives provided in Chapter 8.

Derivatives come into play in basic, everyday life decisions ranging from ordering pizza for delivery at dinnertime to locking-in oil prices to bolster the bottom line of a major multinational corporation (as we shall see, these are examples of a forward and a future, respectively; both are derivatives). Ninety-four percent of Fortune 500 companies use derivatives[3] and of those companies, many use derivatives to manage risks posed by fluctuations in interest rates and foreign exchange rates.

Derivatives are also currently used to combat hunger and malnutrition in lesser-developed countries, as demonstrated in the Introduction.

The prices of virtually everything that we buy, every day, would be higher, were it not for basic hedging strategies which have been put in place by companies throughout the world—companies which must now contend with comprehensive derivatives regulation not only in America, but in other nations using U.S. derivatives reform as their guide since 2010.

This all began in the summer of 2010. Derivatives law and market practice began to change in historic ways on July 16, 2011, when much of Title VII of the Dodd-Frank Wall Street Reform and Consumer Protection Act took effect in the United States. Title VII is dedicated to the reform of the

U.S. derivatives market. This law brought about a complete transformation of the over-the-counter (OTC) derivatives market in the United States and caused reverberations in OTC derivative markets throughout the financial world, as representatives from all G-20 leading industrialized nations committed to settle OTC derivatives by the end of 2012 in a way that is dramatically different from the way these financial tools have been settled in the past. As a result, *almost nothing* in the life cycle of an OTC derivatives trade will be the same as it once was.

Given the widespread use of derivatives and the thick and heavy blanket of new regulation (which some rather naively hope or believe will completely smother the use of derivatives), the need to develop an understanding—or at least to take the first steps toward an understanding—of derivatives has never been greater.

This book is intended to meet that need by providing straightforward descriptions of derivatives and the markets in which they trade, and a guide to the law that now, after July 16, 2011, governs their use in America.

This book is distinctly different from other books on derivatives and futures in a few important respects. First and foremost, it explains derivatives in plain terms with an eye toward developing a greater understanding by a wide swath of our society, from investors, executives, directors, teachers, policy makers, and lawyers to people taking the first steps in their study of this important area of finance.

Although this book is not an advanced treatment on derivatives, derivatives math, or theory, it does enable experienced practitioners to understand or confirm their view of the derivatives mandates in the United States after 2011.

So whereas many books on this complicated subject area require a baseline of knowledge or experience in modern finance, this book does not. The focus of some books is exclusively on one category or family of derivatives. This book describes all or nearly all categories of derivatives. The law on derivatives and industry practice changes frequently, and this guide seeks to capture and describe many of those changes in an understandable way.

This book consists of the following four parts.

Part One sets the foundation by identifying critical developments in public policy, law, and the evolution of financial products that made the 2008 market crises inevitable.

Part Two, the heart of the book, is a summary of early derivative reform efforts. Because comprehensive reform legislation first passed in the United States, the part begins with a description of the futures model which is inherent in U.S. reform and then discusses the transformation and use of this model in other derivatives markets throughout the world.

To enable the reader to see the fundamental changes in the derivatives market, Part Three provides a before and after picture of the market. It begins with a panoramic, historical survey of these products, the market, and derivatives law from practically the beginning of recorded history to the 2008 market crises. As we will see in Chapter 8, derivatives have long been in frequent use because, where there is risk, there also is a need for derivatives. Ancient clay tablets record derivative transactions that are in some ways similar to those which trade electronically today. History is important; however our focus is the post-reform world in which we now live.

A few basic assumptions, or principles, guide this book: First, the law and market practice in this area continue to evolve on a *daily* basis and, for that reason alone, no single book can or should be relied upon as anything other than a snapshot in time of an exceedingly fluid legal and business environment. The reader should not rely on this book as the definitive—or last word—on derivatives, futures, and the complex, multifaceted body of law governing these subjects. As this text went to print, some Republicans in Congress drafted legislation that undercuts key pillars of Title VII, so the law continues to show signs of evolution.

Another basic assumption about the contents of this book is that derivatives require qualified professional counsel. Nothing in this text is, or should be viewed as legal advice, or counsel, on trading strategies or anything else relating to futures or derivatives. Readers are strongly encouraged to consult with a licensed and qualified professional when reviewing, negotiating, and trading any derivative or future. Because the derivatives practice relies upon myriad laws and regulations in the tax, bankruptcy, litigation, finance, and several other disciplines, only the most experienced, licensed professionals who are privy to the reader's specific circumstances should be relied upon for suggestions, advice, or legal counsel, which, again, is not provided or intended to be provided in this text. Neither the publisher nor the author of this work, nor any other person, company, or firm bears any liability for this book or any of its contents or inferences from its contents. The opinions expressed in this text are those of the author alone, and any error or omissions in this book is solely the author's.

Finally, the theory underlying this work is one which posits that because humans are basically good, the greater the number of people who truly understand derivatives and their *utility*, (as opposed to people who use these financial instruments merely for profit), the greater the propensity for the productive use of derivatives in our society.

GORDON F. PEERY

NOTES

1. Tom Lauricella, "Pivot Point: Investors Lose Faith in Stocks." *Wall Street Journal*, September 26, 2011.
2. Comptroller of the Currency, "OCC's Quarterly Report on Bank Trading and Derivatives Activities" Second Quarter 2011.
3. Laurin C. Ariail, "Group of Thirty Survey," in "The Impact of Dodd-Frank on End-Users Hedging Commercial Risk in Over-the-Counter Derivatives Markets," North Carolina Banking Institute (March 2011), www.Law.Unc.Edu/Documents/Journals/Articles/925.pdf.

Acknowledgments

I am deeply grateful for a wonderful group of individuals who made this book possible. At the top of the list is my wife Pamela and children Andrew, Allison, and David. Each gave me the time which I needed to complete this book during an exceedingly challenging and exciting period in our modern financial history.

I am also grateful for my friend Dr. Fabrice Douglas Rouah, co-author of *Option Pricing Models and Volatility Using Excel/VBA* (Wiley 2007), whose ideas during a lengthy bike ride one Saturday in 2009—which he led for most of the way, I might add—in turn led me to John Wiley & Sons and the process culminating in the publication of this book.

I would also like to extend my sincere thanks to the excellent guidance and work by the team at the first-rate publisher John Wiley & Sons, led by Bill Falloon, Meg Freeborn, and Donna Martone, as well as their excellent, patient editorial colleagues and the broader production and marketing teams.

Additional sincere, heartfelt thanks goes to the voluntary, prudent, and cautious editorial assistance of eight partners within the global law firm K&L Gates LLP: Trevor Beadle, who read most of my manuscript, Andrew Petersen (a close friend from years ago, and one of Great Britain's and Europe's leading commercial real estate subordinated debt and securitization practitioners), Larry Patent and Charley Mills (two of the finest futures experts in the market), Philip Morgan, Eric Freedman, Susan Gault-Brown, Howard Goldwasser, Carol Derk of Borden Ladner Gervais LLP (BLG is a full-service Canadian law firm and Carol is a leading derivatives practitioner in Canada who assisted in the shaping of Canadian derivatives law, regulation, and practice) and others who assisted in the review of this book including, at K&L Gates, Carol Terzes, and Sonia Walters (in the graphics and document services departments of K&L Gates).

This may perhaps read like an Academy Award speech and as I've certainly won nothing, the point is that the production and publication of a manuscript such as this in a very busy, fluid statutory and regulatory environment is simply is not possible without the valuable contributions from each of these fine people. Their work is greatly appreciated.

G. F. P.

Introduction

THE CRISES

In 2008, the world began to experience financial devastation of historic proportions. The World Bank estimates that the 2008 market crises resulted in the impoverishment of 64 million people.[1] 2009 was the first year since World War II in which the world economies were officially in recession.[2]

In the United States, statistics from early 2011 indicated that 26 million Americans were out of work and $11 trillion in household wealth vanished at least partially as a result of the financial crisis.[3]

Certainly the world experienced financial crises in the past. From 1970 to 2008, there were 124 systemic banking crises, 208 currency crises, 63 sovereign debt crises, 42 twin crises, 10 triple crises, a global economic downturn around every decade throughout that period, as well as oil, food, and energy price shocks.[4]

The 2008 market crises were different. In the investment world, the crises were like a long, sustained shock to the system, over many trading days and for several weeks at a time. Investors' paper losses in U.S. stocks totaled $8.4 trillion in the year since the market peak in 2007. One manager summed it up this way: "There has never been anything close to what we are experiencing now. . . . Maybe one day in 1987 was close, in terms of absolute riot. But this is happening every day."[5]

This was not just about monetary losses. Some see the precipitous fall of a world power. The recession dealt a psychic blow to the United States both at home and abroad, as at least one commentator in the United States wrote after the fall of Lehman Brothers, in September 2008:

> *But the scary thing is not what will happen to individuals—although a jobless, miserable mess is a very sullen thought—but what this economic crash says about America. Anyone who is too drunk with despair (or drink) right now knows that this all signals a bigger realignment, that our place—our significance—in the world is diminishing. Eight years of this wastrel, spendthrift administration has bankrupted us of our standing and our capital—it's all*

1

gone. Apparently on Wall Street, the bankers now have a saying: "Dubai, Shanghai, Mumbai or goodbye." The future is no longer here. . . . The American century from World War II on—really only about 60 years old—has been a very good time for everybody. The world is about to be a much sorrier place.[6]

Overseas commentary views the fall of Lehman Brothers as emblematic of the fall of America:

There's certainly an idea that the American financial system has gone crazy [indicates Elie Cohen, director of research at the Center for Political Research at the Paris Institute of Political Studies and a member of the Counsel for Economic Advisers]. This has dealt a mortal blow to the timid admiration we had of the American system. But not even the most conservative French person is capable of defending it anymore.[7]

Many believe that derivatives that large firms such as Lehman Brothers entered into caused the 2008 market crises. It is clear that Lehman was an exceedingly active participant in the over-the-counter (OTC) derivatives market. Lehman was a party to 1.7 million derivative transactions.[8] The problem is that few clearly understand derivatives, the role that they played in the crises and the resulting reform.

Following each of the preceding market crises, we saw commitments to reform the system, or at least parts of the system. However, the reform efforts following the 2008 market crises are historic both in geographic breadth and substantive depth. None of the previous crises and resulting reform entailed the global rethink that was launched by governments of the largest economies after the fall of Lehman Brothers and the subsequent market crises. This text is focused on that rethink and reform.

THE GLOBAL RESPONSE

In response to these global financial crises, governments throughout the world first infused hundreds of billions of various currencies into banks and other derivative counterparties. Taxpayers in many countries will ultimately bear the repayment burden for decades for this unprecedented financial outlay. Many blame derivatives.

The belief that derivatives have played a role in the failures of markets over the recent years has given rise to an uncoordinated, sometimes misguided international effort to regulate OTC derivatives and the counterparties which trade them. Distrust is rooted in more than a few of the regulatory initiatives that legislators presented after the 2008 market crises.

The proper framework for reforming derivative markets starts with drawing an analogy that compares derivatives to fire. Wildfires destroy vast stretches of nature. Fires in more urban settings have leveled villages and devastated cities such as Chicago, San Francisco, and elsewhere. In the history of derivatives provided in Chapter 8, a case is made for comparing the 2008 damage caused by derivatives to the destruction caused by fire. Derivatives, like fire, have tremendous utility but exceedingly great potential for destruction.

Those who take the time to understand derivatives will find these financial tools to be rather straightforward. Then, distrust may be put in its proper place. One of the realizations that the reader will have while reading this book is that the most complex derivatives may be deconstructed into manageable parts. The roles played by those parts and the utility of the functions will become self-evident. Our starting point is the simple question: What is a derivative? What is a future?

WHAT ARE DERIVATIVES AND FUTURES?

Derivatives and futures are financial instruments whose value is derived from something else, such as an asset, an index, an event, or even the weather or movie box-office receipts. Like insurance, derivatives are contracts between a party that pays to assume a certain risk, and a counterparty that buys protection against that risk.

Futures contracts, or futures, are standardized derivatives traded on an exchange; they are financial products that come within the broader category of derivatives. Similar to insurance, if there is no insurer collecting premiums then there is no insurance; so with derivatives, if there are no derivatives speculators to receive a fee for speculation, hedging risk is not possible.

Some say that derivatives are nothing more than gambling. Just as we generally do not consider insurance underwriting to be gambling, derivatives transactions should not be labeled as gambling (many derivatives provide financial insurance, and those who provide that insurance are not gamblers; they incur risk and need to be paid for doing so).

One of the key themes within this text is that the world is a far better place with derivatives than without. The utility of derivatives as described in this book helps the reader understand this. The long history of derivatives also brings into sharper focus the dire, legitimate need for derivatives and their sustained use over time. To illustrate, we travel to Malawi, Africa.

Malawi, a land-locked country in the eastern part of Southern Africa, is home to an estimated 14 million people, and nearly all reside in rural areas.[9] The people of Malawi are generally engaged in smallholder subsistence agriculture (including maize production) that is critically dependent on rainfall. Maize, which English-speaking countries of course call corn, is and has been as vital to human sustenance and our economies over the years as any other foodstuff, and this is particularly true for the people of Malawi. A severe drought there in 2005 necessitated hundreds of millions of dollars in international aid for chronic and widespread malnutrition.

The government of Malawi approached the World Bank for programmatic assistance to lessen the adverse financial and human impact of severe droughts.

Among the financial relief that the World Bank provided was a straightforward derivative known throughout the world as an option. The World Bank, which, as we will see in Chapter 8, was a pioneer in over-the-counter derivatives, entered into options with the government of Malawi from 2008 to 2011. These options were index-based weather derivatives, whose basic structure is illustrated in Figure I.1.

In the illustration, the government of Malawi enters into a put option, which we dissect not only in Figure I.1 but in our survey of derivatives in Chapter 10. The Malawi put provides the government with access to a payout if an ingenious, model-driven index on which the put option is based falls below a certain negotiated level.

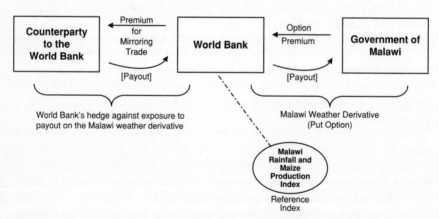

FIGURE I.1   The Anatomy of the World Bank–Malawi Weather Index

The idea of basing a derivative—such as an option—on an index is certainly not new, and these options are ubiquitous. The option is a derivative that *derives* its value from something referenced in the financial tool: in this case, an index.

The index that serves as the underlier of the Malawi weather option includes thresholds that are set by a national maize yield assessment model used by the Malawi Meteorological Office since 1992 for forecasting maize production in Malawi.[10] Data from 20 rainfall stations is collected and integrated in the model, which produces index levels which reflect the impact of the timing, amount, and distribution of rainfall during the maize growing season.[11] The index links rainfall to maize production and numerical values are the product, which in turn provides something of a measuring stick for maize production in a way that is useful to the put option entered into between Malawi, the holder of the option, and the World Bank, the writer of the option.

Malawi pays a premium to exercise its right to a payout under the option. Donors and the U.K. Department of International Development (DFID), which provided budgetary support for the derivative, subsidize the premium.[12] Upon payment of the option premium, Malawi is the *holder* of an option giving it the right to a payout during a one-year, extendable option term. The World Bank is the *writer* of the option.

If precipitation falls below a certain level, the index will then reflect a projected loss in maize production. Under the terms of the 2009 to 2010 option, if maize production in Malawi, as gauged by the index, fell significantly below the historical average, then the option would give Malawi a payout of $4.4 million.[13] In 2009 to 2010, Malawi agreed to use any payout from the option to lock in the price of maize imports before market price increases for maize resulted from the drought.[14]

Simultaneous with the writing of a put option, the World Bank entered into a mirroring trade with a counterparty from Wall Street or other major markets, and paid a premium for the counterparty assuming the risk of the payout to Malawi, thereby hedging against put-option-payout risk. Presumably, the premium paid by World Bank to its mirroring trade counterparty (to the left in Figure I.1) was less than the premium paid by Malawi to the World Bank. The World Bank effectively transfers payout risk to its counterparty on the mirroring trade.

In this way, a classic derivative, a put option, provided the government of Malawi coverage or protection against a specific risk. The derivative was one of a range of impressive financial products designed to offset adversity and risk—in this case drought. Derivatives may be customized to address particular needs of each end user, in this case Malawi.

The derivatives trade is fascinating not only because it is the business of buying and selling risk, but also because it is an inherently creative line of work. It is filled with utility, as the Malawi weather derivative illustrates.

Derivative markets are among the largest of any financial market today, in part because there are no bounds to creating and trading derivatives. There is nothing that cannot be the basis of a derivative. A derivative may be created (and has been created) to hedge against a downturn in a housing market. Derivatives based on weather patterns have existed for years.

In perhaps more familiar terms, when an executive's compensation is based on the issuance of call options to have the right to purchase stock of a company, that executive holds a derivative, an option. As we will see in the first part of Chapter 8, the earliest derivatives were options and other contracts to purchase something in the future, such as grain. These are called *forwards*. Forwards are as fundamental to the economy as traditional cash purchases.

If a forward is traded on an organized exchange, it is called a future, or a futures contract. A future is a contract entered into by one person who wants to sell something to the other party to the contract, the buyer. When the buyer and seller enter into the contract, they agree on a price, quantity, and some point of time in the future to exchange whatever it is that is the subject of the contract.

A futures contract differs from a forward. Whereas a forward can be entered into between two parties in an informal way, without any established market and for any quantity of goods, a futures contract is a standardized contract that is traded on an exchange and cleared through a clearinghouse. The clearinghouse requires collateral to ensure the performance of the parties to the futures contract. Each facet of a forward and futures contract will be discussed in this book.

Unlike a cash purchase at the counter of a grocery store, many modern derivatives and futures are not financial tools for exchanging something that can be eaten or placed on a shelf, although futures contracts can and sometimes do result in the delivery of a physical commodity. More often than not, no physical commodity is exchanged and the parties, instead, enter into these arrangements to manage the risk of something happening (such as a price increase).

Within the field of finance, derivatives are the most dynamic instruments because they have no limits unless the parties, markets, or governments set them. These tools are frequently not based on the availability of cash or hard assets, and they have for decades existed in a largely unregulated trading arena. Derivative transactions are prompted by a range of economic motivations.

WHY TRADE DERIVATIVES AND FUTURES?

People trade derivatives and futures to speculate for profit or manage risk. Chapter 8 tells the history of derivatives and describes in detail how derivatives have been used and the attempts by governments over the years to regulate that use.

Derivatives trading is an extremely lucrative profession that is attractive to many. One derivatives dealer in the early formative days of credit derivatives provides this account:

> *From 1993 to 1995, I sold derivatives on Wall Street. During that time, the seventy or so people I worked with in the derivatives group at Morgan Stanley in New York, London, and Tokyo generated total fees of about $1 billion—an average of almost $15 million a person. We were arguably the most profitable group of people in the entire world. My group was the biggest moneymaker at the firm by far. Morgan Stanley is the oldest and most prestigious of the top investment banks, and the derivatives group was the engine that drove Morgan Stanley. The $1 billion we made was enough to pay the salaries of most of the firm's 10,000 worldwide employees, with plenty left for us. The managers in my group received millions and millions in bonuses; even our lowest level employees had six-figure incomes. And many of us, including me, were still in our twenties.*[15]

Aside from the sheer attraction of profit, business enterprises and traders are drawn to derivatives and futures to manage risk, or hedge. Derivatives are also used to speculate. Two examples bring these fundamental motivations—to speculate or hedge—into sharper focus.

A farmer enters into a contract for the payment for crops as they are planted, with a promise to deliver those crops at some specified later point, after the harvest. The farmer gets paid in advance for crops that will be delivered at some point in the future.

This transaction is a forward. Without a forward, early markets such as Chicago, Illinois would get flooded with commodities after the harvest; forwards provided price support for people, such as farmers, who played critical roles in the more agrarian economies. Within the category of forwards, there are prepaid forwards, in which the farmer is paid, up front, for his crops. Most forwards call for payment and the exchange of goods for the payment simultaneously at some later time, such as six months after the contract is entered into by the farmer and his counterparty. Our farmer may seek this arrangement because he or she wants to lock-in in a payment price in a way that protects the farmer against a possible drop in the price of crops due to oversupply or other factors, such as inadequate storage. The purchaser gets crops at a guaranteed rate; perhaps the purchaser is of the view that the price for the crops will increase.

Real estate developers manage interest rate risk through interest rate swaps. In our second example, a bank provides a loan to the borrower/developer through a credit facility, but charges the developer who borrows under that facility interest on a floating rate of London Inter-Bank Offered Rate (LIBOR) plus 2 percent (LIBOR fluctuates over time). If the interest rate increases over the term of the loan, the developer pays more than if the interest is fixed. To convert that floating-rate loan that is borrowed by the developer to a fixed-rate loan, the developer will turn to a derivatives provider, or a dealer, and pay a fixed amount, similar to a premium for an insurance policy. The dealer will in turn pay the developer whatever LIBOR is over the term of the loan. The dealer remits that payment to the borrower, and the borrower tenders that payment to the bank that provided the loan.

In these two straightforward examples, both the real estate developer and the farmer are protected against adverse changes over time: The farmer locks-in a fixed amount for crops, and the developer transforms a floating interest obligation by, in essence, converting it into a fixed rate product, thereby managing interest rate risk.

The counterparties that enter into separate trades with the farmer and developer take the opposite view: The buyer of the farmer's crops believes that the price for the crops will increase (the farmer is concerned about a crop price decrease and may want the purchase price paid in advance), and the real estate developer is concerned that rising interest rates will drive up his monthly debt service. The provider of the interest rate swap may very well take the view that interest rates will fall. The developer gets a fixed rate from the dealer. The swap obligates the dealer to pay a "floating" obligation. Both the farmer and real estate developer hedge their risks with parties that speculate with respect to those risks.

Derivatives and the markets in which these financial instruments trade have existed in various forms since the beginning of recorded history. In the past 30 years, derivatives have become a pillar of financial markets throughout the world. The Bank of International Settlements estimated that the global OTC derivatives market in 2009 accounted for $615 trillion in notional value.[16] Although this figure makes the derivative market the largest financial market in the world, few understand these instruments, the markets, or even what "$615 trillion in notional value" means. Without that understanding—which this book is designed to provide—many have unjustifiably blamed derivatives for destroying the world, or, more precisely, parts of the world economy from 2007 to 2008.

DID DERIVATIVES DESTROY THE WORLD ECONOMY IN 2008?

The short answer is a clear no. Like fire, which was responsible for destroying nature and urban locales such as major American cities in the nineteenth century, however, derivatives are a force to be reckoned with, and without proper handling, the destructive power of derivatives is almost without bounds. If fire is not carefully guarded, destruction results. Fire, like a derivative, is not evil or a public enemy, but is a powerful force which must be closely guarded and used carefully.

In September and October 2008, when purchasers and dealers of derivatives and other financial products experienced severe liquidity problems, the markets fell dramatically or seized altogether:

- The MSCI World Index of 23 developed markets fell almost 7 percent for the first time in two decades.
- Britain's FTSE 100 Index was down 7.9 percent.
- Germany's DAX lost 7.1 percent.
- France's CAC 40 fell 9 percent.
- Trading was suspended in Russia after the RTS stock index experienced a decline of 20 percent.
- Trading in six bank stocks in Iceland was also halted.[17]

In the face of this adversity, governments throughout the world devised recovery initiatives to stimulate their economies in order to prop-up struggling banks and other key financial institutions that played a role in those economies. Targets of media criticism ranged from government officials to originators of mortgages with various other participants in the market. Of these targets, those frequently cited in the media are users of derivatives.

The market crises that culminated with the bankruptcy of Lehman Brothers resulted in the greatest worldwide reform movement in the history of finance. This reform affects every stage of the derivatives life cycle, from creation and marketing to the trading of products by phone, text messages, and e-mail, to licensure and registration of swap dealers, to real-time reporting, to back office and post-trade activities, to clearing and settlement. Although the reform continues, it is unclear to many in the market what will be required and when. The chapters which follow are designed to provide clarity.

HOW WILL REFORM CHANGE THE DERIVATIVES TRADE?

In Part One of this text, we begin with the causes of the market crises, which led to dramatic reform measures in the derivatives space. Chapter 1 makes the case that many reformers believed that most, if not all, derivatives were to blame for causing the 2008 market crises. This belief was wrong.

What the reformers did in fact see was an interconnected derivatives market, which, due entirely to the way in which many derivatives trade, developed over time to look something like the illustration in Figure I.2.

In Figure I.2, each party to a derivative entered into a mirroring derivative with a counterparty in the same way that the World Bank entered into a derivative simultaneous to its writing a put option to the government of Malawi to lay-off the put option payout risk. The mirroring trade entered into by the World Bank may be found on the left side of Figure I.1 and the World Bank's put option is on the right. The counterparty to the World Bank receives a premium from the World Bank in exchange for bearing the World Bank's risk of the put option payout. As derivatives are formed

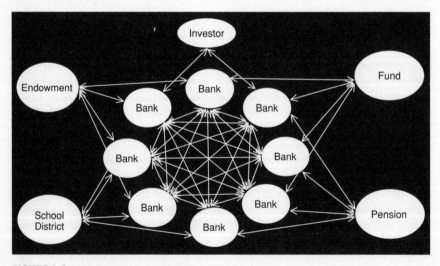

FIGURE I.2   An Interconnected Derivatives Market

and entered into, not one and not two, but myriad additional derivatives result. So, as the different end users (illustrated in the diagram[18] found in Figure I.2, including a range of funds, investors, public entities such as school districts, and also pensions and endowments) enter into derivatives, they and their counterparties also simultaneously, or almost simultaneously, enter into mirroring derivatives, creating not only a web of interconnected transactions, but massive "notational" values within the market.

The dynamic created by mirroring derivative trades has existed for some time; however, in a time of market crises or seizure, when one party fails, the interconnected network experiences a cascading series of failures, jeopardizing the entire financial system, and that is precisely what regulators feared. We carefully pick apart this phenomenon in Chapter 1, which discusses it as a cause of the 2008 market crises, and later in Chapter 3, which explains how the futures model of trading and the futures market were to the regulator a silver bullet for the 2008 market crises.

Reformers, seeing the problem of interconnectivity discussed in the following chapter, are bringing about a completely transformed market structure that resembles the structure in Figure I.3.

When the reader glances at Figure I.2 and its interconnected web, and compares that schematic with the diagram in Figure I.3, he or she is able to grasp the dramatic change in derivatives market structure which is previewed in Chapter 3 and then described in Chapter 9: Market Structure Before and After 2010.

Chapter 3 provides a detailed description of each part of the futures market structure, its historical evolution, functions, and widespread use. The chapter also explains how, during the 2008 market crises, the futures model and structure performed well but, as with every design, there are real and potential flaws—and the reader needs to know about them.

Much of this text is devoted to helping the reader understand the derivatives reformers' belief that the futures market, with each of its component parts depicted in Figure I.3, will prevent future market crises in which derivatives play a role.

In Figure I.3, one critically important component part of the futures market stands in the middle of the entire market: the central clearinghouse. The central clearinghouse, or CCP, requires that only financially fit and risk-monitoring members transact directly with the CCP, and act as a buffer against risk-taking market participants, such as those depicted in Figure I.3: an investor, four funds, a county within a state, and a school district. (All of these entities, including five Wisconsin school districts which in 2006 entered into the most complex derivative, the collateralized debt obligation,[19] have taken exceedingly great risks and lost massive amounts, are described in Chapter 8.) Many of these market participants may still remain in the

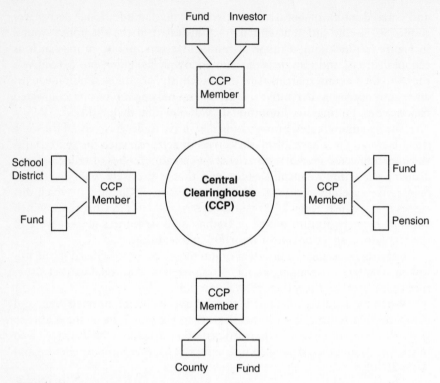

FIGURE I.3   The Futures Market Structure

pre-reform market depicted in Figure I.1 for some time with respect to customized, non-standardized derivatives after derivatives reform mandates are implemented in the timeline suggested in Chapter 2.

After the introduction to the futures model in Chapter 3, Chapter 4 describes the U.S. federal mandate calling for the implementation of that model, and Chapter 5 describes the U.S. government's authority to financially rescue entities that play vital roles and are too big to fail. Chapter 6 gives the reader a primer on existing and next-generation futures documentation, for which the author has played a role in developing for industry-wide use.

WHEN WILL THE REFORMS REQUIRE ACTION?

Chapter 2 addresses this important question. Implementation of ambitious derivative reform, which contemplates a complete paradigm shift and comprehensive reworking of every aspect of the derivatives life cycle, will take some time and, at least in the United States, action will be required in phases, in coordination with the implementation of derivatives reform mandates.

Derivatives reform was heavily criticized by leading members of the 112th U.S. Congress and calls for investigations, hearings, and oversight on the regulatory reach and implementation of derivatives reform existed when this text went to print and will continue for some time. This is a good thing. The derivatives market is among the most important financial markets—and is arguably the largest financial market in modern finance—and a wholesale rethink and reform of such a broad market will take time and careful coordination. Two leading members of the House of Representatives cautioned regulators at the close of 2010:

> *Finally, an overarching concern regarding implementation of Title VII [of the Dodd-Frank Wall Street Reform and Consumer Protection Act] is the need to get it done right, not necessarily get it done quickly. If implemented hastily or without due care, these regulations could damage America's economic engine—the manufacturers, technology companies, real estate developers, and companies that provide vital financing to consumers and American businesses.... We stand ready to work with you even if that means we all consider delaying statutory deadlines or moving forward with legislation to preserve a viable American derivatives marketplace.*[20]

Before we get to the timing issues that are critically important and are addressed in Chapter 2, which provides a timeline for both the market crises and the resulting reforms, we first need to understand the causes of the events leading to reform, and for that we turn to Chapter 1.

NOTES

1. Sher Verick and Iyanatul Islam, *The Great Recession of 2008–2009: Causes, Consequences and Policy Responses* (Institute for the Study of Labor, Deutsche Post Foundation, May 2010), 11.
2. Verick and Islam, *The Great Recession of 2008*, 3.
3. The Financial Crisis Inquiry Report, Final Report of the National Commission on the Causes of the Financial and Economic Crisis in the United States (New York: Public Affairs, 2011), xv.
4. Verick and Islam, *The Great Recession of 2008*.
5. E. S. Browning, Diya Gullapalli, and Craig Karmin, "Wild Day Caps Worst Week Ever for Stocks," *Wall Street Journal*, October 11–12, 2008.

6. Elizabeth Wurtzel, "The World Will Miss Our Heyday," *Wall Street Journal*, October 11–12, 2008.

7. Steven Erlanger, "Wave of 'Toxic Waste' from U.S. Breaking over EU," *International Herald Tribune*, September 20–21, 2008.

8. Alistair Barr, "Lehman Derivatives Auction Described as 'Smooth,'" Reuters, MarketWatch (Oct. 28, 2010) available at www.reuters.com/article/idUSN2814557620101028.

9. "Weather Derivative in Malawi," Global Facility for Disaster Reduction and Recovery (GFDRR), January 2011.

10. IRIN Humanitarian News and Analysis, "Malawi: Derivatives Used to Hedge Against Bad Weather," July 18, 2008.

11. Ibid.

12. World Bank, "Offering Weather Risk Management Solutions in Malawi.

13. "Weather Derivative in Malawi."

14. Ibid.

15. Frank Partnoy, *F.I.A.S.C.O.: Blood in the Water on Wall Street* (New York: Norton, 2009), 13.

16. "OTC Derivatives Market Activity in the Second Half of 2009," Regular OTC Derivatives Market Statistics, Bank for International Settlements, May 19, 2009, available at www.bis.org/press/p100511.htm.

17. CNN.com, "Markets Mayhem after U.S. Bailout Failure," www.cnn.com/2008/US/09/30/us.bailout.deal.markets/.

18. Figure I.2 has been modified from a similar diagram from the International Swaps and Derivatives Association, Inc. diagram illustrating the over-the-counter derivatives market and its interconnected nature as more and more end users and swap dealers utilize mirroring swaps.

19. Gretchen Morganson, "Finger-Pointing in the Fog," *New York Times,* August 20, 2011.

20. Letter from Spencer Bachus, Ranking Member of the Committee on Financial Services and Frank Lucas, Ranking Member of the Committee on Agriculture dated 12/16/10 to Secretary Geitner and Chairmen Gensler, Schapiro, and Bernanke.

One

The Crises That Led to Derivatives Reform

CHAPTER 1

Seven Causes of the 2008 Market Crises

A broken machine cannot be fixed without understanding what caused it to break. In the absence of an accurate understanding of the 2008 market crises, and if effective responses to identified causes are not properly implemented, history may repeat itself. With the fall of MF Global on October 31st, 2011, it may have already.

In fact, in at least some respects recent history repeated itself in September 2011 when massive losses—to the tune of $2.3 billion—at UBS AG resulted from derivatives trades by Kweko Adoboli, a 31-year-old Ghanaian and former UBS trader. Adoboli's trades, based on futures and exchange-traded funds or ETFs, did not set off alarms because the regulatory framework governing those trades did not require trade confirmations for some of Kweko's trades, and proper audit trails, reporting, and monitoring mandates (included in U.S. reforms as we shall see in Chapter 4) were not in place to detect or prevent the trading activity which led to billions in losses.

It is shocking that banks lost billions and the market globally lost trillions in September 2008, and then, exactly two years later, a well-regarded European bank, UBS, sustained billions in loses arising out of ETF and futures trades. One conclusion suggested by this development is that either the causes of the 2008 market crises were not properly identified, or were not in the ensuing years remedied—or both.

This chapter includes the author's short list of primary causes of the 2008 market crises. Although there were more than seven contributing factors, these were the primary causes, or major contributors, that coalesced to result in the 2008 market crises:

1. An incomplete federal response to certain problems that surfaced in the bankruptcy of Enron Corp.
2. The failure of effective regulation (both internally, by means of intra-company controls, and externally, through government regulation) to rein in excessive risk taking and leverage in markets.

3. The development of an unregulated, global, over-the-counter (OTC) derivatives market.
4. The migration of trading from bonds to OTC derivatives due to the implementation of the Trade Reporting and Compliance Engine (TRACE) and the allure of credit derivatives by those who previously traded in the bond and other cash markets.
5. The unrestricted, unmonitored, and reckless use of mortgage origination and private-label residential mortgage-backed securities.
6. U.S. policy that fostered home ownership and government-sponsored enterprise (GSE) mismanagement.
7. Derivatives and structured product accounting practices.

Developing a basic understanding of the causes of the 2008 market crises will help us understand why lawmakers and regulators required certain changes in the derivatives market, and whether the solutions implemented by regulators will prevent later crises.

At least one academic believes that financial services reform legislation enacted in the United States would not have prevented the 2008 market crisis, as reported by the International Financing Review in May 2011:

> The Dodd-Frank Wall Street Reform and Consumer Protection Act—and its mandate of clearing as much of the over-the-counter derivatives market as possible through central counterparties— would not have prevented the financial crisis of 2008, according to renowned derivatives academic John Hall ... Supposing Dodd-Frank was in place five years ago, and around 70% of DTC derivatives went through CCPs [central clearing parties]. I don't think it would have made a whole lot of difference.[1]

There are still other important reasons for developing an understanding of the 2008 market crises. Joseph Stiglitz, in his book *Freefall*, noted:

> If we can understand what brought about the crisis of 2008 and why some of the initial policy responses failed so badly, we can make future crises less likely, shorter, and with fewer innocent victims. We may even be able to pave the way for robust growth based on solid foundations ... to ensure that the fruits of that growth are shared by the vast majority of citizens.[2]

IGNORING THE WARNING SIGNS

As the seven causes are discussed in this chapter, it will become apparent that many saw warning signs but no sufficient, collective action averted the market crises until the damage was done. In some cases, responses to past crises, such as the failure of Enron Corp., missed the true causes and dynamics of the market failures, and the stage was set for the subsequent market crises of 2008. In other cases, such as the most recent responses to the 2008 crises, lawmakers appear in many respects to have overreacted. This suggests that lawmakers need to better hear and act upon the next voices calling attention to factors leading to major losses before the next economic calamity takes root, begins to emerge, and causes systemic losses— yet again.

With respect to the 2008 market crises, even as the global economic machine was breaking, it seemed as if many leading economic policy makers and governments in major markets were collectively surprised by the depth of the downturn, notwithstanding repeated, pervasive and persuasive warnings that fundamental problems were literally all over the place. In a study by the Institute for the Study of Labor, the Institute explains:

> [F]or much of 2008, the severity of this global downturn was under-
> estimated. Subsequently, leading forecasters, including the IMF and
> World Bank, made a number of revisions to its growth forecasts
> during 2008 and into 2009 as the magnitude of the crisis grew.
> Of course there were some voices that issued dire warnings of a
> brewing storm, but they were not enough to catch the attention
> of many who were lulled into a collective sense of complacency in
> the years leading up to the crisis. Some policy makers, after being
> caught by surprise at the seemingly sudden appearance of a global
> downturn, confidently noted that nobody could have predicted the
> crisis.... Following the events of 2008, particularly the collapse of
> Lehman Brothers in September, risk-loving banks and investors
> around the world rapidly reversed their perceptions.... Some com-
> mentators even questioned whether American-style capitalism itself
> had been dealt a deathblow.[3]

Derivatives have long been a source of significant concern as a destabilizing force for the financial system and for the global economy. Some say that in a February 21, 2003 letter to investors, Warren E. Buffett essentially foretold the 2008 market crises:

> The derivative genie is now well out of the bottle, and these instru-
> ments will almost certainly multiply in variety and number until
> some event makes their toxicity clear. Knowledge of how dangerous
> they are has already permeated the electricity and gas businesses, in
> which eruption of major troubles caused the use of derivatives to di-
> minish dramatically. Elsewhere, however, the derivatives business

*continues to expand unchecked. Central banks and governments
have so far found no effective way to control, or even monitor, the
risks posed by these contracts... derivatives are financial weapons
of mass destruction, carrying dangers that, while now latent, are
potentially lethal.*[4]

A recurring pattern in economic crisis and resulting lawmaking is that,
unless comprehensive, intelligent, and carefully coordinated, international
action results from lawmaking, history will repeat itself. We see glimpses of
that—as discussed in this chapter—from the crises and disjointed lawmaking
in the United States that resulted after the savings and loan crisis, the fall of
Long-Term Capital Management L.P., and Enron Corp. After each of the
crises, Congressional inquiries resulted and laws, such as the Sarbanes-Oxley
Act[5] took legal effect but because the resulting laws did not address, in a
careful, coordinated way, many of the *derivatives-related* issues leading to
the failure of Enron and to the 2008 market crises, subsequent losses were
experienced by UBS two years later.

MORE THAN SEVEN CAUSES OF THE 2008 MARKET CRISES

Certainly there were more than seven causes of the 2008 market crises,
but those discussed here played the most significant roles in causing the
greatest economic loss and destruction. None of the causes was the sole or
even greatest cause, yet each *coalesced* over time to create the 2008 market
crises, resulting in a global rethink of how our financial system functions,
how it is structured, regulated—or not—and how the system must change
to prevent future economic crises.

A 10-member U.S. Financial Crisis Inquiry Commission (which is referenced in the pages that follow as the Crisis Commission) published 545
pages of findings in January 2011 that included, in many respects, great dis-
agreement on the causes of the 2008 market crises. The report is comprised
of both a majority and a minority argument, with members of the Crisis
Commission in the minority stating that their written contribution to the
report was limited to nine pages each.[6]

The Crisis Commission undertook an admirable, Herculean effort
to identify the causes of the 2008 crises. Much of what the Commission found and later recorded was, the author believes, on-point and
completely accurate.

However, when the Crisis Commission addressed the role played in the 2008 market crises by derivatives, many of the statements in the report published by the Crisis Commission were overstated or simply wrong.

Many of those statements were wrong because members of the Crisis Commission, writing in the majority, apparently could not tell the difference between the derivatives that many companies in the mainstream use every day to manage risk on the one hand, and derivatives that enabled big players like Lehman Brothers and American International Group Inc. (AIG) to pursue excessive risk taking, on the other. One of many statements in the Commission's report illustrates the lumping together of derivatives-related criticisms by the Crisis Commission:

> *We conclude [that] over-the-counter derivatives contributed significantly to this crisis... when the housing bubble popped and crisis followed, derivatives were in the center of the storm.*[7]

There are, as we will see in our survey of nearly all derivatives in Chapter 10, at least seven categories of derivatives that comprise a global OTC derivatives market, valued at one time as high as $615 trillion, yet only the credit default swap and financial structures based on pools of residential mortgages are later identified by the Crisis Commission as *the primary* cause of the crisis (or if not the primary cause, a leading or at least critically important cause). Even so, as the quote above indicates, *all* OTC derivatives are branded significant contributors to the 2008 crises. The quote above is simply not an accurate statement. It lacks precision.

However, derivatives appear to be so important as a cause of the crises to the Crisis Commission majority that the *Crisis Commission Report* includes six pages of analysis under the heading "The Growth of Derivatives: By Far the Most Significant Event in Finance During the Past Decade."[8] The analysis concludes with this statement:

> *When the nation's biggest financial institutions were teetering on the edge of failure in 2008, everyone watched the derivative markets. What were the institution's holdings? Who were the counterparties? How would they fare? Market participants and regulators would find themselves straining to understand an unknown battlefield shaped by unseen exposures and interconnections as they fought to keep the financial system from collapsing.*[9]

This statement is wrong in several rather obvious respects. First, the statement from the Crisis Commission majority begins with the notion that "everyone watched the derivatives markets." This is simply not possible. The OTC derivatives markets that were used by the biggest financial institutions (i.e., institutions that are generically referenced in the preceding statement were none other than the OTC markets) cannot, by their very nature before 2010, be watched by everyone, as the Crisis Commission majority writes. These are markets of privately-negotiated trades.

In fact, a few pages earlier in their report, the majority refers to the OTC markets in derivatives as markets that are, by their very nature, *not* transparent (and thus cannot be watched); price discovery is neither possible nor available to the public, according to the majority:

> *OTC derivatives are traded by large financial institutions— traditionally, bank holding companies and investment banks—that act as derivatives dealers, buying and selling contracts with customers. Unlike the futures and options exchanges, the OTC market is neither centralized nor regulated. Nor is it transparent, and thus price discovery is limited. No matter the measurement—trading volume, dollar volume, and risk exposure—derivatives represent a very significant sector of the U.S. financial system.*[10]

The Commission majority's statement (i.e., that OTC derivatives caused or were primary drivers of the 2008 market crises) leads the reader to believe that, as Bear Stearns and Lehman Brothers were failing, everyone had their eyes locked on the markets for *all* derivatives and the well-being of the *entire* financial system teetered on bank dependence—and on the performance of—*all* OTC derivatives. This simply is not accurate. Not only did the markets for foreign exchange (FX) and interest rate derivatives properly function, the listed derivatives markets performed properly.

The use in the market of the specific derivatives that the Crisis Commission blames for losses was, in fact, relatively small in comparison to the multitrillion dollar market worldwide, yet all OTC derivatives are seemingly blamed by the majority in the Crisis Commission.

The Hon. Bill Thomas, writing with his Crisis Commission colleagues in the minority on the role played by derivatives in the 2008 market crises, made this lucid comment:

> *While many [of the problems leading to the 2008 market crises] involve the word "derivative," it is a mistake to bundle them together and say, "Derivatives or CDOs caused the crisis." In each case, we assign responsibility for the failures to the people and institutions rather than to the financial instruments they used.*[11]

The takeaway is that, like fire, derivatives can cause and certainly have caused losses; however, no analysis should lay blame solely or even primarily on *all* derivative products in the world today, yet the reality is that many do exactly this.

The result is a flurry of imprecise, fear-laden statements relating to derivatives in the media and, after the crisis and early reform from government, excessive regulation of derivatives. This served as a catalyst for this book.

Some Derivatives Were in Fact Part of the Problem

Just like it is inaccurate to state that all derivatives caused the 2008 crises, it is also inaccurate to state that no derivative contributed to the crises. In fact, two derivatives in the credit derivative family played important roles in the market seizures: the collateralized debt obligation (CDO) and credit default swap (CDS). When critics of derivatives refer to them as "weapons of mass destruction" or "the nuclear option,"[12] the derivatives that in some cases deserve these titles are those structures which were recklessly used in an opaque market. A CDO, however, is not your mainstream, garden-variety derivative, as its structure, depicted in Figure 1.1, suggests.

A more detailed description of the numerous interrelated transactions that comprise a CDO (or as illustrated in Figure 1.1, a CDO^2) is included in Chapter 10: Survey of Derivatives. A summary is provided here, after a few observations. First, the design and structure of the CDO are elegant and have evolved over time in the class of transactions that are labeled "securitization." Essentially, the design converts regular cash flows into securities (bonds), which are issued to investors, and the proceeds from those bond issuances are used to fund the assets (commercial or residential mortgages), which produce the cash flows that are used for repaying the issued bonds. Sounds circular?

The roles of each of the entities within Figure 1.1 can be summarized in this way. The most important entity is the Issuing SPE Trust depicted in the figure. The SPE is a special purpose entity, whose corporate form is a trust, which is formed by a sponsor such as a large bank. The sole function of the SPE (its only, or "special" function or purpose) is to acquire rights to a regular or periodic stream of cash-producing assets (such as residential mortgages, let us say), and then issue bonds whose coupons are based on that stream.

In the top left-hand corner of Figure 1.1, a bank plays the role of loan originator, and the bank's proceeds go to the obligors of the loan, which could be users of credit cards or buyers of a home. These obligors voluntarily

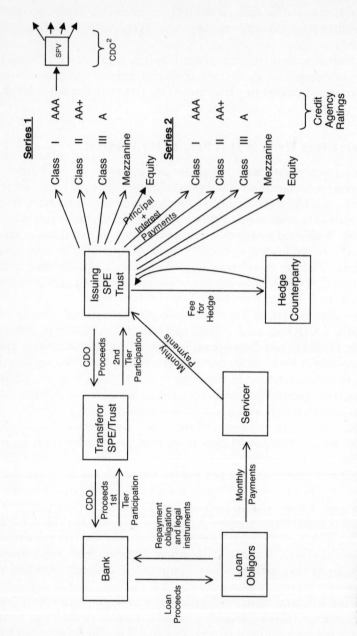

FIGURE 1.1 Collateralized Debt Obligation

or by request or demand by a servicer make monthly payments, which are then cycled through to the SPE, which uses those monthly payments to pay principal and interest on the bonds issued to investors by the SPE. When the obligors execute documents and instruments in exchange for the loan proceeds, that paperwork becomes part of an asset file which is executed and delivered to the bank, which in turn sells the interests (i.e., a participation interest, or sells the assets outright) in the instruments (in the example of a CDO referencing residential mortgages, the mortgages) to a Transferor, which is an SPE organized as a trust, that in turn legally transfers those interests to the SPE issuing the bonds. The SPE issues those bonds in tranches (French for slices), which credit rating agencies rate (except, typically, the mezzanine or equity tranches).

The tranches of bonds issued by the SPE have different risk characteristics, and thus, different ratings. These characteristics are driven in part by the payment stream that begins with the loan obligors. The highest-rated, senior tranches in each series of bond issuances (in Figure 1.1, Class I is rated AAA) are paid first from the cash flows generated by the underlying assets, before the junior securities and equity securities. When an underlying asset such as a mortgage is in default, this interrupts the cash flow to the bond holder, and losses are first borne by the equity and mezzanine tranches (which are typically owned by the sponsor of the securitization; CDO sponsors are in that way said to have "skin in the game" because they stand to lose first), then after that, the more senior bond holders bear losses, all the way to the top, where the senior-most and highest-rated bonds are held.

The entire structure depicted by Figure 1.1 is a derivative within the credit derivative family (the bonds *derive* their value from, among other things, the underlying [mortgage] assets), and derivatives are used within the CDO itself for a number of purposes, including to match the bond repayment obligations owed by the SPE to the bondholders with the cash streams from the underlying obligors. Also, as a source of revenue, some SPEs would enter into credit default swaps (or CDS, which are discussed in this chapter and Chapter 10). The CDO tranches are themselves subject to CDSs in which one party sells protection (like insurance) to another for a fee, in exchange for reimbursement based on the recovery rate of the defaulted tranche. Finally, some buyers of bonds issued by the CDO SPE were themselves trusts, or SPVs (special purpose vehicles, a synonym for SPEs), which, after buying a bond from an SPE, would include that bond in a portfolio of hundreds of other CDO bonds, and then issues bonds based on the payment streams from the portfolio of CDOs.

Certainly the CDO and accompanying derivatives played a role in the global 2008 market crises, but that role was not itself the cause of those crises. These were the seven most significant developments that brought us to the reform that changed the entire landscape of derivatives.

AN INCOMPLETE RESPONSE TO PROBLEMS EXPOSED IN THE ENRON BANKRUPTCY

We begin the discussion of the causes of the 2008 market crises nearly a decade before the crises, with the failure of Enron Corp., and the mentality among finance professionals and financial tools which they used in the years in between the Enron and 2008 market crises.

This is the starting point for the author, because it was in the immediate aftermath of the Enron bankruptcy that I began to work extensively in derivatives and structured finance, and many problems associated with Enron resurfaced nearly a decade later in the 2008 market crises.

Many believe that Enron was an energy company. In fact, it was an aggressive energy *derivatives* trading company and derivatives market—all dressed-up as, and largely regulated as, an energy company. The words dressed-up are used by design because, as we will see later in this chapter, just prior to the 2008 market crises, there were many legal structures (real estate investment trusts, or REITS, are one example) which were dressed up as real estate companies, but really they functioned in some ways as commercial banks—but were not regulated as such.

In 2000, I worked as a fifth-year associate of a leading Washington, DC law and public policy firm which was retained by an international investment bank whose employees were required to appear before Congress in connection with a series of investigations. A series of public hearings on the use of derivatives and structured financial products by Enron prior to its bankruptcy was televised by C-SPAN. Also subject to Congressional inquiry were statements by the bank's analysts, the timing of those statements, and the credit ratings assigned to Enron debt.

Throughout the Enron crisis and thereafter, I became completely submerged in what I call Enron finance, which included, as its key component parts, the widespread use of SPEs and derivatives such as prepaid forwards, which I discuss in Chapter 10. My task then was to first understand Enron finance, translate it into plain English, and distinguish it from lawful business practices. Over time, while watching firsthand in hearings on Capitol Hill in Washington, DC, I witnessed Congressional lawmaking firsthand, frequently interfaced with key lawmakers and their excellent staff, and saw the legislative answer to Enron—and all the destructive fallout that took place after the company filed for bankruptcy on December 2, 2001.

Between December 2001 and April 2002, Congress held numerous hearings that led to its passage of the Sarbanes-Oxley Act[13] on July 30, 2002. Although there is no question that some good came from this law, generally, it was designed to prevent corporate governance and accounting misdeeds.

However, I quickly learned in my Enron-related work that corporate misgovernance was neither the only problem nor even the biggest problem posed by Enron.

Enron was a derivatives trading company whose failure should have caught our collective attention and focused it not only on the need to revamp the corporate governance practices of public companies in the United States, but on the unregulated use of Enron finance.

Enron finance entailed the use of off-balance-sheet structures that were replete with SPEs, intracompany dealings, and, most importantly for purposes of this book, derivatives and other sophisticated transactions which mischaracterized liabilities as assets and otherwise hid from the public the problems that Enron experienced.

Although detailing all the intricacies of Enron finance is outside of the scope of this book, a summary description of Enron finance, Enron, and then its demise is necessary.

Enron Corp. as a Major Derivatives Player

Many thought of Enron as an energy company, but by its last year of corporate existence it was in reality a full-fledged derivatives trading firm with an enormous and highly sophisticated trading floor. Enron began as an energy company but over time used unregulated derivatives and structures both within the company, among its affiliates, and with counterparties that were not affiliates of Enron.

SPEs According to the Powers Report (the February 1, 2002 Report of the Special Investigation Committee of the Board of the Enron Corp., chaired by William Powers, whose outside counsel included a Vanderbilt Law School classmate of the author, Reed Brodsky, then of Wilmer, Cutler, and Pickering), many of the deceptive transactions employed by Enron, in loans and prepaid forwards as well as other structures, included devices used in Enron finance called special purpose entities or SPEs. Accounting rules permitted Enron to establish an SPE, which is itself a corporate entity, and do business with it in such a way that the SPE served and functioned as an independent, outside entity for accounting purposes, provided that, "an owner independent of the company makes a substantive equity investment of at least 3 percent of the SPE's assets, and that 3 percent must remain at risk throughout the transaction; and the independent owner must exercise control of the SPE."[14]

If the foregoing conditions are satisfied, Enron could, with its transactions (including unregulated derivatives) record gains and losses in transactions with its SPEs yet *the assets and liabilities of the SPE are permitted to be omitted from the SPE's counterparty's (i.e., Enron's) balance sheet.*[15]

Although Enron, which was once an exceedingly well-recognized U.S. corporation, began as an energy company when it was created in 1985, its OTC, derivatives-related assets and liabilities increased by more than fivefold from 1985 to 2000, and its consolidated financial statements that year indicated that its nonderivative operations were generating a loss.[16]

Enron's derivatives activities were undertaken both internally, among SPEs and other affiliates, and externally by means of its own trading enterprise, EnronOnline.[17] Testimony by derivatives expert and professor Frank Partnoy in 2002 clearly and cogently stated that Enron, while touted as a successful energy firm, was instead a derivatives firm that covered its own losses:

> *Enron's aggressive additions to revenues meant that it was the "seventh-largest U.S. Company" in title only. In reality, Enron was a much smaller operation, whose primary moneymaking business— a substantial and speculative derivatives trading operation—covered up poor performance in Enron's other, smaller business, including EnronOnline. Enron's public disclosures show that during the past three years the firm was not making money on its non-derivatives business. Gross margins from these businesses were initially zero from 1998 through 2000.*[18]

The federal response to the fall of Enron Corp. in the United States generally brought about reform in the corporate governance of public companies, but it missed almost entirely the misuse of SPEs and structured products which allowed the products described on the previous pages to fuel global financial instability.

At the end of 2001, after filing for bankruptcy, Enron Corp. became the subject of U.S. Congressional investigations, including one by the Senate Permanent Subcommittee on Investigations, which issued a report critical of biased analyst recommendations, conflicts of interest, and the lack of objective credit rating agency ratings regarding complex derivatives and structured products. Members of the Senate subcommittee and members of Congress in the House of Representatives focused on more than $8 billion in deceptive prepay forward transactions and other structured transactions that were provided to Enron for a fee, in order for Enron to manipulate its financial statements or deceptively reduce its tax obligations.

The collapse of Enron occurred at a time when numerous high-profile scandals were the subject of a series of local and federal investigations and televised hearings, all culminating in the passage of comprehensive federal law, Sarbanes-Oxley, which required among other things accountants to certify the accuracy of accounting statements.

ENRON FINANCE USED BY BANKS AND THE LACK OF REGULATION

The problem was that the Enron crisis was viewed as *an accounting crisis*, first and foremost, and the U.S. government failed to see greater, underlying problems that would fuel the market crises that led to the 2008 market crises: the use of off-balance-sheet, SPE-based structures coupled with sophisticated derivatives. This was–or should have been–lesson one.

One of the central problems related to Enron's collapse was the roles played by large investment banks. Years after the repeal of Glass-Steagall (described later in this chapter), the large investment banks which provided derivatives and structured products to Enron were simultaneously recommending Enron securities in published buy recommendations to investors (and supplying Enron with questionable structured products). Economist Joseph Stiglitz stated that one of the remnants of the elimination of key banking regulation was a greater propensity for banks to take risks, and the result of that was internal conflicts of interests within banks that were previously kept in check by federal laws, such as the Glass-Steagall Act:

> The repeal of the Glass-Steagall Act played an especial [sic] role, not just because of the conflicts of interest that it opened up (made so evident in the Enron and WorldCom scandals) but because it transmitted the risk-taking culture of investment banking to commercial banks, which should have acted in a far more prudential manner.[19]

A second major lesson taught by Enron that should have resulted in reform was that Enron finance was anything but regulated, and, for the most part, Enron set into motion this brand of financing privately, off its balance sheets, away from regulators and the market. Part of this is due to the regulation-free environment that developed after the passage of the Commodity Futures Modernization Act of 2000, which, as described later in this chapter and subsequent chapters, such as Chapter 8, ensured the deregulation of OTC derivatives for, among other purposes, the United States to maintain its competitive position in OTC derivatives trading.

Enron failed in a regulatory climate that fostered a hands-off approach by regulators, and the resulting chain reaction in 2008 is illustrated here:

- Banks put at risk, through excessive amounts of leverage, themselves and the financial system.
- By 2008, banks used many thousands of SPEs in complicated financial structures and used accounting, tax, and other practices to push the envelope in ways that were as aggressive as Enron Corp. in

transactions that, while quite different, were the same in some important respects (e.g., many were off-balance-sheet transactions).

- SPEs sponsored by the banks issued bonds or debt.
- Credit-rating agencies rated that debt, but in 2008 failed to measure risk and downgrade many firms, such as Bear Stearns, in much the same way that credit-rating agencies were slow to downgrade Enron.
- Neither the Securities and Exchange Commission (SEC) nor the Commodities Future Trading Commission (CFTC), including the U.S. Federal Energy Regulatory Commission, detected the massive systemic risk posed by the system of SPEs, nor did they rate debt and derivatives that accompanied such debt; the regulators' failure to detect and issue warnings concerning the systemic risk in many ways resembled the regulators' failure to prevent or warn the market of the improper use of structured finance by Enron.
- In April 2010, Congress scrutinized investment banks' purported conflicts of interest in the same way that analysts in banks were scrutinized in early 2002 for their statements and ratings.
- Just as SPEs were an integral part of Enron finance, SPEs were bankruptcy-remote entities that were critically important in taking pools of real estate mortgages from originators and enabling bonds to be issued to investors (which would include other SPEs) in an elegantly complex process described in this chapter and in Chapter 10 as securitization.

If, following Enron, a complete rethink by policymakers would have taken place, and during that process Enron's fall was not viewed as a corporate governance problem but instead as a collection of derivatives, structured finance, conflicts of interest, and accounting problems, then perhaps lawmakers could have been positioned to prevent the 2008 market crises. Perhaps the most egregious misstep by lawmakers and regulators was their failure to view the Enron experience as a major failure within the OTC derivatives market, instead of just as a public company accounting scandal.

THE ABSENCE OF EFFECTIVE REGULATION

Bank regulation is like a game of cat and mouse in which the mouse is smarter, earns more money, and gets to make the first move. Institutions hire bright people to devise ways to exploit loopholes in the system to try to increase profits and stay ahead of competitors and regulators alike. They often succeed, and their success can cost a fortune . . . technological advances had enabled bankers to concoct derivative instruments and so-called structured products like the notorious securitized mortgage loans.[20]

An important contributor to the market seizures in 2008 was the absence of effective, coordinated regulation, a problem that worsened over time as two developments took hold:

1. On the one hand, intelligent bankers, lawyers, and accountants developed financial products that shifted risk (generally risk relating to mortgage origination and secondary-mortgage finance as we will see in the pages that follow), and allowed others to speculate in an unfettered manner with respect to that risk.
2. On the other hand, simultaneously, lawmakers and regulators in the United States did not do enough after prior financial crises (e.g., the savings and loan, 1987 market, Long-Term Capital, and Enron crises discussed in additional detail in Chapter 10) to identify and prevent the recurrence of problems that led to the 2008 market crises.

The starting point in describing this two-part cause is the history that led to an ineffective patchwork of regulation and very active users of derivatives using these financial tools in a way that led to widespread losses in the midst of a regulatory void. Although the discussion that follows provides a summary of this history, a more in-depth dissertation is provided in Chapter 8.

Importance of Banks and Banking Regulation

Federal law in the United States that governed the investment activities of those banks was transformed completely in the twentieth century, and that transformation created an environment for the banks to take the kinds of risks—and to incur unprecedented losses—that led to widespread market seizure and government bailouts throughout the world in 2008. Before describing that transformation, it is perhaps helpful to outline the objectives of banks and the regulations that are meant to govern them.

The market participants with the single greatest influence on the financial crises of 2008 were the large investment and commercial banks in New York and other major financial centers throughout the world. This is not surprising; banks provide the liquidity that functions as the lifeblood of the financial system and the broader global economy. The banks carry out government's monetary policy. Banks also serve as financial intermediaries and provide a range of financial services and financial products to provide an environment in which business may thrive.

When banks fail, as they did in the Great Depression in the United States prior to 1933, and again nearly 75 years later, the banking system gets the attention of lawmakers first, and it is that system that is the first to be reformed.

In the first hundred days of the Franklin Delano Roosevelt administration following the Great Depression, a complete revamp of the banking system was necessitated by a perception that the financial arteries of the U.S. economy were effectively severed:

> *The first priority was the banking system. Before anything else could be done, it seemed imperative to clear the financial arteries of the economy. The outgoing President had asked the President-elect in February to join with him in meeting the banking crisis.... On Saturday night, a few hours after the inauguration [of President Franklin D. Roosevelt], Secretary of the Treasury Woodin agreed to have emergency banking legislation ready for Congress when it convened on Thursday, March 9.... With the declaration of a bank holiday, the Administration bought time—eighty hours until Congress reconvened—to work out a plan for reviving the banks.*[21]

The comprehensive federal laws that followed the Great Depression included the Banking Act of 1933 and the Glass-Steagall Act, which addressed the collapse of the commercial banking system in America in the years leading up to 1933.

Glass-Steagall primarily brought about the separation of commercial banking, in which depositors provided the inflow of cash to the banks from investment banking. Proponents of Glass-Steagall urged federal lawmakers in essence to place a wall in between investment bankers and commercial bankers so that the former could not use and leverage the use of bank depositors' wealth.[22] A response to the proliferation of bank failures during the Great Depression, the 1933 law prevented deposit-taking institutions from owning investment banks and limited the ability of banks to operate across state lines.[23]

In the decades which followed the 1930s, the law that American financial-services businesses tried to circumvent for most of the twentieth century was the Glass-Steagall Act. This circumvention did in fact take place until the overturn of the Glass-Steagall Act. Prior to its repeal, bankers and their lawyers created structures and investment products that led depositors to investments that were certainly far more attractive than simple deposit accounts.

Conrad de Aenlle and Julia Werdigier, writing for the *International Herald Tribune* after the fall of Lehman Brothers in late September 2008, reported:

> *The formation of holding companies that owned consumer and investment banks, as well as subsidiaries in multiple states, weakened Glass-Steagall [according to Jaime Peters, bank analyst at Morningstar]. So did the flourishing in the 1970s of mutual funds and money-market funds that became substitutes for conventional checking and savings accounts... [t]hese developments rendered Glass-Steagall all but moot and the act was repealed in the 1990s. That has led some observers to try to lay the credit crisis at the doorstep of the U.S. Congress, but others see it as an acceptance of the reality that bankers were a step or two ahead of the regulators.*[24]

On November 12, 1999, Congress repealed Glass-Steagall and commercial and investment banks were able to combine, mergers followed, and investment banks were able to leverage the entire assets of commercial-bank deposit accounts and investment-bank assets in the years leading up to the 2008 market crisis.

The Interconnected Nature of the Banking System

If a large bank fails, it is a major problem, as it was when Lehman Brothers filed for bankruptcy. Because large banks were interconnected by short- and long-term financings—traditional and alternative financings—the failure of several banks threatened the entire system. This development was perhaps the greatest cause of the new derivatives reform mandate.

A primary feature of the modern financial system is its interconnectedness. What, in the United States, was once a system of separate and distinct banks in the nineteenth century became an interlocked labyrinth consisting of bank holding companies and affiliates. By 2008, many of the largest banks were simultaneously interconnected with each other and excessively leveraged, a dynamic that threatened the entire financial system. Andrew Ross Sorkin, in his thorough work on the unfolding of the 2008 market crises, wrote that the interconnected labyrinth of bank trades tied the financial system together in one knot:

> *But it was the new ultra-interconnectedness among the nation's financial institutions that posed the greatest risk of all. As a result of the banks owning various slices of [securitized, mortgage-backed*

bonds] *every firm was now dependent on the others—and many did not know it. If one fell, it could become a series of falling dominos. . . . The sudden failure or abrupt withdrawal from trading of any of these large U.S. dealers could cause liquidity problems in the markets and could also pose risk to others, including federally insured banks and the financial system as a whole.*[25]

The intertwined nature of the banking system was nowhere more pronounced than in the OTC derivatives market, because banks facing derivative customers in trades would turn around and hedge their trades with other banks, causing the market over time to resemble the labyrinth described in the Introduction to this text and illustrated in Figure I.2.

Not only were the banks interconnected, they were also voracious risk takers. In 2008, banks on Wall Street were massively leveraged with debt-to-capital ratios of 32 to 1.[26] Prior to the Great Depression in the United States, many individuals, banks, and other market participants relied on large amounts of leverage, which led, in part, to a run on banks and the Great Depression. In 2007 to 2008, not only were the banks and their affiliates interconnected, leveraged risk takers, but the traditional banks also sponsored an entirely new breed of financial services firms and entities: the so-called shadow banks.

THE SHADOW BANKING SYSTEM

The shadow banking system deserves its ominous name because players within the system are not actively regulated as banks are regulated, at least not in the United States. This system consisted of a variety of SPEs as well as other entities which performed certain financing functions of traditional banks, but were not regulated as banks.

Entities in the shadow banking system also include real estate investment trusts (REITS), hedge funds, money-market funds, and other entities. An illustration of a REIT acting as a bank—that is, without the regulatory oversight that should include stringent capitalization requirements to reign in risk taking—is provided in the next section. REITS and other quasi-banking entities in this system occupied the position of a bank in many transactions leading up to the 2008 market crises, yet they did not accept deposits as traditional banks do. However, like banks, the entities were instrumental in the funding of investments in real estate and other assets that became illiquid in 2007 to 2008.

There are no geographic bounds to the system of shadow banks—a description of nonbank financial services firms that entered the financial vernacular around 2007.[27] These institutions emerged and played important roles in financings from 2000 to 2008 in Europe, in the United States, and in other parts of the world, yet the shadow banks are not subject to the vast regulatory regime that governs banks. In the absence of a well-developed body of law to govern shadow banks, these entities became formidable competitors to traditional banks in providing financing for commercial transactions.

The financings of shadow banks included complex derivatives, but also more straightforward forms of financing, such as credit facilities and warehouse and repurchase facilities. The CFTC Chairman Gensler testified before the Financial Crisis Inquiry Commission in May 2010:

> Nearly eight decades ago, after a series of banking crises led to the Great Depression, the United States put in place broad protections over the financial system. These reforms—deposit insurance, prudential rules to limit risk taking by banks, and improved transparency and investor protection in our securities markets—alongside the Federal Reserve's role as lender of last resort, laid the foundation for a more stable banking industry for several decades. Over time, however, the financial system outgrew those protections. A large parallel financial system emerged outside of the framework of protections established for traditional banks. A great diversity of financial institutions emerged to provide banking services to individuals and companies, and they were allowed to operate without being subject to the same constraints applied to traditional banks. The shift in mortgage lending away from banks, the growth of the relative importance of nonbank financial institutions, the increase in the size of investment banks, and the emergence of a range of specialized financing vehicles are all manifestations of this phenomenon.[28]

REITs as Banks

The following is an example of how a REIT, an entity which no one would consider a bank, performs banking functions in the origination of a loan, yet the REIT is not regulated as a bank in the United States.

A REIT may enter into a repurchase facility with a large bank, and it can time the release of funds from that bank in such a way as to enable the REIT to act as a bank and fund the origination of a commercial real estate transaction, as illustrated by Figure 1.2.

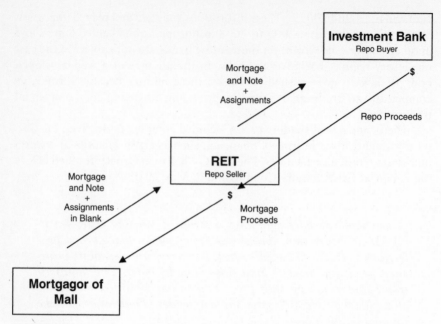

FIGURE 1.2   REITs Performing Banking Functions in a Repurchase Transaction or "Repo"

In Figure 1.2, in the bottom and far left (within a rectangle and called Mortgagor of Mall) figuratively stands a mortgagor as a customer of a bank and borrower which would, in years past, apply to a commercial bank for a commercial real estate loan and mortgage using traditional financing (which continues in existence today, but without the repurchase facility structure that is depicted in Figure 1.2). The mortgagor signs two legal documents, principally: a mortgage, which gives the lending bank legal rights to seize the properly which is subject to the mortgage; and a promissory note, which gives the lender the right to additional recourse to the person signing the mortgage, in order to be made whole if the sale of the property underlying the mortgage is insufficient for the bank to be made whole.

The conference room in which the mortgagor signs the mortgage, promissory notes, and other documents (assignments in blank, as noted in Figure 1.2, which enables the REIT to transfer the legal interests to the ultimate source of mortgage financing, the investment bank at the top, right of Figure 1.2), is not located in a bank, but instead is typically in the offices of the REIT. Usually later in the day, after execution of the mortgage and promissory note and before the wiring cut-off time, the mortgagor receives the mortgage proceeds in its deposit account, but those proceeds do not originate from the REIT. Those proceeds, as illustrated in Figure 1.2, are in fact coming from a large investment bank.

The investment bank in Figure 1.2 has, well before the funding of mortgage for the mall, entered into a completely separate transaction with the REIT in which the REIT:

- Commits to transfer the asset file from the commercial mortgage for the mall to a custodian or the investment bank and assigns the REIT's rights to the underlying mortgage to the investment bank.
- Promises the investment bank to repurchase the mortgage at some later point (thus, the name repo or repurchase facility).
- Pays the investment bank a fee (the fee may be considered interest for the commercial mortgage proceeds provided by the investment bank to fund the mortgage).
- After a period of time which is negotiated with the investment bank, or alternatively, at any time upon the request of the investment bank (the bank can make this request in some repurchase facilities at any time, in its unfettered discretion), the REIT actually repurchases the mortgage and makes the investment bank whole (and then some; a fee is charged and collected by the investment bank for this transaction), and the asset file with the mortgage documentation is transferred to the REIT, which becomes the owner of the mortgage.

In this way, the repurchase facility described above and depicted in Figure 1.2 often serves as a short-term source of financing for a REIT, which, by means of this facility, in essence performs the role of a bank, at least for a period of time. What the customer (the commercial mortgagor in the foregoing illustration) does not see is that several weeks before the closing of the commercial real estate loan at the office of the REIT, the REIT entered into a repurchase facility, or repo, whereby a large investment bank provides repo proceeds to an account held for the REIT moments before the closing of the commercial real estate loan. Just before the loan is funded, the customer executes a promissory note, mortgage, and other documents within the asset file, and those documents are then assigned by the REIT to the investment bank and held in trust. Figure 1.2 illustrates the complete structure of the repo, which enabled the REIT to function as a bank equivalent without banking supervision or extensive or explicit regulatory jurisdiction.

The asset file holding the mortgage may, prior to repurchase of the asset by the REIT in this case, be assigned by the investment bank to a trust, which, in turn, issues tranches of bonds or other securities in a securitization.

Securitizations are described in this part as the fourth factor that contributed to the 2008 market crises.[29]

*   *   *

This is one example of how a REIT acts as a shadow bank, in the context of a commercial real estate loan funded with proceeds from a large repurchase facility that an investment bank provided to the REIT.

Shadow banks, which are highly leveraged, are subject to market risk, liquidity risk, and a host of other risks, and over the years were not subject to capital reserve and other prudent requirements imposed on banks by regulators. More leverage for banks and shadow banks alike meant greater sensitivity to shocks in the market and greater resulting losses. Shadow banks, during market crises, lost access to the sources of financing that were previously provided to them. From 2007 to 2009, we witnessed a rapid deleveraging of the shadow banking industry, especially in the area of real estate, which caused sell-offs of assets and a freefall in asset values.

Banks and Other Financial Services Did Not Have Capital Requirements for Derivatives

Since an early OTC derivatives trade in modern finance, an interest-rate swap between IBM and the World Bank, banks and other derivatives counterparties were not required to comply with stringent, effectively administered capital requirements that would have required these market participants to maintain debt-to-equity ratios in such a way as to prevent risk-taking that led to systemic failure in 2008.

This dynamic developed over a decade, if not longer. Reporters, scholars, and market participants have for many years wrote that bank regulators for at least a decade failed to adequately monitor or even begin to implement effective regulation:

- Banks have not properly disclosed poor lending and investment practices.[30]
- Activities of OTC derivatives market participants suggested the need for greater, if not comprehensive, regulation as early as 1998.[31]
- Leverage and risk concerns relating to derivative use by U.S. banks were discussed at the Basel Committee meeting as early as July 1994, but no effective capital mandate for compliance by those banks was implemented as a part of Basel initiatives.[32]

- Basel Accord's treatment of swaps existed at least 15 years before the 2008 market crises, but it did little to reign in irresponsible risk taking in the OTC derivatives market.[33]

The interconnected, opaque, and shockingly unregulated bank-driven credit derivatives market was a primary cause of the 2008 market crises.

Simultaneous with the inadequate regulation of capital requirements was the development of a market that would be so large that, as of 2008, at least in the United States, the notional value of that market would be 20 times as large as the gross domestic product (GDP) of the United States: the over-the-counter or OTC derivatives market.

DEVELOPMENT OF AN UNREGULATED GLOBAL DERIVATIVES MARKET

The next cause which led to the 2008 market crises was the spectacular growth of the OTC derivatives market worldwide without coordinated regulation. Today the market is the largest market in the world of finance. There is an estimated $300 trillion in OTC derivatives in the OTC market in the United States (in terms of notional value; the difference between notional and actual value is discussed in Part Three), and $615 trillion in notional value worldwide.[34] The first formal OTC trade took place in 1981, as described in greater detail in Chapter 8.

The pace at which the derivatives market developed outstripped the laws that governed the financial marketplace–and not just in the U.S. Commissioner Gary Gensler, Chairman of the U.S. CFTC, opined that other countries' laws also did not regulate derivatives:

> *Over-the-counter derivatives, which started to be transacted in the 1980s, have not been regulated in Europe, Asia, or North America. Until the reforms being debated this year, I am not aware of any major country that had directly regulated these markets over a nearly 30-year period.*[35]

With the enormous size of the derivatives market, why did the largest governments in the world such as the federal government in the United States fail to regulate OTC derivatives? The answer provided by CFTC Commissioner Gensler in 2010 introduces a fundamental position in public policy that needs to be summarized here.

For many years, the most active participants in the derivatives markets were very large banks that were already subject to a complex and well-established regime of law and regulation. Traders that entered positions on behalf of those banks were, along with the firms and banks that employed them, deemed sufficiently sophisticated and, therefore, not in need of careful oversight, according to CFTC Chairman Gary Gensler, who, in answering this question, made this statement, which explains, in part, how the OTC derivatives market was free of government regulation:

> *First, it was claimed that the derivatives market was an institutional marketplace, with "sophisticated" traders who did not need the same types of protections that the broader public needs when investing in the securities or futures markets. This was included in a [U.S.] President's Working Group report in 1999. European regulators held a similar view that sophisticated traders needed less regulation that [sic] the broader investing public. For example, the UK's regulatory approach was different for investment services offered to "sophisticated" investment professionals than the approach for investment services offered to other investors.*[36]

Because the institutions that entered into and traded OTC derivatives were already sufficiently regulated under existing regulatory bodies, their derivatives-related activities do not need to be regulated—or so the claim was stated. As a result, regulators did not regulate the derivatives activities of banks or bank affiliates that were active participants in the derivatives markets. In fact, Gensler stated that these market participants were "lightly regulated."[37]

Central clearing of derivatives has been resisted over the years based on the premise that many OTC derivatives cannot be standardized—and, therefore, cleared—like futures contracts. Chairman Gensler of the CFTC recalled testimony by a Wall Street chief executive officer that as much as 75 to 80 percent of the OTC derivatives market is standard enough to be centrally cleared today.[38] This remains to be seen.

After the fall of Lehman Brothers, the industry, by means of its international trade association, the International Swaps and Derivatives Association (ISDA) spearheaded an effort to standardize credit default swaps (CDS). The ISDA published an international protocol and launched an effort to encourage market participants to enter into, and use, Depository Trust & Clearing Corporation (DTCC) as a trade repository if on a Standard North American CDS Contract (SNAC). However, the author's experience is that the derivatives market has not fully embraced the SNAC CDS, and this experience teaches that the conversion of a customized market with hundreds of trillions of dollars to a centrally cleared market may be more difficult than regulators or even Wall Street executives think. Additional discussion on central clearing reform and the central clearing process are provided in Part Three of this book.

Finally, the United States has not previously regulated its OTC derivatives market because of the concern that U.S. market participants seeking less regulation would take their trades overseas, where countries with less regulation provide attractive, lightly regulated markets for OTC derivatives trading.[39]

In the absence of effective regulation, given the aforementioned factors and developments, the OTC market grew in leaps and bounds from the first interest-rate trade in 1981. By 2008, the global OTC derivatives market was a $615 trillion market in notional value.[40]

The OTC derivatives market was attractive in part because of the transparency that existed in a large, traditional cash market: the secondary bond market, as discussed next.

The TRACE Reporting System and the Allure of Credit Derivatives

The third catalyst or significant factor that led to the 2008 market crises consisted of these two factors:

1. The movement away from a traditional financial instrument, namely, corporate bonds, to OTC derivatives because of the transparency in the bond market resulting from the implementation of the Trade Reporting and Compliance Engine (TRACE).
2. The widespread attraction to credit derivatives.

An important entrant into the OTC market was the former bond trader, who, after the introduction and use of TRACE, sought opportunities to trade in less transparent markets. An integral part of trading successfully is taking advantage of information that is not readily available for any number of reasons.

The interesting aspect of this part of the discussion is that policy makers in derivatives reform have included in that reform the requirement that the current OTC derivatives market become more transparent. The reality is that, as we will see in the case of the introduction of TRACE to the bond market, once a previously opaque market becomes transparent, many of the market players will search for new avenues to trade without transparency.

The Trade Reporting and Compliance Engine

TRACE is a sophisticated reporting system that enables trade details in the secondary bond market to be readily available to the broader market. The corporate bond experience since the adoption of TRACE suggests that the credit derivatives market spiked after the bond market became more transparent after the introduction of TRACE.

In the decades that preceded the use of TRACE, corporate bonds traded in the secondary market, the old-fashioned way: by telephone.[41] Quotations for bonds in the secondary market were accessible by a call to a market professional, because prices for completed bond transactions were not public. Regulators were of the belief that insider trading took place in the opaque secondary bond market before TRACE.

> *First, in an opaque market, well-informed dealers may be able to extract rents from less well-informed customers (Pagano and Roell, 1996), and in fact dealers may well prefer not to disclosure trades that occur, because they profit from the associated reduction in price competition (Madhavan, 1995). Second, increased transparency can facilitate enforcement of rules against excessive "mark-ups" (additions or subtractions in retail price relative to open market) in securities trading.[42]*

In July 2002, this all changed. SEC Chairman Arthur Levitt wanted a database and reporting system to collect the prices of trades on all registered bond offerings.[43] Once consummated, trade details were reported to the predecessor to the National Association of Securities Dealers (NASD), the Financial Industry Regulatory Authority (FINRA), and a computer server made those trade details available through the Internet.

TRACE quickly became the great equalizer of the secondary bond market; with its introduction, bond market participants gained access to the same information. A byproduct of this development, however, which is summarized next, was to push business into the opaque derivatives market.

> *Consider the choice of a trader trying to accumulate a position: trade in the cash corporate market and broadcast your trades to everyone within a few minutes or execute in the credit derivatives market, where there is no reporting system. (The credit derivatives*

market is innovative in structure, but in many ways it operates in the way that the old-line cash corporate market did before TRACE reporting.)[44]

TRACE had a cascading effect in the industry. First, banks that traded in the secondary bond market made less profit, and individual investors traded more efficiently and at less cost. In writing on the subject of transparency in the corporate bond market after the introduction of TRACE, Hendrick Bessembinder and William Maxwell explain how transparency, at least in the previously opaque corporate bond market, resulted in process-related improvements and changes in trade economics:

> *A number of articles in the financial and trade press support the general conclusion of the academic studies that trading costs declined with transaction reporting [through TRACE], particularly for retail traders. A commentator from a fixed income research service stated that "before TRACE, it wouldn't be unheard of for a trader to use the fact that there was no way of verifying the information that he gave about where a bond was trading to his advantage" (as quoted in Bravo, 2003). In contrast, a fixed income trader at an investment company, referring to the post-TRACE environment, was quoted in Vames (2003) as saying, "You don't have to go to three or four different people to find out where something is trading.... [W]hen you have access to (TRACE) information, you have a better idea where things are before you make your first call." A bond trader (as quoted in Laughline, 2005) stated: "increased transparency has clearly helped the small investor and the smaller funds.... [M]any investors now think the real benefit of TRACE lies in knowing that they are not being raked over the coals." A "Lex" (2006) column in the* Financial Times *noted: "[B]ig dealer banks now make less money on each trade. Few observers will lose much sleep over that."*[45]

Bond salesmen lost trading advantages after TRACE. To illustrate, "[i]nstitutional investors paid $1.26 per $1,000 bond to trade last month, according to a review of 5,086 trades involving 22 of the most-active top-rated issues in the investment-grade Bloomberg-NASD bond index. Four years ago [before the introduction of TRACE] it was $2.80 per bond."[46]

In part due to a more transparent market, some bond salesmen lost their work, but those traders who sought pricing advantages in a more opaque market turned to the OTC derivatives market. Derivatives and equity sales offices took the office space previously occupied by bond salesmen.[47] This flight of business from the secondary bond market to the OTC derivatives market occurred over a span of three months, as a former bond salesman explained: "I used to make a good living, and then we were breaking even one month, losing money another," said bond salesman Richard Seifer, 61, whose offices in the old U.S. Express Building at 2 Rector Street are now occupied by companies that trade equities and derivatives.[48]

By the time the participants in the secondary bond market began to migrate to the OTC derivatives market, around 2002 to 2003, financial engineering in the OTC market had nearly completed a full decade of gestation for a new category of derivatives that played a critical role in the 2008 market crises–namely, credit derivatives.

THE RISE OF CREDIT DERIVATIVES AND THE CREDIT DEFAULT SWAP

Financial Times journalist Gillian Tett tells the fascinating story of how several dozen bankers at J.P. Morgan in New York, London, and Tokyo collectively brainstormed at a retreat that seemed more like a fraternity party than a serious think-tank discussion. The product of their brainstorm was a credit derivative that other bankers at the time, or before that time, such as those at Salomon Brothers, developed.[49] Although the elements and processes that combined to make the CDS are described in greater detail in Part Three, a short summary of the evolution of the CDS will help the reader understand its use by AIG and others as a contributor to the 2008 market crises.

The team of J.P. Morgan bankers that Gillian Tett credits with developing credit derivatives, specifically CDS, worked together as an incubator for ideas, led by Bill Demchak, who, at one point, told his colleagues, with the intent to drive innovation, "You will have to make at least half of your revenues each year from a product which did not exist before!"[50] In one of the bankers' brainstorming sessions, the idea of developing an insurance-like derivative based on loans issued by J.P. Morgan developed. The premise, in a nutshell, was that, if derivatives (such as futures) could enable wheat farmers to limit the risk of loss, then derivatives should also be designed to limit losses by a bank from the default of bank customers on bank repayment obligations. In other words, as one trader at J.P. Morgan reportedly said:

> *J.P. Morgan itself had a veritable mountain of loans on its books that were creating regulatory headaches. . . . Would regulators*

permit [CDS] to be sold? If so, what might it mean for the financial world if default risk—the risk most central to the traditional craft of banking—were turned into just another plaything for traders?[51]

Credit derivatives flourished for many reasons, but a primary one is that the market in which they traded was OTC. The result of the development of the CDS by the J.P. Morgan team and other innovators in the late 1980s and early 1990s was a massive global market in credit derivatives. At its peak, the CDS market was a robust $60 trillion market.[52] The entire credit derivatives market was, by 1996, roughly between $100 to $200 billion, and seven years later, it grew to a $3.5 trillion market in notional value, reflecting the growth of the market from 1997 to 2005.[53]

The unregulated use of credit derivatives such as CDS by AIG and other market participants was a major part of the development of the 2008 market crises. However, it was the combination of the unregulated use of CDS with a completely different financial device, securitization, that spread the contagion worldwide and fed the market crises of 2008.

PRIVATE-LABEL RESIDENTIAL MORTGAGE-BACKED SECURITIZATION

Let's be clear: This is an American mess forged by the American genius for newfangled financial instruments in an era where the mantra has been that government is dumb and the markets are smart and risk is nonexistent. The responsibility for undoing the debacle is chiefly American, too.[54]

Most critics of derivatives have a rather vague notion that derivatives were the sole cause of the market crises that led to recessions in many of the largest markets throughout the world in 2008 to 2009. It is probably more accurate to suggest that some combination of certain credit derivatives and securitization were principal causes of the 2008 market crises. Although the markets in interest rate and currency derivatives comprise the majority of the OTC derivative markets, neither segment caused any crash, or the fall of Lehman Brothers, Bear Stearns, AIG, or other financial services firms. These firms sustained debilitating losses, not because of those swaps, or many of the other categories of derivatives that make up the OTC market, but instead because of their misuse of an otherwise positive, powerful financial tool called securitization. If used properly, securitization can properly fuel the growth of an important area of our economy such as the credit card or real estate mortgage industries.

Collateralized Debt Obligations

Perhaps the greatest villain in the 2008 market crises was the irresponsible user or users of collateralized debt obligations (CDOs), which are, as with asset-backed securities (ABS) and MBS, elegant and elaborate financial tools that, if used properly, can be a tremendously positive, powerful force to fund assets such as mortgages and manage risk. However, inexplicable to many, the 2008 market crises saw investors losing massive amounts, before the complete seizure of the CDO market.

CDOs are members of the credit derivative family. Depending on the underlying asset, the derivative may be a collateralized bond obligation (CBO)—a term that has, in more recent years, fallen from trade parlance, as many refer to CBOs as CDOs—or a collateralized loan obligation (CLO). In a CBO structure, a trust owns the bonds, or a pool of high risk, below investment-grade fixed-income securities. A CLO structure includes a trust, typically collateralized by a pool of bank loans, which may include senior unsecured loans and subordinate corporate loans. The pool may include loans that may be rated below investment grade.

As with OTC derivatives, the vast majority of CBOs, CLOs, and other CDOs were privately offered and sold. Provided that certain exemptions to U.S. securities laws apply, ABS are not required to be registered under U.S. securities laws. That being said, for many asset classes, registration is standard.

In 2008 market crises resulted from these "structured products," including structured notes, which are derivative debt securities. The value of that derivative is the principal of, or interest on, structured notes, and it is typically determined by reference to changes in the worth of a reference rate, or index. The interest rate or the principal amount payable upon maturity or redemption may be increased or decreased, depending on changes in the applicable reference.

In the 2008 market crises, structured notes appeared to have included a greater degree of market risk, and they suffered losses, compared to other types of debt securities, because the investor bore the risk of the underlying reference obligations or indices.

These financial products were misused in the years leading up to 2008 in that the users were risk-averse, unregulated, and failed to take into account a collapse in housing markets. The disappointing reality is that the creators, sponsors, and traders of these products who acted in irresponsible ways are the greatest contributors to the financial crises that began in 2006 and culminated in the fall of Lehman Brothers in September 2008. As a result now, all derivatives have become subject to comprehensive financial services regulation worldwide. Although the financial industry contributed in this way, they could not have brought down many pillars in the global financial system without the unwitting help from the regulators.

U.S. POLICY FOSTERING HOME OWNERSHIP AND GSE MISMANAGEMENT

In his opening remarks to a hearing in the U.S. Senate titled "Mortgage Market Turmoil: Causes and Consequences" in March 2007, Senator Christopher Dodd stated:

> *I am going to take a few moments to lay out what I can only call a chronology of neglect: Regulators tell us they first noticed credit standards deteriorating late in 2003. By then, Fitch Ratings had already placed one major subprime lender on "credit watch," citing concerns over their subprime business. In fact, data collected by the Federal Reserve Board clearly indicated that lenders had started to ease their lending standards by early 2004. Despite those warning signals, in February of 2004 the leadership of the Federal Reserve Board seemed to encourage the development and use of adjustable rate mortgages that today are defaulting and going into foreclosure at record rates. So, in sum, by the Spring of 2004, the regulators had started to document the fact that lending standards were easing. At the same time, the Fed was encouraging lenders to develop and market alternative adjustable rate products, just as it was embarking on a long series of hikes in short-term rates. In my view, these actions get the conditions for the perfect storm that is sweeping over millions of home owners today.[55]*

The federal government's policy to foster home ownership spurred in the mortgage industry the use of adjustable mortgages, and securitization spread the securities backed by the adjustable mortgages (and their risks) throughout the world. Over time, many years of securitized mortgages (that fell into default as interest rates rose) were issued in the United States and overseas.

The first link in this chain reaction is a federal policy of fostering home ownership among Americans. The focus of this policy was on the segment of the U.S. population that was economically unable to make the down payment and monthly mortgage payments that, before the advent of more creative mortgage products, were required to own a home.

Encouraging home ownership is a worthy public undertaking. The federal policy in the United States of encouraging home ownership formally began in 1977, when Congress passed the Community Reinvestment Act (CRA). The CRA affirmed the obligation of federally-insured banks and other depository institutions to meet the credit needs of the communities in which the financial institutions lend.[56] For decades after the Great Depression up to the 1970s, before CRA, many of those communities had failed to lend or actively discriminated against poor, often urban communities.[57]

During the early years of the 2000s in the United States, just as securitization of mortgages was becoming a powerful source of mortgage finance, interest rates were low (following the dot-com crisis and the terrorist attacks on September 11, 2001). The Clinton and Bush Administrations encouraged home ownership and inadvertently fostered a business environment which was ripe for aggressive predatory lending by mortgage originators.

Leading economist Joseph Stiglitz argued that it wasn't the CRA policy of encouraging home ownership itself that was to blame, but private mortgage originators that encouraged subprime borrowers to sign mortgages:

> *The conservative critics believe that government is to blame for doing too much. They criticize the Community Reinvestment Act (CRA) requirements imposed on banks, which required them to lend a certain fraction of their portfolio to underserved minority communities. . . . It is America's fully private financial markets that invented all the bad practices that played a central role in this crisis.*[58]

The criticism of Stiglitz's statement minimizes the government's role and is not supported by a consensus. According to Lawrence Harris, a professor of finance, regulators in Washington are deserving of at least part of the blame for spurring home ownership with the awareness that some of the practices were reckless:

> *Political pressure [to increase home ownership]—this is where Washington may bear some blame for the present mess [according to Lawrence Harris, professor of finance at the University of Southern California]. The mortgage leviathans Fannie Mae and Freddie Mac were encouraged to sacrifice safety to keep their great loan machines running at top speed, he said. "Everyone in the administration and Congress wanted money to go into the housing industry," he said. "There was a lot of pressure on them to look the other*

way when receiving undocumented paper that they knew, or should have known, wasn't going to be good. They didn't feel they were all that exposed to risk."[59]

Government-Sponsored Enterprise (GSE)

Viewing government policy to encourage home ownership by those who could afford to pay for mortgages as the sole cause of the 2008 market crises is a mistake. GSEs are corporate entities that enjoy the backing of the federal government. These entities are guarantors of mortgages within securitized pools (of mortgages). However, over time, GSEs became massively overleveraged and were mismanaged. Later known as mortgage leviathans, Fannie Mae and Freddie Mac were each conduits that fueled the subprime crisis. The purpose of these legal entities is to stabilize mortgage lending. In many respects, the GSEs destabilized the system.

Since their creation, the GSEs were part of the problem in many respects, including those identified in the *Crisis Commission Report*. As residential mortgages were originated, the implicit government backing that accompanied a mortgage enabled mortgage originators to underwrite loans that perhaps they would not have underwritten without GSE backing.

The sheer volume of guaranteed and securitized pools of mortgages created a too-big-to-fail mentality with respect to the GSEs, in large part because of these factors that were identified by the Hon. Bill Thomas and his dissenting colleagues in the *Crisis Commission Report:* GSEs were large financial institutions whose failure in and of themselves risked contagion. Yet, they could not go bankrupt because financial institutions throughout the world held GSE debt, and markets depended on the well being of the servicing of that debt. The ongoing mortgage origination system in the United States depended on the existence of the GSEs.[60] Accordingly, the GSEs and a broader federal policy fostering home ownership served as the backbone of the real-estate–based credit crises which emanated in America.

DERIVATIVES AND STRUCTURED PRODUCTS ACCOUNTING PRACTICES

An accounting system that originated in the Middle Ages can't keep track of things like derivative instruments.[61]

I would like to argue that important aspects of crisis are rooted in the failure of accounting theory, standards, regulators, and practice, and we shall have to act to help fix the problems.[62]

One of the many lessons taught by the Enron crisis, which did not get adequate attention by policy makers prior to the crises of 2007 to 2008, was the use of aggressive accounting practices to keep derivatives and structured products off balance sheets. Although this aspect of the Enron crisis, as discussed earlier in this chapter, may have caught the attention of accounting and public policy officials, it did not keep their and other policy makers' attention focused long enough, because even larger accounting problems permitted excessive leverage and resulted in losses leading to the 2008 market crises. As a result:

- *Banks were, and still possibly are, overleveraged:* As this book went to press, U.S. Generally Accepted Accounting Practices (GAAP) did do not recognize gross derivatives exposure on balance sheets. Daniel Gros argues that part of the role that accounting standards and practices play is to accurately and completely disclose the financial well being of enterprises. However, whereas European accounting principles (International Financial Reporting Standards or IRFS) require the disclosure of "positive market values from derivatives," GAAP calls for "derivatives post netting."[63] Gros illustrates the issue by looking at Deutsche Bank, which reports its financials using both GAAP and IRFS. According to Gros, the financials of Deutsche Bank demonstrate that the bank is twice as leveraged under IRFS reporting than under GAAP. The conclusion, according to Gros, is that U.S. banks using GAAP may be under reporting the extent of their derivatives exposure and leverage, even after the 2008 market crises.[64] According to Gros: "properly measured, leverage is still at the same level as the peak of the bubble in late 2007." The conditions for a new systemic crisis are thus still in place according to Gros.[65]
- Accounting practices permitted sponsors of securitization trusts to keep those trusts off the sponsors' balance sheets prior to the 2008 market crises. Bank regulators likely did not recognize how securitization enabled the sponsors to shift liability off of the balance sheets.

Although a proper treatment of the manner in which accounting practices contributed to risk-taking and the broader market failures in 2008 is beyond the scope of this text, any analysis identifying contributors to the market crises which omits mention of the practical application of accounting standards is incomplete.

*　*　*

This chapter was designed to provide a summary of what the author believes are the leading causes to the crises that led to derivatives reform. Clearly, there was no sole cause for the crisis, and critics of derivatives who point their fingers at derivatives as a leading (or the only) cause of the economic crises are disregarding the adverse effects of government policy, government-sponsored enterprises, loopholes left by laws past after former crises, and several other factors in the crises that are discussed in the preceding pages.

Although derivatives did play a role in the 2008 market crises, it was not a leading role. The risk management function of credit default swaps had the effect of luring executives in failed financial service firms into a false sense of security. Did these executives realize and act rationally after reaching that conclusion? Absolutely not.

In fact, some commentators point to a human element in the financial crisis. Instead of realizing that their balance sheets were weighed down excessively with assets that were of little value, instead of entering into damage control, executives of major firms that failed in 2008 undertook even greater risks, according to the president of Atlantic Investors, a $3.5 billion investment-management company and hedge fund:

> *I've been talking about [the market crises of 2008] for years.... But I started to notice it in the fall [of 2008]. Because if you think about it, if you have all this nuclear waste on your balance sheet, what are you supposed to do? You're supposed to cut your dividends, you're supposed to raise equity, and you're supposed to shrink your balance sheet. And they [Lehman Brothers and Bear Stearns & Co.] did just the opposite. They took on more leverage. Lehman went from twenty-five to thirty-five times leveraged in one year. And then they announce a big stock buyback at $65 a share and they sell stock at $38 a share. I mean, they don't know what they're doing. And yet they get rewarded for doing that. It makes me sick.*[66]

This analysis suggests that human error in the form of irresponsible risk taking was a primary cause in the crises, as opposed to any financial product such as a derivative. It is unclear that the massive reform effort which resulted in 2010 and thereafter gets to the heart of the problem: excessive risk taking. Therefore, it is also not clear that the reform which this book details will in fact prevent the next market crisis. Certainly an uncoordinated international reform effort will change almost nothing.

With the timeline of the crisis and an understanding of how it unfolded, as provided in the next chapter of this book, at least we will be in a better position to identify and prevent the exacerbation of the next financial crisis before it is too late.

NOTES

1. *International Financing Review*. 2011. "Clearing Houses Would Not Have Prevented Financial Crisis." May 17.
2. Joseph E. Stiglitz, *Freefall: America, Free Markets and the Sinking of the World Economy* (New York: Norton, 2010), xxv.
3. Sher Verick and Iyanatul Islam, *The Great Recession of 2008–2009: Causes, Consequences and Policy Responses* (Bonn: Institute for the Study of Labor, Deutsche Post Foundation, May 2010), 3–4.
4. Warren E. Buffett, Chairman of the Board, Berkshire Hathaway, Annual Report (Feb. 21, 2003).
5. Pub. L. 107-204.
6. *The Financial Crisis Inquiry Report: Final Report of the National Commission on the Causes of the Financial and Economic Crisis in the United States* (New York: BBS Public Affairs, 2011) (hereinafter *Crisis Commission Report*), 443.
7. Ibid., xxiv–xxv.
8. Ibid., 45.
9. Ibid.
10. Ibid., 46.
11. Ibid., 426.
12. George White, "William Seidman on Culprits of the Financial Crisis," TheDeal .com, November 10, 2008. www.thedeal.com/dealscape/2008/11/william_sei dman_on_culprits_of.php.
13. The Sarbanes-Oxley Act of 2002 (Pub. L. 107-204), 116 Stat. 745.
14. "Report of Investigation by the Special Investigative Committee of the Board of Directors of Enron Corp.," February 1, 2002 (Powers Report), 5.
15. Ibid., 5.
16. Frank Partnoy, "Enron and the Use of Derivatives," (Testimony before the Senate Committee on Government Affairs, March 2002), 2, 20.
17. Ibid., 19.
18. Ibid.
19. Joseph Stiglitz, "The Anatomy of a Murder: Who Killed America's Economy?" *Critical Review* 21, no. 2–3 (2009).
20. Conrad de Aenlle and Julia Werdigier, "Regulation 101: First, Bend the Rules," *International Herald Tribune*, September 20–21, 2008.
21. Arthur M. Schlesinger, Jr., *The Coming of the New Deal* (Pennsauken, NJ: Windmill Press, 1960), 3–4.
22. De Aenlle and Werdigier, "Regulation 101."
23. Ibid.
24. Ibid.
25. Andrew Ross Sorkin, *Too Big To Fail* (New York: Viking, 2009), 5.
26. Ibid., 4.
27. Bill Gross, "Beware Our Shadow Banking System," *Money*, CNN.com, November 28, 2007.
28. Gary Gensler: "Current Legislation 'Strong, Comprehensive and Historic,'" FuturesMag.Com (July 1, 2010), www.futuresmag.com/News/2010/7/Pages/

Gensler-Current-legislation-strong-comprehensive-and-historic.aspx (Accessed on January 6, 2011).

29. See "Private-Label Residential Mortgage-Backed Securitization" on page 45 in this chapter.
30. George Graham, "Warning on Poor Lending Standards," *Financial Times,* October 15, 1998, 8.
31. David Barboza and Jeff Gerth, "On Regulating Derivatives," *New York Times,* December 15, 1998, C1.
32. Barbara C. Matthews, "Capital Adequacy, Netting and Derivatives," *Standard Journal of Law, Business, and Finance* 167 (1995): 169–170.
33. See Bruce S. Darringer, "Swaps, Banks and Capital: An Analysis of Swap Risks and a Critical Assessment of the Basel Accord's Treatment of Swaps," *University of Pennsylvania International Business Law* 259 (1995): 16.
34. Gensler, "Current Legislation."
35. Ibid.
36. Ibid.
37. Ibid.
38. Ibid.
39. Ibid.
40. "OTC Derivatives Market Activity in the Second Half of 2009," Bank for International Settlements (May 11, 2010). www.bis.org/press/p100511.htm.
41. Hendrik Bessembinder and William Maxwell, "Transparency and the Corporate Bond Market," *Journal of Economic Perspectives* (Spring, 2008): 3. Available in abstract, http://ssrn.com/abstract=1082459.
42. Ibid.
43. Mark Pittman and Caroline Salas, "Bond Traders Lose $1 Million Incomes as Transparency Cuts Jobs," *BondsOnline,* October 24, 2006. www.bondsonline .com/News_Releases/news10240601.php.
44. Dave Boberski, *CDS Delivery Option* (New York: Bloomberg, 2009), xv.
45. Bessembinder and Maxwell, "Transparency and the Corporate Bond Market."
46. Pittman and Salas, "Bond Traders Lose $1 Million."
47. Ibid.
48. Ibid.
49. Gillian Tett, *Fools Gold* (New York: Free Press, 2009), 3.
50. Ibid., 7–8.
51. Ibid., 21.
52. Gensler: "Current Legislation."
53. George Chacko et al., *Credit Derivatives: A Primer on Credit Risk, Modeling and Instruments* (Philadelphia, PA: Wharton School Publishing, 2006), 53.
54. Roger Cohen, "The Fleecing of America," *International Herald Tribune,* September 22, 2008.
55. U.S. Senate Committee on Banking, Housing, and Urban Affairs, March 22, 2007, referenced in Michael Lewis, *Panic: The Story of Modern Financial Insanity* (New York: Norton, 2009), 309.
56. Speech by Chairman Ben S. Bernanke, Community Affairs Research Conference, Washington, DC, March 30, 2007.

57. Ibid.
58. Joseph Stiglitz, "The Anatomy of a Murder."
59. De Aenlle and Werdigier, "Regulation 101."
60. *Crisis Commission Report*, 425.
61. Daniel Gros, "Are We Primed for Another Crisis?" http://wallstreetpit.com/15236-are-we-primed-for-another-crisis.
62. Ibid.
63. De Aenlle and Werdigier, "Regulation 101."
64. Shyam Sunder, Yale School of Management, Accounting Research Symposium, Hangzhou, China Slide Presentation, December 16–17, 2009.
65. Gros, "Are We Primed for Another Crisis?"
66. William D. Cohan, *House of Cards: A Tale of Hubris and Wretched Excess on Wall Street* (New York: Doubleday, 2009), 3.

CHAPTER 2

The Crises and Reform Timeline

Chapter 1 presented seven causes of the 2008 market crises that led to the subject of this book: derivatives reform.

One takeaway from the previous chapter is that many over-the-counter (OTC) derivatives did *not* lead *or even contribute at all* to the massive losses that began in 2007 to 2008. Many thousands of interest-rate swaps and foreign-exchange derivatives, for example, had no bearing whatsoever on the losses sustained by large banks, investors, and individuals in the markets. In fact, these and many other categories of derivatives were and continue to facilitate everyday business, yet, as we will see, comprehensive regulation of derivatives came about after a series of events that are highlighted in this chapter.

In this chapter, we begin on the eve of the 2008 market crises, right after the fall of Bear Stearns & Co. on March 16, 2008, and then follow a timeline that helps the reader see how Federal officials eventually voted, enacted and signed into law on July 21, 2010 the single greatest body of derivative mandates in U.S. history: Title VII of the Dodd-Frank Wall Street Reform and Consumer Protection Act.

So that the reader has the entire timeline in one place with six of the most important milestones detailed in the pages that follow, we begin with Figure 2.1. So as not to get lost among the trees, that is, the details of the events described in the pages that follow, the reader is presented with three distinct phases of the timeline, as illustrated in Figure 2.1:

1. The collapse of the U.S. housing market.
2. The adverse and long-lasting effect of the housing market collapse not only on financial markets, but especially on holders of securities whose value derived principally from pools of mortgages, and those mortgages began to default after 2006.

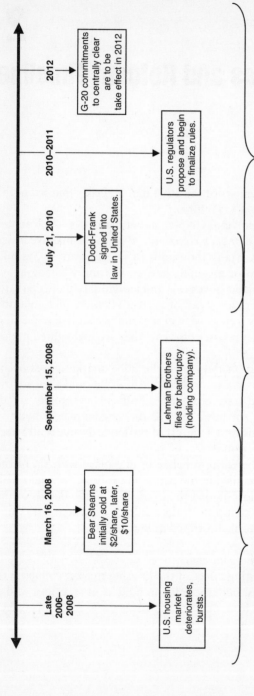

FIGURE 2.1 Crises and Reform Timeline

3. Government responds to the financial crises, including the enactment of federal law, the recapitalization of large financial services firms, and the promulgation of extensive regulations on, among other aspects of the financial services industry, the over-the-counter derivatives market.

Because the market crises and resulting reforms took place first in the United States and emanated outward, this chapter puts the reader in downtown New York in 2008, in the early months of the market crises. It then takes the reader through the eve of reform and through the early regulatory timeline in 2011. The focus of this timeline is derivatives reform; the trillions in currencies that the United States and other governments provided to save major players in marketplaces are well documented elsewhere and are outside the scope of this work. The early players and guiding principles for U.S. reform are introduced as a prelude to the global response and broader reforms which are the subject of Chapter 3.

MARCH 17, 2008: BEAR STEARNS IS SOLD

We begin in the middle of March 2008, where we find a prominent investment bank Bear Stearns & Co., in utter chaos and on the brink of collapse. With over 15,000 employees in markets throughout the world in the earliest days of the twenty-first century, Bear Stearns, established in 1923, weathered the Great Depression and a World War. Just a year earlier, in 2007, its shares traded at $172.00.

After counterparties fled the firm, generally because of its excessive leverage and, particularly, because of its overuse of mortgage-backed securities and related derivatives, Bear Stearns executives, directors, and shareholders had no choice but to sell the firm at $10 per share to JPMorgan Chase & Co. on March 17, 2008.[1]

Instrumental in that sale was the head of the New York Federal Reserve, Timothy Franz Geithner. He firmly believed that without the financial support by the United States for the purchase of Bear Stearns by JPMorgan Chase & Co., the bankruptcy of Bear Stearns "would have caused a run on the entire market. That, in turn, would have made it impossible for other investment banks to fund themselves," according to a New York Federal Reserve official.[2]

Geithner and then-Secretary of the Treasury Henry "Hank" Paulson Jr. on the eve of the sale of Bear Stearns feverishly worked to facilitate the sale of Bear Stearns to prevent collapses throughout the financial system. Their efforts eventually resulted in the Federal Reserve providing credit support for $29 billion in residential mortgage-based structured products and other assets of Bear Stearns, as a condition to JPMorgan Chase acquiring Bear Stearns.[3]

MARCH 27, 2008: BARACK OBAMA INTRODUCES REFORM PRINCIPLES

Ten days after the sale of Bear Stearns, Illinois Senator Barack Obama, while campaigning for the U.S. presidency, delivered an influential speech on March 27, 2008, at Cooper Union in New York. The then-senator proposed an exceedingly aggressive, broad reform mandate to the audience in attendance, which included Paul Volcker, the former chairman of the Federal Reserve Board and Michael Bloomberg, the mayor of New York.

In his speech at Cooper Union, where first president George Washington took the oath of office, Obama presented six principles of reform. These principles, according to Obama, were necessary to guide financial reform efforts because America's historically inherent "sense of shared prosperity" has been lost due to private dealmaking in "board rooms, on trading floors and in Washington . . . decisions made in New York's high rises have consequences for Americans across the country."[4] Then-Senator Obama said at in Lower Manhattan on March 27, 2008:

> *Now, as most experts agree, our economy is in recession. To renew our economy and to ensure that we are not doomed to repeat a cycle of bubble and bust again and again and again, we need to address not only the immediate crisis in the housing market, we also need to create a twenty-first century regulatory framework and we need to pursue a bold opportunity agenda for the American people.[5]*

It was in downtown New York City, on March 27, 2008, that an entirely new regulatory framework, that included a comprehensive reworking of derivatives trading at least in the United States, was born. This rework of derivatives-trading regulation cannot be more comprehensive; it affects every stage of the life cycle of a derivatives trade.

The broader resulting reform of financial services in the United States within which derivatives reform was a part is even more remarkable. This is because the reform does not focus exclusively on primary causes of the 2008 market crises, namely, the excessive leveraging of investment banks in mortgage-backed securities, coupled with the collapse of the housing markets. Instead, the reform that Obama seemed to have in mind as a presidential candidate as early as March 27, 2008, involved a wholesale re-ordering of government agencies and coverage of all or nearly all financial services, from the issuance of credit cards to the marketing of mortgage-backed securities, and everything in between. Very little was off of the regulatory reform table. These six principles were outlined by then-Senator Obama as guideposts for the required reform:

1. Borrowers of government funding during a crisis should be subject to oversight.
2. No financial institution should be free from effective regulation and financial services reform must include new capital requirements for firms that invest in "complex financial instruments like some of the mortgage securities that led to our current crisis."
3. Current financial regulation and the agencies that carry out that regulation need to be streamlined.
4. Institutions need to be regulated "for what they do, not who they are. Over the last few years, commercial banks and thrift institutions were subject to guidelines on subprime mortgage that did not apply to mortgage brokers and companies. Now, it makes no sense for the Fed to tighten mortgage guidelines for banks when two-thirds of subprime mortgages don't originate from banks."
5. "We must remain vigilant and crack down on trading activity that crosses the line to market manipulation. On [sic] recent days, reports have circulated that some traders may have intentionally spread rumors that Bear Stearns was in financial distress while making market bets against the country [company]."
6. "Sixth," we need a process that identifies systemic risks to the financial system."[6]

Obama's state of mind in this early vision of financial services reform does not include any mention of mainstream derivatives such as interest rate and currency swaps, but instead pinpoints, accurately, mortgage-backed securities as a root cause of the market crises.

However, after Obama became president, the Obama Administration's need to reform *all* OTC derivatives translated into a major component of the law that President Obama eventually signed on July 21, 2010.

SEPTEMBER 15, 2008: A BANKRUPT LEHMAN BROTHERS

The largest bankruptcy filing in the history of the United States took place on this date, with Lehman holding over $600 billion in assets, and many thousands of cash and derivative trading counterparties now had to contend with their bankrupt broker-dealer. Following this event, the cataclysmic series of market failures described in the Introduction and Chapter 1 took place.

NOVEMBER 2008 TO JANUARY 2009: AMERICAN LEADERSHIP ASCENDS

On November 4, 2008, Barack Obama was elected president of the United States, and Obama appointed Timothy Geithner as Secretary of the U.S. Treasury. Geithner's first day as Treasury Secretary was January 26, 2009.

MARCH 26, 2009: GEITHNER PROVIDES TESTIMONY TO CONGRESS ON REFORM

Two months after his first day as Treasury Secretary, Timothy Geithner testified to the chamber within Congress that acts first on derivatives reform, the U.S. House of Representatives. Before the House Financial Services Committee, Secretary Geithner testified about "the most severe global financial crisis in generations."[7]

Geithner testified that Americans were saddled with financial obligations which they did not understand. It appears from his testimony that he referred not only to home owners, but also to traders and executives associated with the largest investment banks in America. Geithner also described President Obama's approach to financial services reform:

> On February 25 [2009], after meeting with the banking and financial services leadership from Congress, President Obama directed his economic team to develop recommendations for financial regulatory reform and to begin the process of working with the Congress on new legislation. The Treasury Department has been working with the President's Working Group on Financial Markets (PWG) to develop a comprehensive plan of reform. This effort has been and will be guided by principles the president set forth earlier this year and in his speech as a candidate at Cooper Union in March 2008.[8]

In this testimony, we first hear one of President Obama's principal spokespersons for new financial service regulation identify derivatives reform within a broader plan to reduce systemic risk. Geithner testified that the U.S. government should "establish a comprehensive framework of oversight, protections and disclosure for the OTC derivatives market, moving the standardized parts of these markets to central clearinghouse [sic], and encouraging further use of exchange-traded instruments."[9] So it was on

March 26, 2009 that we first heard that the Obama Administration would convert the OTC market to an exchange-traded market.

MAY 13, 2009: GEITHNER WRITES A LETTER TO HARRY REID

In one of his earliest written statements on derivatives as Treasury Secretary, Geithner opens his letter, addressed to powerful members of the U.S. Congress, including Senate Majority Leader Harry Reid (D-NV), by referencing his testimony before the House earlier in March. Then, in the second sentence of the letter, he explained that OTC derivatives are largely excluded from regulation by current law. He next indicated that after consultation with federal security and commodity regulators, Geithner seeks the amendment of federal security and commodity laws to include a comprehensive new body of law governing derivatives.

Geithner's recitation of the categories of new derivatives regulation echoed many of the principles of financial services reform that were outlined by then-Senator Obama on the campaign trail a year earlier: management of systemic risk caused by OTC derivatives; the protection of unsophisticated market participants; and the improvement of the regulatory regime to ensure that the Securities and Exchange Commission and the Commodity Futures Trading Commission have "clear, unimpeded authority" to regulate and prevent manipulation.[10]

The cornerstone of Geithner's new comprehensive reform is the amendment of federal law to require "all OTC derivatives dealers" and other market participants to be subject to more rigorous laws including—most important—a clearing mandate; trading based on regulated, electronic exchanges and trade-execution systems; the timely reporting of trades for market transparency and regulatory oversight; the collateralization of trades by margin requirements; and capital requirements for large banks.[11]

JUNE 2, 2009: AN EARLY VOICE SPEAKS OUT AGAINST THE CLEARING MANDATE

On June 2, 2009, a Washington, DC-based publication, *The Hill*, publishes a compelling article written by the Hon. Mike McMahon (D-NY) of the U.S. House of Representatives, in which McMahon accurately places the blame for the misuse of derivatives on AIG and others that poorly managed their derivatives-trading books. McMahon, who acknowledges that derivatives played a role in the 2008 market crises, nevertheless indicated that the Obama Administration's mandate to require all or nearly all OTC derivatives to be exchange-traded and cleared to be an overreaction to the market crises that will damage corporations using derivatives in the ordinary course of business.[12]

JUNE 22, 2009: AMERICAN CORPORATIONS LOBBY AGAINST CENTRAL CLEARING MANDATES FOR OTC DERIVATIVES

Another champion in Congress for the legitimate use of derivatives by main-stream companies was Senator Michael Crapo (R-ID), and on June 22, 2009, the Senator posted a series of letters from industry leaders explaining that a mandate to require all derivatives to be centrally cleared would, in the case of Cargill Risk Management, divert working capital in excess of $1 billion from its operations. David Dines, President of Cargill, wrote that if this amount is multiplied "across all companies in the U.S. . . . [the] ramifications are enormous, especially at a time when credit is critically tight." Senator Crapo subsequently posted a letter addressed to him by the Director of Risk Management of beverage giant MillerCoors in which the director stated that increased collateral costs would result from central clearing, notwithstanding the extensive team and prudent derivatives trading practices already in effect at MillerCoors.[13]

JULY 22, 2009: INTRODUCTION OF LEGISLATION FAVORING EXEMPTIONS TO THE CLEARING MANDATE

Early legislative efforts favoring the preservation of OTC derivative trading in limited circumstances continue on this date with the introduction by U.S. Representative Mike McMahon and Members of the New Democrats Coalition of H.R. 3300, whose intent to exempt certain derivatives from central clearing is illustrated:

> *Clearinghouses require that participants pledge only liquid collateral, such as cash or short-term government securities, to support their positions in the market without regard to the credit quality of the company. However, companies need their most liquid assets for the working capital and investment purposes. Requiring a company to post cash as collateral means removing cash from the company's core business, which hurts the company and its employees, as well as the overall economy of the United States.*[14]

The bill would create an Office of Derivatives Supervision within the U.S. Treasury and require traders of derivatives to register with regulators. End users of derivatives that obtain funds in debt markets on an uncollateralized basis were, under this bill, relieved from any margin requirements related to derivatives.

JULY 30, 2009: INTRODUCTION OF BROAD OUTLINES OF THE NEW LAW

Rep. Barney Frank (D-MA), Chairman of the House Financial Services Committee, and Collin Peterson (D-MN), Chairman of the House Agriculture Committee, announced what would become the framework, generally, of the law that would be enacted on July 21, 2010. Broad mandates were included in a concept paper. These mandates included the mandatory clearing of OTC derivatives, with two exceptions: if a regulator determines that a product is not sufficiently standardized or if one party to a trade is not a "major market participant," as determined by an appropriate regulator.

The exception to the clearing mandate was actually far more restrictive than legislation passed by the House of Representatives in December 2009 and the legislation signed into law by the president on July 21, 2010.

SEPTEMBER 8, 2009: THE INDUSTRY DEMONSTRATES COMMITMENT TO CENTRALIZED CLEARING

Fifteen major OTC derivative dealers committed, in a letter to the Federal Reserve Bank of New York, to meet certain specified clearing targets for clearing interest rate and credit derivatives. Although this was an important development milestone, clearinghouses have over the years cleared the derivatives that were the subject of the September 8, 2009 commitment. Moreover, the clearing that is the subject of the dealers' commitments is among banks, not end users such as airlines, real- estate developers, or many of the other companies that use and require interest rate swaps to manage interest-rate risk.

OCTOBER 2, 2009: HOUSE RELEASES DRAFT OF OTC DERIVATIVE LEGISLATION

Rep. Barney Frank (D-MA) continued his leadership in the OTC derivatives legislative realm by releasing a 187-page discussion draft of legislation, which, in many ways, formed the foundation of the legislation that was signed into law a year later. The bill, titled the Over-the-Counter Derivatives Markets Act of 2009, introduced key terms such as "major swap participant" and "major security-based swap participant," and other early concepts were introduced by this draft legislation, such as excluding derivatives that were entered into for hedging purposes from the determination of whether a market participant is categorized among the most active derivative players.

NOVEMBER 11, 2009: SENATE RELEASES DRAFT OF OTC DERIVATIVE LEGISLATION

Senator Chris Dodd (D-CT), Senate Banking Committee Chairman, released a bill in discussion draft form called for a major overhaul of financial services regulation. The draft called for the creation of an independent watchdog, the Consumer Financial Protection Agency, to ensure that consumers get clear and accurate information on financial products, including mortgages.

The proposed law was based on many of the precepts that form the basis of the law now in effect in the U.S., including:

- Regulators in the United States lack authority to require, and there is no regulatory mandate that requires that derivative development and trading activities be closely monitored and regulated. The Senate's discussion draft gives the SEC and the CFTC authority to regulate derivatives.
- Clearing derivatives is a cornerstone of the proposed law. The CFTC and SEC are to determine which trades must be centrally cleared.
- For those trades that are not centrally cleared, the proposed law requires the parties to those derivatives to post collateral in order to offset risk posed to the system.
- Swap repositories and clearinghouses are to collect and publish data to make the derivatives market in the United States more transparent to the public and accessible to regulators.

DECEMBER 11, 2009: HOUSE PASSES THE WALL STREET REFORM AND CONSUMER PROTECTION ACT OF 2009

The House led the Senate in derivatives reform by passing comprehensive legislation that would completely transform the derivatives trade in the United States. The legislation passed by the House would then be considered along with the legislation to be passed by the Senate by a conference committee comprised of representatives of both the Senate and the House in 2010. Then the president would sign the product of that committee on July 21, 2010.

One key feature of the Wall Street Reform and Consumer Protection Act of 2009 is the exception to the clearing requirement, which was drafted in a way that allowed more end users to trade OTC as opposed to settling trades via a clearinghouse. As long as a party to a derivative that is mandated for clearing is not a major swap participant (or a major security-based swap participant), is not a dealer of derivatives, and uses the trade to hedge risk (including balance sheet risk), the trade need not be centrally cleared. The importance of this is that many mainstream companies that need derivatives to manage risk (such as the risk of rising energy prices) may continue to negotiate and trade derivatives OTC with customized collateral arrangements. This legislation would, at least in reference to exceptions to clearing, meet many of the needs expressed earlier by large corporations in letters (see the entry in this timeline for June 22, 2009).

JANUARY 1, 2010: THE NEW YORK FED PUBLISHES *THE POLICY PERSPECTIVES ON OTC DERIVATIVES MARKET STRUCTURE*

The Federal Reserve makes clear that, although OTC derivatives were not the central cause of the 2008 market crises, the complexity of derivatives and the opaque nature of the OTC derivative market in the United States exacerbated the problems relating to the crises. This influential paper discussed the ways in which regulators, including the New York Fed, could better monitor and regulate derivatives in the OTC market in the United States. Included among the recommendations were the need for higher capital requirements, more transparency in pricing of derivatives and supervision of clearinghouses. The white paper, which referenced dealer initiatives to clear derivatives (see the September 8, 2009, entry in this timeline) recognized that clearinghouses, which effectively guaranteed trades previously settled over-the-counter, do not eliminate counterparty risk (a clearinghouse bears the risk of clearing member default to some extent), and because of that, regulators need to more closely monitor and ensure that the centralization of risk will not pose problems to the financial system. This paper was revised in March of 2010.

APRIL 7, 2010: FINANCIAL CRISIS INQUIRY COMMISSION BEGINS HEARINGS

As noted in Chapter 1, the Financial Crisis Inquiry Commission formed by Congress began its hearings on the causes of the 2008 market crises on April 7, 2010. Although a Herculean effort was mader, some questioned the timing of the Commission, as members of Congress in both chambers had begun and in some cases completed substantial work in preparing drafts of legislation—well before January 2011, when the Commission published its findings concerning the causes of the 2008 market crises.

APRIL 16, 2010: SENATOR LINCOLN INTRODUCES THE WALL STREET TRANSPARENCY AND ACCOUNTABILITY ACT OF 2010

Many regarded Senator Blanche Lincoln's legislation as the most stringent legislation on OTC derivatives to ever be introduced in Congress. Although many of the provisions were integrated into the legislation that was signed by President Obama on July 21, 2010, the timing of Senator Lincoln's re-election campaign, and her eventual loss, had a negative effect on the viability of some of the more stringent aspects of her bill. For example, Senator Lincoln's draft severely limited the ability of banks to engage in the proprietary trading of derivatives. Her plan called for banks to spin-off their derivatives trading desks (or separately capitalize those activities). A modified version of this feature made its way into the legislation signed into law by the President, but a four-year phase-in period was included for banks to make arrangements for severing proprietary trading, including derivatives trading, from banking operations.

APRIL 22, 2010: PRESIDENT OBAMA RETURNS TO COOPER UNION TO SPEAK ON REFORM

Bank executives assembled on this date at Cooper Union heard President Obama urge them to support financial services reform, so that the economy could improve. President Obama referenced in his speech the visit that he made to Cooper Union as a candidate for president:

> Now, since I last spoke here two years ago, our country has been through a terrible trial. More than 8 million people have lost their jobs. Countless small businesses have had to shut their doors. Trillions of dollars in savings have been lost—forcing seniors to put off retirement, young people to postpone college, entrepreneurs to give up on the dream of starting a company. And as a nation we were forced to take unprecedented steps to rescue the financial system and the broader economy... but you're here and I'm here because we've got more work to do.... As I said on this stage two

years ago, I believe in the power of the free market.... I've spoken before about the need to build a new foundation for economic growth in the twenty-first century. And the importance of the financial sector requires that Wall Street reform is an absolutely essential part of that foundation. Without it, our house will continue to sit on shifting sands, and our families, businesses, and the global economy will be vulnerable to future crises. That's why I feel so strongly that we need to enact a set of updated, commonsense rules to ensure accountability on Wall Street and to protect consumers in our financial system.[15]

APRIL 26 TO 27, 2010: SENATE VOTES TO DELAY DEBATE ON DERIVATIVES REFORM

In two votes with the same outcome of 57 to 41, a procedural measure to move forward on debate on financial services and derivatives reform failed in the U.S. Senate, effectively stalling movement toward new derivatives law. Sixty votes are required in the U.S. Senate to move forward on legislation towards passage into law. The result: Senators were sent back to reach agreement on open issues.

Before the Senate vote that eventually brought Dodd-Frank to the floor for debate, reconciliation, and enactment later in July of 2010, key Republican senators stalled passage of the bill. However, these key members of Congress could not delay reform efforts much longer, after oversight hearings:

Among the challenges for Republicans was explaining how they could participate in an oversight hearing on Tuesday criticizing Goldman Sachs executives and proclaiming the need to tighten regulation on Wall Street, but then go to the Senate chamber and vote to block debate of the financial reform regulatory bill.[16]

APRIL 27, 2010: THE GOLDMAN HEARING

A key catalyst to the implementation of reform was the "Goldman hearing" in late April 2010:

The Goldman hearing on April 27, 2010, involved, in one room, several hundred members of the media, including at least fifty camera-toting journalists seated on the floor in front of a large rectangular table, rows of officials seated behind the table where witnesses from Goldman sat, leaving standing room only for security guards, who had to pacify approximately fifteen members of the public who were dressed in prison garb and hissed during the hearing when bonuses of Goldman employees were announced.

The obvious intent of the members of Congress who interviewed the Goldman Sachs officials, which included Chief Executive Officer Lloyd Blankfein and the head of Goldman's mortgage unit Daniel Sparks, was to bring to light perceived unethical practices involved in the design and sale of collateralized debt obligations (CDOs) and other transactions. However, to the public, it was as if two worlds (one from Wall Street and the other from Washington, DC) collided, leaving little resolved, as one Washington commentator wrote:

> *It was as if people from different planets had finally come together in the Dirksen Senate Office Building for Tuesday's big hearing on Goldman Sachs and its role in fomenting the financial crisis. From Planet Washington were the members of the Senate's Permanent Subcommittee on Investigations, aging and slightly rumpled*

Senator Carol Levin and his staff spearheaded a lengthy investigation that culminated with a hearing that brought public attention to the market-making role of Goldman Sachs. Seated behind Senator Levin were his longtime chief investigators, aidses and staff members with whom the author interfaced some ten years earlier during hearings related to Enron: Robert L. Roach and Elise J. Bean, Counsel and Deputy Chief Counsel to Sen. Levin, within the Senate Permanent Subcommittee on Investigations (April 27, 2010) (author's photography).

politicians of varying sophistication who had spent several months tutoring themselves about the fine points of synthetic CDOs and who only wanted the aliens before them to acknowledge how much havoc they had wreaked on the markets and the economy. . . . Sitting opposite were four brilliant young men from Planet Wall Street, each impeccably tailored in dark suits, white shirts and subtly colored ties, and each sporting that one-day growth of facial hair that holds some mysterious attraction to females in Lower Manhattan. Tutored by Goldman's army of lawyers, the four responded to each question with a question. . . . The Fab Four made clear that there was no such thing as a bad deal or a crappy security. . . . Finally, after five frustrating hours of talking past each other, everyone simply gave up. A new, slightly older and more accommodating panel of Goldman aliens was ushered in, followed finally by the firm's chief executive. The results were largely the same: The issues were never really joined, the conflicting viewpoints never resolved, the full story never told.[17]

Demonstrators wearing striped mock prison garb holding "Wanted" notices with pictures of Lloyd Blankfein and trader Fabrice Tourre of Goldman. During the hearing, at the mention of certain facts such as the bonuses of Goldman traders, the demonstrators would hiss, causing security to ask the demonstrators to remain silent (April 27, 2010) (author's photography).

Although the Goldman hearing in late April 2010 yielded little in the way of clarity on the issue of whether Goldman broke the law or is culpable for the financial crisis, the hearing resulted in Goldman's shares falling to a nine-month low, losing $21 billion in market value by May 1, 2010, and the Democrat leadership in the U.S. Senate succeeded in bringing about a final vote on legislation that would be the basis for new U.S. derivatives law.[18]

A nearly ten percent drop[19] in Goldman's share price after the Goldman hearings coincided with renewed momentum for derivatives lawmaking in the U.S.

APRIL 28, 2010: SENATE VOTES AGAIN TO PROCEED WITH FINANCIAL SERVICES REFORM

The third time is the charm—but not in derivatives reform. For the third time in three days, on April 28, 2010, the Senate voted 56 to 42 to continue to block formal derivatives and financial services reform.

On the morning of April 29, 2010, Politico.com reported that late in the evening of Wednesday, April 28, 2010, the Senate voted to proceed with legislation:

> *And by late Wednesday—after three days of negative headlines and an 11-hour grilling Tuesday of Goldman Sachs executives by frustrated senators—Republicans backed down. But they won a few concessions, most notably the removal of a $50 billion industry-financed fund to wind down doomed companies. The standoff ended with a whimper, as Republicans agreed to proceed to the bill on a voice vote, declining an opportunity to put their position on record.... "It's time for Wall Street to come out of the shadows and out into the light of day," said Washington Sen. Patty Murray. "And it's time for negotiations to come out of the backroom and onto the Senate floor.... It's time to put an end to obstruction and begin working for American families, so I'm glad that we're finally now on this bill."*[20]

MAY 20, 2010: SENATE PASSES ITS VERSION OF THE LEGISLATION

The Senate passes its version of the legislation over five months after the House passed its version on December 11, 2009. The bill passed by the Senate on May 20, 2010 embodied the fundamental changes called for by earlier reform efforts, including taking what was previously a privately-negotiated bilateral marketplace and converting it into a transparent, futures-like market; in fact the cornerstone of the derivatives portion of the legislation is the mandate setting into motion the transformation of the OTC market into a futures market, which is the subject of Chapters 3 and 4 of this text.

JUNE 30, 2010 AND JULY 15, 2010: CONGRESS APPROVES LEGISLATION AND SEEKS THE PRESIDENT'S APPROVAL

On June 30, 2010, legislation passed by a 237 to 192 vote in the U.S. House of Representatives and one month later, on July 15, 2010, after returning from recess, the U.S. Senate passed by a 60 to 39 vote the Dodd-Frank Wall Street Reform and Consumer Protection Act.

JULY 21, 2010: PRESIDENT OBAMA SIGNS DODD-FRANK INTO LAW

The most historic derivatives reform was signed into law, together with the most comprehensive financial services reform, on this date, when President Barack Obama signed the Dodd-Frank Wall Street Reform and Consumer Protection Act into law.

The balance of the book will describe that law, derivatives, and the markets following the enactment of the greatest body of derivatives law ever passed in history.

From the sale of Bear Stearns on March 17, 2008 to the signing of Dodd-Frank into law on July 21, 2010, an impressive frontal assault on many of the merely perceived or actual problems, as well as areas of finance that were not problematic—such as interest rate derivatives and other derivatives—took place. Many thousands of the brightest minds from main street, Wall Street and in Washington, DC debated, wrote articles and legislation, and collaborated. The end result of this effort over the better part of two and a half years was the Dodd-Frank Wall Street Reform and Consumer Protection Act, which not only fundamentally changed the way derivatives are traded, but created new federal authorities, powers, and agencies, and left a larger Washington footprint on the financial services industry than arguably any law that government has enacted in 70 years.

For perspective, however, it should be pointed out that, though the 2008 market crises and the resulting lawmaking were certainly historic, the pace of reform was much slower than the reform that followed the Great Depression. Arthur M. Schlesinger, Jr., author of *The Age of Roosevelt: The Coming of the New Deal*, wrote:

> In the three months after [President Franklin Delano] Roosevelt's inauguration, Congress and the country were subjected to a presidential barrage of ideas and programmes unlike anything known to American history. On adjournment on June 15, 1933, the President and the exhausted 73rd Congress left the following record:
>
> March 9—the Emergency Banking Act
>
> March 20—the Economy Act
>
> March 31—establishment of the Civilian Conservation Corps
>
> April 19—abandonment of the gold standard
>
> May 12—the Federal Emergency Relief Act, setting up a national relief system
>
> May 12—the Agricultural Adjustment Act, establishing a national agricultural policy, with the Thomas amendment conferring on the President powers of monetary expansion
>
> May 12—The Emergency Farm Mortgage Act, providing for the refinancing of farm mortgages
>
> May 18—The Tennessee Valley Authority Act, providing for the unified development of the Tennessee Valley
>
> May 27—the Truth-in-Securities Act, requiring full disclosure in the issue of new securities
>
> June 5—the abrogation of the gold clause in public and private contracts
>
> June 13—the Home Owner's Loan Act, providing for the refinancing of home mortgages
>
> June 16—the National Industrial Recovery Act, providing both for a system of industrial self-government under federal supervision and for a $3.3 billion public works programme
>
> June 16—the Glass Steagall Banking Act, divorcing commercial and investment banking and guaranteeing bank deposits
>
> June 16—the Farm Credit Act, providing for the reorganization of agricultural activities.
>
> June 16—the Railroad Co-ordination Act, Setting up a federal Co-ordinator of Transportation.

This was the Hundred Days; and in this period Franklin Roosevelt sent fifteen messages to Congress, guided fifteen major laws to enactment, delivered ten speeches, held press conferences and cabinet meetings twice a week, conducted talks with foreign Heads of States, sponsored international conferences, made all the major decisions in domestic and foreign policy, and never displayed fright or panic and rarely even a bad temper. His mastery astonished many who thought they had long since taken his measure.... No one would ever know, General Hugh S. Johnson later said, how close we were to collapse and revolution.[21]

U.S. RULE MAKING IN 2010 AND 2011

Once President Obama signed Dodd-Frank into law, the primary regulators for derivatives in the United States, the CFTC and the SEC, began their solicitation of thousands of comment letters, held open meetings and proposed and promulgated over a hundred rules to implement the statutory mandates of Dodd-Frank, often in collaboration with the rest of the regulatory world.

As a leading regulator implementing Dodd-Frank, the CFTC spent 2010 to 2011 proposing almost all of the rules that will govern trading of swaps and stated that final rules will be phased-in over time to permit market participants time to come into compliance with the new regulatory regime. The next part of this chapter describes the timing proposed by the CFTC in 2011 for CFTC rulemaking in key areas. Figure 2.2 provides a flow chart, which the reader can read from top to bottom to understand the conceptual order of U.S. derivatives rulemaking.

Viewing Figure 2.2 from top to bottom, among the hundreds of derivative rules that U.S. regulators are required to put into final form, the author believes that definitions of derivatives reform in the United States may be conceptualized as three distinct categories of reform. Chapter 4 thus divides all U.S. derivatives reform into these categories:

1. Products
2. People
3. Platforms.

A close review of the new statutory law of derivatives suggests that for regulators to carry out the statutory law by promulgating rules, the regulators first must put into final form the definitions of derivative products. This is important because market participants need clarity as to which regulator governs them and their derivatives, where those derivatives are to be traded

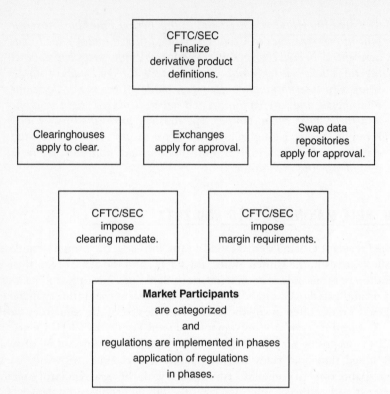

FIGURE 2.2 Top to Bottom Order of Rulemaking and Compliance

and how entities are to function. Much of this is determined by the type of derivative used, where it is used and by whom. The dividing line between the regulation of swaps by the CFTC and security-based swaps by the SEC is also product-driven.

Because the finalization of product-related derivatives is therefore a critical first step, Figure 2.2 places this step at the top of the diagram. Next, underneath that step, as illustrated in Figure 2.2, is a process whereby those trading platforms apply and receive regulatory approval:

- Exchanges and approved markets for derivatives.
- Clearinghouses affiliated with, owned by, or clearing trades independent of exchanges.
- Repositories for swap and security-based swap data.

Then, once product definitions are finalized and platforms for trading are approved and regulated in an ongoing way, the regulators will begin to impose mandates, such as the critically important mandate to centrally clear a trade or maintain margin.

Market participants who are among the most active users and traders of derivatives will be among the first in line to be required to comply with the new mandates, according to CFTC rulemaking in 2011; market participants and the timeline for market compliance are classified by their degree of market activity. A timeline for their compliance with new rules is described next.

At its open meeting on September 8, 2011, the CFTC proposed regulations to establish a schedule to phase-in the effective dates of future final rules governing swap trading documentation, margin requirements for uncleared swaps, and mandatory swap clearing and trade execution pursuant to Dodd-Frank. CFTC Chairman Gary Gensler announced that the CFTC would not complete the adoption of all of the final rules implementing Dodd-Frank until the first quarter of 2012, shortly after this text went to print. Chairman Gensler stated that among the rules that will not be adopted until the first quarter of 2012 are those governing swap execution facilities and the segregation of margin for uncleared swaps. He also stated in September 2011 that the CFTC is considering further exemptive relief from Dodd-Frank's requirements for swaps. The CFTC announced in September 2011 a further postponement of certain key provisions such as position limits, in light of the fact that in connection with all proposed CFTC rulemaking, the Commission received 13,000 written comment letters on proposed position limits and other rules.[22]

Clearing and Trade Execution

Section 723(a) of Dodd-Frank amended the Commodity Exchange Act to establish mandatory clearing requirements for virtually all swaps that are not entered into by a commercial end user. The new Commodity Exchange Act (CEA) Section 2(h)(2) authorizes the CFTC to determine whether a swap must be cleared. The new Section 2(h)(1) of the CEA[23] makes it illegal to engage in a swap that is required to be cleared unless that swap is submitted for clearing to a regulated clearing organization. Finally, Section 2(h)(8) requires all swaps subject to the clearing requirement to be executed on a designated contract market (DCM) or a swap execution facility (SEF), unless no DCM or SEF makes the swap available for trading.

Based on the CFTC's pronouncements to date regarding the implementation of its final swap rules, it appeared when this book went to print that mandatory clearing of swaps would not go live until late 2012. Pursuant to the CFTC's proposed schedule to phase in the swap-clearing requirements, a market participant's compliance date will depend on the type of market participant it is. For these purposes the CFTC has grouped market participants into four categories:

- **Category 1 Entities**: Swap Dealers (SDs), Security-Based Swap Dealers; Major Swap Participants (MSPs); Major Security-Based Swap Participants; and Active Funds. The CFTC's proposed creation of a new category of market participant known as an Active Fund is defined to mean "any private fund as defined in section 202(a) of the Investment Advisors Act of 1940, that is not a third-party subaccount and that executes 20 or more swaps per month based on a monthly average over the 12 months preceding the CFTC issuing a mandatory clearing determination under section 2(h)(2) of the Act."[24] The requirements of the proposed rules, of course, raise a new set of issues for such entities.
- **Category 2 Entities**: Commodity pools; private funds as defined in Section 202(a) of the Investment Advisors Act of 1940 other than active funds; employee benefit plans as defined in paragraphs (3) and (32) of section 3 of the Employee Retirement Income and Security Act of 1974 (ERISA);[25] or persons predominantly engaged in activities that are in the business of banking, or in activities that are financial in nature as defined in Section 4(k) of the Bank Holding Company Act of 1956 (provided that the entity is not a third-party subaccount).
- **Category 3 Entities**: This category appears to be a catch-all category that would include Category 2 entities that are third-party subaccounts, plus all other entities that do not fall into Categories 1 or 2.
- **Category 4 Entities**: All other entities not excluded from the mandatory clearing requirement.

U.S. regulators designed the implementation of new rules in such a way as to require most active market participants (i.e., Category 1 Entities) to comply first with the new regulatory mandates. For example, pursuant to Section 2(h)(2) of the CEA, the CFTC will issue a mandatory clearing determination for a swap that is under consideration for review, in accordance with Dodd-Frank mandates. This will trigger the proposed compliance schedule as follows (unless the CFTC believes phasing is unnecessary for a particular swap):

- **Phase 1**: For swap transactions between Category 1 Entities, the mandatory clearing requirement will take effect 90 days after the CFTC issues its determination.
- **Phase 2**: For swap transactions between Category 2 Entities, or between a Category 2 Entity and a Category 1 Entity, the mandatory

clearing requirement will take effect 180 days after the CFTC issues its determination.

- **Phase 3**: For all other swap transactions involving Category 3 or Category 4 Entities, the mandatory clearing requirement will take effect 270 days after the CFTC issues its determination.

As set forth in Section 2(h)(8) of the CEA, all swaps that are subject to mandatory clearing will be required to be executed on DCMs or SEFs. The CFTC proposed to phase-in compliance with this trade execution requirement at the same time as the clearing requirement is phased-in, or 30 days after the swap is made available for trading, whichever is later.

When Does the Clearing Clock Begin to Tick?

The author believes that the process whereby the OTC derivatives market begins to convert to more of a futures market will begin shortly after publication of this book. The CFTC determined that, before market participants could be required to comply with a mandatory clearing determination, the CFTC must first:

- Adopt final rules related to the end-user exception to mandatory clearing established by Section 2(h)(7) of the CEA.
- Finalize rules jointly proposed with the Securities and Exchange Commission (SEC) that would further define the terms swap, swap dealer, and major swap participant.
- Adopt final rules relating to the protection of cleared swaps customer contracts and collateral.

Similarly, before market participants could be required to comply with a trade execution requirement, the CFTC must:

- Finalize all of the above rules related to the clearing requirement.
- Adopt final rules related to SEFs and DCMs including registration rules for SEFs that provide procedures for the provisional registration of SEFs.

Documentation and Margin Requirements

Section 731 of Dodd-Frank amended the CEA by adding Section 4s, which sets forth registration and regulation provisions to govern SDs and MSPs. Pursuant to Section 4s(i), the CFTC released proposed rules (§23.504) governing documentation standards for SDs and MSPs on January 13, 2011.[26] Pursuant to Section 4s(e) the CFTC released proposed rules (§§23.150-23.158) establishing margin requirements for SDs and MSPs that are not banks (and therefore are not under the oversight of a prudential regulator) for all uncleared swaps.[27]

Mirroring the phasing schedule for clearing discussed above, the CFTC proposes to phase-in compliance with documentation standards on a 90/180/270 day timeline, depending on the category entities that are involved in the swap transaction:

- **Phase 1:** For swap transactions between Category 1 Entities, compliance with proposed §23.504 and §§23.150-23.158, no later than 90 days from the date of adoption of final rules.
- **Phase 2:** For swap transactions between Category 2 Entities, or a Category 2 Entity and a Category 1 Entity, compliance with proposed §23.504 and §§23.150-23.158 no later than 180 days from the date of adoption of final rules.
- **Phase 3:** For all other swap transactions involving Category 3 or Category 4 Entities, compliance with proposed §23.504 and §§23.150-23.158 no later than 270 days from the date of adoption of final rules.

When Does the Documentation Clock Begin to Tick?

Before SDs and MSPs are required to comply with trading documentation (§23.504) requirements, the CFTC must:

- Adopt final rules for trading documentation.
- Adopt regulations governing confirmation of swap transactions and the protection of collateral for uncleared swaps.
- Finalize rules jointly proposed with the SEC that would further define the terms swap, swap dealer, and major swap participant.
- Adopt registration rules, including procedures for the provisional registration, of SDs and MSPs.

Before SDs and MSPs are required to comply with margin requirements (§§23.150-23.158) the CFTC must:

- Adopt final rules for trading documentation (the proposed margin requirement rules cross-reference provisions in the trading documentation proposed rule and, as such, the final trading documentation rule must be published *before* requiring compliance with margin requirements).
- Adopt final rules for margin requirements.
- Finalize rules proposed with the SEC that would further define the terms swap, swap dealer, and major swap participant.
- Adopt registration rules, including procedures for the provisional registration, of SDs and MSPs.

The CFTC's proposed schedules were thus dependent on a host of other rulemakings becoming final—for the clearing compliance schedule, five rulemakings must first be finalized, and in fact were not finalized when this text went to print. The phase-in proposals illustrate the interconnectedness of the various rulemakings authorized by Dodd-Frank and the fact that, if any rulemaking is delayed or stayed by an agency or a reviewing court, the impact on the new regulatory framework could be widespread together complicate the picture illustrating the new market in derivatives.

Many important substantive provisions of Dodd-Frank were meant to be effective, according to the statutory text of Dodd-Frank, on or before July 16, 2011. Section 754 of Dodd-Frank states that unless a provision within Dodd-Frank provides otherwise, the derivatives title (Title VII) within the law "shall take effect on the later of 360 days after the date of the enactment of [Dodd-Frank], or, to the extent a provision of [Title VII] requires rulemaking, not less than 60 days after publication of the final rule or regulation implementing [Title VII]."[28]

In other words, the provisions within Title VII, the derivatives title of Dodd-Frank, are to take effect on the later of July 16, 2011 (which was the 360th day after President Obama signed Dodd-Frank into law), or, if a regulation is required to implement Dodd-Frank, then 60 days after that regulation became effective.

Some provisions did not require, from the text of Dodd-Frank, an implementing regulation, so many within the U.S. derivatives market, as it approached July 16, 2011, grew anxious concerning the legal effectiveness of certain Dodd-Frank provisions.

On June 17, 2011, the CFTC published for final comment a proposed order which would grant temporary exemptive relief from certain provisions of the new law governing derivatives, and the CFTC extended comment periods for its rulemaking. The effect of that regulatory action was to put market participants more at ease and allow the CFTC to propose the phasing-in of Dodd-Frank regulations that had not yet been finalized.

While regulations continued to be published in the Federal Register by both the CFTC and SEC, this text went to print. Readers are therefore encouraged to follow SEC and CFTC rulemaking by visiting www.DerivativesGuide.com.

U.S. REFORM BLAZES THE TRAIL FOR GLOBAL DERIVATIVES REFORM

This chapter summarized the milestones in the development of the law of derivatives. In many ways it is fitting that this law was first enacted in the United States. Many of the financial products that became illiquid and brought about losses in fact originated in the United States and were sold overseas. Therefore, many in the market expected the United States to take the lead to fix a problem that became global and resulted in widespread financial devastation. However, as illustrated by Chapter 1, the problems are multifaceted, complex, evolved over time and are certainly not the responsibility of any one person or country.

The focus of the timeline provided in Chapter 2 is derivatives reform in the United States. Lawmakers and regulators in the United States have, to varying degrees, coordinated U.S. reform efforts with those undertaken in countries with major derivatives markets. In many ways, the guiding principles underlying U.S. derivatives law are shared by leading governments reforming derivatives in the Group of Twenty Finance Ministers and Central Bank Governors, or G-20, and U.S. reform that is the focal point of this book became the prelude to the global response and reform that is the subject of the next chapter.

NOTES

1. *New York Times*, "Could Bear Stearns Do Better?" Dealbook Blog, March 17, 2008.
2. William D. Cohen, *House of Cards: A Tale of Hubris and Wretched Excess on Wall Street* (New York: Doubleday, 2009) (quoting an unnamed New York Federal Reserve official), 65.
3. Yalman Onaran, "Fed Aided Bear Stearns as Firm Faced Chapter 11, Bernanke Says," Bloomberg.com, April 2, 2008.
4. Transcript: Obama on "Renewing the American Economy," NYT.com, March 27, 2008.
5. Ibid.
6. Ibid.
7. *Wall Street Journal,* Text of Geithner's Testimony on Regulating Risk, March 26, 2009.
8. Ibid.
9. Ibid.
10. Letter of Secretary of the Treasury Timothy Geithner to the Hon. Harry Reid, U.S. Senate, May 13, 2009.
11. Ibid.
12. The Hon. Rep. Mike McMahon, "Misunderstanding Derivatives Endangers Main Street," *The Hill*, June 2, 2009.
13. U.S. Senator Mike Crapo, http:/crapo.senate.gov/issues/banking/6_22_09_os_letters.cfm.
14. Text of H.R. 3300.
15. Remarks by the President on Wall Street Reform, Cooper Union, New York, April 22, 2010. www.whitehouse.gov/the-press-office/remarks-president-wall-street-reform.

16. David M. Herszenhorn and Edward Wyatt, "As G.O.P. Relents, Regulation Bill Moves to Floor," *New York Times*, April 29, 2010.

17. Steven Pearlstein, "Planet Washington Meets Planet Wall Street," *The Washington Post*, April 28, 2010.

18. Herszenhorn and Wyatt, "As G.O.P. Relents."

19. Graham Bowley, "Goldman's Market Value Plunges $21 Billion," *New York Times*, May 1, 2010.

20. Carrie Budoff Brown and Meredith Shiner, "GOP Relents as Wall Street Debate Moves Forward," www.politico.com, April 29, 2010.

21. Arthur M. Schlesinger, Jr., *The Age of Roosevelt: The Coming of the New Deal* at 19–20 (Toronto: Heinemann, 1958), 19–20.

22. Jamila Trindle, "CFTC Postpones Vote on Position Limits," *Market Watch*, September 27, 2011.

23. 7 U.S.C. 1 *et seq.*

24. The CFTC believed that the proposed numerical threshold for Active Funds as proposed would be appropriate because a private fund that conducts this volume of swaps would be likely to have sufficient resources to enter into arrangements that comply with the clearing and trade execution requirement earlier than other types of market participants, and sufficient market experience to contribute meaningfully to the buy-side perspective as industry standards continue to develop.

25. This phrase is another example of confusion caused by Dodd-Frank. All employee benefit plans are defined in paragraph (3) of section 3 of ERISA. This includes many types of plans that are *not* subject to ERISA requirements, such as government plans (i.e., employee benefit plans for government employees), which are more fully defined in paragraph (32) of section 3 of ERISA. By including the separate reference to the more detailed definition of government plans in section 3(32) of ERISA, a question has been raised, but not yet resolved by regulators at the time this text went to print, as to whether *all* employee benefit plans are meant to be included in the phrase "employee benefit plans as defined in paragraphs (3) and (32) of section 3 of ERISA," or only those employee benefit plans subject to ERISA and government plans.

26. 17 CFR Part 23, "Swap Trading Relationship Documentation Requirements for Swap Dealers and Major Swap Participants," 76 FR 6715, February 8, 2011.

27. 17 CFR Part 23, "Margin Requirements for Uncleared Swaps for Swap Dealers and Major Swap Participants," 76 FR 23732, April 28, 2011.

28. Dodd-Frank Section 754.

PART TWO

Derivatives Reform

In America, when we get knocked down, we don't stay down. In the last 80 years, America has experienced 13 economic recessions. And fought back with 13 economic expansions. It was never easy, but it was always possible. If you're bullish on America, and we are, then you're bullish on getting up and coming back. That's not a belief, that's history.

—Merrill Lynch Global Wealth Management advertisement, *Wall Street Journal*, October 11 to 12, 2008

INTRODUCTION TO PART TWO

We began in the Introduction with statistics demonstrating that the 2008 market crises were the worst financial calamaties in 70 years. The crises created economic devastation in more countries than many of the other calamitous events in the past century. In fact, the 2008 market crises created such widespread financial destruction that policy makers in major economies throughout the world called for extensive research on the causes of the market crises and vowed to do whatever it took to prevent a recurrence. From the author's experience and research, Chapter 1 describes the seven causes that arguably were most responsible for the market crises. Comprehensive reform efforts began, as we saw in Chapter 2. These are the takeaways:

- The 2008 market crises created historic, widespread, and pronounced dislocations in the world economy, massive losses, and widespread human suffering and turmoil.
- There were at least seven causes of the 2008 market crises, all were interrelated and each cause fed off of the other.
- 2008 was a year in which established, over-leveraged financial services firms failed within an interconnected, global financial system, and each firm's failure destabilized the modern global economy.
- Notwithstanding the fact that much of the 2008 market crises emanated from the United States, and resulted in the U.S. to become the target of worldwide criticism, lawmakers in the United States took two years to enact new derivatives law in statutory form.
- The implementation of new regulations in the United States (and elsewhere) is a slow process that implicates myriad operational, technological and legal issues.

With these takeaways in mind, the reader perhaps next asks: after the financial devastation caused by the 2008 market crises, what have policy and lawmakers seized upon as the solution to address these crises and prevent future ones?

Chapter 3 provides the answer: lawmakers, first in the U.S., responded to the 2008 market crises with a wholesale rejection of over-the-counter or OTC derivatives trading in favor of the futures model, which is the focus of this chapter.

Introduction to Futures, Margin, and Central Clearing

Before launching into futures, the reader is reassured that this chapter, and indeed the entire book, is not designed to be a tedious recitation of derivatives law and practice. This would be rather boring for everyone, actually.

This chapter takes advantage of what is arguably the most dynamic transformation which has taken place in the history of modern finance: the transformation of the over-the-counter (OTC) derivatives market to an exchange-traded, and centrally cleared, market. This is the policy makers' solution to the 2008 market crises; it is in many ways a dynamic, controversial, and extremely aggressive solution. It is also, in many ways, overkill: *a few* categories of derivatives played important roles in the 2008 market crises, yet *all* OTC derivatives in the United States are subject to reform.

Derivatives reform is in fact dynamic, sometimes creative, and always rapidly evolving, and so is this chapter and the author's website accompanying this text, www.DerivativesGuide.com. Chapter 3 is designed to build a foundation for the reader to understand the specific reform mandates discussed in Chapter 4 and the chapters that follow. This is designed for the reader with little or no familiarity with futures contracts or what the author describes as the futures model. In writing about the new law of derivatives, it became readily clear to the author that the reader needs to have a background in futures and not all readers have that; this chapter fills the gap in futures experience and understanding, if the reader has one.

We begin with arguably the three greatest failures in the OTC derivatives markets that threatened the modern financial system and perhaps the global economy. In revisiting these failures, the discussion is not historical in nature. Instead, the author suggests that in the course of crisis management during three crises, policy and lawmakers in essence acted in the same way as a central clearinghouse would act if one of its members failed by making special assessments to members to preserve the stability of the market. The task of this chapter is to unpack the preceding sentence for the reader and explain, using first the failures of prominent U.S. financial services firms—LTGM, Bear Stearns, and Lehman Brothers—to demonstrate how the previous way in which OTC derivatives traded actually made the crisis management carried out by U.S. government officials far more difficult than if these three failed financial services firms traded only futures contracts by means of exchanges and clearinghouses. As the reader views in the pages that follow the extensive efforts by financial regulators to cobble together a safety net in which each of these three financial services firms would fall, the reader, putting himself or herself in the shoes of a U.S. regulator, may think:

> *Our work as regulators managing the fallout from this crisis would have been much easier if all derivatives were traded and regulated like futures contracts. The futures markets seemed to have weathered the storms over the years quite nicely. The opaque OTC derivatives market has on the other hand caused the greatest anxiety and the crises within those markets just keep coming. Let's change the entire U.S. OTC derivates market in the United States and make it look a lot more like the futures market.*

In fact, this is what has happened. While the OTC derivatives and structural products markets were seizing in 2007 to 2008, futures markets continued to function. Markets for futures contracts functioned and price discovery was achieved (in contrast to the markets for residential mortgage-backed securities and CDOs, among others).

The advantages of the futures market were glaringly obvious during the 2008 market crises. The transparency, regulatory, and price discovery attributes of the futures market presented so many advantages to lawmakers during and after the crisis. The way in which the New York Federal Reserve, for example, crisis-managed in the case of three historic collapses of firms (each of which were heavy users of derivatives) resembles in several respects the remedies which a central clearing party or clearinghouse would bring to bear to prevent a collapse in the system, as will be explained.

The problem now, however, is that for many, the futures market is not well understood.

To regulators, the three case studies of failing U.S. financial service firms pointed to the need for the futures model, and after the responses to those failures are discussed here, the history, basic concepts, players, markets, products, clearing facilities, and regulators are introduced, as illustrated in this table of contents for Chapter 3.

Beginning readers should continue to read each part of this chapter as presented. More experienced readers should pick and choose parts to supplement their existing understanding; this chapter is designed to provide a foundation for reform concepts (e.g., the clearing mandate) which are highlighted in later chapters.

This chapter concludes with the beginnings of derivative reform initiatives in several leading market places throughout the world.

With this summary of reform initiatives throughout the world, and a baseline understanding of how futures markets and the contracts which trade within them work, the reader will be prepared for a guide forward through specific reform initiatives, which Chapter 4 provides.

THREE CRISES AND THE NEED FOR THE FUTURES MODEL

In past market crises, the New York Federal Reserve at least twice attempted to cobble together a network of banks that could perform the crisis-management function of a central counterparty (CCP), which generally is synonymous with a clearinghouse (but not an exchange; these terms are explained in Chapter 9, which details market structure). In one instance, the Federal Reserve succeeded, and in another, it failed. In both circumstances, a CCP structure would have possibly prevented both crises in the OTC market.

Long-Term Capital Management (LTCM)

LTCM was informally rescued by its lenders under the leadership of William McDonough, the then-president of the New York Federal Reserve. Although the Federal Reserve did not formally intervene in LTCM with an infusion of liquidity, it rather forced a rescue of LTCM by a hastily-organized syndicate of 20 lenders, each committing to pay $3.65 billion.[1] The Fed provided an example of how a financial market disaster could be averted by assembling a large circle of individual sources of private financing to recapitalize LTCM, a $7 billion hedge fund that used leverage ratios in the 18 to 20 range.[2]

By 1997, LTCM had many thousands of trades and hundreds of trading relationships: some were cash market transactions, mostly in bonds;[3] others were derivatives. In an effort to sustain 40 percent annual returns, LTCM traders went into markets and placed trades that they did not fully understand, such as currency trading and equity arbitrage. Finally, in 1998, after acquiring Russian sovereign debt, LTCM, along with other Russian bondholders, heard that Russia would default. This development, coupled with a wave of collateral calls, effectively ended LTCM.[4]

The point of the LTCM experience, for purposes of this chapter, is not to learn how or why LTCM failed, or even the extent of LTCM's use of derivatives, but to explore the manner in which the Federal Reserve informally brought about the rescue of this heavy user of derivatives to prevent a broader crisis. The Fed played an informal role in bringing about a private solution to a problem that posed a serious threat to the financial system. In many ways, the Fed's crisis management was a prelude to the New York Fed's interventions in 2008, with respect to Bear Stearns and Lehman Brothers (and also AIG). Though U.S. credit support was not necessary, the Fed assembled major Wall Street and European bankers, LTCM's counterparties, in much the same way that a clearinghouse in the futures model (discussed in the pages that follow) would turn to its members. Leadership of 14 banks rescued LTCM by contributing $3.65 billion in liquidity.[5]

> *The Fed's intervention in the LTCM crisis was widely and inaccurately construed as a public bailout, although no taxpayer money was involved. The rescue capital all came from banks that had profited mightily from LTCM's business; [Federal Reserve Bank of New York President, William McDonough] in effect strong-armed them into disgorging some profits for the public good.*[6]

The informal consortium of lenders arranged by the Fed, with each bank circling the Fed in the crisis management effort to handle the LTCM crisis looked much like a member-clearinghouse structure.[7]

With respect to the informal network of banks that were asked by the Fed to provide liquidity, and as discussed in the pages that follow, the Fed undertook subsequent efforts to cobble together sources of liquidity, with varying degrees of success in the 2008 market crises.

One of the more interesting takeaways from the LTCM experience is that despite being implored by the Fed, Bear Stearns did not agree to provide any part of the cash infusion into LTCM in contrast to that provided by 14 other banks. Bear Stearns eventually failed in March 2008, as described later in this chapter.

Bear Stearns' refusal to infuse liquidity into LTCM was not a function of its lack of awareness or familiarity with LTCM's trading. Bear Stearns cleared its trades as LTCM's clearing broker.[8] It cleared bonds and other financial products for LTCM and, in fact, made a $500 million margin call to LTCM that triggered the rescue of LTCM.[9]

With $100 billion in derivative positions, a shockingly massive trading book at the time, the failure of LTCM jeopardized not only LTCM's counterparties but the entire system. Because of the private, opaque and unregulated nature of LTCM's trading, it was unclear about how extensive losses would be realized by market participants. According to one senior banker in the UK, "We will never know quite how close we came to financial Armageddon."[10]

Apparently Bear Stearns failed to participate in the LTCM bailout because it cast a disapproving eye on LTCM equity, according to the *New York Times* comparison of the LTCM and Bear Stearns failures:

> *Bear was warned to raise more capital by selling stock, but its senior executives, led by James Cayne, the chief executive, thought the company's stock was cheap, and refused. Cayne, who was an original investor in Long-Term Capital, should have remembered that the hedge fund's most obvious flaw was its excessive borrowing, or leverage. Before its* annus horribilis, *Long-Term Capital had intentionally reduced its equity to a mere 3 percent of assets. It was a fatal mistake.*[11]

Looking at the crisis-management efforts at the impending failure of LTCM, it seems, in hindsight, that the Fed cobbled together a private consortium of major banks in much the same way that a central counterparty or clearinghouse would impose assessments recommitted by a default of a fellow clearing member.

In the case of LTCM, the consortium successfully averted a major hit to the financial system. The markets calmed after the rescue of LTCM, and, as we saw in Chapter 1, U.S. regulatory officials, in fact, called for the *deregulation* of derivatives after LTCM. Although the Fed did play a role in arranging the rescue of LTCM, it found, 10 years later, that it couldn't by itself save the one firm that failed to contribute to the LTCM rescue.

Bear Stearns & Co.

In the case of the failure of Bear Stearns in March 2008, the New York Fed, as in the LTCM crisis, again played an important role in crisis management by soliciting massive cash infusions from private sources, but this time for the firm that failed to contribute to the LTCM bailout: Bear Stearns & Co.

The Fed's efforts in early March 2008 were designed to bring about a financing conduit to essentially take the book of Bear Stearns. However, the Fed's ability to directly finance Bear Stearns was limited due to regulatory constraints:

> *The Federal Reserve, in response to the broader financial crisis unwinding globally, was in the process of making arrangements to lend to investment banks if necessary. Such a program was hoped to be in place by month's end and the attorney inquired if "there was something that could be done to speed the program along." Although the Federal Reserve Act allows the Federal Reserve to lend to institutions that are outside the commercial banking system, it has never done so in its 96-year history. There were technical problems as well since investment banks do not have accounts at the Federal Reserve Bank and therefore some conduit involving a commercial bank would need to be arranged. In addition, Bear Stearns was not regulated by the Federal Reserve and its true condition would take some time to determine. A central bank does not lend to bankrupt companies.[12]*

Unlike the LTCM experience, the Fed in the last days of Bear Stearns was unable to arrange a consortium of banks as lenders to Bear Stearns. The Fed facilitated the rescue of Bear Stearns, however; in the end, the Fed, through JPMorgan Chase & Co. as a conduit, provided $30 billion in proceeds.[13]

The circle of financiers could not be assembled to provide a bailout for Bear Stearns, providing a lesson to policy makers that a network of financial support cannot be cobbled together in every crisis; instead, a consortium of members to a system or model for consolidating counterparty risk must already be in place, so that, if one of the members fails, the others may take the book or provide credit support to prevent losses and act as a buffer against a shock to the financial system. That is precisely what a central clearinghouse is designed to do. The Bear Stearns near-collapse in March 2008 was a dry run for a catastrophic financial failure of historic proportions: the fall of Lehman Brothers.

Lehman Brothers

As with the LTCM experience, the New York Fed attempted, on September 12, 2008, to assemble a circle of Lehman counterparties to solicit sufficient credit support from each to prevent massive losses from the fall of Lehman Brothers, and the gravity of their undertaking, coupled with the then-fragile state of the system were reported by William Cohan in his excellent text *House of Cards*:

> *When the most powerful men in American capitalism convened at the New York Federal Reserve Bank's Italianate palazzo in lower Manhattan on Friday evening, September 12, to try to save Lehman Brothers from certain death, what confronted them was the knowledge that whatever actions they did or did not take that weekend could push the financial system into the abyss. "We went into the weekend knowing it was very dark," explained Tim Geithner, then the president of the New York Fed and eventually the Secretary of the Treasury. "There was nobody that was part of this process that did not believe the world was exceptionally fragile and that Lehman was systemic and that the consequences of its default would be traumatic. There was nobody in that room—from the Treasury, the Fed, or from the Federal Reserve Board or from the private sector—that could have told you exactly what would happen or what the consequences would be. I made it clear over and over again in that room that if we didn't solve this, everything else would be harder to deal with. Solving this was not going to make all the other problems go away, but we did not feel we had the ability to insulate the markets from the broader consequences of default.*[14]

The first option that Timothy Geithner, President of the New York Federal Reserve at the time, and Henry Paulson, Secretary of the U.S. Treasury, wanted to implement resembled the emergency consortium used to bail out LTCM.[15] In the weeks and then days leading up to the fall of Lehman Brothers on September 15, 2008, the leaders of the Fed and Treasury worked together to convene meetings to save Lehman, perhaps in a similar way that the Fed managed in the LTCM private bail out.

The September 12, 2008, meeting at the New York Fed failed to save Lehman; it and many of its affiliates filed for bankruptcy and much about the financial world has never been the same.

On and after September 18, 2008, many thousands of counterparties to the various Lehman entities that filed for bankruptcy experienced great difficulty retrieving collateral and canceling trades.

By the time the reader opens this text, a significant part of the Lehman experience has been uncovered and understood, and, therefore, should not be discussed here, as this part delves into the futures world, which is quite different from OTC trading, as we will see.

Whereas the OTC cash and credit default swap markets seized for a time after the fall of Lehman Brothers, the futures markets, although not perfect, experienced fewer losses or delays in recovering assets when compared to the OTC derivative markets in 2008. Where did this market come from?

A BRIEF HISTORY OF FUTURES CONTRACTS AND MARKETS

Why do futures contracts and markets exist, and when did they develop? While the history of derivatives and futures provided in Chapter 8 describes cuneiform tablets from 1700 B.C. evidencing barley contracts, derivatives and futures markets came into formal existence at least as early as seventeenth century Japan and likely well before that period of time, in ancient Greek and Roman markets, where, at the height of the Roman Empire, trading centers called *vendalia* (sales markets) served as distribution centers for commodities brought to the markets from the outer reaches of the empire.[16]

The First Market: Osaka, Japan and its Rice Tickets

As in other countries, early Japan had an agrarian economy organized by a feudal system in which absentee landlords collected rice crops from workers on their land.[17]

> *A typical landlord would haul and sell his rice shortly after harvest in the Osaka spot market and use such cash to finance his expenses until the next harvest time. History reveals that most nobles often had to raise cash between harvests to meet some unforeseen financial emergency. They often did so by selling forward contracts, that is by agreeing to deliver during the next harvest season a pre-agreed quantity of rice for a pre-agreed price, provided the merchant who bought such a forward contract was willing to offer the landlord a cash down payment. Over the decades, these forward contracts, called rice tickets became standardized in terms of rice grades (there were four grades available) and contract term (the year was divided into three 4-month periods.)*[18]

Rice tickets became negotiable and were traded. If, after purchasing a rice ticket an adverse development (e.g., bad weather) drove up the price of rice, the value of that rice ticket would increase, creating an opportunity for the initial buyers of the ticket to re-sell it, at a profit. Over time, the issuance and re-sale of rice tickets spurred enough active trading to support a formal market, and thus what is believed to be the first commodity exchange began in Osaka, Japan, in 1650.[19] A clearinghouse for these standardized forward contracts (i.e., futures) accompanied the Osaka futures exchange.

A similar evolution of futures markets took place years later in the United States, in present-day Chicago, Illinois, in the early to mid-nineteenth century.[20] Like the rice harvest in Japan, farmers harvested corn, wheat, soybeans, and other foodstuffs in quantities that exceeded market demands at the time of harvest. Simple economic theory tells us that prices would drop to precariously low levels and shortages of storage facilities and transportation challenges worked against the farmers.

In the year 1859, as we read in Chapter 8, The History of Derivatives and Futures, saw the incorporation of the Chicago Board of Trade to even-out distribution and significant savings in spot prices.[21] Farmers, grain elevators, and food processing companies all traded with grain speculators and others; as a result, futures crops and inventories over time and relatively speaking were protected from price uncertainty.

The Osaka rice markets and Chicago Board of Trade experiences illustrate that futures markets develop to counter seasonable production, price volatility, or both, in what we in Chapter 9 refer to as the cash markets.

Early Clearinghouses in the United States: The General Cash Office

This chapter discusses at length the concept of clearing. Well before futures and derivatives clearing, the financial infrastructures within the leading markets settled trades in cash markets (i.e., markets for stocks, bonds, etc.). Former U.S. Secretary of the Treasury, Albert Gallatin, made the first suggestion for a bank clearing system in 1831. Secretary Gallatin borrowed bank clearing concepts from London and Scottish clearing systems.[22]

Gallatin's plan called for the establishment of a general cash office, capitalized by select member banks, which would replace the early nineteenth century routine in the United States in which every bank would send porters to other banks in order to collect and pay credit and debt balances.[23] The general cash office would maintain books in which each bank would daily be credited or debited and balances would be written in relation to "quotas" for each bank. Each bank which drew from the general cash office in excess of its quota would have to "replenish its quota" whenever the quota "was diminished [by] one half or any other proportion agreed on," according to Gallatin.[24]

Some twenty years after Treasury Secretary Gallatin proposed daily settlement by means of a general cash office, in 1853, 52 banks in New York City organized the New York Clearing House Association, comprised of each of these as member banks.[25] Each member bank designated a delivery clerk (who, as the name implied, delivered claims against other banks) as well as a settling clerk (who received packages of checks or currency from other bank delivery clerks).[26]

If 50 banks cleared, and each bank had a payment relationship with all the other banks, then the clerks had to service 2,500 accounts. The whole operation took place at ten o'clock in the morning each day. The delivery clerks formed a military-like procession as they circulated the stationary to settling clerks and presented them with accounts due. The proof clerks in the employ of the clearinghouse recorded the sums and struck balances for the amounts due from or to each bank. The whole procedure customarily took 35 to 40 minutes.[27]

In the throes of a liquidity crisis—during bank closings or market seizures—member banks of the New York Clearing House Association turned to the clearinghouse as the lender of last resort (much as troubled U.S. financial services firms turned to the Federal Reserve in 2008). This actually took place during the Panic of 1857, in the 1860s, and again during the Panics of 1873, 1889, 1893, and the Panic of 1907, which is described in Chapter 8.[28]

The early clearinghouses in the cash markets, where stocks, bonds, and other fungible assets traded, developed around the same time that clearinghouses for futures contracts developed (in contrast to derivatives markets, where contracts for future delivery of assets, or rights, or obligations trade).

1848: The Modern Era of Futures Begins

The modern era of futures began in the United States in 1848 with the establishment of the Chicago Board of Trade (CBOT) by 82 merchants,[29] and continued as the world's oldest, formal futures and options exchange, until its 2007 merger with the Chicago Mercantile Exchange (CME).

The Chicago Board of Trade enabled farmers and other market participants to enter into forwards, on an exchange (and thus futures contracts, as opposed to forwards, which are derivatives in the over-the-counter [OTC] market), to hedge against low prices due to macroeconomic factors. BOTCC, the Board of Trade Clearing Corporation, an independent corporation that settled all trades for CBOT, acted as guarantor to clearing members, reconciled all clearing member accounts, and set adjusted clearing member margins as prices fluctuated.[30]

The late nineteenth century and early parts of the twentieth century in the United States saw a disbursed collection of exchanges in addition to the Chicago Board of Trade:

> *In May 1884, the New York Produce Exchange took possession of new premises. By 1911, it was trading in meat, wheat, corn, rye, oats, barley and other grains, flour, meal, hops, hay, straw, seeds, port, lard, tallow, greases, cotton-seed oil, animal and vegetable oils, naval stores, butter, and cheese, in quantities from single packages to entire cargoes.*[31]

The legal and economic relationships that were formed in futures trading in the early years of the Chicago Board of Trade continue to be formed today, although the process of creating those relationships is faster, more efficient, and international in nature, as we will see in later chapters. Today the Chicago Board of Trade is joined by over a dozen other futures exchanges, all providing an effective forum for trading futures contracts, which are frequently the subject of other derivative and financial arrangements.

As regional exchanges and clearinghouses sprouted in the United States in the mid- to late-nineteenth century, the OTC derivatives market did not thrive due to, in large part, to key decisions handed down by the courts in the United States.

Futures markets were legally enforceable in the United States in part because contracts traded on those markets involved an identifiable interest in a commodity, such as a grain. For cases in which neither party to a contract has such an interest, the courts in the United States have not in periods described later in Chapter 8 enforced those arrangements after one party defaulted. For example, an 1884 U.S. Supreme Court decision found that a contract in which the parties speculated as to whether goods would be delivered in the future was not enforceable:

> *[I]f, under guise of such a contract, the real intent be merely to speculate in the rise or fall of prices, and the goods are not to be delivered, but one party is to pay the other the difference between the contract price and the market price of the goods at the date fixed for executing the contract, then the whole transaction constitutes nothing more than a wager, and is null and void.*[32]

After World War I, the depression that followed the war generated intense speculation in grain futures.[33] As a response to this speculation, the

U.S. Congress passed the first federal law regulating the futures trade: the Futures Trading Act. Then the U.S. Supreme Court declared it unconstitutional. In 1925, the first clearinghouse was formally established in the United States, at the Chicago Board of Trade, two years after Congress passed another act, the Grain Futures Act, rooted in the constitutional power embodied in the interstate commerce clause of the U.S. Constitution.[34] This act permitted futures trading in specific commodities, but only on exchanges that were licensed to transact futures, and these licenses could be revoked.[35]

Years later, after the onset of the Great Depression, in 1936 the U.S. Department of Agriculture conducted studies which led to the enhancement of federal government futures regulatory power in the Commodity Exchange Act of 1936 (CEA). This created the Commodity Exchange Commission, which was responsible for licensing futures exchanges, imposing registration requirements for intermediaries in the market such as the futures commission merchant, set trading limits for speculative trading, and was the source of other foundational powers and restrictions which continue today. This act is a primary statutory basis for new U.S. derivatives law, which followed the 2008 market crises.

The CEA required futures commission merchants (FCMs), discussed below, to segregate customer margin from FCM funds and laid the foundation for many other regulations whose application to derivatives was revisited (and expanded to apply to "swaps," as we shall see in Chapter 4, after the 2008 market crises).[36]

The development of financial futures resulted from a dynamically changing global economy following World War II, the explosion of U.S. government-issued debt, and an increasingly volatile interest rate environment.[37]

In the 1950s and 1960s, the Bretton Woods international monetary system, a fixed exchange rate regime, prevailed, with currencies pegged to the U.S. dollar at set parities, and the U.S. dollar was anchored to U.S. government gold reserves at a rate of $35 per ounce of gold.[38]

This all changed on August 15, 1971. The U.S. suspended its obligation to exchange gold reserves for U.S. dollars accumulated by foreign banks.[39] The U.S. dollars then in circulation were out of proportion to U.S. gold reserves, so currency exchange rates were allowed to flow, volatility resulted, and a byproduct of these developments was a futures market developed at the Chicago Mercantile Exchange to facilitate risk distribution.

During the early 1970s, the affluence of many of the world's industrially developed countries coincided with declines in crop production in several major crop-producing nations.[40] By late 1974, it was estimated that the world feed-grain supplies had dwindled to a month's supply.[41] It was during this time that members of the U.S. Congress began to question the adequacy of existing futures market regulation, including the reach of the CEA into futures trading not covered by that Act. As a result of Congressional hearings, Congress passed the Commodity Futures Trading Commission Act of 1974. This act:

- Amended the CEA and created an independent Commodity Futures Trading Commission (CFTC), which today is a leading U.S. regulator of futures and certain derivatives, now referred to as swaps, which we will see in the chapter that follows this one.
- Called for the consolidation in the CFTC of the Commodity Exchange Authority (previously an agency within the USDA).
- Called for the appointment by the President and confirmation by the U.S. Senate of five full-time Commissioners serving staggered terms.[42]

The Commodity Futures Trading Commission Act was reauthorized in 1978 under the Futures Trading Act, and in later years, including in 1982 (in which the U.S. Congress adopted the Shad/Johnson Accord Index Act, which defined the jurisdiction of the CFTC and the Securities and Exchange Commission).

Between 1921 and 1983, over 180 separate futures markets were in existence.[43] A thorough historical treatment of early futures markets is beyond the scope of this text; the reader is directed to the exceptional recent work by Emily Lambert, *The Futures: The Rise of the Speculator and the Origins of the World's Biggest Markets* (Basic Books, 2011). During the 1921 to 1983 periods, there were over 20 separate futures exchanges, but only 11 were authorized by the CFTC.[44] Since 1925, there are claims that no customer within or outside of CBOT lost money due to default on a futures position.[45]

The first financial futures contracts were based on Government National Mortgage Association, or Ginnie Mae, mortgage-backed certificates at the Chicago Board of Trade.[46] In the absence of a Federal Reserve pursuit of interest rate stability in the 1970s, financial institutions became reluctant to make long-term fixed-rate loans, thereby shifting interest-rate risk to each borrower. This dynamic played a role in the development of U.S. Treasury futures for purposes of fixing interest-rate risk, locking-in financing rates, and even creating low cost synthetic debt instruments.[47]

One of the most impressive aspects of the modern history of futures is the rate of the development of financial futures contracts. It took over a century for a market to develop for trading futures contracts based on foodstuffs and agricultural products, yet financial markets, where financial futures are traded, sprung up in less than 15 years and overtook more traditional agricultural futures markets in many respects.[48]

The 1982 Reauthorization and the Shad/Johnson Accord

Under the terms of the Shad/Johnson Accord Index Act, Congress vested the CFTC with exclusive jurisdiction over stock index futures and options on stock index futures contracts, while the Securities and Exchange Commission received jurisdictional authority from Congress over the trading of options on any security or index of securities, or options on foreign currencies traded on a U.S. exchange.[49] The jurisdictional divisions in enacted statutes by Congress continued to influence Federal lawmaking after the 2008 market crises. Chapter 4 highlights and explains these divisions.

In 1992, Congress again re-authorized the CFTC by means of the Futures Trading Practices Act and included a range of new mandates to address new futures industry trends. These mandates included the requirement to develop audit trails (a part of the new law for cleared derivatives, discussed in the next chapter) and added floor traders to the individuals that are required to register with the CFTC, which by this time included floor brokers, floor traders, commodity pool operators, commodity trading advisors, and associated persons.[50]

As of 1992, the Federal Reserve Board was, under the Futures Trading Practices Act, given margin oversight authority with respect to stock index futures contracts. As discussed in Introduction to the Futures Model and Basic Futures Concepts part of this chapter below, "margin" means an asset that is pledged by a futures trader in support of its obligations under a futures contract. Day-to-day responsibility for setting margins previously remained with the exchanges, and changes in margin or exchange rules for stock index futures trading had to be approved by the Federal Reserve and CFTC.[51]

THE COMMODITY FUTURES MODERNIZATION ACT OF 2000

On December 21, 2000, the Commodity Futures Modernization Act (CFMA) was signed into law, severely restricting the CFTC's and the SEC's ability to regulate OTC derivatives,[52] and generally resulting in a degregulated, trading environment.

An important theme which weaves through the provisions of CFMA is the liberalization of derivatives and futures regulation to free-up from regulation the more sophisticated derivatives and futures traders, such as large banks, in order to permit them to compete with their non-U.S. competitors.

To this point, we have described the evolution of the futures trade over thousands of years, and the law in the United States, as that trade developed in nineteenth- and twentieth-century America. One of the key takeaways is that Congress and regulators sought the confinement of futures trading activity to regulated exchanges. In centralizing futures (and options) on exchanges, traders could put on and trade out of positions with relative ease and without causing price disruptions, and centralized markets would provide price discovery as well as other advantages, such as the ability to monitor and regulate trades.[53]

The CFMA brought about radical changes to the CFTC's authority and deregulated the exchange-traded derivatives space. The law created a new class of market participants, eligible contract participants (ECPs), and eligibility requirements for ECPs, and once those requirements were met, ECPs were largely emancipated from CFTC oversight.[54] This is an important historical theme: regulation occurs in cycles, and just as derivatives ingenuity and trading volumes exploded after 2000, the U.S. deregulated futures and derivatives.

Another key theme was that regulation by the CFTC would not be evenly applied across the board, but instead would depend on the sophistication of the party trading the product and the market within which it traded. This part of the CFMA, the selective regulation of some but not other parties, has been repealed.

Key features of the CFMA, which constitutes the most comprehensible reworking of derivatives (and futures) in the United States prior to Dodd-Frank, included:

- Reduction of regulation of futures markets to promote innovation.
- The establishment of core principles and standards to permit clearing-houses and exchanges in futures to satisfy regulatory mandates such as managing risks associated with clearing.
- Clarifying the legality of privately-negotiated swaps, provided that certain conditions were satisfied.[55]

The CFMA also directed the CFTC to recognize and regulate differently the distinctly separate functions of an exchange and clearinghouse (those are described in detail in the pages that follow).

* * *

Since 2008, the futures market has performed well, but not perfectly, during a time in which market seizures took place (most notably the markets for collateralized debt obligations and private label mortgage-backed securities). The history of the futures market includes, in fact, instances of failures among clearing members, and this chapter later references a few of those failures. Even so, the futures market remains a robust, widespread, powerful market led by international exchanges providing a range of product offerings, trading platforms, and methods and opportunities to trade electronically at all hours. As an example, CME, the Chicago Mercantile Exchange, once considered the embarrassing little sister to the Chicago Board of Trade,[56] today is one of the world's leading exchanges, offering around-the-clock trading via Globex, a premier electronic trading platform. In the 1980s, cash settlement on futures contracts, instead of physical delivery of a commodity, became an innovation of CME.[57] The Chicago Mercantile Exchange is a leading financial marketplace in the world in this space, in terms of open interest—the number of futures contracts and options outstanding at the close of trading.[58]

Other leading international exchanges include Liffe, now owned by NYSE Euronext, as NYSE Euronext LIFFE. Liffe (pronounced "life") opened in 1982 and enjoyed leading futures trading volumes.[59] Individual equity option trading migrated to LIFFE CONNECT, a computer-based electronic platform. Additionally, world exchange leaders include Eurex (with CME and NYSE Euronext LIFFE, the "big three"), Hong Kong Exchanges and Clearing (HKEx), Tokyo Commodity Exchange and Tokyo Stock Exchange, Singapore Mercantile Exchange (SMX), Singapore Exchange (SGX) and Singapore Commodity Exchange (SICOM), Bursa Malasia, National Stock Exchange of India (NSE), China Financial Futures Exchange (CFFEX), and the Intercontinental Exchange, or ICE.

INTRODUCTION TO THE FUTURES MODEL AND BASIC FUTURES CONCEPTS

With the foregoing discussion as background, we are now ready to explore the component parts of the futures model, as a prelude to the post-2008 market crises reform. Before we go any further, however, and in order to ensure that the reader has at least a basic foundation for understanding the clearing mandate that is a critical part of derivatives reform, which began after the 2008 market crises, the author begs the indulgence of the more experienced reader to address a few most basic questions:

- What is a futures exchange?
- What is clearing?

- What is a clearinghouse?
- Is a clearinghouse an exchange?
- If a clearinghouse is *not* an exchange, what exactly is it and what does it do?

What Is a Futures Exchange?

A futures exchange is a venue for trading futures contracts, which as we'll see later in this chapter, are standardized derivatives calling for the delivery at a specified price and set time of an asset or financial commodity. In contrast to trading over-the-counter (OTC), where trades are consummated privately and off-market, exchanges in the cleared derivatives and futures trade are highly organized, regulated, and typically automated on electronic platforms.

Regulators impose position limits on exchanges, which, in turn, set the maximum number of derivatives that a party can hold on one side of the market. Once a trade is executed, the two parties to the trade will allege and affirm the trade, which must then be properly margined.

Exchanges began as non-profit associations and, as discussed, have precursors in the non-derivative cash markets. Today, leading exchanges are for-profit and publically traded (as in the case of CME). Exchanges converting from non-profits to for-profits are said to demutualize, and members receive shares of stock, in one or more classes of stock.

In early organized exchanges, futures were traded exclusively, on exchanges in a system called "open outcry," where traders cry out their bids to go long and offers to go short; this took place in a pit,[60] but much of the trading activity today takes place via electronic trading platforms. Open outcry still exists. However, since 1982 the direction of the industry is to route trades electronically through an exchange, and then to settlement via the clearinghouse.

Members of an exchange were permitted to participate directly in the early exchange proceedings, which resembled auctions in many respects. Traders and brokers would stand on the trading floor in times past; traders would capture the spread: the traders stand ready to buy at the bid price, and then sell at the offer price, and collect the difference in between those prices. Brokers would also be standing on the trading floor and would execute trades on behalf of their clients, for a fee. Those clients would open an account with their broker, call and verbally convey to their broker an order, which would then be related to the order desk of a brokerage firm for execution on the floor. A clerk at the brokerage firm would time stamp the order, then hand a written request to a runner, and once the trade was executed, the brokerage firm would contact the customer. The trade at that point is "executed," but it is not "settled;" it must clear. A trade was filled at the exchange, but it is settled at a clearinghouse.

The exchange accepts market orders (open orders to buy or sell at the best available price), limit orders (orders which specifically set the price at which the order is to be executed, or not executed at all), or other orders such as market if touched, which indicates to the broker that the broker is to buy or sell at the best available price.

The vast majority of exchange activities are conducted through an electronic platform. A leading example is the Globex electronic trading platform at the CME Group, whose hubs are located in several markets throughout the world, thereby dramatically expanding access to the trading forum, or exchange. Parties seeking to trade via CME are entitled to open access to Globex, provided that an end user license agreement is executed and the parties have an account with a clearing member of the CME clearinghouse. Most parties connect with a clearinghouse by means of an electronic platform or through their brokers, which have platforms for trading at multiple exchanges.

What Is Clearing?

Paradoxically, the term clearing is used often, defined rarely, and is, as a result, far from always clear.[61]

Clearing is a process that commences at the point of execution of a trade and ends at maturity and settlement or termination. When two traders enter into a trade, whether by phone, e-mail, or in person, that point in the derivatives life cycle is referred to as execution. An anatomy of which is provided in Chapter 7. By executing a trade, a derivatives buyer, with a seller, creates a legal obligation to buy or assume risk (on an asset) which we call an "underlying;" the two parties execute that trade with an eye to settle, at which point the legal obligation at execution is fulfilled.

In the early years of futures trading, once a trade was executed on an exchange-trading floor, floor traders or brokers would take their transaction cards to a brokerage firm that clears trades. That firm would transmit the buy or sell details to a clearinghouse (either owned by the exchange or in some way affiliated with the exchange, but technically separate from the exchange). The task of the clearinghouse is to match each buyer with each seller and settle their trades. If trade details (from a buyer and a seller) do not match, then the trade does not clear. Once matched, the clearinghouse stands in between the buyer and seller; then, the clearinghouse is the buyer to each seller, and the seller to each buyer.

Customers trading via CME's Globex benefit from the Globex computer matching system, which matches sellers and buyers by means of a matching, or allocation algorithm (e.g., FIFO, or first-in, first-out). By the time a trade is submitted for clearing it has either been matched or is submitted on a pre-matched basis.

The word *clearing* is meant to capture the activities that take place in between execution and settlement. The reader will see, in the anatomy of a cleared derivative provided in Chapter 7 (the first analysis in a published work), a transition from execution to settlement, during which positions are processed, monitored, and readied for settlement at maturity. Prior to maturity, outstanding options, futures, and other cleared derivatives at the end of each trading day are referred to as "open interest."[62]

Figure 3.1 illustrates the clearing process and distinguishes it from the earlier, execution phase of a futures contract or cleared derivative.

As discussed in the preceding pages and summarized in Figure 3.1, the first step is the placement of an order by the customer (and the customer may in some cases do this directly, or via a clearing broker, or a brokerage firm). Next, the order is filled and it is sent to the exchange by the brokerage firm. As described in greater detail in Chapter 7 the trade terms sought by the customer are routed through the customer's broker to an exchange and, once filled, the order is restated and approved by the customer. That restatement and approval is known in trade parlance as affirming and alleging, terms that will be discussed in Chapter 7. This completes the first phase of the futures contract or cleared derivatives life cycle, the execution phase.

EXECUTION PHASE			CLEARING PHASE		
I. ORDER	II. EXCHANGE	III. EXECUTION	IV. CLEARING	IV. CLEARING (cont.)	V. OFFSET or SETTLEMENT
o Customer places order with brokerage firm	o Order electronically routed to execution facility, the exchange o Alleged/Affirmed	o Execution (Buyer and Seller form legal Contract) (After execution the trade is reported, see Chapters 4 and 7)	o Executed Trade "Taken-up" and submitted to Clearing House	o Match trade data o Margin	o Settlement/ Offset o Settlement Reported

FIGURE 3.1 Comparison of Execution and Clearing Phases

Once the customer or their broker/intermediary approve the trade, a legal contract is, generally at that point, formed, and as we will see in the next chapter, Chapter 4, the new law requires the real time (or as close to real time as possible) reporting of that trade to a data repository.

In Figure 3.1, the clearing phase begins once the trade has been executed. If the customer's broker or its affiliate is a member of a clearing house that will clear the trade, then the trade will be immediately submitted. If the broker/broker affiliate is not a clearinghouse member, then the trade must be given up to an entity that is a member of an exchange (a clearing broker or FCM, or futures commission merchant), which will then take up the trade and submit it to the clearinghouse also for clearing. The clearinghouse will require margin both initially and going forward (as discussed below), confirm that the trade is properly matched (buyer to seller, seller to buyer), then will, by a process called novation, step in between the buyer and seller as the counterparty to both, thereby guaranteeing the trade. The clearinghouse will then collect trade data, adjust the clearing broker/FCM account details initially and through the life of the trade, and bring about settlement or other disposition of the trade, such as termination.

What Is a Clearinghouse?

The clearinghouse steps into the life cycle of a trade following execution to handle post-execution tasks and facilitate the orderly disposition of the trade. The clearinghouse also actively manages the daily reports and modifications concerning open positions,[63] and it conducts during each trading day risk exposure calculations to determine, set, and call for collateral, which, in the cleared derivatives industry, is typically referred to as "margin."

The clearinghouse, with the remedial, crisis-management measures that are integral to the clearinghouse system, is designed to manage and substantially limit the counterparty risk of default that we saw earlier in this chapter (in three failures of prominent financial service firms). The clearinghouse does this by carrying out at least two vital functions:

> It warranties the financial integrity of each futures contract that it clears and it supervises deliveries made against futures contracts by holders of short positions. To create the funds necessary to guarantee the financial stability of the futures markets it clears, the clearing house requires that each of its clearing members posts a guaranty deposit. The amount required is substantial. It may be in cash or a letter of credit. If a member defaults, these funds may be drawn on to ensure that no public futures customer loses money as a result of the default. If the total of the guaranty deposits on hand is still not

enough to cover the defaulting member's debts, the clearing house is authorized to levy a special pro rata assessment on its members to make up the difference.[64]

Chapter 8, the history of the OTC derivatives and futures, describes early clearinghouses in ancient temples, churches, and in fairs and on wharves. Modern clearinghouses originated in trading centers, such as those in grain markets in nineteenth century Chicago. Because one cannot understand the futures model without first understanding a futures contract, we now turn to a more detailed discussion about these contracts, and the manner in which they settle, or "clear."

Clearinghouses clear trades in a way that is quite different from clearing in the cash (non-derivative) markets. Since a picture tells a thousand words, we begin our introduction to the futures model with the following diagram, which illustrates fundamental differences between how a transaction settles in the futures model, as compared to the manner in which a transaction settles in other non-futures markets, without a clearinghouse.

In the top half of Figure 3.2, two parties, a buyer and a seller "face off" against each other in the OTC, or over-the-counter derivatives market. This arrangement is familiar to all of us; one party has an asset to buy, the other party has an asset to sell, and the parties exchange, in legal parlance, legal consideration). So far, so good.

In the bottom half of Figure 3.2, the seller and buyer, after their trade is matched and ready to settle, are pushed to the outer edges of the diagram,

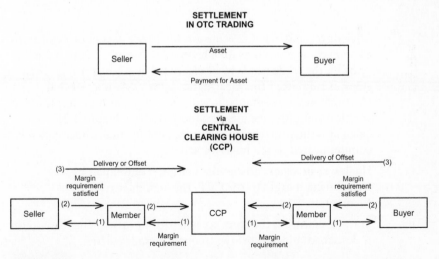

FIGURE 3.2 Comparison of Settlement in OTC and Centrally Cleared Trades

and inserted in between them are new parties (in rectangles and a large square), and we see the clearing mechanics, represented by a series of arrows, along with numbers in parentheses. All of this is actually quite straightforward yet it is mysterious to many.

Figure 3.2 picks-up in the process right after execution. A buyer and seller in a futures trade are said to execute a trade when they agree on the trade details. The point of execution is the moment at which a legal contract is formed by the buyer and the seller. This point exists in both the futures model and in cash market trades. The fundamental difference between cash and derivative market transactions is that a period of time elapses between agreement and settlement.

Figure 3.2 illustrates the most significant difference between an OTC trade and a centrally cleared trade in the futures model: the use of a clearinghouse in the settlement process. Figure 3.2 includes clearing members (represented by the word "Member" in rectangles outside of the clearinghouse in the bottom half of Figure 3.2), which in many ways are the agent to each party. Each of these will be described at length; this is an overview of the settlement structure (which is separate and distinct from the execution structure, but both the execution and settlement structures will be combined in this text's description of the full life cycle of a trade, which is introduced in this chapter and fully described with other aspects in a more fulsome way in Chapter 7). The participants in clearing and the sequence of events in bringing about settlement will next be described, in a series of steps, by reference to the numbers in parentheses in Figure 3.2:

(1)   After Buyer and Seller execute a trade (trade execution) by means of an exchange (such as, in Chapter 4, a Swap Execution Facility or SEF), the trade needs to be cleared. The trade, through these steps, is submitted to a clearinghouse by a Member of that clearinghouse. Simultaneous with the submission of that trade to the clearinghouse, the clearinghouse (CCP in Figure 3.2) calculates the initial margin requirement for that trade, which is communicated to the buyer or seller.

(2)   The buyer or seller satisfies the margin requirement by transferring margin to the CCP, through their respective Members.

(3)   At trade maturity, the contract is settled or offset. The offset term is described in detail below; frequently trades offset.

Is a Clearinghouse an Exchange?

By this point, the reader should readily answer this question with a resolute no. There is some confusion in the market, and the terms exchange and clearinghouse sometimes are used interchangeably, but the terms refer to distinctly different legal entities and very different goals and functions. Part of the confusion may stem from the reality that many clearinghouses are owned by or are divisions within exchanges; in other cases, such as that of the Options Clearing Corporation, the largest equity derivatives clearing organization, the clearinghouse is entirely independent of exchanges. To review, a clearinghouse is, as the name suggests, a financial utility that handles the clearing functions, described previously.

An exchange is a financial utility that, as the name suggests, is a physical or electronic venue or medium through which assets such as securities (or derivatives) are bought and sold. An exchange is a price-discovery mechanism—that is one of the primary functions of an exchange, and, as we saw in Chapter 1, the absence of a transparent exchange (and a regulated exchange) was a shortcoming within certain segments of the structured finance and OTC derivatives markets in the 2008 market crises.

If a Clearinghouse Is *Not* an Exchange, What Is It and What Does It Do?

To review: A clearinghouse is a legal entity which is either a division of an exchange or is entirely separate in all respects from the exchange. Its functions are discussed above, but to underscore the most critical of its functions, we continue to discuss the clearinghouse and its roles here.

The clearinghouse is a solution to global counterparty risk in the OTC derivatives market (that has been thought of before by regulators but never introduced on a large scale outside the futures arena).

Losses arising out of the Great Recession of 2008, and the inability of the New York Federal Reserve to construct a safety net, together provided the impetus to impose central clearing requirements on the $300 trillion OTC derivatives market in the United States. There was no clearinghouse to save the day in the case of the OTC derivative positions of the three financial services firms we discussed at the outset of this chapter, so policymakers made the mandate to centrally clear trades at the heart of the derivatives reform that followed the 2008 market crises. Commitments were made by representatives of the G-20 industrialized countries to bring about central clearing under the futures model, and early steps have been taken in this direction, as described in the conclusion of this chapter.

Until we get there, it bears repeating that the clearinghouse is a backstop. A clearinghouse substitutes its own credibility for all traders by standing in the middle of each trade (as the seller to every buyer and the buyer to every seller) through a legal process referred to as novation. In Chapter 7, the Lifecycle of a Cleared Derivative, we examine that process more intensively.

Clearinghouses guarantee the obligations of each part of a trade, and they do this by elaborate systems of financial safeguards. One system, sometimes referred to as "good to the last drop," entails the clearinghouse committing its capital to satisfy any default obligations not covered by posted margin by members or a separately capitalized guarantee fund.[65]

"Live another day" is another name of a safeguard model, in which members of clearinghouses receive protection primarily with guarantee funds; however, in this model the core clearinghouse is not committed to satisfying all obligations.[66] Upon a default, remaining members not in default must assume unpaid amounts. The clearinghouse makes no commitments beyond what its members are themselves willing to commit. CCorp, The Clearing Corporation, which was acquired by ICE in 2009 is an example of this model in practice; it provides clearing services to ICE Clear Credit and ICE Clear Europe. Clearinghouses have guaranty funds, to which admitted members must contribute and, as we will see in Figure 3.4, margin and these funds play an important role in preventing losses due to clearing member or customer default.

One of the most important component parts, then, of the futures model, is the clearinghouse. It provides support to the market in the case of a default of a clearing member or trader where the Federal Reserve could not (at least in the case of Lehman's bankruptcy). Before we discuss that in greater detail, it is important for the reader to understand the basic features of a cleared derivative such as a futures contract.

What Are the Basic Features of a Futures Contract?

Standardized Forwards   As described in the introduction to this text, a futures contract, much like a forward, is a binding agreement to buy or sell an asset, usually a financial instrument or commodity, at some point later in the future. However, unlike a forward, a futures contract is subject to an organized, orderly, standardized, and systemic trading process that affects every aspect of the trade, from pricing to settlement. The price for the purchase (later in time) is discovered through futures trading on an exchange, which is subject to daily settlement and margining procedures. These contracts are standardized according to certain specifications of the asset as well as the delivery date, time, and location.

Whereas a forward may be entered into by parties for purposes of buying and selling at any later point in time *any* asset and *any* amount, grade, or quantity of that asset, a futures contract is by necessity *more standardized* in terms of the grade or quality of the asset, the quantity, and when the asset is to be settled, or, in futures parlance, "delivered." As an example: A futures contract for corn on the Chicago Board of Trade (CBOT) calls for 5,000 bushels of No. 2 yellow corn, within set months for delivery, March, May, July, September, and December.[67] The pricing for the contact is determined by the offers to purchase and sell the futures contract on an established exchange, which sets the terms of the contract (e.g., the grade, quantity, and delivery date for settlement).

Offset   Futures contracts are standardized, thereby enabling parties to, in essence, terminate and get paid for their contracts by entering into offsetting transactions—or a reversing trade to bring the trader's net position to zero.

As an example, if a trader bought one December CBOT mini-sized silver contract but does not want delivery of that amount of silver, the trader must sell one December CBOT mini-sized silver contract before the delivery date and time stated in the contract.[68] A seller of a contract, who is obligated to sell an asset at a later date, can offset its obligations under that contract by buying the contract back in the futures market, thereby relieving the seller from having to sell the asset under the initial contract. On the other hand, a buyer of a contract can sell the contract in the futures market and be relieved of the obligation to purchase the asset under the first contract.[69] For offsetting to take place, the contracts need to be standardized. That is a prerequisite to clearing.

Futures contracts may call for the physical delivery but most are offset; physical delivery does not take place. Exchanges have over the years increasingly called for cash settlement.

A rather unique aspect of futures trading is the manner in which a buyer enters its obligation to purchase by later selling the contract. To deconstruct this important concept, a buyer under a futures contract, who of course has a contractual obligation to purchase, can later sell the contract in the very liquid futures market and thereby relieve the buyer of the obligation to purchase. In a similar way, a seller of an asset in a futures contract can buy the contract back in the futures market, thereby relieving the party of the obligations to sell the object of the futures contract.

Unlike OTC derivatives trading, futures contracts involve more than just two counterparties: the futures customer interacts with a clearing broker or futures commission merchant or FCM, an exchange, and an annex, affiliate of that exchange, or a separate legal entity altogether called a clearinghouse. The clearinghouse associated with an exchange margin.

Margin   An important aspect of futures contracts is the concept of margin. Margin (or collateral) requirements are determined on a case-by-case basis.

Many readers are familiar with the way in which collateral is exchanged in the OTC market,[70] however that process is quite different from the way collateral (or, in futures parlance, margin) is exchanged in connection with a futures contract or other cleared derivative.

Clearinghouses require clearing firms to deposit margin on behalf of their customers, the parties that initiate the trades. Margin acts as a financial safeguard. When the clearing member posts proper margin, it ensures the performance of the trade. Clearing margins are set by a risk committee within the clearinghouse and excess margin above and beyond what the clearinghouse requires may be set and required by the clearing member. Dodd-Frank alters this, as we shall see in the next chapter. All assets to satisfy margin requirements are generally the assets of the customer placing the trade.

The clearinghouse demands deposits from clearing members to cover all initiated or open positions that are carried by the clearing member. Clearinghouses typically collect margin from clearing members on a net basis, while clearing members collect from their customers on a gross basis. A nonclearing broker is to post margin with the clearing broker.

Initial and Variation Margin   Initial margin is the minimum amount of proceeds that must be deposited by a customer with the clearing broker (or the FCM; FCM and clearing broker will be used interchangeably in this chapter) to initiate and maintain an open position. Initial margin may be thought of as a good faith deposit to commence a trade. Maintenance margin is the amount (generally less than the initial margin) which must be maintained during the life of the futures contract. During the life of a trade, assets in a customer account may decline and the customer must then deliver additional margin. A margin deposit is analogous to a cash performance bond (although it is not technically an extension of credit, but it instead is meant to help offset against adverse market movements). It assures the customer's performance of the futures contractual obligation.

Daily Settlement   At the end of each trading day, the clearinghouse establishes a settlement price for each contract (usually an average of the prices of the last few trades of the trading day) and, using this settlement price, the accounts are marked-to-market. The difference in the then-current settlement price and the previous trading day's settlement price is determined and if that difference is positive, then the dollar amount is credited to the margin accounts of those holding long positions (the buyers), and debited from those holding short positions (the sellers under the contract). If the settlement price has decreased and the difference is negative, then the opposite outcome takes place (the dollar amount is credited to the holders of the short positions and charged to those holding long positions).[71]

Futures contracts are customarily bought and sold on initial margin that represents a very small percentage of the aggregate purchase or sales price of the contract (ranging upward from less than 2 percent). Because of margin requirements, price fluctuations occurring in the futures markets may create profits and losses that, in relation to the amount invested, are greater than are customary in other forms of investment or speculation. Adverse price changes in the futures contract may result in margin requirements that greatly exceed the initial margin. In addition, the amount of margin required in connection with a particular futures contract is set from time to time by the clearinghouse associated with the exchange, on which the contract is traded, and it may be modified from time to time during the term of the contract.

The clearing organization sets original margin that a clearing member must post to clear a position for a customer. Once that is done and the position remains open, it is marked to market daily (and even intraday) to reflect unrealized gains and losses. Market movements produce the variation *pays* to the clearing organization (required if the market movement is *adverse*), and variation *collects* from the clearing organization if market movements are *favorable*. Initial margin is deposited by the customer with its FCM (which may or may not be the clearing member—if the FCM is not a clearing member of the relevant clearing organization, it must submit the trade for clearing on an omnibus basis through a clearing member), and that minimum customer initial margin is generally about 25 to 30 percent above the original margin level that the clearing member must deposit with the clearing organization. There is also a customer maintenance margin level, which is about 70 to 75 percent of the customer initial margin level. If the customer's account equity erodes to the maintenance margin level, a margin call goes out to the customer to restore his account to the initial level. This minimizes the need for daily calls on customers if there are relatively small market movements.

Brokerage firms carrying accounts for traders in commodity interest contracts may not accept lower amounts of margin as a matter of policy for protection again default. The clearing brokers require futures customers to make margin deposits equal to exchange minimum levels for all commodity interest contracts. This requirement may be altered from time to time at the discretion of the FCM as clearing member. Initial margins are established with reference to historical price volatility, the speculative nature of the trade, and other factors that are similar to those used by the credit desk of a derivatives provider in OTC trading, discussed in the pages that follow.

After posting initial margin, market fluctuations may and often do cause open position values to fluctuate. A decline in value of a cleared contact may result in a margin call being issued to the customer by the FCM/clearing member. All open positions must satisfy a certain margin level referred to as maintenance margin. If the initial margin that is posted by the customer falls below that maintenance margin level, the customer must then post additional margin back up to the initial margin level.[72] In the event that the customer fails to satisfy the margin call and the account still has positive equity, the FCM will typically be able, assuming that market-standard legal documentation is in place, to liquidate one or more contracts before suffering a loss. A margin call is typically issued when an account has about 70 percent in equity remaining in the account, so if the customer fails, the FCM may recover first from equity existing in its customer's account (when the customer fails to respond to the margin call). The FCM also has various other rights and remedies that it may exercise upon a default by the customer. To further protect the FCM or clearing member from sustaining losses due to a customer default, excess margin may be collected from the customer.

Excess Margin In addition to initial margin, a futures customer or an end user of a centrally cleared derivative may be required to post additional margin over and above what is required by a central clearinghouse. The clearinghouse through its own methodology, in line with applicable law and regulation, generally sets margin levels. A clearing member or FCM may, based on factors that include the derivatives traded and the credit profile of the futures customer or end user, require that additional margin (or, in industry parlance, excess margin) be pledged to the FCM/clearing member.

REGULATION OF FUTURES

In the brief history of futures provided earlier in this chapter, the development of the statutory law governing commodities and futures contracts, and the evolution of the regulatory regime—including the futures regulator, the CFTC—in the United States has been introduced. What follows are certain key aspects of the regulation of futures, many of which are important within the post-reform derivatives market for cleared derivatives.

Accountability Levels and Position Limits

Designated contract markets have established accountability levels and position limits on the maximum net-long or net-short futures contracts in commodity interests that any person or group of persons under common trading control (other than a hedging party) may hold, own, or control. Regulatory authority for these limits has been further established in new U.S. reforms, as we shall see in the next chapter.

Accountability levels and position limits are designed to prevent a corner or squeeze on a market or undue influence on prices by any single trader or group of traders. The position limits imposed by the CFTC apply to certain agricultural commodity interests such as oats, soybeans (including soybean oil and soybean meal), corn, wheat, and cotton, but not to interests in energy products.

Dodd-Frank added level requirements for exempt metals and energy commodities, as well as agricultural commodities.

Certain exchanges or clearing organizations also set limits on the total net positions that may be held by a clearing broker (but if the CFTC sets a limit, the limit set by the exchange cannot be lower than that limit set by the CFTC). The net position is the difference between an individual or firm's open long contracts and open short contracts in any one commodity. In general, no position limits are in effect in forward or other OTC contract trading or in trading on non-U.S. futures exchanges, although the clearing brokers may trade in such markets and may impose such limits as a matter of credit policy.

Daily Price Limits

Most U.S. futures exchanges (but generally not foreign exchanges) may limit the amount of fluctuation in some futures contract or options on a futures contract prices during a single trading day. Once the daily limit has been reached in a particular futures or options on futures contract, no trades may be made at a price beyond the limit.

Futures contract prices have occasionally moved to the daily limit for several consecutive trading days, thus preventing prompt liquidation of positions and subjecting the trader to substantial losses for those days. The concept of daily price limits is not relevant to OTC contracts, including forwards and swaps.

Commodity Prices

Commodity prices are volatile and, although ultimately determined by the interaction of supply and demand, are subject to many other influences, including the psychology of the marketplace and speculative assessments of future world and economic events.

Examples of Futures and Other Listed Products

Options are written and traded in both the OTC- and exchange-traded markets, however, their close-out mechanics differ. An exchange-traded option may be closed out only on an exchange, which provides a liquid secondary market for an option of the same series. An OTC option may be closed out only with the other party to the option transaction.

Options on Futures Contracts

Options on futures contracts are standardized contracts traded on an exchange. An option on a futures contract gives the buyer of the option the right, but not the obligation, to take a position at a specified price (the striking, strike, or exercise price) in the underlying futures contract or underlying interest. The buyer of a call option acquires the right, but not the obligation, to purchase or take a long position in the underlying interest, and the buyer of a put option acquires the right, but not the obligation, to sell or take a short position in the underlying interest.

Centrally Cleared Swaps

Cleared swaps involve two counterparties first agreeing to the terms of a swap transaction, then submitting the transaction to a clearinghouse that acts as the central counterparty. Once submitted to the clearinghouse, the original swap transaction is novated and the central counterparty becomes the counterparty to a trade with each of the original parties based on the trade terms determined in the original transaction. In this manner, each swap counterparty reduces its risk of loss due to counterparty nonperformance because the clearinghouse acts as the counterparty to each transaction.

A FUTURES CONTRACT IN ACTION

To see how each component part works together, we next turn to a few days in the life of a futures contract. The reader's attention is first drawn in

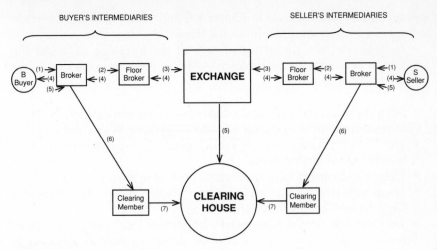

FIGURE 3.3   The Life of a Futures Contract

Figure 3.3 to the two sets of intermediaries, the Buyer's Intermediaries on the upper left, and the Seller's Intermediaries on the upper right. The numbers in parentheses are included in the schematic to give a sense of chronological order to the process.

At the outset, both the buyer and the seller, who generally will not know each other (in contrast to the OTC derivatives trade, in which the two parties must know each other very well as each bears counterparty risk, or default, failed performance or bankruptcy/insolvency with respect to the other) instruct their broker (or, if no broker, directly submit an order via, for example, CME's Globex) to enter into a futures contract. The buyer is, in industry parlance, referred to as a long, and the seller is the short.

Many years ago, the broker for each buyer and seller would then communicate their clients' respective trade orders to a floor broker, which would then execute the trade in the exchange. Today, much of the process is simplified and carried out electronically, obviating the floor broker intermediary.[73] In any event, the exchange communicates back to the brokers and ultimately, to the buyer and seller, that the seller has a buyer, and the buyer has a seller. The trade is, as described in more detail in Chapter 7, alleged and affirmed (that is, confirmed, electronically), and both brokers, on behalf of the buyer and seller, proceed to bring about the central clearing of the trade and once the trade is matched and affirmed, the trade is submitted to the clearinghouse, but only if the intermediaries utilized in the trade up to this point are members of a clearinghouse where the trade is cleared. If they are not, another intermediary, the clearing member, is retained by means of a give-up agreement (discussed in Chapters 6 and 7) to "take up" the trade and submit it for clearing via the clearinghouse.

To illustrate how the timing of each of the foregoing steps and the application of margin principles described in the preceding pages work, we use the following example:

- First, the futures strategy of the customer is communicated to the FCM for execution on an exchange after documentation is finalized.
- The FCM previously satisfies various prudential requirements to be a member of the clearinghouse.
- These requirements include collateral posting by the FCM.
- These requirements also bring about, typically, the capitalization of a large default fund by the clearinghouse.
- The clearinghouse will handle an FCM's default by allowing other members to acquire pro rata portions of the defaulting members position. If the other members do not, in essence, acquire the defaulting member's position, the exchange will draw on its default fund to satisfy remaining positions of the defaulting member.
- On Monday, the FCM posts to the clearinghouse an aggregate amount of margin that the clearinghouse requires of the member. This amount includes initial margin amounts for every individual position to be centrally cleared.
- On Tuesday morning, the FCM will communicate to the futures customer an amount that is required by the FCM of the customer, and this amount will include the following:
  - Margin required under U.S. Federal law (for short and long positions, as initial margin; initial margins can normally range from 5 to 20 percent of the full value of the futures contract).
  - Margin over and above federal requirements, that is, margin required by the house rules of the FCM.
  - Fees/charges unrelated to the margin required by the FCM.
- On Wednesday, in our example, if the position moves in the customer's favor, the amount in excess of the initial margin requirements, over and above the maintenance margin level, may either be withdrawn or used for margining additional positions. If the market moves against the customer, the customer will be required to deposit additional margin.
- So on Wednesday, a margin call takes place when the customer's account value falls below the maintenance margin requirement, which may be about 75 percent of the initial margin requirement. When this happens, the customer will have to deposit sufficient funds to bring the equity balance in the account back up to the level of initial margin

requirements. Clearinghouses establish initial and maintenance margin requirements. All clearing members, however, may establish margin requirements in excess of federal requirements for specific traders. From time to time, the clearinghouses may adjust margin requirements on various contracts.

- The FCM of the exchange acts as the conduit and facilitator of the daily margin variations and cash flows.

This chapter next turns to certain problems in the futures trade.

DEFAULT BY A CLEARING MEMBER IN THE FUTURES MODEL

No system is perfect. It is important to briefly illustrate imperfection in the cleared derivatives marketplace. When compared to OTC market failures, futures and exchange traded derivative failures are relatively small in comparison. In order for the futures model to perform, the performance of the clearinghouse and clearing members must take place, but full and timely performance or claims of non-performance have been reported.

- **MF Global** transferred hundreds of millions of dollars in customer assets from client accounts to its own securities brokerage accounts before declaring bankruptcy on October 31, 2011.
- **Citibank's 2011 claim involving Lehman Brothers foreign exchange clearing.** In 2011, Citigroup Inc. claimed in litigation that the failure of Lehman Brothers resulted in $1.26 billion in unpaid expenses relating to the clearing of foreign exchange contracts. Lehman claimed it was entitled to a return from Citi of $1 billion in collateral, but Citi is claiming, as this book goes to print, $260 million in losses relating to cleared FX trades, according to Reuters in 2011.[74]
- **J.P. Morgan Futures Inc.** On September 9, 2009, this registered FCM was subject to a CFTC order and sanctions for improperly under-segregating funds in the course of transferring $1.45 billion of assets into its house account and drawing upon the FCM's customers' assets in a way that violated the Commodity Exchange Act asset protections. The FCM failed to properly notify the CFTC and JPMFI's employees were not properly supervised in the course of their handling customer assets.[75] A $300 million penalty and cease and desist order were among the sanctions imposed by the CFTC.
- **Refco Bankruptcy.** A large and well-known New York foreign exchange and commodity brokerage house, and one of the main futures brokers

on the CME, was forced into filing bankruptcy in 2005. This filing was facilitated by loans from the fourth largest bank of Austria, Bawag PSK. Refco represented to customers that Refco had properly segregated their 17,000 retail brokerage accounts from the assets of Refco; however, the subsequent bankruptcy proceedings revealed that segregation in fact did not take place. In the end, creditors recovered one-half of the $2.4 billion in total fraud.[76] The CFTC found on January 23, 1996, that Refco violated customer segregation requirements and failed to supervise employees in violation of CFTC cease and desist orders in 1983, 1988, and 1990.[77]

- **Klein and Co. Futures Inc.** In May 2000, broker Klein and Co. Futures Inc.'s omnibus account was liquidated by New York Clearing Corporation. As in the case of Volume Investors (summarized below) 15 years earlier, Klein's account held all of its customers' margin, not just the margin of Klein's customers who could not meet margin calls after those customers sustained substantial losses.[78]
- **Volume Investors.** In 1985, a futures broker and clearing member of NYMEX (Commodity Exchange Inc., a division of NYMEX), Volume Inventors, defaulted.[79] The default was caused by the failure of customers of Volume Inventors. After a significant change in the value of prices for gold futures, the customers could not meet margin calls. The customers' failure to meet the margin call caused Volume Investors to default on the clearinghouse's margin call, which exceeded Volume's assets. The clearinghouse seized the entire accumulated margin posted by Volume on behalf of all of its customers in order to pay other clearing members. This action left the non-defaulting customers (whose broker and clearing member was also Volume Investors) with no margin at the clearinghouse and no timely means of obtaining their assets from the failed broker their margin (i.e., amounts held in Volume's omnibus account).[80] After the collapse of Volume Inventors, the CFTC required a minimum amount of margin on all short option positions, even those that were deep out of the money.[81]

In the event a clearing member fails, the futures model includes within it a series of remedies that clearinghouses apply, typically in a particular order. The application of clearinghouse remedies enables the clearinghouse to, in essence, serve as a guarantor (which it is, although it executes no written guaranty in favor of a trader as a beneficiary of such a guaranty). In principle, so long as the daily changes in the price of a futures contract does not exceed margin deposits, then the margin deposits held by the clearinghouse (together with margin held by clearing members) would in principle be sufficient to meet the obligations of both buyers and sellers of trades cleared via the

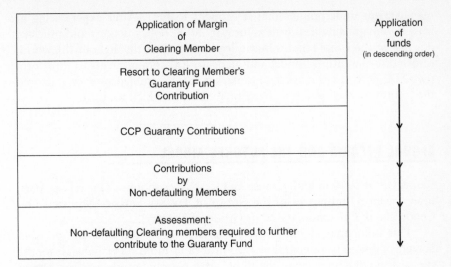

FIGURE 3.4 Clearinghouse Waterfall

clearinghouse. In this way, in principle, the buyers and sellers are protected against the default or delayed performance, so long as margin is properly and timely calculated and collected.

No clearinghouse is the same as the others, of course. Figure 3.4 illustrates the basic principles that govern, and the remedies which are set into motion upon, the default of a clearing member.

As illustrated in Figure 3.4, upon a clearing member's default, the clearinghouse first resorts to the member's margin, then to its contribution to a guaranty fund. Some, not all, clearinghouses will, at the third step in the waterfall, make their own contribution to prevent losses from occurring if the failing clearing member's margin and fund contribution are insufficient. Next, the clearinghouse will turn to the other (non-defaulting) members for contributions or give those other members the opportunity to buy, pro rata or by clearinghouse rules, the book of the failed clearing member.

Then, if the foregoing remedies are insufficient to prevent loss due to a failed clearing member, the clearinghouse will make a special assessment and require all non-defaulting clearing members to further contribute to the clearinghouse (specifically, the guaranty fund of the clearinghouse). It is this last step that the New York Fed, in essence, attempted to do to avert the three crises summarized in the beginning of this chapter. If all of the open contracts that LTCM, Bear Stearns, and Lehman Brothers were centrally cleared, the Fed would likely never have been faced with the crisis management undertakings that it brought to bear. After experiencing at least two major financial firm failures in 2008, policy makers and officials, not just in the United States but in leading markets throughout the world, resorted to the futures model and made critical commitments to transform the OTC derivatives market to a market that resembled or even mirrored the futures market, and it is that global effort to which we turn.

GLOBAL REFORM AND THE FUTURES MODEL

Reform after 2010 in both eastern and western economies has, in large part, been driven by initiatives of the Group of Twenty Finance Ministers and Central Bank Governors (G-20 or Group of Twenty).

This influential global body, comprised of the top financial decision makers of nineteen countries and the European Union, are responsible for the stewardship of 85 percent of the global gross national product, 80 percent of world trade, and two-thirds of the population of the world. The G-20 traces its roots to the last stages of the Asian financial crisis of 1999. Since that time, the G-20 has held regular meetings among its members, including finance ministers and central bank governors, with the G-20 heads of government meeting in Washington, DC, in November 2008, as the global financial crises took hold. For that meeting the body enlarged to include representatives of Spain and the Netherlands, and international financial institutions (i.e., the International Monetary Fund and World Bank), as well as the United Nations. Recent G-20 summits have created massive stimulus packages to support the global economy and have also, in the 2009 summit in Pittsburgh, Pennsylvania, produced this statement, which has become the single most influential mandate in the area of derivatives reform: "All standardized OTC derivatives contracts should be traded on exchanges or electronic trading platforms, where appropriate, and cleared through central counterparties by end-2012 at the latest."[82]

After the 2008 market crises, almost no aspect of the global financial system and no category of cash or synthetic market or trades within it are free from reform mandates. Members of the G-20 have begun to implement these primary derivatives reform mandates:

- Central clearing of vast swaths of the global OTC derivatives market.
- Imposition of stronger capital requirements to reign in the excessive use of leverage by financial services firms, banks, and funds.
- Reporting of derivative trading activities to bring about a more transparent market that is more easily monitored and regulated.

These were some of the early derivatives regulatory developments within the G-20.

European Union

Derivatives reform has been a priority of the European Union (EU).[83] The European Commission (EC)[84] issued in 2010 its Proposal for a Regulation of the European Parliament and of the Council on OTC Derivatives, Central Counterparties and Trade Repositories, which provided an early, comprehensive framework for derivative reform. On the first page of that proposal is the September 2009 G-20 commitment that all standardized derivatives are to be traded on an exchange and centrally cleared, as well as the G-20's reaffirmation of that commitment in Toronto, Canada, in June 2010. The proposal also states that its mandates are within a "broadly identical scope of application"[85] of the Dodd-Frank derivatives mandate, the subject of this text.

Initially, the response of the EU focused on the use of credit default swaps by Lehman Brothers, but then broadened its regulatory review to include these measures:

- Holding a series of bilateral and multilateral conferences in 2008 to determine a careful and comprehensive response to the 2008 market crises.
- The establishment of the Derivatives Working Group that included government and market representatives.
- The formation of a Member States Experts Working Group on Derivatives and Market Infrastructures. The group held a series of meetings in the first half of 2010.
- Extensive public consultations from July 2010.[86]

In order to develop uniform clearing mandates, a process developed at the EU-level for determining which derivatives are to be mandated for clearing. The aim of this process is to prevent regulatory arbitrage that could result if one or more individual member states develop less stringent derivatives reform, which would then attract some opportunistic market participants.

The EU proposal for derivatives reform includes seven titles on these subject areas:

- Title I—Definitions and scope of derivatives reform.
- Title II—Clearing, reporting and risk mitigation of OTC derivatives.
- Title III—Authorization and supervision of clearinghouses.

- Title IV—Clearinghouse requirements.
- Title V—Interoperability of the derivative market, including post-execution activities in the OTC market for derivatives in the EU.
- Title VI—Regulation and surveillance of trade repositories.
- Title VII—Requirements for trade repositories.[87]

Many of the mandates in the titles enumerated in this list mirror those within statutory reform in the United States which is embodied in Title VII of Dodd-Frank, the subject of the next chapter.

In comparing Title VII derivatives reform mandates with publicly available summaries of derivatives reform initiatives by the EC, the CFTC highlighted these regulatory features:

- Date of Effectiveness: EC derivatives legislation is to be effective 20 days after the publication in the Official Journal of the EU, with technical standards to be completed by June 30, 2012.
- Clearing Requirements and Process: A clearinghouse within the EU is to request authorization from its national regulator to clear a category of derivatives. The EU authority that has an important role in this undertaking is the European Securities and Markets Authority (ESMA), which may, on its own, determine categories of derivatives that are subject to a mandatory clearing requirement.
- Foreign Clearing Houses: A clearinghouse that is established outside the EU may only provide clearing to entities in the EU if the clearinghouse is recognized by ESMA.[88]
- Reporting Requirement: Any financial counterparty, and a nonfinancial counterparty whose net non-hedged positions exceed a threshold, must report to a registered trade repository the details of any derivative that it has entered into and any modification or termination, not later than the working day following the execution, clearing, or modification of the contract, and if a trade repository is not available to receive the report, then financial counterparties to the trade must report to the national regulator.[89]

Canada

As with other members of G-20, Canada firmly and aggressively adopted G-20 derivative commitments to reform the Canadian OTC derivatives market. Important players in this effort include the Bank of Canada, the Department of Finance, the Office of the Superintendent of Financial Institutions, the Autorité des marchés financiers (the securities regulatory authority in Quebec), including the Centre of Excellence for Derivatives led by Derek West, and the other securities regulatory authorities in Canada that comprise the Canadian Securities Administrators (CSA). In particular, the Canadian OTC Derivatives Working Group (the Working Group) and the CSA Derivatives Committee are spearheading Canadian reform.

The Working Group, which is chaired by the Bank of Canada, is an interagency working group that emerged at the end of 2009 in Canada. It is composed of members of the Bank of Canada, the Office of the Superintendent of Financial Institutions, the Federal Department of Finance, and three provincial securities regulators. The primary objective of the Working Group is to execute the commitments made by Canada as a part of the Group of Twenty Finance Ministers and Central Bank Governors, or G-20.[90]

G-20 commitments, made in September 2009 at a summit in Pittsburgh, Pennsylvania, and reinforced at the summit in Toronto, Canada, in June 2010, included an ambitious goal of trading all standardized OTC derivatives on exchanges or electronic trading platforms and cleared through central counterparties by the end of 2012.

To bring about the execution of this commitment within Canada, leading market participants, including the Canadian Market Infrastructure Committee comprised of major dealers and buy-side participants that are active in Canadian derivatives markets, provided policy recommendations to the Working Group. On October 26, 2010, the Working Group published a white paper on the reform of OTC derivatives markets in Canada.[91] This white paper sets out the Working Group recommendations in five key categories:

- **Capital Incentives and Standards:** The Working Group recognizes the need for the Basel Committee on Banking Supervision to develop a definitive international capital regime and for the widespread, consistent application of that regime to market participants in Canada and elsewhere.
- **Standardization:** The Working Group places a high value on the standardization of derivative contracts in Canada and encourages the setting of specific milestones for Canadian derivatives industry players to accomplish standardization throughout the industry in Canada. The Working Group also recognizes the need for standardization to be harmonized internationally.
- **Central Clearing:** It is suggested that the merits of a Canadian-based central clearing counterparty with links to international infrastructures be considered. For noncentrally cleared derivative contracts, the Working Group recommends the adoption of best practices for counterparty risk management. Target dates are to be set for clearing certain classes of derivative products that are appropriate for clearing.

- **Trade Repositories:** Whenever a derivatives trade involves a Canadian counterparty, the Working Group recommends the reporting of salient details of each such trade to a trade repository to which the Canadian authorities have appropriate access (no matter where the repository is located geographically).
- **Trading Venues:** The Working Group recommends that Canadian authorities encourage the migration of standardized OTC trades to transparent, electronic public-trading venues that would enable all market participants to determine market activity and valuations.[92]

On November 2, 2010, the CSA Derivatives Committee issued a comprehensive and influential white paper, Consultation Paper 91-401 on Over-the-Counter Derivatives Regulation in Canada. This paper examines the same subject areas as, and makes recommendations that are similar to, the Working Group. In addition to the five areas summarized in the preceding list, the Consultation Paper also addresses capital and collateral requirements and the need to establish end-user exemptions from certain regulatory proposals. With regard to capital and collateral requirements, the CSA Derivatives Committee recommends a risk-based approach that reflects appropriately the risks that an entity assumes. Specifically, higher capital and collateral requirements for noncentrally cleared bilateral arrangement are suggested. The Consultation Paper also acknowledges the need for further analysis before making a recommendation with respect to the segregation of collateral that supports derivative trades. The CSA Derivatives Committee suggests that further study is needed in order to define the categories of end-users that should be exempt from the regulatory proposals, as well as to establish the conditions that end users will need to satisfy to be able to rely on the exemptions.[93]

Reform in Canada is largely consistent with the reform initiatives in the United States, and early reform efforts indicate that, although Canadian reform has been set into motion, the enactment of those reforms will take place later than the "go-live" of law in America. Industry leaders and officials from the Bank of Canada met on a regular basis to put in place the market infrastructure to enable Canada to meet its G-20 commitments.[94]

Canada is an important trading jurisdiction in the global derivatives market (particularly the interest rate and currency-based derivative markets) as well as in the foreign exchange markets. In particular, foreign exchange transactions are used by both Canadian financial and nonfinancial entities. In 2009, $319 billion of foreign exchange contracts were booked with nonfinancial counterparties in Canada.[95] Canada is also exceedingly important to the United States because of the level of sophistication of many of its derivatives counterparties, including leading Canadian banks that trade with those in the United States.

The Far East and Southeast Asia

Asian members of the G-20 also committed to bring about central clearing of OTC derivatives by the end of 2012. As Reuters reported on July 25, 2011, many financial supervisors within Asian G-20 countries believe that meeting the 2012 clearing deadline will be difficult in part due to the labored process to bring about central clearing on a wide scale in the United States and EU.[96]

In Japan, in May 2010 an amendment to the Financial Instruments and Exchange Act (FIEA) brought about mandates to clear large-scale derivative transactions, the reporting and storage of trade data, and greater regulation generally of firms that trade derivatives. Derivatives that are subject to mandatory clearing are to be designated for clearing by a cabinet office ordinance no later than November 18, 2012.[97]

After the May 2010 amendment, the Japanese government issued a proposal to combine the trading of financial derivatives and commodity futures to a single trading venue by 2013.[98]

As of the date this text went to print, Singapore, Hong Kong, and Korea were also taking significant steps toward centralized clearing. Hong Kong joined Japan in making clear its commitment to mandate central clearing of derivatives previously traded OTC by the end of 2012.[99] According to IFC Review in June 2011, Hong Kong will require financial institutions incorporated in Hong Kong to clear all interest rate swaps and non-deliverable forwards at an authorized central clearinghouse and then report those trades to a local, Hong Kong central bank trade repository. Hong Kong Exchanges and Clearing (HKEx) is reported to invest initially HK$180 million on information technology and staff for a new clearing division. The Singapore Exchange launched derivatives clearing services and initially offered dollar interest rate swap clearing on a voluntary basis.[100]

Perhaps the most pronounced aspect of the mandates is that many are based on a wholesale rejection of the bilateral OTC derivatives market structure in favor of one in which traders enter into trades that are priced by regulated exchanges and cleared by means of a central clearinghouse. Because of the widespread adoption of the centrally cleared market in derivatives, the foregoing discussion of the futures model was necessary before we look at the U.S. derivatives reform mandates in Chapters 4 and 5.

* * *

With the foregoing discussion about futures, the need for the futures model, existing futures regulations, and a brief description of futures contracts and other exchange-traded derivatives as background, we now turn to Chapter 4, which includes a description of the specific legislative mandates concerning derivatives in the United States.

NOTES

1. Charles R. Morris, *The Two Trillion Dollar Meltdown* (New York: Public Affairs, 2008), 53.
2. Ibid, 51.
3. Ibid.
4. Ibid.
5. "Long Term Capital Management: It's a Short Term Memory," *New York Times*, September 7, 2008, http://www.nytimes.com/2008/09/07/business/worldbusiness/07iht-07ltcm.15941880.html?pagewanted=all
6. Morris, *The Two Trillion*, 53.
7. Ibid., 52–54.
8. Ibid.
9. Andrew Garfield, et al., "Bear Stearns $500m Call Triggered LTCM Crisis," *The Independent*, September 26, 1998, http://www.independent.co.uk/news/business/bear-stearns-500m-call-triggered-ltcm-crisis-1200636.html. See also *Toronto Centre Case Study on Bear Stearns* (Toronto: Toronto Leadership Centre, 2010), 11. http://siteresources.worldbank.org/FINANCIALSECTOR/Resources/J2-BearStearnsCaseStudy.pdf
10. Ibid.
11. "Long Term Capital Management: It's a Short-Term Memory," *New York Times*, September 7, 2008.
12. *Toronto Centre Case Study on Bear Stearns* (Toronto: Toronto Leadership Centre, 2010), 11.
13. Ibid., 11.
14. William D. Cohan, *House of Cards: A Tale of Hubris and Wretched Excess on Wall Street* (New York: Doubleday, 2009), 434.
15. Ibid., 433.
16. Chicago Board of Trade, *The Chicago Board of Trade Handbook of Futures and Options* (New York: McGraw-Hill, 2007), 97.
17. A.G. Malliaris, *Futures Markets,* Vol. 1 (Elgar Reference Collection, 1997), xii.
18. Ibid., xii.
19. Ibid., xii.
20. Ibid., xii.
21. Ibid., xii.
22. Ibid.

23. Ibid., 379.
24. Ibid., 379.
25. Ibid., 379.
26. Ibid., 379.
27. Ibid., 380.
28. Ibid., 381–82.
29. Nick Battley, *The World's Futures Options Markets* (New York: John Wiley & Sons, 2000), 25.
30. Ibid., 27.
31. Chicago Board of Trade, *The Chicago Board of Trade Handbook of Futures and Options*, 89.
32. Ibid.
33. Ibid.
34. Ibid.
35. Ibid.
36. Ibid., 94.
37. Battley, *The World's Futures & Options Markets*, 26.
38. Ibid., xiii.
39. Ibid.
40. Chicago Board of Trade, *The Chicago Board of Trade Handbook of Futures and Options*, 90.
41. Ibid.
42. Ibid., 91–92.
43. Malliaris, *Futures Markets*, Vol. 1, 256.
44. Ibid., 26.
45. Ibid., 27–28.
46. Chicago Board of Trade, *The Chicago Board of Trade Handbook of Futures and Options*, 108.
47. Ibid.
48. Ibid.
49. Ibid., 92.
50. Ibid.
51. Ibid.
52. Philip McBride Johnson and Thomas Lee Hazen, *Derivatives Regulation* (New York: Aspen Publishers) (2011 Cumulative Supplement), 83.
53. Ibid.
54. Ibid.
55. Ibid.
56. Emily Lambert, *The Futures* (New York: Basic Books, 2011), 32.
57. Battley, *The World's Futures & Options Markets*, 37.
58. Ibid., 40.
59. Ibid., 82.
60. Robert W. Kolb and James A. Overdahl, *Futures, Options, and Swaps* (New York: Blackwell, 2007), 14–15.
61. Ibid., 18.

62. Ibid.
63. Ibid.
64. Ibid.
65. Ibid.
66. Ibid.
67. Ibid.
68. Ibid.
69. Ibid.
70. Collateral is transferred between counterparties during the term of an OTC transaction based on the changing value of the transaction, whereas independent amounts are fixed amounts posted by one or both counterparties at the start of an OTC transaction. Distinctions between OTC trade documentation and exchange traded derivatives documentation are discussed in Chapter 6. Customers in the futures and listed derivatives markets do not deposit margin directly with the clearing organization; only clearing members make that deposit. There generally is no privity (or contractual relationship) between the clearing organization and the customer, which is one of the issues in the handling of customer funds in a default situation.
71. Don M. Chance and Robert Brooks, *An Introduction to Derivatives and Risk Management* (Thomson South-Western 2007), 267.
72. Kolb and Overdahl, *Futures, Options, and Swaps*, 18.
73. Chance and Brooks, *An Introduction to Derivatives and Risk Management*, 266–70 and Figure 8.2 (Figure 8.2 is the basis for Figure 3.3 in this text, which modifies Chance and Brook's Figure 8.2). Chance and Brooks illustrate in Figure 8.2 the steps that futures contract participants and intermediaries took to clear a futures contract in the open outcry system, which continues to exist today, but to a lesser extent due to the electronic platforms in existence today such as CME's Globex.
74. "Citi Seeks to Keep $1 Billion Lehman Collateral," Reuters (May 26, 2011, available at www.reuters.com/assets/print?aid=us.
75. In the Matter of J.P. Morgan Futures Inc., U.S. Commodity Futures Trading Commission Order (CFTC Docket 09-12, September 9, 2009).
76. "The Refco Bankruptcy and its Impact on Retail Forex Trading," www.forexfraud.com/forex-articles/the-refco-bankruptcy-and-its-impact-on-retail-forex-trading.html.
77. "Refco Agrees to Pay a $925,000 Civil Penalty to Settle," Commodity Future Trading Commission Release (No. 3888-96) (January 23, 1996).
78. Kolb and Overdahl, *Futures, Options, and Swaps*, 19.
79. "Futures Commission Merchant Activities," Comptroller of the Currency (November 1995), 16.
80. Kolb and Overdahl, *Futures, Options, and Swaps*, 19.
81. "Futures Commission Merchant Activities," Comptroller of the Currency (November 1995), 16.
82. G-20 Leaders' Statement, the Pittsburgh Summit (September 24–25, 2009), 9.

83. Created in the aftermath of the Second World War, the EU is a political and economic partnership made up of 27 European countries that has brought about a half of a century of prosperity, peace, and stability. The EU launched a single European currency and built a Europe-wide market. Europa—basic Information on the European Union—is available at http://europa.eu/about-eu/basic-information/index_en.htm.

84. The EC is both an institution and a College of Commissioners, one Commissioner from each EU country. Since 2002, the EC has set out to simplify and improve EU regulatory environment, and in this vein the EC has examined and re-examined new initiatives (e.g., financial service reform) for potential social and environmental impact. The European Commission at Work—Basic Facts—European Commissioner, available at http://ec.europa.eu/atwork/basicfacts/index_en.htm.

85. European Commission, "Proposal for a Regulation of the European Parliament and of the Council on OTC Derivatives, Central Counterparties and Trade Repositories," 2010, 3.

86. Ibid., 3.

87. Ibid.

88. ESAMA is an independent EU authority that fosters the stability of the EU's financial system by ensuring the proper and efficient functioning of EU Securities Markets. ESAMA, like U.S. financial system regulators (e.g., the Securities and Exchange Commission and Commodity Futures Trading Commission) also fosters inventor protection and supervisory convergence among securities regulators and financial sectors by working closely with other European authorities. The European Securities and Markets Authority: www.esma.europa.eu.

89. "Derivatives Reform: Comparison of Title VII of the Dodd-Frank Act to International Legislation," CFTC Staff for the Global Markets Advisory Committee (October 5, 2010).

90. OTC Derivatives Working Group, "Reform of Over-the-Counter (OTC) Derivatives Markets in Canada: Discussion Paper from the Canadian OTC Derivatives Working Group" (October 26, 2010).

91. Ibid.

92. Ibid., 4.

93. Canadian Securities Administrators Derivatives Committee Consultation Paper 91–401, Over-the-Counter Derivatives Regulation in Canada, November 2, 2010.

94. "In Canada, Derivatives Reform Slowly Takes Shape," FINCAD News, http://derivative-news.fincad.com/derivatives-regulations/in-canada-derivatives-reform-slowly-takes-shape-993/.

95. OTC Derivatives Working Group, "Reform of Over-the-Counter (OTC) Derivatives Markets in Canada: Discussion Paper from the Canadian OTC Derivatives Working Group," no. 41 (October 26, 2010), 23.

96. "Asia May Struggle to Meet G-20 Derivative Deadline-ISDA," Reuters, July 25, 2011.

97. Atsumi & Partners, "Japan Moves to Centralize Clearing of OTC Derivatives," PLC Global Finance Email Update, May 4, 2010.
98. "Japan Could Unify Financial and Commodity Derivatives by 2013," *FOW: Let's Talk Derivatives*, August 6, 2010.
99. "Hong Kong Lawmakers to Enforce Mandatory CCP by the End of 2012," *IFC Review*, June 6, 2011.
100. Ibid.

CHAPTER 4

U.S. Derivatives Law in Title VII of Dodd-Frank

This chapter is your guide for developing an understanding of the mandates relating to derivatives included within Title VII of the Dodd-Frank Wall Street Reform and Consumer Protection Act (Dodd-Frank) as signed into law by President Barack Obama on July 21, 2010. The legislative and regulatory regime governing derivatives in the United States continues to evolve. For that reason, what follows should not be read to be the definitive or "final say" on derivatives law in the United States, even though the author describes in this chapter some of the finalized rules implementing Dodd-Frank which were available before this book was published.

ORGANIZATION OF DODD-FRANK

Before setting a framework for understanding Title VII derivatives mandates, it is necessary to outline the broader structure of Dodd-Frank. The organization of Dodd-Frank reveals the importance of certain critical features of the new legal framework and regulatory regime. The law begins with the statement that the Dodd-Frank Wall Street Reform Consumer Protection Act is a law that is designed to "... promote the financial stability of the United States by improving accountability and transparency in the financial system, to end the concept of too big to fail, to protect the American taxpayer by ending bailouts, to protect consumers from abusive financial-services practices, and for other purposes."[1] There are a total of 16 titles within Dodd-Frank:

Title I: Financial Stability.
Title II: Orderly Liquidation Authority.

Title III: Transfer of Powers to the Comptroller of the Currency, the Corporation, and the Board of Governors.

Title IV: Regulation of Advisers to Hedge Funds and Others.

Title V: Insurance.

Title VI: Improvements to Regulation of Bank and Savings Association Holding Companies and Depository Institutions.

Title VII: Wall Street Transparency and Accountability.

Title VIII: Payment, Clearing, and Settlement Supervision.

Title IX: Investor Protections and Improvements to the Regulation of Securities.

Title X: Bureau of Consumer Financial Protection.

Title XI: Federal Reserve System Provisions.

Title XII: Improving Access to Mainstream Financial Institutions.

Title XIII: Pay It Back Act.

Title XIV: Mortgage Reform and Anti-Predatory Lending Act.

Title XV: Miscellaneous Provisions.

Title XVI: Section 1256 Contracts.

Hundreds of Rules

Dodd-Frank set into motion rule making of historic proportions. The number of rules that implement Dodd-Frank is breathtaking if not overwhelming. Approximately one-third of all rules relate to derivatives! U.S. regulators were charged with the task of finalizing the rules numbered to the right of their names (the number of rules include rules on subjects other than derivatives):

- Securities and Exchange Commission (SEC) (95).
- Commodity Futures Trading Commission (CFTC) (61).
- Financial Stability Oversight Council (56).
- Federal Deposit Insurance Corporation (FDIC) (31).
- Bureau of Consumer Financial Protection (24).
- U.S. Department of Treasury (9).[2]

Title VII of Dodd-Frank is effective on the later of (a) 360 days after the enactment of Dodd-Frank (Dodd-Frank was signed into law on July 21, 2010) or (b) 60 days after the promulgation of a final rule, if a rule is required for the implementation of a Title VII mandate. Substantial political pressure was applied to the CFTC and SEC to finish its rule-making processes by mid-July 2011 but these two regulators were unable to meet that deadline.

Because many of the rules on derivatives have not been finalized by the time this book went to press, the reader is encouraged to follow the derivatives rule-making process with reference to the additional materials provided at the conclusion of this book, including the website: www.DerivativesGuide.com.

Preventing Regulatory Turf Battles

For U.S. regulators, Dodd-Frank constitutes a radical change from their historical roles. In Chapters 3 and 8, the reader will find discussions on U.S. law on derivatives and financial services prior to Dodd-Frank, including the Commodity Futures Modernization Act and Gramm-Leach-Bliley Act. These two critically important laws in essence prohibited the SEC from regulating a significant category of derivatives now entrusted to the SEC, security-based swaps. Title VII repeals that prohibition, gives the SEC jurisdiction over security-based swaps (and security-based swap dealers), and also includes mandates for the two primary U.S. derivatives regulators, the SEC and CFTC, to work harmoniously with each other in the promulgation of derivative regulations.

Dodd-Frank changes the way that the market will look at derivatives. Section 762 of Title VII amends the two primary U.S. securities laws, specifically, Section 2A of the Securities Act of 1933 and Section 3A of the Securities Exchange Act of 1934. The import of this amendment is to exclude swaps (as defined in Section 206 of the Gramm-Leach-Bliley Act) from the definition of security, while subjecting security-based swaps to antifraud provisions, and also to the reporting obligations under Section 16 of the 1934 Act, which will have significant consequences for security-based swaps on equity underliers.

Dodd-Frank unifies derivatives law. Chapter 8 also discusses the hodge-podge efforts of states to regulate derivatives in the past. Title VII includes, in Section 722 and 767, prohibitions for states to regulate credit default swaps (CDS) as insurance. Title VII now bars earlier efforts at the state level, including those by the New York State insurance commissioner, to treat CDS as insurance and regulate that derivative as such.

Title VII also includes provisions that clarify the applicability of state law to derivatives. Section 767 of Title VII proscribes the application of any state law regarding the offer, sale, or distribution of securities as a part of a security-based swap or security futures product (state antifraud law applies to that transaction, however).

As discussed earlier, Dodd-Frank's jurisdictional provisions do not prevent turf battles, especially when considering that the CFTC is given jurisdiction over, for example, security-based swap agreements, yet the SEC has existing regulatory power to regulate fraud or insider trading involving those agreements.

INTRODUCTION TO TITLES VII AND VIII

Included within Dodd-Frank are two important titles relating to derivatives, Title VII and Title VIII, both of which bring about fundamental changes to the way derivatives are entered into, settled, and cleared in the United States. They also affect the process outside of the United States, to the extent that derivatives activities have a direct and significant effect on U.S. commerce or are undertaken to circumvent Title VII. Chapter 4 is dedicated to Title VII, and the subject of Chapter 5 is Title VIII.

The Wall Street Transparency and Accountability Act of 2010, which we call Title VII, is the act within Dodd-Frank that changes literally every phase of the life cycle in a derivatives trade. These changes are brought about for purposes of advancing these public policies:

- **Shine light on the OTC derivatives market.** As we saw in Chapter 1, in the months leading up to the passage of Dodd-Frank, regulators and members of Congress expressed their view that the problems in the OTC derivatives market basically crept up on Washington, DC. To enable these policy makers to develop a greater awareness of the market, the way in which derivatives trade, and the market size, greater reporting obligations of at least the largest players in the OTC market is necessary.

- **Replace private trading with centrally-cleared trades.** As discussed in the preceding pages, Congressional history leading to the passage of Dodd-Frank identified the need for the futures model, as opposed to private trading OTC, in light of the various shortcomings of the OTC market, such as inadequate collateralization and disputes by the traders over trade and collateral value. These market deficiencies all pointed toward the regulated, transparent exchange and clearing through the futures-style system that survived market seizures in 2008. A central mandate of Dodd-Frank is the requirement that trades be centrally cleared *if* the CFTC or the SEC mandates those trades to be centrally cleared.

- **Manage Counterparty Risk by Collateralizing Trades.** The posting of collateral is generally the most effective way to secure performance on trades. In the largely unregulated OTC market before Dodd-Frank, many active participants had collateral practices that were not uniform in nature, and losses on major defaults created system-wide damage. The Dodd-Frank mandates call for regulators to mandate certain derivatives for central clearing (and thereby make them illegal to consummate outside a central clearing system). As we will see in this chapter, swap dealers and major swap participants who trade derivatives that are mandated for central clearing have to initially execute those trades through a regulated exchange facility, and they must clear these transactions through a DCO or other regulated clearing entity. In this new trading system, swap and security-based swap dealers, as well as major swap and security-based swap participants must comply with capital and margin requirements and a host of other business-conduct standards.

- **Eliminate turf battles among regulators in Washington, DC.** A primary cause of the 2008 market crises was the regulatory void in the derivatives area. The reasons for absence of comprehensive and effective derivatives regulation were discussed in Chapter 1. As they drafted Dodd-Frank, members of Congress were mindful of the long history of division among the regulators on questions, such as which derivative product is to be regulated by which regulator and to what extent. Dodd-Frank's Title VII attempts to clarify the regulatory jurisdiction regarding derivatives. However, several areas of ambiguity remain and, as this text goes to print, the SEC and CFTC continue to evaluate proposed regulations on jurisdiction.
- **Regulation of the largest OTC market participants is needed.** The drafters of Dodd-Frank believed that substantial regulation of the most active OTC derivative-market participants was necessary. This led to the creation of major-swap-participant and swap-dealer concepts.

Most of these public policies are advanced by the text of the Dodd-Frank. However, the details continue to be put in place as of the publishing date of this book. Over 140 of the 520 rule makings and many of the 81 studies and 93 reports are devoted to the implementation of the new law of derivatives.[3]

Additionally, with the election of 2010 in the United States resulting in significant changes within the leadership of Congress, the legal and regulatory landscape continues to take form perhaps in some ways which surprise even some Dodd-Frank lawmakers. At the last stage of the Dodd-Frank lawmaking, Congressman Barney Frank (D-MA) stated that Congress would consider a bill that follows Dodd-Frank for purposes of addressing technical issues and the exception for the clearing of derivatives.[4] On April 15, 2011, key members of the U.S. House of Representatives introduced legislation, H.R. 1673, which would make December 31, 2012, the earliest date for the effectiveness of Title VII mandates. This would bring the timeline for the implementation of many of the U.S. derivative mandates (e.g., the mandate calling for regulators to require the central clearing of certain categories of derivatives previously traded OTC) in line with G-20 mandates, as discussed earlier in this book.

Title VII completely overhauls the U.S. OTC derivatives market and includes, as its cornerstone, a mandate calling for regulators to designate certain derivatives as subject to exchange (or swap execution facility) trading and central clearing (or else the derivative would be illegal if settled bilaterally).

Title VII is subdivided into two parts, Subtitles A and B, and then Subtitle A is further subdivided into two parts: first, the division of regulatory authority between the CFTC and SEC, and then the division of authority over derivative products. Subtitle A is essentially designed by the lawmakers to apply to the CFTC. The second half of Title VII, referred to as Subtitle B, applies to the SEC. Title VIII is the subject of Chapter 5.

Title VII did not, by itself, create entirely new provisions that had no relation to existing law. Dodd-Frank's Title VII amends most often the Commodity Exchange Act or CEA, but also significant amendments are made to the Securities Exchange Act of 1934 (the 1934 Act) and the Securities Act of 1933 (the 1933 Act), as well as the Investment Company Act of 1940.

Title VII of Dodd-Frank is effective on the later of two dates, according to the text of Title VII:

- July 16, 2011, a date that is 360 days after President Barack Obama signed Dodd-Frank into law.

- The sixtieth day after the publication of the final rule that implements Title VII of Dodd-Frank.

THE APPROACH TO UNDERSTANDING NEW DERIVATIVES LAW IN THE UNITED STATES

This chapter presents a new approach to conceptualize Title VII's comprehensive rework of the derivatives market in the United States as not one but three spheres, or, as demonstrated in the diagram which follows, three categories of new law and regulation. Some aspects of the law concern products, others concern people within the U.S. derivatives market, and finally a third "sphere" of the new law concerns the platforms on which the people trade the products. The reader is directed to Figure 4.1 and what follows.

As we saw in Chapter 2, in the discussion regarding the timing and order in which U.S. derivatives law and regulation would be finalized and effective in the marketplace, it is important to first have an understanding of the derivatives, or products, and the way in which they are regulated. This is true for a few reasons. First, how a product is conceptualized by lawmakers

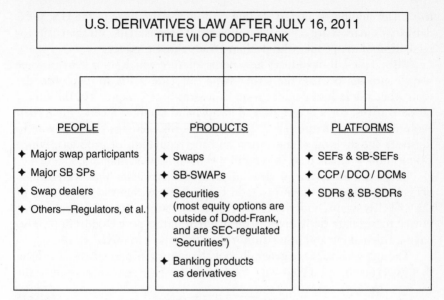

FIGURE 4.1 Products, People, and Platforms of Title VII

and regulators, and defined with precision in final rulemaking will determine which regulator (i.e., the CFTC or SEC) will regulate that product, and that will in turn telegraph to the market which set of regulations must be followed (i.e., the CFTC's, the SEC's, or both, in the case of mixed swaps, discussed further on) and when (the reader is directed to Figure 2.2 in Chapter 2, which illustrates how the finalization of the product definitions precedes the implementation in final form of the vast majority of CFTC and SEC rules).

This chapter discusses Dodd-Frank's Title VII mandates within each of the three categories, and we begin with the new law governing derivative products.

PRODUCTS

The starting point in the Title VII analysis is a discussion on how derivative instruments, or products, are now regulated in America. Title VII of Dodd-Frank divides the universe of OTC derivatives (as opposed to futures, options on futures, and other listed derivatives) in a way that may be confusing without an understanding of how the two primary regulators, the CFTC and the SEC, regulated these products in the past. Chapter 3, in its discussion of the history of futures regulation, and Chapter 8, in its retelling of the history of derivatives and Futures, provide some perspective on that front. Developing an understanding of how the products in the U.S. OTC derivatives market are regulated is important because Title VII then calls for regulation of the people who deal and trade those products.

Also, Title VII introduces new nomenclature which is, at least in some ways confusing because the term "swap" in Title VII is so much broader than what the industry understood as a swap (see Chapter 10, the survey on derivatives, for a description of swaps, and Chapter 8 concerning their evolution). As a picture tells a thousand words, perhaps the best way to illustrate the division of authority, and the regulation of products, which Dodd-Frank's Title VII set into motion is the following diagram, Figure 4.2.

In the author's view, a clear majority of derivatives that were traded OTC before the enactment of Dodd-Frank come within the jurisdiction of the CFTC as swaps, with the CFTC (as the regulator with arguably the most power to regulate derivatives it the United States, post-Dodd-Frank) also having rulemaking and other authority with respect to mixed swaps.

Though securities are generally not thought of as derivatives (a subject that governments grappled with for hundreds of years, as discussed in the

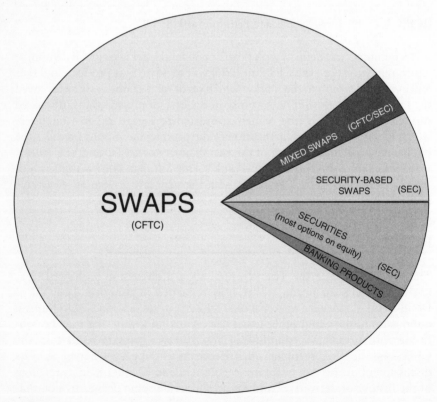

FIGURE 4.2 Division of Authority, Jurisdiction and Product Overview

panoramic history of derivatives in Chapter 8), Figure 4.2 includes securities as a slice of the OTC market in the United States, because the ubiquitous stock option, a classic derivative, is generally treated as a security (not a swap!) and governed by the SEC under Federal law (e.g., the U.S. Securities Exchange Act of 1934), not Dodd-Frank, unless the equity referenced by the option is a restricted security under the 1934 Act. Certain banking products that, technically speaking, are derivatives, are regulated by neither the SEC nor the CFTC, but banking regulators with jurisdiction over the entity providing the derivative as discussed later in greater detail.

Swaps—Regulated by the CFTC

Most of the OTC derivatives products traded OTC are swaps that are now, according to Title VII, regulated by the CFTC.

It is rather unfortunate that Title VII uses the term "swaps" to cover this vast category of derivatives. This is because, for many years, the derivatives industry referred to swaps in a way that flies in the face of the new definition of swap in Section 721 of Title VII (which amends the Commodity Exchange Act or CEA), which covers not just exchanges of payments (swaps) but a vast array of derivatives. In fact, 22 derivative products, ranging from interest-rate swaps, floors and caps, to energy, metal, and at least some credit default swaps are included within the defined term swap. Subpart 47 of Section 721 of Title VII includes these categories of derivatives within "swap."

1. A put, call, cap, floor, collar, or similar option that is entered into for the purchase or sale (or is based on the value of) one or more interest or other rates, currencies, commodities, securities, instruments of indebtedness, indices, quantitative measures, or other financial or economic interests of property of any kind (a contract or option on a contract for the sale or future delivery is excluded from the term swap).
2. Derivatives that provide for any purchase, sale, payment, or delivery that is dependent on the occurrence, nonoccurrence, or the extent of the occurrence of an event or contingency associated with a potential financial, economic, or commercial consequence.
3. Derivatives that provide for an exchange of payments, on an executory basis (i.e., parties to an executory contract expecting the execution or performance of that contract at some point in the future), based upon the value or level of interest or other rates, currencies, commodities, securities, debt instruments, indices, quantitative measures, or other financial or economic interests or property of any kind that transfers financial risk without transferring ownership risk, including 22 derivative products listed in Section 721(47) of Dodd-Frank, ranging from interest-rate swaps, floors and caps, to energy, metal, and at least some credit default swaps.

The import of this definition is that, if a product is a swap, then that product, the dealer of that product, and the exchange where it is traded—all come within the jurisdiction of the CFTC, and the CFTC only.

Exclusions from the Term Swap

Financial products that are not swaps include:

- A contract calling for the sale of a commodity for future delivery (i.e., a forward, discussed in Chapter 10) or option to enter into such a contract.
- Any sale of a nonfinancial commodity or security for deferred delivery, as long as the transaction is intended by the parties to be physically settled.
- Options on assets (other than restricted securities) that are governed by the 1933 Act or 1934 Act or options on foreign currencies that are entered into by means of a national securities exchange.
- Notes, bonds, or other debt that is covered by the 1933 Act.

In Chapter 8, The History of Derivatives and Futures, we see other governments addressing the reality that, in the early stages and Futures of entering into a derivatives contract, it certainly is not always clear whether a contract is entered with the intent to bring about physical delivery. As noted earlier, Section 721 of Dodd-Frank excludes any "sale" of a "nonfinancial" commodity or security for "deferred shipment or delivery" as long as the transaction is "intended to be physically settled."

This is an important exclusion from the term "swap," because many commercial entities which engage in buying and selling physical commodities will likely rely on this exclusion for all of their forward contracts (forward contracts are discussed in Chapter 10 in greater detail). The availability of the exclusion from the term swap in Section 721 will then turn on the intent of the parties to physically settle. This brings to the forefront the importance of intent in the minds of regulators over the past centuries, as discussed in Chapter 8. It is likely that, over time, there will need to be proof of intent as a part of the availability of the physical delivery exclusion in Section 721.

SEC jurisdiction is discussed next. Even though swaps come under the CFTC's jurisdiction, the SEC retains authority to regulate fraud and insider trading of certain instruments, such as a security-based swap agreement, which, under Section 721 of Dodd-Frank, comes within the definition of swap, and is, therefore, within the jurisdiction of the CFTC *and the SEC.*

Security-Based Swaps—Regulated by the SEC

Title VII defines a "security-based swap" as a swap that is based on:

- A narrow-based security index.
- A single security or a loan.
- The occurrence, nonoccurrence, or the extent of the occurrence of an event relating to a single issuer of a security or the issuers of securities in a narrow-based security index.

An option on a security is not a security-based swap unless the security is restricted under the 1934 Act. A narrow-based security index is generally defined as an index:

1. That has nine or fewer component securities.
2. In which a component security comprises more than 30 percent of the index's weighting.
3. In which the five highest-weighted component securities, in the aggregate, comprise more than 60 percent of the index's weighting.
4. In which the lowest weighted component securities comprising, in the aggregate, 25 percent of the index's weighting, have an aggregate dollar value of average daily trading volume of less than $50 million (or in the case of an index with 15 or more component securities, $30 million), with special ranking rules for certain securities that have an equal weighting.

To illustrate how the definitions in Title VII work in practice, a derivative that is based on a basket of seven securities is a security-based swap, and if a derivative is based on an index with seven components, that derivative would also be a security-based swap, because it has as its reference obligations components of a narrow-based security index. Terms such as *reference obligations* are discussed in our survey of derivatives in Chapter 10.

In the foregoing illustrations, the SEC is vested with regulatory power under Title VII of Dodd-Frank to regulate both of the derivatives discussed in the preceding paragraph. The dealers of these derivatives are security-based swap dealers, and their obligations under Title VII are discussed in this chapter, in the sphere of regulation that applies to people, and people within banks, firms, companies, and organizations.

To make sure that the reader understands the sphere of product regulation under Title VII, if a derivative is based on the S&P 500 or some other index with many dozens of components (i.e., FTSE), that derivative is regulated by the CFTC—not the SEC—even though the reference obligation of the derivative has all the hallmarks of the kind of entity that the SEC would regulate (i.e., issuers of equity in the United States). Dealers of that derivative are referred to as swap dealers (not security-based swap dealers) and, as we shall see, those dealers must register with the CFTC and take on many of the kinds of obligations that futures commission merchants or FCMs have under the CEA, as discussed in the previous chapter.

Mixed Swaps—the SEC and CFTC Share Jurisdiction

If the world of derivatives were simple, there would only be swaps and security-based swaps in the product sphere that is subject to Title VII. The underliers of many derivatives include both equities (equity shares of an issuer, by themselves, would, if the subject of a derivative, pull that derivative into the jurisdiction of the SEC), as well as other non-equity underliers that would, on their own, give the CFTC sole jurisdiction. These are derivatives that have attributes of swaps and security-based swaps. These are called "mixed swaps" under Title VII, with respect to which the CFTC and SEC have joint jurisdiction.

There will, even after Dodd-Frank, continue to be regulatory tension between the CFTC and the SEC for a variety of reasons, as long as both regulators exist. One example of how tensions will continue to exist has already been mentioned: a security-based swap agreement (i.e., one that meets the definition of swap agreement, as defined by Section 206A of the Gramm-Leach-Bliley Act [15 U.S.C. 78c note] of which a material term is based on the price, yield, value, or volatility of any security or any group or index of securities or interest therein) is a swap under CFTC's jurisdiction but also comes under the SEC's antifraud and insider trading regulatory jurisdiction.

Joint rule making concerning mixed swaps is required by Title VII.

Credit Default Swaps

An important derivative discussed in greater detail in Chapters 1, 8, and 10 is the credit default swap, or CDS. Although not completely clear from a reading of the jurisdictional terms of Title VII, if a CDS has as its underlier shares of a publicly traded company, then it is likely that the CDS will be regulated by the SEC as a security-based swap (same result if the CDS references a narrowly-based index). If, however, a CDS is on a broad-based index, such as the S&P 500, Title VII requires that the derivative, although based on components of an index that represent the equity of publicly traded companies, comes under the jurisdiction of the CFTC as a swap.

Foreign Exchange Derivatives

Dodd-Frank entitles the U.S. Department of Treasury (Treasury) to make a determination that two categories of foreign exchange derivatives (as described later, foreign-exchange forwards and foreign-exchange swaps) are not swaps under Dodd-Frank.

On April 29, 2011, Treasury proposed to exempt foreign exchange swaps and foreign-exchange forwards from the definition of swaps. Because it is important to understand exactly which products the Treasury proposed to be outside the definition of swaps (and the CFTC's regulatory reach), the definitions of these two derivatives, within Section 721 of Dodd-Frank, are summarized here:

- A foreign-exchange forward is a transaction which involves the exchange of two different currencies on a future date at a fixed rate, which the parties to the trade agree upon at execution.
- A foreign-exchange swap is a transaction which has two legs: first, an exchange of two different currencies on a specific date at a fixed rate which is agreed upon at execution, and second, a reverse exchange of the two currencies exchanged in the first leg, on a specific date and at a fixed rate that is agreed upon at the execution of the contract.

These definitions suggest this question: What exactly is the difference between a foreign-exchange swap (which Treasury proposes to exclude from the definition of swap) and a currency swap, which remains within the definition of swap within Section 721 of Dodd-Frank?

The short answer is that currency swaps include at least one component in addition to the two legs stated in definition of foreign-exchange swap (see the preceding bullet points) such as an interest-rate payment that is made at some point after the first exchange of currencies at the first leg, and the reverse exchange in the second leg of the swap.

Treasury proposed that foreign exchange swaps and foreign-exchange forwards be taken out of the term swap because the manner in which these two derivatives settle is different from the settlement process for other currency-based forwards. Many foreign-exchange swaps and forwards are traded in the interdealer market, and the vast majority of trades are settled via the clearinghouse CLS, which is the largest multicurrency cash-settlement system. This system substantially limits settlement risks in large part because it entails a payment-versus-payment (PVP) settlement process in which, in foreign exchange trades, one party does not tender currency unless the other party does so (almost simultaneously).

Energy and Environmental Derivatives

Energy derivatives, like the other products, also present difficult jurisdictional issues because of existing regulation and the division of authority put in place by Congress. The practical result of this is that market participants in the energy derivatives area may be under the jurisdiction of both the CFTC and the Federal Energy Regulatory Commission (FERC). As with numerous other provisions in Dodd-Frank's Title VII, the provisions in the title on energy and carbon markets and products remain unresolved in final, complete form, as this text went to press.

Title VII requires FERC and the CFTC to enter into a memorandum of understanding to establish procedures for resolving jurisdictional conflicts over energy derivatives.

Under Title VII, financial derivatives (as opposed to forward contracts that call for future physical delivery of commodities including energy commodities such as oil, which are carved out of the definition of swaps) are swaps under Section 721 subpart 47(A)(iii)(XI) (an energy swap is a subcategory of swaps under Section 721 of Dodd-Frank's Title VII).

Dodd-Frank mandated an intensive study of the viability of a carbon credit market, and the law also establishes the Energy and Environmental Markets Advisory Committee. The law set into motion an interagency working group comprised of the chairman of the CFTC, the secretary of Agriculture, the secretary of the Treasury, the administrator of the Environmental Protection Agency, and other federal energy officials to study the development of a transparent and efficient carbon market. Although the committee does not have a specific charter under the text of Title VII, it is to conduct public meetings and submit white papers to the CFTC.

In early 2011, a federal interagency working group led by the CFTC released a report on existing and proposed oversight of carbon markets. The working group included the chairman of the CFTC, as chair of the working group, the secretary of Agriculture, the secretary of the Treasury, the chairman of the SEC, the administrator of the Environmental Protection Agency, the chairman of FERC, the chairman of the Federal Trade Commission, and the administrator of the Energy Information Administration. These were the key guideposts identified by the working group to guide existing and proposed rule making on carbon markets:

- **Objective 1:** Facilitate and protect price discovery in the carbon markets. The first objective of rule making is to ensure that rules will be promulgated that foster and protect price discovery so that market pricing reflects supply and demand.
- **Objective 2:** Ensure appropriate levels of carbon market transparency. Just as a key objective of Dodd-Frank was to ensure a transparent market, the working group stated in their report that carbon market regulatory oversight must also ensure a transparent carbon market.
- **Objective 3:** Allow for appropriate, broad market participation. Regulatory oversight is to enable entities with emission compliance obligations to efficiently meet their obligations and allow offset credit providers to bring those credits to market.
- **Objective 4:** Prevent manipulation, fraud, and other market abuses. The fourth objective stated by the federal interagency working group was that carbon markets are to be free from manipulation, fraud, and other market abuses.

The working group recommended that the existing regulatory oversight program, as enhanced by Dodd-Frank, be retained for present and future carbon allowance and offset derivatives markets.

Stable Value Contracts

Stable value contracts are popular investments in retirement plans which offer investors safe investment opportunities with a reasonable guaranteed rate of return and capital preservation (as the principles underlying the transaction).

Title VII of Dodd-Frank calls for the CFTC and the SEC to conduct a joint study (within 15 months of enactment of Dodd-Frank) to determine whether stable value contracts fall within the definition of a swap.

Banking Products

Agreements, contracts, or transactions with a Federal Reserve-regulated bank (or the federal government or agency) that is expressly backed by the full faith and credit of the United States are excluded from the definition of swap. Deposit accounts and other banking products, although not intuitively derivatives, are deemed derivatives and come within the jurisdiction of the banking regulator that oversees the bank that provides them.

Certain "identified banking products" are excluded from the jurisdiction of the CFTC and the SEC (and the definitions of security-based swap and security-based swap agreement).[5] However, the appropriate federal banking agency that has jurisdiction over a swap dealer is authorized to make an exception to the exclusion for any particular identified banking product that it determines, in consultation with the CFTC and the SEC:

1. Would meet the definition of swap or security-based swap (SBS).
2. Is known to the trade as a swap or SBS or otherwise has been structured to evade the CEA or the 1934 Act.

If the bank is not under the jurisdiction of an appropriate federal bank regulatory agency,[6] the identified banking products exclusion will not apply, even if the aforementioned conditions are satisfied.[7]

Review: What Is this Derivative and Who Regulates It?

The easiest way to answer this question is to focus first on the underlier of the derivative. This approach, although simplistic, at least provides a starting point in the analysis. If the underlier is an equity (or a narrow-based index), then the derivative is likely a security-based swap within the SEC's jurisdiction. If not, it is likely that the derivative is a swap under the jurisdiction of the CFTC. There are a few additional examples that perhaps will clarify the foregoing division of regulatory authority over products in the U.S. derivatives market:

- An equity swap in which shares of Microsoft are the underlier of a derivative structured as a total return swap, in which one party pays a fee (plus depreciation) to the other in exchange for the appreciation of Microsoft stock; is a security-based swap and is regulated after Title VII by the SEC.
- An option to purchase shares of Microsoft is not a security-based swap; it is instead a "security" within the jurisdiction of the SEC under the Federal law (e.g., 1934 Act).
- A financial derivative (as opposed to one in which physical delivery of a commodity is contemplated, which would not be a swap but would continue to be regulated by the CFTC under the CEA) based on a commodity is a swap that is regulated by the CFTC.
- A derivative whose value is driven both by a commodity and an equity is a mixed swap, and both the SEC and CFTC share jurisdiction and jointly regulate that product.

Questions and ambiguity exist in the area of product regulation. Title VII anticipates this and, in fact, Congress mandated in Section 712 of

Dodd-Frank that the CFTC and the SEC coordinate with each other before the commencement of rule making that is required by Dodd-Frank in order to assure the development of a consistent regulatory regime. Congress was also mindful of the turf battles which existed and in fact contributed to the regulatory lapses that led in part to the 2008 market crises, as discussed in Chapter 1. With this in mind, early in the text of Title VII of Dodd-Frank are restrictions imposed on the CFTC and SEC to prevent both regulators from issuing regulations on products (as well as on dealers and repositories of those products) which fall within the jurisdiction of the other regulator.

In the year following the enactment of Dodd-Frank, numerous market participants submitted public comments on the subject of the division of regulatory authority over derivative products. In the absence of such coordination, players within the derivatives market may take advantage of uneven rule making and carry out regulatory arbitrage to the detriment of others in the market.

PEOPLE

Within the next regulatory sphere are the people that play a role in the new world of derivatives after Dodd-Frank, including:

- Regulators.
- Derivative counterparties (i.e., dealers and end users).
- Leadership within the counterparties (e.g., chief compliance officers and directors on subcommittees evaluating uncleared derivatives trading, traders, and front- and back-office staff in the offices of the most active users of derivatives).
- Advisers.
- Custodians.
- Eligible Contract Participants.
- Taxpayers.
- Whistleblowers.
- Bad actors.

Regulators: Four Critical Regulatory Bodies in the U.S. Derivatives Market after Dodd-Frank

One of the primary causes of the 2008 market crises that we discussed in Chapter 1 was the lack of an effective system to regulate derivatives and excessive risk taking by the users of these financial tools. In the weeks that followed the height of the market crises in the fourth quarter of 2008, spirited debate took place over whether a new regulatory body was needed to govern the use of derivatives. In the timeline provided in Chapter 2, at least one piece of legislation called for the creation of a new agency for derivative regulation in the United States.

As enacted, Dodd-Frank strengthened and clarified existing authority and created the Financial Stability Oversight Council, which plays a critically important role in the payment and clearing of financial transactions including derivatives, as discussed in Chapter 5 on Title VIII of Dodd-Frank. Dodd-Frank empowers these regulators as the principal rule-making and rule-enforcing bodies in the U.S. derivatives market:

- **Commodity Futures Trading Commission (CFTC).** The CFTC is viewed as the regulator with the greatest, most expansive authority under the Dodd-Frank Title VII regime. Dodd-Frank should be viewed as significant because it rejects the way business was done in the OTC industry in favor of the futures-style way of doing business. The regulator with the most experience in handling this is, of course, the CFTC, which is given broad, powerful authority under the Commodity Exchange Act, as amended by Title VII of Dodd-Frank, to regulate a new and very expansive category of derivatives called swaps. As discussed previously, swaps are essentially all derivatives other than futures contracts and security-based and mixed swaps, and the CFTC is given great powers to regulate these instruments, the dealers of these instruments, and the clearing and reporting of these derivatives. The CFTC has, under Dodd-Frank, the most enhanced authority among derivative regulators.
- **Financial Stability Oversight Council (Council).** The Council, which is established under the terms of Section 111 of Title I of Dodd-Frank, is another regulatory authority that oversees derivatives rule making. The Council is the coordinating and dispute-resolution body that would, for example, mediate a dispute between the CFTC and the SEC.
- **Securities and Exchange Commission (SEC).** As discussed in the preceding pages, whereas swaps are regulated by the CFTC, security-based swaps come under the jurisdiction of the SEC, according to Dodd-Frank. The SEC has jurisdiction over dealers of security-based swaps as well as the clearing and reporting of these instruments, which were described in greater detail earlier in this book.
- **The U.S. Department of Treasury and Other Regulators.** The final category of governmental authorities to regulate derivatives is the U.S. Treasury and prudential regulators, which include the Board of Governors of the Federal Reserve and other regulators of banks such as the

Federal Deposit Insurance Corporation, Office of the Comptroller of the Currency. Also within this category are federal regulators of housing finance and securitization, the Federal Housing Finance Agency and the Farm Credit Administration. Finally, the U.S. Department of Treasury, which is empowered by Dodd-Frank to take two categories of derivatives, foreign-exchange forwards, and foreign exchange swaps out of the definition of swaps, is included in this important category of regulators. The previous section of this chapter included a description of the Treasury proposal relating to these derivatives. Under Dodd-Frank, these prudential regulators are required to oversee derivative activities of banks.

The Regulatory Long Arm and Its Reach Outside the United States

One of the more controversial aspects of Dodd-Frank and its Title VII is the ability of U.S. regulators to impose Title VII mandates on non-U.S. entities under certain circumstances.

Title VII does not empower the CFTC and SEC with jurisdiction over swap (and security-based swaps under the jurisdiction of the SEC, as discussed in the preceding pages) activities *outside* of the United States, unless those activities "have a direct and significant connection with activities in, or effect on, commerce of the United States" or evade or circumvent the law or CFTC or SEC rules that implement Dodd-Frank mandates.

It is also important to note that the SEC and CFTC have powers that extend the reach of their rule-making and enforcement authority over fraudulent activity. The SEC is empowered by expansive antifraud provisions in the 1934 Act, for example. Federal district courts in the United States are empowered by Dodd-Frank with jurisdiction to hear lawsuits filed by the U.S. Department of Justice or the claims filed by the SEC *in activity that is outside the United States* that involves conduct that has a *foreseeable and substantial* effect on the United States, as well as activity that takes place inside the United States for purposes of setting into motion activity that would be in violation of Dodd-Frank.

The authority vested in the SEC and CFTC by Congress in Section 715 is particularly interesting in light of the United States Supreme Court case of *Morrison v. National Australia Bank*.[8] In *Morrison*, the United States Supreme Court (U.S. S.Ct. or Court) restated the long-standing principle of American jurisprudence that legislation of Congress is meant to apply only *within* the territorial jurisdiction of the United States. In *Morrison*, the National Australia Bank (NAB), a bank incorporated in Australia with equity traded on the Australian Stock Exchange (and on other exchanges outside the United States) purchased a mortgage servicer headquartered in the United States. When, in 2001, NAB wrote down the value of its holdings in the mortgage servicer, certain residents of Australia who owned NAB shares sued NAB, alleging fraud under, among other provisions, Section 10(b) of the Securities and Exchange Act of 1934 (the 1934 Act). The U.S. S.Ct. in *Morrison* affirmed an earlier dismissal of the plaintiffs' lawsuit, and in doing so, the Court noted the unpredictable and inconsistent application of prior cases in which courts have used two tests to determine the regulatory reach of the SEC in *antifraud cases*:

- *The Conduct Test* (i.e., whether the fraudulent conduct occurred in the United States).
- *The Effects Test* (i.e., whether the fraudulent conduct had a substantial effect in the United States or on citizens of the United States).

Justice Antonin Scalia of the Court, in delivering the decision in *Morrison*, pointed out the inconsistent application of these tests by U.S. courts over the years, and included language in the *Morrison* decision to suggest that the SEC's extraterritorial reach must be abundantly clear in the statute providing justification for the CFTC and SEC to regulate derivatives activity outside the United States. Because the plaintiffs and defendant in *Morrison* were all Australian, and NAB was incorporated in Australia it's not at all clear that the plaintiffs in *Morrison* would be permitted to sue NAB under Dodd-Frank, especially in light of the *Morrison* Court's apparent rejection of the Conduct Test and Effects Test.

Section 715 of Dodd-Frank gives the SEC and CFTC the authority to prohibit a non-U.S. person or entity from doing business in the United States if that person or entity's country is deemed to have permitted derivatives activities in a way that undermines the stability of the United States.

Given principles in international law such as comity (which generally calls for deference to foreign jurisdictions) and the existing, numerous pre-Dodd-Frank organization of international banking activities that were certainly not designed to evade Dodd-Frank mandates, which followed those activities, the author sees significant work ahead for the U.S. regulators to harmonize Title VII mandates with international financial services structures and non-U.S. mandates (and not just those of the G-20 industrialized countries), and possibly the adjudication of the extraterritorial reach of Dodd-Frank. Title VII directs the primary U.S. regulators of derivatives to develop a body of regulation that is harmonious with non-U.S. derivatives law and regulation.

Regulations That Apply to a Wide Range of Market Participants

Derivative regulations apply in some cases to newly created categories of individuals and entities (as discussed below, e.g., major swap participants), but in other cases, such as those outlined next, apply to all existing persons, companies, firms, and other entities entering into derivatives under the jurisdiction of the U.S. regulators. This is what market participants must do.

Everyone Must Report   Well, nearly everyone. In order to bring about transparency in the U.S. OTC derivatives market (which was largely absent and accordingly the lack of transparency was one of the causes of the 2008 market crises, as noted in Chapter 1), Congress required a widespread reporting requirement as a part of Title VII.

Dodd-Frank's reporting obligations bring to life a new entity that was completely nonexistent prior to Dodd-Frank: the swap data repository or SDR.

An SDR is an entity that collects and maintains information or records concerning swaps entered into by third parties for purposes of providing market transparency, price discovery and more effective monitoring and regulation of the derivatives market in the U.S. SDRs are completely new entities which Dodd-Frank introduced to the U.S. market.

On October 31, 2011, the CFTC's final rule imposing SDR duties, standards, and core principles became effective.

Dodd Frank and its implementing regulations mandate that all SDRs (and security-based swap data repositories, which for purposes of this chapter will also be referred to as SDRs) register, comply with numerous duties and core principles, and other requirements. Specifically, SDRs must:

- Accept data submitted from various sources, including SEFs or swap execution facilities.
- Confirm with swap (and SBS, or security-based swap, counterparties) the accuracy of submitted data.
- Maintain data according to regulatory standards.
- Provide direct access to data by regulators.
- Provide public reporting of data as mandated by regulators.
- Establish automated systems for monitoring and analyzing data (including the appropriateness of the use of key exemptions from Dodd-Frank mandates such as the end-user exemption to the clearing mandate).
- Maintain the privacy of end users.
- Establish and maintain business continuity and disaster recovery procedures.

SDRs are to designate chief compliance officers with specified duties, establish transparent governance arrangements, and establish and enforce rules to minimize conflicts of interest.

These reporting obligations, which apply to one or both parties to virtually all derivatives in the U.S. market, now apply to these market participants, among others:

- **Parties to Uncleared Trades Must Report.** The central clearing requirement is discussed below; it is a critically important component of derivatives reform generally, but especially in the United States under Title VII. Although the U.S. regulators recognize that some parts of the U.S. market will remain in the OTC sphere, all trades that are entered and settled OTC must be reported to a swap data repository (discussed below and in Chapter 9). Title VII contains open-ended language imposing broad reporting requirements with respect to parties to uncleared swaps. Title VII gives the SEC and CFTC authority to require reporting and also require retention of internal records and transaction documentation and other related data for regulatory inspection.
- **Certain Parties to Cleared Trades Must Report.** Swaps and security-based swaps that are centrally cleared are to be reported to swap data repositories, as discussed in Chapter 9 in greater detail.
- **Beneficial Owners and Investment Managers.** The SEC, which, as discussed earlier, is the regulator charged by Title VII to govern security-based swaps, is authorized to amend Section 13 of the 1934 Act to extend that act's SEC reporting requirements to persons in cases where the SEC deems such persons to have beneficial ownership by means of a security-based swap such as, for example, an equity swap that gives an investor dividends without owning the actual shares which are the subject of that security-based swap.
- **Large Traders.** Title VII gives authority to the CFTC to establish quantitative levels at which the CFTC would impose reporting requirements on certain swap positions. All persons (or entities) that hold swap positions at or over CFTC-prescribed levels must either report to the CFTC regarding those holdings or reduce positions to fit under CFTC levels. The SEC is given authority under Title VII to establish large security-based swap ceilings and reporting requirements.

Eligible Contract Participants (ECP) This first requirement, applicable across the board in the United States, has ramifications for certain derivatives that are entered into by retail investors. Unless you are an ECP, it is not lawful to enter into a swap unless the swap is executed by means of an exchange regulated by the CFTC. The same thing is true for security-based swaps; those transactions cannot be entered into by any non-ECP unless the transaction is entered into via a regulated national securities exchange. Retail customers, that fall outside of the ECP definition are only permitted to trade swaps on designated contract markets—as opposed to SEFs—and cannot trade bilaterally.

Also, the registration requirement of Section 5 of the 1933 Act applies (unless each counterparty to a security-based swap is an ECP), so it is illegal for anyone to offer or sell a security-based swap to someone who is not an ECP, unless it is registered with the SEC first and it is in full compliance with the 1933 Act.

What is an ECP? An ECP is, generally speaking, a financial institution, an insurance company, investment company (these three categories are not subject to asset, net worth, or investment requirements); commodity pool, corporation, or other legal entity; or an employee benefit plan, governmental entity, or certain other types of entities and individuals. Each case (except financial institutions, insurance companies, and investment companies, which do not need to meet asset, net worth, or investment requirements) has a minimum of required total assets, net worth, or total amount invested and other specified requirements need to be fulfilled.

Abusive Swaps Section 714 of Title VII is ominously titled "Abusive Swaps" and directs the SEC and CFTC to collect information because the regulators need to issue a report concerning the users of these swaps that are detrimental to the financial system.

TAXPAYERS

Though certainly not all taxpayers are active users of derivatives, U.S. taxpayers were in the minds of the members of Congress as they drafted and conferred with each other with respect to the taxpayer bailout of the banks and financial-services firms that were thought of as too big to fail.

Title VII sets into motion a two-year phase-in period for a complete prohibition on any swaps entity from receiving enumerated categories of federal funding, access to federal funding, and credit support. As written, the Title VII provision imposes the prohibition to entities that are active in trading interest-rate swaps, FX swaps, government securities, AAA-rated debt instruments, or swaps to hedge risk.

The prohibition on U.S. federal assistance also precludes the use of taxpayer funds to prevent the receivership of any swap entity resulting from that entity's swap activity, if the entity is FDIC-insured or has been designated as systemically important. If an FDIC-insured or systemically important institution is put into receivership or declared insolvent because of swap activity, then its swap activity will be subject to termination or transfer in accordance with applicable law. All funds that are expended on the termination or transfer of swap activity of a swaps entity must be recovered, either through the disposition of assets of the swap entity or by assessments, including on the financial sector. Title VII expressly provides that taxpayers are to bear no loss as a result of the exercise of any authority related to winding up the swap activity of an entity that is FDIC-insured or systemically important, and no taxpayer resources are to be used for the orderly liquidation of any swap entity that is not FDIC-insured or systemically important.[9]

Regulating the Most Active Market Participants: Dealers and Major Swap Participants

Once an understanding of how products are regulated by Dodd-Frank is achieved, many of the new terms introduced in Title VII of Dodd-Frank become clear. Dodd-Frank grants to the CFTC extensive new authority over commodities derivatives markets as well as over swaps, as described earlier, and the dealers that provide a market in swaps, which Dodd-Frank refers to as "swap dealers."

The SEC has jurisdiction over security-based swaps, and those dealers who trade these swaps, which are referred to as "security-based swap dealers." There are limited differences between the swap dealer and security-based swap dealer terms; perhaps those differences reflect differences between SEC and CFTC regulations, which continue to evolve.

An important takeaway for the reader is that the most onerous and burdensome requirements imposed by Dodd-Frank are imposed on the most active derivative market participants: the swap dealers, security-based swap dealers, as well as major swap participants and major security-based swap participants. In the pages that follow, the author's references to swap dealers and major swap participants will also be to security-based swap dealers and major security-based swap participants, because the law and regulation governing entities in each of these categories is largely the same. After discussing the manner in which an entity may be included in the definitions of swap dealer and major swap participant, this chapter will then describe the requirements of each under Title VII.

Swap Dealers

The first category within the Dodd-Frank universe of the most active OTC market participants is the swap dealer for swaps, and the security-based swap dealer for security-based swaps (these dealers will be referred to as "swap dealers"). Under Title VII, a swap dealer is any person who:

1. Holds itself, himself, or herself out as a dealer in swaps.
2. Makes a market in swaps.
3. Regularly enters into swaps with counterparties in the ordinary course of business for its own account.
4. Engages in any activity causing the person to be commonly known in the trade as a dealer or market maker in swaps.

A person (or corporate entity) may be designated as a swap dealer if any of the foregoing points of the definition apply for a single type or single class or category of swap (even if the person or entity is not engaged in swap activities with respect to other categories of swaps).

The term swap dealer, however, does not include a person who enters into swaps for such person's own account, either individually or in a fiduciary capacity, outside their regular business.

The volume of the dealing activity is important. Regulators are authorized to exempt from designation as a swap dealer any entity that engages in *de minimis* swap dealing.

A critical development in the law of derivatives in the United States is the rule making that followed the enactment of Dodd-Frank. Title VII requires the CFTC and the SEC to define the component parts of the swap dealer and security-based swap dealer definitions, including the term "substantial position." Title VII requires these two regulators to do so in a way that is prudent for the effective monitoring, management, and oversight of entities that are systemically important or can significantly impact the financial system of the United States.

There is much at stake in the development of final rules on this and other key concepts of Title VII. For example, many market participants such as energy companies engage in derivative trading activities in the ordinary course of business that could conceivably bring those companies into the definition of swap dealer. Energy companies, in particular, could and often do take large positions that could, unless the CFTC otherwise determines by final rule, be treated as swap dealers such as major banks—and both entities would be subject to the requirements provided next.

Major Swap Participants

The next category within the Dodd-Frank universe of the most active OTC market participants is the major swap participant for swaps, and major security-based swap participant for security-based swaps. Both are referred to as major swap participants. A major swap participant is one who falls within any of three categories (each has a test associated with the category, illustrated in Figure 4.3), namely, a non-swap dealer which:

MAJOR PARTICIPANT TESTS

Major Participant Test One: Substantial Position Test

Current Exposure.

The CFTC and SEC require the calculation of both current and current + future swap and security-based swap (SBS) exposures, calculated separately, for major swap and security-based swap participant characterization (MSP and MS-BSP). In this column, we discuss the component parts of the current exposure calculation, which, for each trade category, will then be added to potential exposures (to the right). Calculations of current exposures are to be brought about for all categories of swaps and SBSs, separately (categories and other key terms are discussed in the accompanying Glossary).

First Step: After netting treatment, and excluding positions held by ERISA funds and those for hedging or mitigating commercial risk, calculate the then-current mark-to-market replacement cost of each swap (and, separately, each SBS), on a category-by-category basis, and for each category of swaps and SBSs. This calculation is with respect to exposure to all counterparties. For each day in the past quarter, calculate the average daily exposure for each category, and this value will be referred to below as (A).

Second Step: Calculate the value of eligible collateral, minus haircuts, posted in support of the trades referenced above; this value is (B).

Third Step: Subtract (B) from (A), yielding current exposure, or (C).

Fourth Step: Apply (C) for swaps to the thresholds for each swap category:

In order for an entity to not be a MSP regulated as such by the CFTC:

C < $1 billion for trades in the credit, equity, or commodity swap categories

C < $3 billion for rate swaps

Fifth Step: Apply (C) for SBSs to the thresholds for each SBS category:

In order for an entity to not be an MS-BSP regulated as such by the SEC,
C < $1 billion for security-based credit swaps and C < $1 billion other security-based swaps.

Sixth Step: If (C) > the (above) thresholds, then the entity is a MSP or MS-BSP, regardless of potential exposure calculations (to the right).

(Note that the "active fund" development needs to be further clarified by the CFTC.)

Potential and Current Exposure Combined.

This test takes into consideration both current, net, uncollateralized, non-commercial hedging, non-ERISA trading exposure (to the left), as well as potential future exposure (calculated with adjustments, if applicable, below) in the major categories of swaps and SBSs. The regulators require each entity to add (C) to potential exposure values in the aggregate, (Y), which takes into account certain factors, such as clearing and the existence of netting agreements, as applicable and as detailed below.

First Step: Determine potential exposure for each trade ("trade" means a swap or SBS) by multiplying the notional value of each swap and SBS using a conversion factor in the table that follows; the risk factor percentages range from .00 to .15 (or 15%), based on the type and tenor of the swap or SBS, and this value, for each trade, is (T).

Second Step: Apply discounts, or offsets against (T) for three factors which may or may not exist: (i) the existence of a netting agreement, see (U), below; or (ii) if the trade is centrally-cleared (multiply (T) by .20 and the result is (V)); or (iii) if the trade is subject to daily mark-to-market collateralization (multiply (T) by .20) (W).

Netting: In calculating potential exposure, and in the case where master netting agreements exist with respect to a trade, the regulators are proposing to allow entities to take into account the following risk adjustment. However, to get "credit" for netted positions, trade-by-trade calculations and ratios of netted trades to non-netted trades are involved in this calculation:

$$(U) = [(T) \times 0.4] + [(T) \times NGR \times 0.6]$$

(where NGR is a ratio of net current exposure to gross current exposure)

(U) is the value of an entity's exposure to one counterparty for a single trade that is covered by a netting agreement. For every trade that is subject to a netting agreement, (U) needs to be derived, and then aggregated with all other trades in each category of swaps and SBSs, as contemplated in the third step.

Third Step: Aggregate, for each category of trades, the values of all (T)s + (U)s + (V)s + (W)s to get, for all trades in each category, an aggregate value, (X), and, (C) + (X) = (Y). Fourth Step: In order to not be a MSP, (Y) < $2 billion for credit, equity, or commodity swaps, and (Y) < $6 billion for rate swaps; in order to not be a MS-BSP, (Y) < $2 billion for security-based credit trades and (Y) < $2 billion for other SBSs.

FIGURE 4.3 The Widespread Reporting Requirements of Title VII

Major Participant Test Two: The AIG Test

Current Exposure.

The CFTC and SEC require for Test Two the calculation of aggregate counterparty exposure. This test, which I call "the AIG test" is designed to determine the degree of derivatives-based exposure to the financial system. Reported commentary suggests that the CFTC commissioners seek by means of this test to pull into the MSP category those users of swaps which, due to the risk posed to the financial system by their swaps, pose a danger to that system.

In contrast to the First Test, and according to Section 721(a)(16) of Dodd Frank:

- There are no carve-outs for hedges or positions maintained by ERISA accounts.

- The thresholds are higher.

- The calculations are to be made across all categories of trades (not bucket by bucket).

but this test also requires the calculation of current exposure.

First Step: After netting treatment, calculate the then-current mark-to-market replacement cost of each swap (and, separately, each SBS). This calculation is with respect to exposure to all counterparties. For each day in the past quarter, calculate the average daily exposure for each swap or SBS, and this value will be referred to below as (**A**).

Second Step: Calculate the value of eligible collateral, minus haircuts, posted in support of the trades referenced above; this value is (**B**).

Third Step: Subtract (**B**) from (**A**), yielding current exposure, or (**C**).

Fourth Step: Apply (**C**) for swaps to the threshold for all swaps

In order for an entity to not be a MSP regulated as such by the CFTC:

C < $5 billion for all swaps

Fifth Step: Apply (**C**) for SBSs to the threshold for all SBSs:

In order for an entity to not be a MS-BSP regulated as such by the SEC:

C < $2 billion for all SBSs

Sixth Step: If (**C**) > the (above) thresholds, then the entity is a MSP or MS-BSP, regardless of potential exposure calculations (to the right).

Potential and Current Exposure Combined.

This test takes into consideration both current, net, uncollateralized, non-commercial hedging, non-ERISA trading exposure (to the left), as well as potential future exposure (calculated with adjustments, if applicable, below) in the major categories of swaps and SBSs. The regulators require each entity to add (**C**) to potential exposure values in the aggregate, (**Y**), which takes into account certain factors, such as clearing and the existence of netting agreements, as applicable and as detailed below.

First Step: Determine potential exposure for each trade ("trade" means a swap or SBS) by multiplying the notional value of each swap and SBS using a conversion factor in the table that follows; the risk factor percentages range from .00 to .15 (or 15%), based on the type and tenor of the swap or SBS, and this value, for each trade, is (**T**).

Second Step: Apply discounts, or offsets against (**T**) for three factors which may or may not exist: (i) the existence of a netting agreement, see (**U**), below; or (ii) if the trade is centrally-cleared (multiply (**T**) by .20 and the result is (**V**)); or (iii) if the trade is subject to daily mark-to-market collateralization (multiply (**T**) by .20) (**W**).

Netting: In calculating potential exposure, and in the case where master netting agreements exist with respect to a trade, the regulators are proposing to allow entities to take into account the following risk adjustment. However, to get "credit" for netted positions, trade-by-trade calculations and ratios of netted trades to non-netted trades are involved in this calculation:

$$(U) = [(T) \times 0.4] + [(T) \times NGR \times 0.6]$$

(where NGR is a ratio of net current exposure to gross current exposure)

(**U**) is the value of an entity's exposure to one counterparty for a single trade that is covered by a netting agreement. For every trade that is subject to a netting agreement, (**U**) needs to be derived, and then aggregated with all other trades in each category of swaps and SBSs, as contemplated in the Third Step.

FIGURE 4.3 (continued)

Major Participant Test Three: Highly Leveraged Financial Entities

The Third Test is designed to pull into the definitions of MSP and MS-BSP those entities which (a) are not required to comply with Federal banking agency capital requirements and regulations; and (b) maintain substantial positions as highly leveraged financial entities.

Regulators are intending this test to be used to pull into the definition of MSP and MS-BSP those entities with smaller books of derivatives (that would not trigger classification under the First and Second Tests) but with greater leverage relative to assets due to those books.

Financial Entity

One of the following:

- Swap dealer or MSP.
- Commodity pool.
- Private investment fund.
- Person involved in predominantly banking or financial activities.

Substantial Position

The proposed substantial position test for this prong of the MSP definition is the same test used for the First and Second Tests, but hedging and ERISA positions are not carved-out of the calculations (i.e., those positions are included).

Thresholds are not clear as of the time this book went to print.

Highly Leveraged

Liabilities/Equity = 8/1 or 15/1

The liabilities to equity ratio are not clear as of September 22, 2011.

"For these reasons, we propose two possible definitions of the point at which an entity would be 'highly leveraged'—either an entity would be 'highly leveraged' if the ratio of its total liabilities to equity is in excess of 78 to 1 or an entity would be 'highly leveraged' if the ratio of its total liabilities to equity is in excess of 15 to 1." 75 Fed. Reg. 244 at 80199 (Dec. 21, 2010).

Third Step: Aggregate, for each category of trades, the values of all $(T)s + (U)s + (V)s + (W)s$ to get, for all trades in each category, an aggregate value, (X), and, $(C) + (X) = (Y)$.

Fourth Step: Apply (Y) for swaps to the threshold for all swaps

In order to not be an MSP, (Y) for swaps (includes all swaps, not just major category).

Fifth Step: Apply (Y) for SBSs to the threshold for all SBSs:

In order for an entity to not be a MS-BSP: **$4 billion.**

FIGURE 4.3 (*continued*)

CONVERSION TABLES FOR POTENTIAL EXPOSURE

Swaps

Residual maturity	Interest rate	Foreign Exchange Rate	Gold	Precious metals (except gold)	Other commodities
One year or less.........	0.00	0.01	0.01	0.07	0.10
One to five years.........	0.005	0.05	0.05	0.07	0.12
Over five years.........	0.015	0.075	0.075	0.08	0.15

Residual maturity	Credit	Equity
One year or less.........	0.10	0.06
One to five years.........	0.10	0.08
Over five years.........	0.10	0.10

Security-Based Swaps

Residual maturity	Credit	Equity	Other
One year or less	0.10	0.06	0.10
One to five years.........	0.10	0.08	0.12
Over five years.........	0.10	0.10	0.15

FIGURE 4.3 (*continued*)

GLOSSARY

Conversion factor—On a position-by-position basis using the tables cited in the previous page.

Current Exposure—This is meant to pick up an entity's average daily uncollateralized, netted exposure as measured in a way that is based on values derived in the tests described at the beginning of this figure at the close of each business day, beginning on the first business day of each calendar quarter and continuing through the last business day of that quarter, with respect to both Swaps and Security-Based Swaps.

Daily average—The arithmetic mean of the applicable measure of exposure at the close of each business day, beginning the first business day of each calendar quarter through the last business day of that quarter. To correctly calculate daily averages for the substantial position tests, take the mean of the daily average measured as of the close of business over each calendar quarter.

DCO—Derivatives Clearing Organization registered with the CFTC.

Eligible Collateral—Regulators are not presently prescribing the methodology for measuring the value of collateral supporting positions. As long as the collateral practice is "consistent with counterparty practices and industry practices generally" then the practice used will be acceptable.

Gross Counterparty Exposure—Total current exposure, not taking into account applicable netting provisions.

Haircuts—A percentage that is subtracted from the market value of an asset that is being used as collateral. In such cases, the amount of collateral pledged to the counterparty will be greater than the current exposure.

Hedge, Hedges, Hedging Positions—The CFTC seeks comments to define "hedging" ("As a general matter, the CFTC preliminarily believes that whether a position hedges or mitigates commercial risk should be determined by the facts and circumstances at the time the swap is entered into, and should take into account the person's overall hedging and risk mitigation strategies. At the same time, the swap position could not be held for a purpose that is in the nature of speculation, investing or trading. Although the line between speculation, investing or trading, on the one hand and hedging, on the other, can at times be difficult to discern, the statute nonetheless requires such determinations. The CFTC expects that a person's overall hedging and risk management strategies will help inform whether or not a particular position is properly considered to hedge or mitigate commercial risk."). This critically important term remains unclear. 75 Fed. Reg. 244 at 80195 (Dec. 21, 2010).

Major Swap Categories

- **Rate**—Any swap primarily based on one or more reference rates, such as swaps of payments determined by fixed and floating interest rates, currency exchange rates, inflation rates, or other monetary rates.

- **Credit**—Any swap primarily based on instruments of indebtedness, including but not limited to any swap primarily based on one or more indices related to debt instruments, or any swap that is an index credit default swap or total return swap on one or more indices of debt instruments.

- **Equity**—Any swap primarily based on equity securities, such as any swap primarily based on one or more indices of equity securities, or any total return swap on one or more equity indices.

- **Commodity**—Any swap not included in the first three categories, which generally includes any swap for which the primary underlying item is a physical commodity or the price or any other aspect of a physical commodity ("commodity" as defined in CEA Section 1a(9), and CFTC Rule 1.3(e)).

Mark to market—A swap is considered to be subject to mark-to-market margining if, and for as long as, the counterparties follow the daily practice of exchanging collateral to reflect changes in the current exposure arising from the swap (after taking into account any other financial positions addressed by a netting agreement between the counterparties).

Minimum Transfer Amount and Threshold Rider—If the fund is permitted by agreement to maintain a threshold for which it is not required to post collateral, the total amount of that threshold (regardless of the actual exposure at any time) shall be added to the fund's aggregate uncollateralized outward exposure. If the minimum transfer amount under the agreement is in excess of $1 million, the entirety of the minimum transfer amount shall be added to the fund's aggregate uncollateralized outward exposure.

Net Counterparty Exposure—Total current exposure reduced by applicable netting provisions.

Netting Agreement—An agreement, coming within Section 362(b)(17) of the U.S. Bankruptcy Code, providing for the exercise of rights, including rights of netting, setoff, liquidation, termination, acceleration, or close out, under or in connection with one or more contracts entered into between an entity and a single counterparty. MSP calculations only account for netting permitted under the relevant netting agreement, which must be enforceable. Netting may be across different categories of derivatives.

FIGURE 4.3 (*continued*)

Potential Exposure—Potential exposure is determined by the total notional principal amount of open positions, their tenure or duration, as adjusted by certain risk factors. The risk factors are set forth above. This part of the major swap (and security-based swap) participant test accounts for the aggregate potential outward exposure. Adjustments are critically important to this aspect of the substantial position test.

Swap—As defined in Title VII of Dodd-Frank, includes the following products:

- credit default swaps referencing a broad-based security index;
- credit default swaps referencing more than one loan or any loan index;
- total return swaps referencing a broad-based security index (whether comprising debt securities or equity securities);
- total return swaps referencing more than one loan;
- equity variance and dividend swaps referencing a broad-based security index;
- correlation swaps referencing a broad-based security index and any commodity or commodity index (including FX, rates and rate indices/indexes);
- interest rate swaps;
- OTC options on or referencing any asset other than an option on a security or a certificate of deposit, or group or index of securities, including any interest therein or based on the value thereof;
- commodity swaps;
- weather, energy, and emissions swaps;
- other swaps referencing broad-based (as opposed to narrow-based) securities indices, government securities and most other reference assets; and
- swaptions on any of the above.

Please note that Treasury has proposed that Foreign Exchange Forwards and Foreign Exchange Swaps, as defined in Dodd-Frank (below) are to be exempted from the definition of "swap":

- Foreign Exchange Forward: a transaction that solely involves the exchange of two different currencies on a specific future date at a fixed rate agreed upon on the inception of the contract covering the exchange.
- Foreign Exchange Swap: a transaction that solely involves **(A)** the exchange of two different currencies on a specific future date at a fixed rate agreed upon on the inception of the contract covering the exchange and **(B)** a reverse exchange of the two currencies described in subparagraph **(A)** at a later date and at a fixed rate agreed upon on the inception of the contract covering the exchange.

Security-Based Swap—As defined in Title VII of Dodd-Frank, includes the following products (note that most equity options are "Securities," not Security-Based Swaps (!)):

- total return swaps referencing a single security or loan;
- total return swaps referencing a narrow-based index of securities;
- OTC options for the purchase or sale of a single loan, including any interest therein or based on the value thereof;
- equity variance or dividend swaps referencing a single security or narrow-based index of securities;
- single-name CDS; and
- CDS referencing a narrow-based index of securities.

* * *

FIGURE 4.3 *(continued)*

161

1. Maintains a substantial position in swaps for any of the major swap categories as determined by the CFTC (excluding positions held for hedging or mitigating commercial risk; positions maintained by any employee benefit plan for the primary purpose of hedging or mitigating any risk directly associated with the plan's operation are also excluded from the substantial-position threshold).
2. Has substantial counterparty exposure that could have serious adverse effects on the financial stability of the U.S. banking system or financial markets.
3. Is a financial entity (as discussed later) that is highly leveraged relative to the amount of capital it holds, is not subject to the capital requirements of a federal banking regulator, and maintains a substantial position in outstanding swaps in any major swap category.

The definition of major swap participant excludes entities whose primary business is to provide financing, but that use swaps (or security-based swaps for purposes of hedging commercial risks related to interest rate and currency exposures) in circumstances in which at least 90 percent of the risk hedged against arises out of financing that facilitates the purchase or lease of products, if 90 percent or more of the products are manufactured by the entity's parent company or another subsidiary of the parent company.

As with the definition of swap dealer, the final regulatory interpretation of the Title VII wording is critically important. Title VII requires the CFTC and the SEC to define with precision the terms "substantial position" in a prudent way, so that these regulators can effectively monitor, manage, and provide oversight of the most active derivative market participants, as well as those whose derivatives activities pose systemic risk to the U.S. financial system

As for the third part of the major swap participant definition, the term financial entity is broadly defined in Title VII, and it includes swap dealers (and security-based swap dealers as well as major swap participants and major security-based swap participants) as well as commodity pools, private funds, employee benefit plans, and financial-services firms and other entities that are predominantly engaged in banking or financial activities. Even if an active user of derivatives sidesteps the three categories outlined in the preceding list, many other provisions of Title VII would still continue to apply. The definitions in the Commodity Exchange Act of commodity pool operators, commodity trading advisers, and commodity pools (three important categories of users of futures or swaps that were discussed in Chapter 3 and once again will be discussed in the pages that follow in the context of Title VII requirements) were enlarged by Dodd-Frank so that, even if those entities are not major swap participants, they would still be regulated by the CFTC in important ways.

In late December 2010, the entire market poured over the proposed rules for the major participant designations (i.e., the rules for determining whether an entity is a major swap participant, or major security-based swap participant). The three prongs discussed above were the subject of proposed rules when this text went to print, and the illustrations on the following pages, in Figure 4.3, bring into sharper focus the proposed manner in which non-dealer market participants are to determine whether they are major swap participants.

This is critically important because, if an entity is a major swap participant or major security-based swap participant, the most onerous obligations of Title VII within Dodd-Frank apply, and these are discussed next.

Obligations of Dealers and Major Participants

In order to prevent many of the abuses in the OTC derivatives market (and perceived abuses; the distinction is discussed in the causes of the 2008 market crises in Chapter 1), Title VII imposes obligations on the most active market participants within two categories discussed in this chapter: swap dealers (and security-based swap dealers) and major swap participants (and major security-based swap participants). There are a total of seven categories of obligations that Title VII imposed, and each is summarized in the pages that follow.

1. Registration Requirements   Swap dealers and major swap participants are required to register as such under the CEA or Commodity Exchange Act, and major security-based swap dealers and major security-based swap participants are obligated to register with the SEC under the 1934 Act. Title VII requires banks that come within these categories to register even if the banks are already subject to a different regulatory regime in the U.S. (or elsewhere).

2. Capital and Margin Requirements   Perhaps the most onerous part of Title VII is the requirement that swap (and security-based swap) dealers and major swap (and security-based swap) participants adhere to capital and margin requirements.

Title VII requires the CFTC or the SEC to confer with banking regulators to establish capital requirements. These requirements were imposed in part to prevent the leverage and risk taking discussed in Chapter 1 as causes of the 2008 market crises. Title VII also requires that the CFTC impose margin requirements on swap dealers and major swap participants (and security-based swap dealers and major security-based swap participants) so as to ensure that trades are properly collateralized. The title looks to clearinghouses to impose margin (as discussed in the previous chapter) in the first instance, but it also requires regulators to ensure that the two most active derivative market participants in practice fully and appropriately collateralize their trades.

This part of the law is among the most controversial. Prior to Dodd-Frank, collateral obligations relating to OTC derivatives were freely negotiated, and many trading relationships permitted customization in the exchange of certain categories of collateral, such as cash and liquid securities, like U.S. Treasuries, as well as other individualized aspects of collateral relationships, such as the posting of letters of credit in energy derivative transactions. An ongoing subject of debate is whether Title VII has brought about unnecessary rule making in parts of the derivatives market where trading neither contributed to the 2008 market crises (as discussed in Chapter 1), nor necessitated regulatory intervention.

As an early part of this ongoing debate that was discussed in Chapter 2, the International Swaps and Derivatives Association, Inc. (ISDA) issued a press release on June 29, 2010, referenced in the final meeting of the Congressional conference committee, which stated that U.S. companies may be faced with $1 trillion in capital and liquidity requirements due to the requirements of Title VII.

3. Recordkeeping and Reporting Requirements Swap dealers and major swap participants (and their security-based counterparts under Subpart B of Title VII) are required to maintain records, as long as the CFTC and SEC require, in order to be able to, among other things, construct an audit trail, maintain daily trading records of swaps and all related records (including related cash or forward transactions), as well as transcriptions and recordings of communications, electronic mail, instant messages, and other daily trading records for each customer or counterparty.

A primary cause of the financial crisis was the failure of regulators to monitor and impose discipline on market participants, as discussed in greater detail in Chapter 1, which outlines seven causes of the 2008 market crises. Although regulators did little in a comprehensive way to regulate the OTC derivatives market, that market pre-Dodd-Frank grew to a $615 trillion market when measured in 2009.

One of the earliest regulatory reform measures became final on October 1, 2010, the date on which the CFTC passed a final interim rule on the reporting of many derivatives that existed on July 21, 2010, when President Obama signed Dodd-Frank. CFTC and the SEC published interim final rules to implement the reporting requirements imposed by the Dodd-Frank Act, which added Section 4R to the Commodity Exchange Act, or CEA.

One of the most important missions that the Dodd-Frank Act seeks to accomplish is to create mechanisms to allow regulators to monitor the size of the derivatives market in the United States (and that part of the non-U.S. market that has a direct and significant connection with commerce in the United States). To enable U.S. regulators to monitor the derivatives market, the drafters of Dodd-Frank included in that Act a comprehensive recordkeeping and reporting scheme. On October 1, 2010, as the earliest rule that implements Dodd-Frank focuses exclusively on reporting and recordkeeping, giving the first indication of the comprehensive and labor-intensive reworking of the derivatives market. This rule requires retention of confirmations evidencing swaps in existence on July 21, 2010, as discussed in the following.

The recordkeeping requirements of Dodd-Frank introduce yet another new acronym to the derivatives market: Swap Data Repository (SDR). The Swap Data Repository is discussed earlier in this chapter and in Chapter 9. In amending the CEA, Section 723 of Dodd-Frank requires that swaps be reported to an SDR that is registered with regulators. If there is no SDR that would accept the swap, the swap is to be reported to the CFTC (and security-based swaps are to be reported to the SEC).

An important consideration in the reporting requirements of Dodd-Frank is the effective date of the swap, that is, the date on which the parties to the swap intend for the swap to be legally effective. If the effective date for the swap is prior to the enactment of Dodd-Frank (July 21, 2010), then it is referred to in Dodd-Frank as a pre-effective swap. Section 723 of Dodd-Frank (which adds Section 2(h)(5) to the CEA) includes a requirement that pre-enactment swaps be reported to a registered SDR or to the Commission. This reporting must take place no later than 180 days after the effective date of that subsection. However, reporting requirements were delayed during early rule making because some critical aspects of Dodd-Frank (e.g., the regulation of Swap Data Repositories) were slow to be proposed.

Swaps that are not accepted for clearing by a derivatives clearing organization or clearinghouse (in Title VII parlance, a DCO, which is discussed in Chapter 9) are to be reported to an SDR (or to the SEC or CFTC, depending on whether the trade is a swap or security-based swap, if no SDR accepts the swap for reporting).

New derivatives reform requires trade details to be reported at various stages of the derivatives trade lifecycle. Both cleared and OTC trades are required to be reported in the U.S. Dodd-Frank reporting mandates included in Sections 727 and 766 of Dodd-Frank. All swaps (SBS), whether exchange-traded and cleared or OTC, are required to be reported in real time, unless a transaction is a very large trade which meets a minimum block trading size set by the regulators, in which case transaction reporting is subject to delay. Prior to the publication of this text, there were time delays in reporting that the two regulators proposed:

- CFTC: 15-minute reporting delay for block trades.
- SEC: 8- to 26-hour reporting delay of the notional amount of the trade (execution and pricing are still to be reported, in real time to the extent possible).

The real-time reporting requirements of Dodd-Frank raised a number of concerns in the U.S. derivatives marketplace, including:

- Derivative reporting would reveal positions.
- Derivative reporting would affect pricing.
- Derivative reporting would result in the mistaken publication of trades.
- Derivatives reporting would involve third-party service providers that may not properly handle trade information.

The author is an active participant in a trade group charged with the responsibility of developing reporting conventions, some of which are introduced here. Minimum block trading sizes are determined generally by SDRs. SDRs aggregate swap products within asset classes into smaller groups called swap instruments. Public dissemination of the notional amounts of transactions is subject to a rounding convention. This convention provides that notional principal of contracts in excess of $250MM be reported in the "$250MM+" category in reporting fields. The explanation of the proposed rules cites the rounding convention as providing a degree of anonymity. The minimum block trading sizes are then subject to a two-part test:

- The first part, called the Distribution Test, is the notional amount that is greater than 95 percent of the transactions of a swap instrument, where the rounding convention has first been applied.
- The second part, called the Multiple Test, is the result of multiplying a block multiple by the social size of the swap instrument. The block multiple is proposed to be five and the social size is the largest of the swap instrument's mode, median, or mean. (The minimum block trading size is then simply the higher of the results produced by the Distribution Test and the Multiple Test).

As for the SEC, that regulator proposed rules to require that all security-based swaps be reported in real time, unless a transaction meets minimum block trading size. The proposed rules specify general guidelines for setting block trading thresholds but do not set specific levels.

Under rules proposed by the SEC, block trades will still require real-time reporting of execution and pricing, to the extent possible, but the notional size will be suppressed for a minimum of eight hours and a maximum of 26 hours, based strictly on the time of day a transaction is executed, under the SEC's proposal introduced before this book went to press.

4. Compliance with Business Conduct Standards One of the most important aspects of Dodd-Frank is that it requires, in Title VII, the fulfillment of certain business conduct requirements by swap dealers and major swap participants (and their security-based counterparts under subpart B of Title VII). These requirements include:

1. Verifying that any counterparty is an "eligible contract participant."
2. Disclosing to counterparties that are not major swap participants or swap dealers (or major security-based swap participants or security-based swap dealers):
   a. Information about the material risks and characteristics of the swap.
   b. Any material incentives and conflicts of interest associated with the swap transactions.
   c. The derivatives clearing organization's daily mark for cleared swaps, if the counterparty requests it.
   d. The swap dealer's or major swap participant's daily mark for uncleared swaps.
3. Communicating in a fair and balanced manner based on principles of fair dealing and in good faith.

5. Duties Owed to Special Entities Swap dealers and major swap participants (and their security-based counterparts under subpart B of Title VII) owe special duties to special entities, including governmental entities, pension plans, and endowments.

If a swap dealer or security-based swap dealer acts as an advisor to a special entity, it must act in the best interests of the special entity and have a reasonable basis for determining that any swap recommended to the special entity is in the best interests of the special entity.

If a swap dealer, a security-based swap dealer, a major swap participant, or a major security-based swap participant acts as a counterparty to a special entity, it must have a reasonable basis to believe that the special entity has a representative independent of the swap dealer, security-based swap dealer, major swap participant, or major security-based swap participant that is capable of evaluating the risks of the transaction, is not subject to a statutory disqualification from registration, and will act in the best interests of the special entity. After the passage of Dodd-Frank, certain special entities voiced concerns about the independent representative requirement as one that gave swap dealers and major swap participants too much control over who may and who may not represent a special entity.

The swap dealer and major swap participant must also disclose in writing before the initiation of the transaction the capacity in which it is acting. In any dealings with special entities, swap dealers and major swap participants are prohibited from engaging in fraudulent, deceptive, or manipulative acts. This provision of Title VII replaces a proposal in an earlier U.S. Senate bill that would have imposed a fiduciary duty on swap dealers or security-based swap dealers that provide advice regarding, offer to enter into, or enter into a swap or SBS with a government entity or agency, pension plan, endowment, or retirement plan. This part of Title VII was highly controversial because of the concerns of state governments and retirement plans that the imposition of a fiduciary duty would effectively close the market for swaps and security-based swaps to Special Entities. After the enactment of Dodd-Frank, some commentators have taken the position that the SEC and CFTC are, by regulation, essentially requiring the imposition of a fiduciary duty.

6. Obligations Concerning Conflicts of Interest Under Title VII, swap dealers, security-based swap dealers, major swap participants, and major security-based swap participants must implement conflict-of-interest policies. The conflict of interest requirements imposed by Title VII appear to evolve at least in part from initiatives of Senators in the Goldman Sachs hearings in late April 2010 (discussed in Chapter 2).

The requirement here is to separate, by appropriate information barriers within a swap dealer or major swap participant (and their security-based counterparts under Subpart B of Title VII), employees conducting research or analysis of the price or market for any swap, commodity, or security-based swap, as well as employees providing clearing activities or making determinations about accepting clearing customers on the one hand, from the review, pressure, and oversight of persons involved in pricing, trading, or clearing activities on the other.

7. Designation of a Chief Compliance Officer In order to make chief compliance officers of futures commission merchants accountable, the swap dealers and major participants must designate a chief compliance officer who has met certain new requirements under Title VII; these compliance officers must bring about the filing of compliance reports as well as the ratification of those reports. The compliance officer's duties under Title VII include:

- Developing and putting in place compliance policies.
- Resolving conflicts of interest.
- Monitoring issues in derivatives use so as to identify noncompliance.
- Draft, certify, and execute annually a compliance report.
- Establish remedial measures and procedures for incidents of noncompliance.

WHISTLEBLOWERS

Persons in the commodities industry receive additional protection (in addition to protections under the Commodity Exchange Act prior to the enactment of Dodd-Frank) for whistleblower activities under the provisions of Section 748 of Dodd-Frank, "Commodity Whistleblower Incentives and Protections," which state that:

- The CFTC will pay whistleblowers, under certain circumstances, not less than 10 percent and not more than 30 percent of the monetary sanctions imposed in a successful enforcement action.
- Legal counsel must represent whistleblowers.
- Retaliation against whistleblowers is prohibited.

Whistleblowers who knowingly provide false information are subject to prosecution.

Final whistleblower incentives and protection rules were effective on October 24, 2011, after the CFTC closed a public comment period earlier in 2011, on February 4, 2011.

The final rules included provisions that require a whistleblower to come forward voluntarily, before the whistleblower or his or her representative receives an official inquiry or demand; a whistleblower award is not available after the person is first questioned about a matter.

Other factors for determining whether and to what extent an award is to be given to the whistleblower include the significance of the information, the extent to which the information is original in nature and the degree of assistance provided.

To provide whistleblowers with protection against retaliation, the new rules provide a federal cause of action against an employee and other relief such as reinstatement, back pay, and compensation for expenses such as reasonable attorney's fees.

Whistleblowers are entitled to appeal CFTC decisions, including denials of awards for whistleblowing, and such appeals are to be filed with the appropriate U.S. Circuit Court of Appeals.

Directors of Public Companies Using the End-User Exception to the Clearing Requirement

As we will see in the next section within this chapter, the SEC and CFTC designate categories of derivatives that must be centrally cleared (and executed on a swap execution facility or board of trade) or else not traded at all. An exception to that clearing requirement, in Section 723 of Dodd-Frank, permits certain end users to continue to trade OTC notwithstanding the SEC or CFTC mandate (under certain important conditions discussed in the Platforms part of this chapter, described next).

However, Section 723 also requires an appropriate subcommittee of the board of directors or other governing body of public companies (i.e., those that have SEC reporting obligations under the 1934 Act) utilizing the clearing exception to review and approve the decision to enter into derivatives, subject to the use of the exception to the clearing requirement. Director approval of the use of the end-user exception is proposed to be required on a swap-by-swap basis.

Custodians

Section 724(c) of Dodd-Frank gives parties to uncleared swaps and security-based swaps the right to have initial margin supporting those uncleared trades be deposited in accounts maintained by independent custodians, and invested until the maturity of the derivative in investments approved by the SEC and CFTC. Prior to the effective date of Title VII, this collateral arrangement (or similar arrangements) was permitted only if certain regulatory requirements exist in certain circumstances, such as if the end user is a registered investment company governed by the U.S. Investment Company Act of 1940.

PLATFORMS

Arguably the most important part of U.S. derivatives reform that has been brought about by Dodd-Frank is the federal mandate that covers the vast majority of derivatives only through certain highly regulated trading systems, or platforms, settled by means of a central clearinghouse, and reported to a swap data repository. Compared to that new federal mandate, there is nothing more revolutionary that has happened in at least 70 years in the U.S. financial system. Because of their importance, Chapter 9 is dedicated to market structure, including the new trading venues and platforms that are introduced here.

This mandate requires a fundamental rethink about how derivatives are created, executed, collateralized, cleared, and traded, as well as which technology is used and how quickly that technology can be utilized in order to lawfully trade derivatives.

The Dodd-Frank mandate also requires the market to understand institutions that are now mandated as a part of federal law in the United States but which have never existed before: swap data repositories, SDRs and swap execution facilities, or SEFs.

Because of the importance of central clearing and exchange trading, two chapters of this book have been dedicated to these institutions: Chapter 3, Introduction to Futures, Margin, and Central Clearing, of which SEFs and clearinghouses are a vital part, and Chapter 9, Market Structure Before and After 2010, which discusses in greater detail the new trading venues. I would like to thank my K&L Gates colleagues who authored with me an investment alert published immediately after the passage of Dodd-Frank in 2010, entitled "Congressional Overhaul of the Derivatives Market in the United States," by Gordon F. Peery, Charles R. Mills, Anthony R. G. Nolan, Lawrence B. Patent, and Edward Eisert, *Financial Services Reform Alert* (July 21, 2010); I rely on that alert in this chapter.[10]

Trading Venues: DCMs and SEFs

Swaps will generally be required to be entered into via designated contract markets (DCMs), exchanges or a type of newly-created facility referred to as a SEF. Security-based swaps will need to be entered into by means of a security-based SEF. Unlike an SEF, a DCM can also serve as a trading platform for futures. This chapter refers to security-based SEFs and SEFs collectively as SEFs.

Title VII requires that both DCMs and SEFs satisfy certain core principles, which were already included in the CEA before Dodd-Frank's Title VII amended much of it. In order for cleared swaps to be traded on SEFs, the SEFs must satisfy criteria imposed by Title VII, which include:

1. Prohibiting trading of derivatives that are susceptible to manipulation.
2. Imposing internal controls to monitor the trading of swaps to prevent manipulation, price distortion, and disruptions in trade processing.
3. Facilitating information dissemination to regulators.
4. Implementing rules that are in line with those set by the SEC and CFTC (e.g., rules on position limits).

Derivatives Clearing Organization (DCO)

It is important to recognize that Title VII does not require that all derivatives in the U.S. OTC derivatives market be centrally cleared. The general rule is that, if the CFTC or SEC determines that a swap or security-based swap (as appropriate) must be cleared, then counterparties to that swap or security-based swap are prohibited from entering and settling that instrument unless they submit it to a derivatives clearing organization (DCO), or clearing agency (in the absence of an exception to the clearing requirement). If the CFTC or SEC takes no action, but a DCO accepts for clearing instruments of the relevant type, an end user may elect that the swap be submitted to the clearing organization for clearing in accordance with that organization's rules and procedures or the derivative may be settled OTC, but other requirements (e.g., reporting and recordkeeping) still apply to the trade.

In order to be authorized to clear a derivative, a DCO must file an application with the CFTC or SEC, as applicable. The CFTC or the SEC must act on the submission within 90 days, unless the DCO agrees to an extension of time. A DCO must provide for swaps or security-based swaps to be cleared on a nondiscriminatory basis, whether they were executed bilaterally or through an unaffiliated exchange. In addition, if no DCO is requested to clear a particular swap or security-based swap otherwise subject to mandatory clearing (that is, neither party thereto qualifies for an exemption from mandatory clearing), the CFTC must conduct an investigation and issue a public report within 30 days, and take such action as the CFTC deems necessary and in the public interest, which may include requiring the parties to retain adequate margin or capital. However, the CFTC could not require a DCO to clear a swap (and the SEC could not require the clearing of a security-based swap by a clearing agency) if the clearing of that instrument would threaten the financial integrity of the DCO or clearing agency. If a security-based swap must be cleared under Title VII, the counterparties to the security-based swap must submit the security-based swap to a DCO or a clearing agency.

Clearing Mechanics, Documentation, and Technology

As described in Chapters 3 and 10, DCOs, through novation by the counterparties to a swap or security-based swap, in essence step in between the counterparties to an executed trade and become the buyer to the counterparty that is the seller, and the seller to the counterparty that is the buyer, thereby attempting to ensure that the performance of both counterparties' obligations under the swap. Although the sections within Title VII do not expressly mandate or describe the clearing mechanics, documentation, and technology, a brief discussion of how clearing works in the Dodd-Frank regulatory regime is necessary. For more detail, the reader is directed to Chapter 7, the Life Cycle of a Cleared Derivatives Trade.

To centrally clear those swaps or security-based swaps that are designated for clearing, a member of a DCO must be designated to submit the swap to the DCO. Not all swap counterparties are members of DCOs. DCO membership, which is not prescribed by Title VII or other provisions of Dodd-Frank, is open to parties to swaps that meet certain prudential and other requirements, which typically include a certain level of assets, as well as other undertakings, such as the posting of collateral to a large default insurance fund of the DCO. During the Dodd-Frank rule-making process, tension developed between setting high financial requirements for clearinghouse membership on the one hand, and not setting the financial requirements for clearing membership so high that they restrict access.

In the current OTC derivatives market, generally only the largest dealers and end users are members of DCOs. If neither of the two counterparties that face each other in the executed derivatives transaction is a member of a DCO, at least one must relinquish the swap to a member of a DCO by entering into a contract with a DCO member, which in turn clears the swap through the DCO. Derivative clearing organizations' members generally guarantee the performance of the swap by the original counterparties and help bring about the application of certain remedies and other mechanisms in the event of member default.

Not all requirements (including documentation and margin arrangements) are the same for all DCOs, and not all members of DCOs use the same technology or margin arrangements. Title VII does not harmonize the divergent clearing arrangements that exist in the market today.

The documentation that is required to centrally clear a swap or security-based swap under Title VII varies according to the DCO that clears the swap or security-based swap and is the subject of Chapter 6. In some early cases, the DCO adds an annex to the existing ISDA Master Agreement, Schedule, and Credit Support Annex documentation; the annex supplements the existing ISDA and incorporates new clearing requirements for covered transactions that are subject to the DCO rules. Title VII does not prescribe any particular technology to satisfy the clearing requirements imposed by the SEC or the CFTC. Each DCO generally has a clearing platform that is adopted by end users and members to a cleared trade.

Swaps and security-based swaps will not be subject to Title VII clearing (and exchange-trading and margining) requirements if the counterparties entered into the transactions before the enactment of Dodd-Frank, or prior to the effectiveness of a clearing requirement that is imposed by the SEC or CFTC, if the end-user exception is met (as described next), or if certain other requirements are satisfied, as described next.

The End-User Exception to the Clearing Requirements; Treatment of Eligible Contract Participants

There is an exception to the requirement that certain swaps or security-based swaps be centrally cleared under Title VII for instruments to which one of the counterparties is a commercial end user (a term that is not defined in Title VII but means, in industry parlance, the party that faces the dealer in the derivative) that hedges or otherwise manages commercial risk through the swap. A counterparty that qualifies for this exception:

1. Is not a financial entity.
2. Uses swaps to hedge or mitigate commercial risk.
3. Notifies the appropriate regulatory agency how it meets its financial obligations related to noncleared swaps.
4. Is not a swap dealer or major swap participant.

The exclusion of financial entities from the commercial end-user exception means that a large swathe of participants in OTC derivatives markets is not eligible for this exemption. The term "financial entity" for this purpose is broadly defined and includes swap dealers, security-based swap dealers, major swap participants, major security-based swap participants, commodity pools, private funds, employee benefit plans and entities predominantly engaged in banking or financial activities. However, there are important exceptions to the definition of financial entity, particularly for the financing arms of manufacturers. Furthermore, the CFTC and the SEC also may exempt small depository institutions, farm credit system institutions, and credit unions with total assets of $10 billion or less.

In the case of publicly traded companies reporting to the SEC under the 1934 Act, the commercial end user exemption from clearing and exchange-trading of swaps is available only if an appropriate committee of the board or governing body reviews and approves (on a swap-by-swap basis, according to a proposed rule) its decision to enter into OTC derivatives trades. The end user may use an affiliate to conduct its swap activities, provided that the affiliate is not a swap dealer, security-based swap dealer, major swap participant, major security-based swap participant, private fund, commodity pool, or a bank holding company with over $50 billion in consolidated assets.

However, under Title VII, a person who is not an eligible contract participant as defined in the CEA (as discussed earlier in this text, an ECP) may not enter into a swap or security-based swap except via a designated-contract market, and a security-based swap is subject to the registration requirement of Section 5 of the 1933 Act, unless each counterparty to the security-based swap is an ECP. Subject to the foregoing limitations, it appears that ECPs will continue to be able to enter into nonstandard derivatives that are not centrally cleared and exchange-traded, as long as the SEC and the CFTC do not require that the derivatives be centrally cleared.

Prior to the passage of Dodd-Frank in the House of Representatives on June 30, 2010, the Congressional conference committee on Dodd-Frank (the Committee) reconvened on June 29, 2010, to consider a \$19 billion bank tax, which the Committee removed from Dodd-Frank. During its June 29, 2010, meeting, the Committee considered an amendment to re-open Title VII to clarify the end-user exemption, but the amendment failed on a 6-to-6 vote among the members of the Committee from the Senate. Congressman Barney Frank on the Committee (and the "Frank" in Dodd-Frank) subsequently stated on the record that he expects that a bill in early 2011 would be necessary not only to make technical corrections to Dodd-Frank, but also to make more substantive changes to clarify the end-user exception. As of December 1, 2011, no such correction amendment passed.

Since the final meeting of the Committee, Senators Christopher Dodd and Blanche Lincoln wrote a letter to House leadership stating that the design of the end-user exception (and the scope of the definition of major swap participants) is intended to enable certain classes of end users that hedge or otherwise manage commercial risk through derivatives to continue to be able to use derivatives for those purposes, without having to centrally clear or collateralize their trades.

Because central clearing constitutes such an important part of the post-Dodd-Frank world of derivatives in the United States (and in other countries as well), and because clearinghouses actually concentrate counterparty risk, the U.S. Congress saw fit to include Title VIII within Dodd-Frank an entire title dedicated to the regulation of payment systems and clearing (and not just with respect to derivatives, but repurchase facilities and other ubiquitous fund transfer arrangements), Title VIII.

NOTES

1. Preamble to the Dodd-Frank Wall Street Reform and Consumer Protection Act.
2. Joseph Neu, "What Comes After Dodd-Frank Regarding Rulemaking and Derivative Exemptions?" August 2, 2010, www.neugroup.com/what-comes-afterDodd-Frank-regarding-rulemaking-and-derivative-exemptions.

3. U.S. Chamber of Commerce, *Financial Regulatory Reform—Uncertainty Grows*, www.chamberpost.com/2010/07/financial-regulatory-reform-uncerta inty-grows.html.

4. Congressman Frank made this statement on the record during the final day of Congressional conference committee deliberations on June 29, 2010.

5. Identified banking products consist of: deposit accounts, savings accounts, certificates of deposit, or other deposit instruments issued by a bank; banker's acceptances; letters of credit issued or loans made by a bank; debit accounts at a bank arising from a credit card or similar arrangement; and participations in a loan which the bank or affiliate of the bank (other than a broker or dealer) funds, participates in, or owns, that is sold to certain persons. The exclusion from jurisdiction and from the definitions of swap and security-based swap does not extend to agreements that would otherwise qualify as identified banking products under Section 206 of the Gramm-Leach-Bliley Act.

6. Dodd-Frank defines this term by reference to the Federal Deposit Insurance Act (i.e., the Comptroller of the Currency, the Director of the Office of Thrift Supervision, the Board of Governors of the Federal Reserve System, or the Federal Deposit Insurance Corporation), the Federal Reserve Board in the case of a noninsured state bank, and the Farm Credit Administration for farm credit system institutions.

7. Gordon F. Peery, Charles R. Mills, Anthony R.G. Nolan, Lawrence B. Patent, and Edward Eisert, "Congressional Overhaul of the Derivatives Market in the United States," *Financial Services Reform Alert*, July 21, 2010, www.klgates .com/congressional-overhaul-of-the-derivatives-market-in-the-united-states-07-21-2010/

8. *Morrison et al. v. National Australia Bank Ltd., et al.* (U.S. SCt., Slip op.) (June 24, 2010).

9. Peery *et al.*, "Congressional Overhaul of the Derivatives Market in the United States."

10. Available at www.klgates.com/newstand/detail.aspx?publication=6562.

CHAPTER 5

Title VIII of Dodd-Frank

Perhaps the most important and somewhat overlooked part of U.S. financial-services reform consists of a mere 13 sections of U.S. law which comprise Title VIII of Dodd-Frank, titled the Payment, Clearing, and Settlement Supervision Act of 2010. As Title VIII—and Title VII and many other parts of Dodd-Frank—continued to be in a state of regulatory flux when the publisher printed this text, the early outlines did however begin to take form for the new law on clearing, settlement, and payment systems, and this chapter provides a guide to this new U.S. law.

The impact of this law will be evident not only in the OTC derivatives market in the United States, but in other financial markets where financial activities involve any of the following, as long as they have a relation with U.S. commerce and if the activities are deemed "systemically important":

- Fund transfers.
- Securities contracts.
- Contracts for sale of a commodity for future delivery.
- Forward contracts.
- Repurchase agreements.
- Swaps.
- Security-based swaps.
- Swap agreements.
- Security-based swap agreements.
- Foreign exchange contracts.
- Financial derivatives contracts.
- Any similar transaction that "the Council," a new regulatory body introduced in the pages that follow, determines to be a financial transaction for purposes of Title VIII.[1]

Title VIII requires the U.S. Financial Stability Oversight Council, to designate those financial market utilities or payment, clearing, or settlement activities which are or may likely become systemically important.

Once the label of systemic importance is bestowed on any of the foregoing market activities, or on the financial market *utility* that carries out those activities, Title VIII gives great latitude to U.S. regulators to regulate that activity or utility as they see fit.

Section 804 of Title VIII mandates the determination, after public hearing and comments, of a payment, settlement, or clearing activity that is systemically important. That determination is to be made by two-thirds of the members serving on the Council. This Council is established pursuant to Section 111 of Dodd-Frank, and is comprised of these members:

- Secretary of Treasury (the chairperson of the Council).
- Chairman of the Board of Governors of the Federal Reserve System.
- Comptroller of the Currency.
- Director of the Bureau of the Consumer Financial Protection.
- Director of the Federal Housing Finance Agency.
- Chairman of the Securities and Exchange Commission.
- Chairperson of the Federal Deposit Insurance Corporation.
- Chairperson of the Commodity Futures Trading Commission.
- An independent member appointed by the president having insurance expertise.

OPPOSITION TO TITLE VIII

The potential invasiveness of regulation that may implement Title VIII was the subject of this minority view lodged in the record by four U.S. senators in their opposition to the title:

> *This title is another example of the bill's inclination to leave difficult decisions to regulators. Forcing regulators to determine when someone or something ought to be regulated is an inappropriate delegation of Congressional power.... Private enterprises that are deemed to be of systemic importance will have to get preapproval from the Fed before making any material changes in their operations.*[2]

Though the four U.S. senators were correct when they wrote that private enterprises would come under greater regulation, that regulation, *if implemented properly in relation to private trading*, may very well have been helpful, but it was almost entirely absent in the decades that preceded the market crises of 2008. The senators are each correct in their assessment that the Title VIII language is exceedingly broad and gives substantial power to the Federal Reserve.

The reach of the new law embodied in Title VIII is almost limitless: Any transfer of funds is fair game to the enumerated regulators if that or other activity is designated as systemically important. Central clearing and exchange trading utilities are now subject to a potentially massive overlay of federal regulation under Title VIII. Title VIII, unlike Title VII discussed in the previous chapter, is effective as of July 21, 2010.

It is well established that clearing institutions in the United States prior to the enactment of Title VIII generally performed well. Unlike the privately negotiated structured finance market and one segment of the OTC derivatives market—the market for credit default swaps (CDS)—the centrally cleared futures markets, listed options, and other cleared derivative markets performed admirably in many respects during the 2008 market crises. A governor of the Board of Governors of the Federal Reserve System wrote of the record of central counterparty (CCP) risk management success:

> *I have often cited CCPs for exchange-traded derivatives as a prime example of how market forces can privately regulate financial risk very effectively. Indeed, it is hard to find fault with the track record of derivatives CCPs, many of which have managed counterparty risk so effectively that they have never suffered a counterparty default.*[3]

Even during the 1987 market crises, as discussed in Chapter 8, exchange and clearinghouse performance was generally sound.

Given this history of performance, the massive reach of regulation mandated by Title VIII may appear to be misguided at the outset to many, especially to those who do not appreciate the vast OTC derivative market that will, over time, be converted to a centrally cleared market, as described in Chapters 3 and 4.

However, another angle to this development must be viewed: the OTC market in the United States is a $300 trillion (in notional) market. The futures market is a fraction of that size, and the CCP and futures model that are utilized by the futures market has never in its history been tested with volumes of that magnitude. With the CFTC and SEC imposing mandates that require central clearing pursuant to Dodd-Frank Section 723 (discussed in Chapter 4), the payment, clearing, and settlement utilities, workflows, and performance records have, with vastly greater volumes of trading, been largely untested. This means the risk of future failure of a large, untested centrally-cleared market is very real.

The risk that, after the clearing mandate, one or more clearing houses may be too big to fail and require federal support or even a bailout is too great to relieve clearing systems from oversight and regulation. Section 806 of Title VIII highlights that risk of clearinghouse failure. In that section,

Congress authorizes the Federal reserve to permit discount and borrowing privileges in unusual circumstances to enable clearing houses and other "designated financial market utility[ies]" to borrow from the government in a time of crisis.

This development in the law yields at least these questions:

- Before this new law, which governmental bodies were responsible for regulating payment, clearing, and settlement?
- What exactly does Title VIII set into motion, and when?
- What is a "systemically important activity" and how may it be regulated?
- What is the practical result of this new law?

BEFORE TITLE VIII

At the outset, it is important to begin with some historical background. As demonstrated in Chapter 1, a primary cause of the 2008 market crises was the absence of effective regulation (principally over private trading) that neither prevented, monitored, or provided an early warning of financial activity that destabilized not only the financial system in the United States but in many markets in the world.

In hindsight, the problem was not that there were no federal bodies that studied and provided guidance on payments, clearing, and other settlement activities. As we will see, federal and international analysis did, in fact, exist on these important aspects of our financial system. The problem instead was that regulation did not exist in the markets where most of the losses were, at least initially, experienced by investors and swap participants: the structured product and the CDS market.

In November 2004, the Bank for International Settlements (BIS) published Recommendations for Central Counterparties, within a report of the BIS Committee on Payment and Settlement Systems and the IOSCO Technical Committee. In that report, the committee noted that, although central clearing, in fact, is a system with great potential for reducing counterparty risk, "a CCP also concentrates risks and responsibility for risk management in the CCP."[4]

The 2004 report provided recommendations for counterparties in 15 areas: Legal risk, participation agreements, measurement and management of credit exposures, margin requirements, financial resources, default procedures, custody and investment risks, operational risk, money settlements, physical deliveries, risks in links between CCPs, efficiency, governance, transparency, and regulation and oversight. The recommendations made in each of these important areas, although outside the scope of this text, provide an effective roadmap for regulators carrying out the mandates of Title VIII.

One of the important questions raised in the 2004 report of the BIS Committee on Payment and Settlement Systems is the following:

Are the laws and regulations governing the operation of a CCP and the rules, procedures and contractual provisions for its participants clearly stated, internally coherent and readily accessible to participants and the public?[5]

For those of us in the United States, there is no question that the answer, prior to the Dodd-Frank derivatives regime, is a clear no, primarily because those laws and regulations have only recently been extensively revamped, so the educational process undertaken by market participants—of which this text is a small part—is currently underway.

In 2007, one year before the fall of Lehman Brothers, BIS again published a report titled "General Principles for International Remittance Services," which was the product of the World Bank and the Committee on Payment and Settlement Systems. In his forward to the report, Timothy F. Geithner, the then-chairman of the Committee on Payment and Settlement Systems and eventual U.S. Treasury Secretary, wrote, with a World Bank vice president, Michael U. Klein, that little regulatory attention and few reports have been devoted to the practical realities of transferring money.[6] The report is noteworthy because it identifies several impediments to international and national payment systems (as of 2007), including a lack of transparency and understanding by those who use the system, poor or disproportionate regulation, and a generally weak legal framework under which payment systems perform. This 2007 report suggests the need for federal regulators in the United States and elsewhere to undertake the study, monitoring, and more effective regulation of payment systems that are mandated by Title VIII.

Around the same time of the 2004 study discussed in the preceding pages, within the BIS Committee on Payment and Settlement Systems, the primary federal regulator of derivatives (i.e., futures contracts), the Commodity Futures Trading Commission, reorganized its Division of Trading and Markets (or T&M) and created two new divisions, the Division of Market Oversight and the Division of Clearing and Intermediary Oversight.[7] This division is charged with daily market trading and surveillance analysis and the responsibility of disclosing market-sensitive data to the National Futures Association (NFA, introduced in Chapter 3). However, the mandate of the Division of Clearing and Intermediary Oversight only extends to financial products, markets, and market participants in the futures—and now swaps—category; Title VIII reaches into any systemically important activity (not just an activity involving OTC or exchange-traded derivatives).

As we can see from the foregoing initiatives in 2004 and 2007, the problem was not that federal and international bodies did not study, monitor, and seek to regulate payment and clearing functions. They did. The problem which Title VIII seeks to prevent and regulate is the seizure of clearinghouses and payment systems, and the Title does this by means of implementing another new, even historic, body of law.

WHAT EXACTLY DOES TITLE VIII SET INTO MOTION AND WHEN?

The mandates of Title VIII were effective immediately upon the enactment of Dodd-Frank on July 21, 2010. The new law creates a framework for more robust regulation of payment, clearing, and settlement activities to the extent that those activities are designated as "systemically important," an important phrase that is discussed later.

Title VIII establishes a new framework for another new breed of acronyms:

- **FMUs.** Designated, systemically important financial market utilities (FMUs) which are people who manage or operate multilateral systems for the purpose of transferring, clearing, or settling payments, securities, or other financial transactions among financial institutions or between financial institutions and the person.
- **PCSs.** Designated, systemically important payment, clearing, and settlement (PCSs) activities (e.g., an activity carried out by one or more financial institutions to facilitate the completion of financial transactions but not any offer or sale of a security or any quotation, order entry, negotiation, or other pretrade activity or execution activity) conducted by FIs.
- **FIs.** Financial institutions (FIs) include banks (depository institution) and organizations operating under Sections 25 or 25A of the Federal Reserve Act; a branch or agency of a foreign bank; a credit union, a broker or dealer, an investment company, an insurance company, an investment adviser, a futures commission merchant, a commodity trading advisor, or a commodity pool operator and any company engaged in activities that are financial in nature or incidental to a financial activity, as described in Section 4 of the Bank Holding Company Act of 1956.[8]

FMU and PCS activities (as long as they are systemically important, as described later) will be subject to risk-management standards imposed by regulators, including the CFTC, SEC, and others including supervisory agencies which are federal agencies with primary jurisdiction over FMUs. If multiple regulators have jurisdiction over an FMU, then Section 803 of Dodd-Frank requires that one regulator be designated to be the supervisory agency.

Section 813 of the title requires that, within a year of July 21, 2010, the CFTC, the SEC, and the Federal Reserve jointly report to committees within Congress (i.e., the Committee on Banking, Housing, and Urban Affairs and the Committee on Agriculture, Nutrition, and Forestry of the U.S. Senate; the Committee on Financial Services and the Committee on Agriculture of the U.S. House of Representatives) recommendations for the following:

- Improving consistency in SEC and CFTC regulatory oversight of clearing functions.
- Promoting robust risk management (and risk management oversight) by designated clearing entities.
- Improving regulators' ability to monitor the potential effects of designated clearing entity risk management on the stability of the financial system of the United States.

WHAT IS A SYSTEMICALLY IMPORTANT ACTIVITY?

A critical part of Title VIII is the definition of "systemically important" and "systemic importance."

If an activity is designated as systemically important, in the application of the factors illustrated in Figure 5.1 (i.e., factors which Dodd-Frank Section 804 [a][2][A]-[E] require the U.S. Financial Stability Oversight Council to consider and two-thirds of the Council, including its chairperson, approve), and the terms apply to payment, clearing, and settlement activities (i.e., PCSs), and the utilities that are used to carry out those activities (i.e., FMUs), then Title VIII applies, and those activities become subject to whatever regulation is deemed within the broad mandate of Title VIII.

According to Section 803 (9) of the title, these two terms are defined as follows:

> The terms *"systemically important"* and *"systemic importance"* mean a situation where the failure of or disruption to the functioning of a financial market utility or the conduct of a payment, clearing, or settlement activity could create, or increase the risk of significant liquidity or credit problems spreading among financial institutions or markets and thereby threaten the stability of the financial system of the United States.[9]

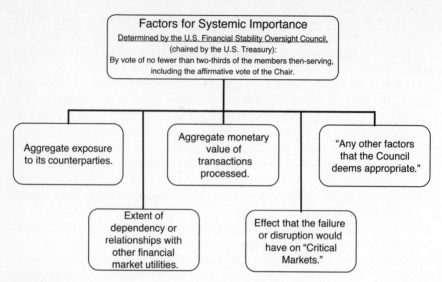

FIGURE 5.1   Factors for Determining Systemic Importance

The Council (as discussed earlier, the Council created in Section 111 of Dodd-Frank, which is chaired by the U.S. Secretary of Treasury) is to use any factors that it deems appropriate to bring about the designation of the systemically important label, including aggregate money value, exposure to the system, the interdependent nature of the utility or payment system, and the resulting effect to the financial system that the failure of the utility, payment, or clearing activity would have.

The determination of systemic importance, which may be rescinded, may only be brought about by a proposed determination, advance notice to the public of that determination and a hearing, and an opportunity to submit comments unless the circumstances are so emergent that, by two-thirds vote of the Council, the hearing and commend period may be suspended. The Council is to provide a final determination within 60 days of its hearing on the proposed determination.

Title VIII gives great latitude to these regulators to regulate that activity as they see fit in the event the label of "systemic importance" attaches to any FMU or PCS. It is unclear as of the date on which this book went to print how exactly systemically important utilities and systems would be regulated—especially in light of the existing Dodd-Frank rulemaking efforts.

PRACTICAL RESULTS OF THE NEW LAW

Title VIII is a rather ominous delegation of authority to regulators to pass a wide range of new regulations that govern designated payment, clearing, and settlement activities in the post-Dodd Frank markets—and not just with respect to derivatives and futures markets, but cash markets and any system that involves the transfer of funds. There are the seven practical observations:

1. Title VIII will, therefore, bring about a new set of Federal regulations in the United States that will include risk management policies that will apply to designated FMUs and PCSs (i.e., those financial market utilities and payment, clearing, and settlement activities that are designated as systemically important). These regulations must be proposed and put into final form by the Fed to promote the safety and soundness of the system and bring about robust risk management.
2. A designated financial market utility must provide advance notice of any proposed change to its operations, rules, or procedures that could *materially* affect the nature or level of the risks presented by the FMU (the term *materially* is to be the subject of rule making that is to follow after the date on which this text was published).
3. A designated FMU must submit information, data, and records that may be requested by the Financial Stability Oversight Council in order to assess the systemic importance of the FMU.
4. Title VIII requires the CFTC and the SEC to consult with the Fed prior to exercising certain of their authority in the areas of payment and settlement under the Commodity Exchange Act (with respect to the CFTC) and federal securities laws such as the Securities and Exchange Act of 1934, and both regulators (i.e. the SEC and CFTC) are to coordinate with the Fed to develop the report called for by Section 813 of Dodd-Frank, as summarized earlier.
5. The SEC or other regulator with primary jurisdiction over a designated FMU is mandated by Section 807 of Dodd-Frank to conduct examinations with respect to the risks posed to the system by the FMU and its safety and soundness. The Fed may also conduct an examination under its back-up enforcement authority under Section 808.
6. Title VIII empowers the Federal Reserve to take emergency enforcement action against a designated FMU.
7. A designated financial market utility or FMU may be authorized by the Federal Reserve to draw Fed proceeds in a time of crisis in a way which surprises many who believed that Dodd-Frank did away with the "too-big-to-fail" doctrine.

* * *

With so many mandates imposed on new categories of market participants (such as designated financial market utilities, which were the subject of this chapter, and major swap participants, which were the subject of Chapter 4), we next turn in Chapters 6, 7, and 8 to a discussion of the practical realities of implementing the new Dodd-Frank mandates in derivatives trading.

NOTES

1. Section 803(7)(B) of the Payment, Clearing, and Settlement Supervision Act of 2010, within the Dodd-Frank Wall Street Reform and Consumer Protection Act.
2. Minority Views of Senator Shelby, Senator Bennett, Senator Bunning, and Senator Vitter, S. Rept. 111–176 (April 30, 2010 Committee Reports).
3. Randall S. Kroszner, "Central Counterparty Clearing: History, Innovation and Regulation," *Federal Reserve Bank of Chicago Economic Perspectives* (4Q2006), 37.
4. Bank for International Settlements (BIS), "Recommendations for Central Counterparties," Bank for International Settlements, November 2004, 1.
5. Ibid., 14.
6. CPSS/World Bank, "General Principles for International Remittance Services," January 2007, iii.
7. Philip McBride Johnson and Thomas Less Hazen, *Derivatives Regulation* (New York: Aspen, 2004), 961.
8. Payment Clearing and Settlement Supervision Act of 2010, Section 803(5).
9. Section 803(9) of Dodd-Frank.

A Primer on Legal Documentation

I n a volatile market where brokers, dealers, banks, funds, and other counterparties default, merge or possibly fail altogether, there is arguably nothing more important than having protective legal documentation in place.

The purpose of this chapter is to provide an introduction to derivatives
documentation in both the over-the-counter (OTC) and centrally cleared
markets.

This chapter is designed to provide a starting point for readers, but it is
not intended to be—and it certainly should not be used as—the sole or even
primary resource for understanding, drafting, or negotiating derivatives documentation. Like the rest of this text, Chapter 6 is for general, introductory,
and informational purposes and is not intended to constitute legal advice. It
is important to note that legal documentation is driven in part by local law,
and also by market practice. Accordingly, this chapter is designed to provide
a baseline foundation for handling documentation. There is no substitute
for customized, thoughtful legal counsel by a qualified, licensed attorney
with extensive experience in the area of derivatives documentation for the
market or markets in which you or your organization trade.

This introduction, at this point in the text, is designed to pull together
various concepts already introduced to the reader, including:

- Exposure to widespread counterparty risk in OTC trading led to systemic failures (as discussed in the Introduction and Chapter 1, in the
  years leading to the 2008 market crises, each party to OTC derivatives
  was directly exposed to the other).
- An unregulated, extensively interwoven OTC marketplace entails the
  risk of system failure, especially if complex products trade in that marketplace, as the default of one party exposes the rest of the system to
  market seizure, massive losses, or both (Chapter 1).

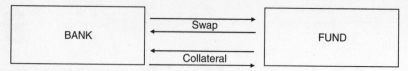

FIGURE 6.1   Bilateral OTC Derivative Trade

- The failure of at least three major international financial services firms resulted in regulators searching for, and seizing upon a new model for derivatives: the futures model (see Chapters 2 and 3).
- Central clearing and central clearing utilities were at the heart of not only global reform mandates (see the conclusion of Chapter 3), but also Dodd-Frank Title VII (Chapter 4) and Title VIII (Chapter 5).

The necessity for a primer on documentation is also self-evident from the differences in transaction structure in OTC trading, as illustrated in Figure 6.1, as compared to the moving parts and structure in the centrally-cleared, exchange-traded, centrally cleared derivatives market (as it existed at the time this book went to press) illustrated in Figure 6.2.

In Figure 6.1, two parties face each other, in any one of the many OTC derivatives summarized in Chapter 10, Survey of Derivatives. The series of arrows represents collateral that is exchanged by one or both of the parties, in support of the swap depicted by the set of arrows near the top of

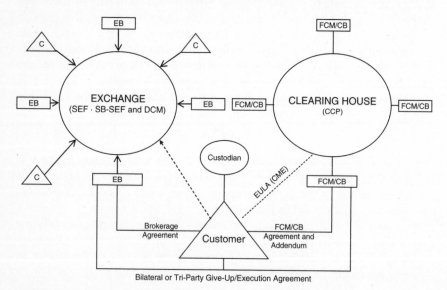

FIGURE 6.2   Trading Structure in the Centrally Cleared Environment

Figure 6.2 Abbreviation listing	
Abbreviation	**Meaning**
EB	**Executing Broker,** also known as an introducing broker. A customer or end user may place an order with an executing broker as opposed to a member of a regulated exchange. Executing brokers are responsible for executing orders on a regulated market on behalf of the customer, and then submitting the trade to a clearing member by means of an execution agreement (or give-up), which is discussed at the conclusion of this chapter.
C	**Customer.** These market participants are commonly referred to as customers in futures (and options on futures) trades, but also other cleared derivatives. In Figure 6.2, the primary customer for discussion purposes finds itself in the middle of the schematic, centered near the bottom, and other customers circle the exchange; all customers in Figure 6.2 are in triangles.
FCM/CB	**Futures Commission Merchant or Clearing Broker.** An FCM may be a Clearing Broker that is a member of a regulated clearinghouse (in the United States, a DCO) and it may be an EB, or Executing Broker as well. FCMs are regulated by the CFTC (Commodity Futures Trading Commission).
Custodian	**Custodian.** As we will see in the pages that follow, many end users have OTC (and some exchange-traded and centrally cleared) derivatives trading relationships that contemplate their custodians holding collateral that is pledged to the custodian in favor of the swap counterparty. Some pioneers in the cleared derivatives space have sought to continue this custodial relationship in the clearing of all derivatives under Dodd-Frank clearing mandates and the author has been involved in that effort.

(continued)

Figure 6.2 (continued)	
Abbreviation	Meaning
SEF and SB-SEF and DCM	**Swap Execution Facility and Security-Based Swap Execution Facility**; these are Dodd-Frank terms which mean exchanges. DCM stands for designated contract market. These terms are discussed at length in Chapters 7 and 8.
CCP/ Clearinghouse	Discussed at length in Chapter 3, this entity is separate and performs tasks that are completely different from the exchange.
EULA	**End User License Agreement**, which is, in essence, a license agreement that entitles the end user to use Globex of CME to clear.

Figure 6.1. The newer, post-Dodd-Frank world of trading is the focus of Figure 7.1 and Chapter 7. Key features of the trading relationship illustrated by Figure 6.1 include the ability of either party to freely negotiate triggers for determining which and how much collateral is to be exchanged and when. Many of these features are completely absent in the trading arrangement in the exchange and centrally cleared world, best illustrated by Figure 6.2, which presents a startling contrast in complexity with the OTC arrangement depicted in the previous illustration in Figure 6.1.

The reader is encouraged to visit www.DerivativesGuide.com after reading this chapter to receive updates to the set of documentation and trading relationships that are depicted in these figures. Some of the key features and documentation within the centrally cleared trading environment are discussed in this chapter, and the abbreviations in Figure 6.2 are provided.

Before we discuss the key component parts and documentation within the centrally cleared, exchange-traded environment, we begin our discussion at the logical place: the beginning of derivatives trading, about 30 years before this book was published, and the evolution of documentation to those used in the arrangement illustrated by Figure 6.2 is discussed next.

BACKGROUND

As discussed in greater detail in the next chapter (Chapter 7, The Life Cycle of a Cleared Derivatives Trade), derivatives are executed in a way that differs from deal execution in many other areas of finance. The first difference has to do with speed. The pace of derivative deals is so rapid that derivative traders typically initiate transactions electronically or by phone, and affirm trades with a bare minimum of documentation. Typically, the process starts with a verbal agreement among traders, which is then confirmed by e-mail or electronically affirmed—often in an hour or even in seconds.

Although both parties to a trade are legally bound by the traders' initial verbal agreement in many jurisdictions, that oral agreement offers very little in the way of relief for disputes, which invariably arise throughout the life cycle of derivative transactions. To illustrate, initial verbal agreements and even subsequent e-mails between the parties typically do not address triggers for events of default, and the method for computing damages.

"LET'S USE AN ISDA"

In the world of OTC derivatives leading up to the 2008 market crises, many parties entered into ISDAs. What's an ISDA? ISDA is an acronym for an influential trade industry, the International Swaps and Derivatives Association, Inc. Practitioners pronounce it "Is-dah," but the receptionists at the offices of the trade association cheerfully answer incoming phone calls with "I-S-D-A, may I help you?" No matter what you call it, or how you say it, in derivatives documentation parlance, an ISDA refers to the ISDA Master Agreement, which is boilerplate documentation that members of ISDA have developed over the years. A Schedule, a Credit Support Annex to the Schedule, and one or more confirmations which evidence trades "under the ISDA" generally modify this master agreement.

The ISDA closes the documentation gap left by traders moving seemingly at the speed of light. As for ISDA negotiations, however, they frequently do not exactly move at the speed of light, especially when inexperienced negotiators are involved.

Although traders negotiate and settle transactions in the OTC market between themselves, or bilaterally, as illustrated in Figure 6.3, in the exchange-traded derivatives market, including the futures markets, the process is completely different (as we saw in Chapter 3 and will see in Chapter 7).

Most OTC derivatives are evidenced by the ISDA Master Agreement and accompanying schedule (which customizes the master agreement), credit support annex to the Schedule, and a trade Confirmation for each trade, which is typically generated by the swap dealer (in financial derivatives).

The purpose of this documentation is to minimize certain risks which are inherent in OTC derivatives transactions, primarily counterparty risk. An important way to manage counterparty risk is to negotiate and execute documentation requiring the posting of collateral by the counterparty to the trade.

In Figure 6.3, the fund and bank have entered into a swap, and both parties are obligated under the swap terms to exchange either payments or

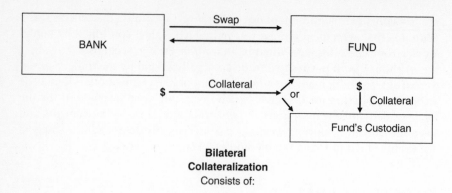

FIGURE 6.3   Bilateral OTC Derivatives Collateralization

assets, or both, and this exchange is illustrated by the arrows between the bank and fund.

In some OTC derivative trading platforms, one party requires its counterparty to deliver collateral. That party is referred to as the secured party (or pledgee) in the Credit Support Annex, which is discussed in great detail later in this chapter. If, under the Credit Support Annex, a party never will be obligated to deliver collateral to its counterparty, then that party is said to be in a unilateral collateralization relationship. This relationship may have been the product of uneven bargaining power, or it may be quite customary in some derivatives, such as interest rate swaps accompanying real estate financings.

Figure 6.3 illustrates a bilateral, or two-way, collateral arrangement where both parties may be obligated to post pledge collateral to the other. The arrow near the center of the diagram under "collateral" represents U.S. dollars as collateral being posted by the bank, under the terms of the Credit Support Annex, in favor of the fund, as secured party. The dollar proceeds may be deposited in a deposit account held at the fund's bank, or in an account maintained by the fund's custodian.

Figure 6.3 illustrates the OTC swap structure in a manner that is most advantageous to the fund (depicted by the box to the far right) which faces a bank as its counterparty to the swap. Not all funds succeed in negotiations in bringing about this trading arrangement. Funds governed by the Investment Company Act of 1940 in the United States (1940 Act), such as mutual funds, succeed in getting the tri-party structure illustrated in Figure 6.3 because of a regulatory requirement (imposed by the SEC at the time when this text went to print) embodied in 1940 Act Rule 17f-1, which requires 1940 Act—governed entities to maintain their assets (including collateral supporting OTC trades) pursuant to a written contract ratified by the fund's board. 1940 Act companies have interpreted this rule to require the segregation of their OTC derivative collateral and maintenance of that collateral in their fund custodian's account, as illustrated in the structure depicted in Figure 6.3. If, under the terms of the Credit Support Annex, the bank requests margin from the fund, the fund transfers that requested collateral not to the bank, but to the fund's custodian, and the fund grants a lien to the bank, which may obtain the custodied assets upon a default by the fund.

The utility and importance of this arrangement is underscored in new derivatives law in the United States, which is expected to serve as a model in markets outside of the United States. Dodd-Frank includes Section 724(c), which requires a swap dealer or major swap participant to notify its OTC derivatives counterparty of the right to require collateral segregation with respect to the initial margin (in ISDA documentation parlance, "Independent Amounts") of uncleared derivatives. This means that all end users—not just entities governed by the 1940 Act—facing swap dealers and major swap participants, are entitled to maintain their initial margin supporting uncleared trades with custodians, provided that certain requirements are satisfied. The documentation required for this arrangement is listed in Figure 6.3: an ISDA Master Agreement and Schedule, a bilateral Credit Support Annex (the fund could also take advantage of the tri-party structure described here with a unilateral credit support annex in which only the fund is collateral transfer obligations), and a Control Agreement (also known as a Special Pledge and Custody Agreement or Tri-Party Control Agreement). The third of the three documents listed here is entered into among the fund, the fund's counterparty, and the custodian of the fund. The fund's counterparty is entitled to receive under the Control Agreement certain rights to immediately retrieve collateral maintained by the fund's custodian under the terms of the Control Agreement in the event that the fund defaults under the terms of the ISDA Master Agreement or the Schedule or Credit Support Annex to the Schedule.

As this book went to print, the author was on his way to the CFTC to help bring about improvements to the system following the collapse of MF Global.

With the passage of the Dodd-Frank Wall Street Reform and Consumer Protection Act (Dodd-Frank), and the principal mandate of Title VII of Dodd-Frank concerning the central clearing of derivatives, many market participants, especially those clearing trades through CME, believe that the ISDA Master Agreement will no longer be used to document derivatives trading.

Notwithstanding this view, ISDA documentation continues to be important because the conversion of the OTC derivatives market to a centrally cleared market will take place in phases; even then, some derivatives trades will be so unique that they will be documented under master agreements and confirmations, which are summarized next.

HISTORY OF THE ISDA

Prior to 1985, swap dealers in the OTC derivative markets used their own customized forms for trade documentation, and legal counsel for each side expended an exceedingly great—and often unnecessary—amount of time reviewing documentation for each trade. The lack of standardization in derivative documentation resulted in delayed processing (or, in some cases, no processing at all), only to be followed by high legal fees.

Many other areas of modern finance lack standard documentation but, because of the enormous global market for derivatives and the rapid pace at which these financial products trade, standardization became necessary, and the lack of standardized derivatives documentation limited the growth of derivative products and impaired secondary markets in swaps and other complex instruments of finance. Over time, dealers used other dealers' forms, but standardization eluded market participants prior to the mid-1980s.

Derivatives gradually transformed from novel financial transactions (accompanying complicated deals or as stand-alone arrangements) into widely-used transactions. Over time, the need for standardization of terms and documentation among dealers to reduce costs and facilitate liquidity became apparent. Most importantly, a steadily-increasing number of participants required speed in their execution of trades, and ISDA has made rapid execution of trades possible via Confirmations.

The Beginnings of ISDA

In June of 1985, ISDA published its Code of Standard Wording, Assumptions, and Provisions for Swaps, which focused on cash flows and payments upon termination. Most swap dealers in the United States approved the 1985 Code.

In August 1985, the British Bankers' Association (BBA) introduced the British Bankers' Association of Interest Rate Swaps (BBAIRS) guidelines, which primarily were used for swaps between banks. In 1986, ISDA revised and expanded its code, and in doing so it facilitated the development of the ISDA Master Agreement. Subsequently, in 1987, 1992, and again in 2002, ISDA refined its Master Agreement and released standard definitions and forms of Confirmations for derivatives.

ISDAs in the Post-Reform World

Today, ISDA represents over 800 member institutions, businesses, and governmental entities that hail from 60 countries on six continents in the OTC derivatives market. With the globalization of markets, improved technology, and simultaneous growth of complex derivative products, process and documentation have evolved dramatically and continue to change every day. The international capital markets expansion in the 1980s and beyond was largely facilitated to a significant extent by swap documentation pioneered by ISDA and used since then by many thousands of market participants.

Today, the ISDA Master Agreement remains the overarching legal document evidencing the rights and obligations of the two sides to a derivatives trade, but only if that trade is not centrally cleared as a part of the reform mandates. Documentation for derivatives that are centrally cleared, such as futures and derivatives that are subject to the Dodd-Frank clearing mandate, are described later in this chapter.

Before discussing some of the important details within the OTC documentation and its umbrella structure, it is necessary to reinforce the reader's understanding of why OTC derivatives documentation will still be used in the post-reform world.

ISDAs will continue to be used for two primary purposes: first, as a means for traders to document derivatives that are not standard and as such are not subject to a governmental mandate to centrally clear; and secondly, as a means to calculate a non-defaulting party's damages when a trade that is mandated for clearing is rejected because one of the parties to the trade has not complied with margin, position limits, or other rules or requirements imposed by clearinghouses, members of those clearinghouses, or the law (as described in Chapters 4 and 5). Some clearinghouses, such as ICE, contemplated the further use of ISDAs as the basis for cleared trades. Because not all categories of derivatives will be immediately mandated for central clearing by regulators, and due to the reality that an OTC market for some unique trades will likely continue to exist, the ISDA Master Agreement and the OTC documentation architecture remain important, so a brief discussion follows on that subject.

BASIC OTC ARCHITECTURE

There are essentially three levels of documentation in a typical trade. At the top of the documentation hierarchy is the Master Agreement, a document with content that never changes; its dispute resolution and other broad terms apply to every trade, unless varied by the parties. Next, there are two documents that modify the terms of the master agreement in several important respects: the Schedule and Credit Support Annex. Finally, the economics of each trade and other details are evidenced by confirmations, which further custom-make the transaction to fit the needs of the parties and the derivative product. Unless the parties state otherwise, the Master Agreement (as amended by the Schedule, Credit Support Annex, and Confirmation) governs the derivatives traded by the parties.

Master Agreement

This is the umbrella agreement that covers all derivative deals (i.e., transactions) by the counterparties at any time during the open-ended term of the Master Agreement (the Master Agreement terminates by mutual agreement or pursuant to the termination mechanics described in greater detail in the agreement itself). This document covers the vast array of derivatives, from interest rate swaps to foreign exchange trades to various combinations of the products. As with the vast majority of derivatives documentation, the Master Agreement published by ISDA includes many terms that are frequently used in the derivatives trade, and certain key terms are summarized in a glossary following the conclusion of this chapter. As with everything else in the derivatives trade, terms are used in customized, unique ways, and questions regarding their use should be directed to the author via www.DerivativesGuide.com.

This standardized umbrella approach appealed because it reduced paperwork and made negotiations more efficient when key terms governing all trades between them were part of a signed Master Agreement. Further, parties favored the approach because they believed that, if a counterparty became insolvent, the trustee or debtor in possession in insolvency proceedings would not be able to cherry-pick individual trades most favorable to the bankrupt party and reject transactions unfavorable to the nondefaulting creditor. Also, multiple trades under a master agreement helped parties reduce multiple payments by gathering their trades to one payment. Parties to a master agreement could then better view their credit exposure from multiple trades under a single umbrella agreement. Over-the-counter derivatives described in greater detail in Chapter 10 that come under an ISDA include:

- Foreign exchange-based derivatives, including forwards.
- Options.
- Interest rate swaps.
- Commodity and energy swaps.
- Inflation derivatives.
- Weather derivatives.

Most of the terms in the master agreement (e.g., certain events of default, etc.) are mutually applicable to the two counterparties to the Master Agreement. Some of the key features of this agreement include: covenants to regularly furnish information or documentation; standard representations that are typically included in other finance documentation; events of default (including the failure to pay or deliver upon settlement of a trade; breach of the agreement unless remedied within a certain period, such as 30 days; failure to provide or maintain collateralization; breach of representations and other enumerated defaults under the master agreement, including the declaration of bankruptcy by either party); and provisions setting forth the consequences of default.

ISDA published two Master Agreements, one in 1992, and the other in 2002, after market crises necessitated adjustment to the 1992 version. As with all other legal documentation, licensed and qualified legal counsel must be consulted to ensure that the proper master agreement is used, and to ensure that the agreement is customized to fit unique facts and circumstances.

Prior to the publication by ISDA of its 1992 Master Agreement, the OTC market used standardized forms typically for interest rate derivatives (e.g., swaps, caps, collars, and floors, as discussed in Chapter 10) and options. In 1987, ISDA adopted the predecessor to the 1992 Master Agreement, at which point parties began to use a Master Agreement as an umbrella for numerous trades among them.

A key consideration for the reader is the law that governs the Master Agreement and accompanying agreements and annexes that follow. To properly handle this consideration, qualified legal counsel is required.

Schedule

The Schedule is designed to customize the Master Agreement to fit the credit, tax, and other legal needs of the parties arising out of their unique credit profiles. A Schedule typically includes customized termination provisions referred to as additional termination events, or ATEs (one ATE, for example, entitles the end user to terminate its ISDA with its counterparty swap dealer if the credit ratings of the dealer fall below a certain level), as well as credit-related terms and a wide array of covenants and representations that add to, limit, or reduce the covenants and representations within the Master Agreement. Schedules include these component parts:

- Part 1: Termination provisions, such as cross-default terms and ATEs.
- Part 2: Tax language and obligations to provide tax forms.
- Part 3: Deliverables for one party to the ISDA to provide to the other, including, for example, financial documents.

- Part 4: Miscellaneous provisions such as contact details for providing formal notices.
- Part 5: Other provisions, such as unique representations and warranties which one party requires from the other.
- Part 6: Terms for currency or other derivatives.

Credit Support Annex

This OTC document, referred to as the Annex or CSA, is similar to the Schedule and confirmation because the parties customize it to address and accommodate credit risks noted in the master agreement. There is a New York form annex, and a separate CSA for trading under English law. The CSA states the party's or parties' duties to deliver and return collateral; it specifies the collateral (and credit for the kind of collateral) that may be posted in response to a margin call; it grants a security interest (in the New York form CSA), and it includes other rights, remedies, and covenants with respect to the collateral, as well as its custody and return to the party that pledges the collateral.

An important means to manage OTC counterparty risk is to obtain collateral from a counterparty to the OTC trade. In the OTC trading world, in which no central counterparty or clearinghouse exists (as discussed in Chapter 3), bilateral CSAs are the best way to limit risk of loss from the default of a counterparty. In many cases in negotiations involving OTC derivatives documentation, one party will supply the other with its set of derivatives documentation that, although based on forms published by ISDA, favors the party that supplies the documentation, and that documentation is signed without review or negotiation. The CSA, like the ISDA Schedule, is customized to address needs relating to the parties signing the documentation. The principal reason for executing a CSA is to limit or manage counterparty credit risks or the risk of default by the use of collateral practices. However, without properly reviewing, drafting, and negotiating the CSA, its intended purpose may never be realized.

The CSA is one of a few documents that are referred to in the ISDA Schedule as Credit Support Document, which may also include guaranties, letters of credit, financial guaranty insurance, or surety bonds (and Control Agreements, discussed later). Although counterparties negotiate the list of Credit Support Documents, more often than not in most OTC derivative trading relationships, the CSA is then the only document listed in the ISDA schedule as a Credit Support Document.

Calculating the Delivery Amount

Parties executing a CSA agree to a framework for collateralizing OTC derivative positions, or obligations under the ISDA Master Agreement. Collateral is to be delivered in a Delivery Amount, as security to the counterparty under the ISDA Master Agreement. When overcollateralized, a Return Amount is tendered to the overcollateralized party. It is important to develop an understanding of how these two amounts are calculated.

Parties to an ISDA Master Agreement designate a Valuation Agent to calculate delivery amounts and return amounts and to provide notice of those amounts. If the parties do not designate a Valuation Agent, then the party on the ISDA Master Agreement making the demand for collateral is the Valuation Agent.

On a Valuation Date, and a Valuation Time (both of which may be negotiated by the parties to the ISDA), the Valuation Agent marks-to-market the exposure. The Valuation Agent performs these tasks:

- Values collateral already posted.
- Makes a determination about whether the pledgor under the CSA is entitled to interest or distributions.
- Calculates the value of any excess collateral in the Return Amount.
- Provides notice of its valuation no later than the notification time (e.g., 1:00 p.m. New York City time unless otherwise negotiated and specified), one local business day after its valuation, and by the notification time in order to be entitled to receive requested collateral by the next local business day.

Calculation of Credit Support Amount

Under New York law, the Valuation Agent in the CSA determines the amount that a Pledgor (the Pledgor is the party that provides collateral to support its derivative payment obligations to the Secured Party) is to transfer by means of the following formula, whose component parts are described as follows:

	Exposure of the Secured Party
+	Independent Amounts Attributable to the Pledgor
−	Independent Amounts (of the Secured Party)
−	Threshold (applicable to the Pledgor)
=	Credit Support Amount

Each of the component parts is briefly described here.

- **Exposure** is generally the amount that the one party would owe the other if the ISDA Master Agreement were terminated.

- **Independent Amount** is an amount that one party may demand from the other party to reflect a number of factors, such as the credit profile of the counterparty, the derivatives traded or volatility. Independent Amounts have the effect of increasing posting obligations and relieving or acting as a buffer against collateral posting requirements.
- **Threshold** is an amount of risk that one party is able to tolerate before calling for collateral.
- **Minimum transfer amount** or **MTA**. If the amount that the Valuation Agent calculates is less than the MTA, no collateral need be transferred. This component part functions to obviate *de minimum* amounts that are required under the CSA to be transferred.
- **Credit support amount** means the amount that must be tendered to the Secured Party, minus the value of any previously posted collateral (as determined by the calculations of the Valuation Agent), yielding an amount that is referred to as the **Delivery Amount**.

Parties may base the settings for MTAs and Thresholds or factors including credit ratings of the rated debt of the end user who is a party to the ISDA Master Agreement and CSA to the Schedule.

Confirmations

Confirmations include the economic terms of the derivative, and they come in either the short- or long-form variety. A long-form confirmation is essentially a shortened version of the Master Agreement with many of the key Schedule and Credit Support Annex terms imported by the parties to the trade. Parties who, for various reasons, are unable to negotiate and execute (in time for a trade, for example) an ISDA Master Agreement instead put in place a long-form Confirmation with a covenant to finalize and execute a master agreement at some later point.

Like a long-form Confirmation, a short-form Confirmation identifies the derivative product, the length of the transaction with respect to that derivative, the ISDA definitions that are unique to that derivative, the entity that will make determinations and calculations relating to the performance of the derivative, and, most important, the cash flows and termination payments for the derivative. The parties may elect to vary the terms of the master agreement, and, unless they agree otherwise, the terms of the Confirmation take precedence over the terms of the ISDA Master Agreement and its Schedule.

Control Agreement

Collateral is tendered under the terms of the Credit Support Annex. Another collateral-related document is referred to in market parlance as a Control

Agreement, Tri-party, or Tri-party Control Agreement, which is, as its name suggests, a written agreement among the derivatives dealer (or other counterparty), the end user who the dealer faces under the ISDA Master Agreement, and the custodian of the end user. Under the terms of the Control Agreement, upon receipt of a margin call from the derivatives dealer, the end user pledges or tenders the requested collateral, not to its counterparty under the ISDA, but rather to its own custodian to hold unless and until the out-of-money trade or trades necessitating collateral mature or terminate. Prior to Dodd-Frank, generally only end users regulated by the SEC as 1940-Act funds under the Investment Company Act of 1940[1] were able to successfully persuade swap dealers to enter into Control Agreements, with few exceptions. Depending on a few factors, including the requirements of the parties, the law governing the activities of the parties and, to a lesser extent, market practice, a Control Agreement may be required for purposes of evidencing, among other things, the custodial duties relating to the posted collateral. A Control Agreement, therefore, evidences the arrangement whereby a custodian establishes one or more accounts to hold posted collateral. The party in whose favor collateral is posted is able to access that collateral only upon the occurrence of an event of default, termination event, or Additional Termination Event under the terms of the ISDA Master Agreement and its Schedule.

Section 724(c) of Dodd-Frank, previously discussed in greater detail in Chapter 4, calls for independent custodians to hold initial margin for uncleared derivatives or at least the notification to the end user of the right to have an independent custodian to hold initial margin for uncleared trades. This part of U.S. reform has provided a foundation for more Control Agreements to be put in place by a wider range of end users, so that end users receiving a margin call from their counterparty can respond to that call by posting collateral in favor of the calling party in the end user's accounts maintained by their custodian.

Ancillary Documents, Including Those for Credit Support

Depending on the credit needs of the respective parties, a guaranty of the performance of one party may be exchanged, along with documents called for in the schedule (e.g., formation documents for a corporate counterparty, tax forms, and the like) upon the execution and delivery of the Master Agreement.

Ancillary documents include forms of credit support such as guarantees, letters of credit, and insurance. This credit support is typically provided upon execution of the master agreement so that a backstop of support for the obligations of the parties under the ISDA may exist before trading.

Letters of credit, which are frequently used in energy derivative transactions, and financial guaranty insurance policies, used especially before the 2008 market crises, frequently serve as the functional equivalents of guarantees. In derivatives accompanying structured financial products, parties in whose favor insurance policies were issued often obtained commitments that allow the beneficiary to terminate the trading relationship, obtain additional collateral, or obtain a more credit-worthy insurer—or some combination of the foregoing—in the event the insurer's (or its affiliates) debt ratings were downgraded by a credit-rating agency.

THE ISDA DOCUMENTATION IN PRACTICE, AND PROBLEMS IN 2008

In the third quarter of 2008, many in the OTC derivatives market contended with the failure of Lehman Brothers and its derivatives trading arm, Lehman Brothers Special Financing Inc. (LBSF). Additionally, the purchase of Bear Stearns by J. P. Morgan Chase & Co., also described in Chapters 2 and 8, gave rise to a host of important legal implications, which are outside the scope of this chapter.

Although Lehman Brothers, the parent and holding company of Lehman affiliates, filed for bankruptcy on September 15, 2008, it was not until October 3, 2008, that LBSF filed for bankruptcy, causing many in the OTC derivatives market to experience weeks of uncertainty. Some (nondefaulting) counterparties to LBSF sought to terminate their trades with LBSF only after October 2, 2008; those parties did not have in place an ISDA Master Agreement with a Schedule (those documents would have given those parties express contractual remedies to terminate positions, offset amounts owed, and seize excess collateral); those parties only had long-form Confirmations, which were described earlier in this chapter.

In many cases, the pace of derivatives trading outstripped the parties' ability to properly review and execute, or sign trade confirmations. In other cases, especially before 2008 but also more recently, one party has assigned (or novated) trades without the proper consent of the remaining party. Ideally and in most cases, one counterparty (usually a bank if it is a party to a derivatives trade) generates a Confirmation promptly after a trade is initially negotiated, and that confirmation is reviewed via an electronic trading platform; if the trade details are consistent with the initial conversation by the traders, the trade is affirmed.

Regulators before and after the 2008 market crises became concerned with the reality that many confirmations were not generated, properly reviewed, or executed by both parties to the trades. A backlog of confirmations suffering from those defects developed over time. Each of these problems, and especially those that were highlighted after the failure of Lehman Brothers, suggested to policy makers and market participants alike the protections that are inherent in the market for listed derivatives. Regulators also became concerned that one party to a negotiated, executed trade assigned its rights to a third party, without securing the consent of the original party that remained in the trade. This concern has resulted in years of successful efforts led by the largest banks to electronically confirm derivative trades.

The Appeal for Listed Documentation

Although, as the October 31, 2011 failure of MF Global illustrates, no market is perfect in the sense that its participants are never immunized from losses or challenges in trading, after the 2008 market crises, the futures and other listed derivatives markets were viewed with great, widespread appeal. This is, in large part, because the markets for listed derivatives are transparent and heavily regulated, and for the most part generally well-regulated.

In discussing the causes of the 2008 market crises, Chapter 1 included commentary from regulators who were surprised by the extent of losses and market seizure in segments of the OTC derivatives and structured-finance markets. Because the markets for listed derivatives (primarily futures) are already heavily regulated, and include a central clearinghouse, electronic trading, and other platforms whereby market participants can enter into and readily confirm transactions, there was much about these markets that appealed to policy makers and market participants alike from 2007 to 2010. Coupled with these advantages is the reality that losses experienced by participants in the listed derivatives and futures markets were much smaller than those experienced by many in the markets for structured products and OTC derivatives.

Differences in OTC Trading and the World of Exchange-Traded Derivatives

As illustrated by Figure 6.1 and Figure 6.2, the manner in which derivatives are entered into and settled is completely different in the exchange-traded space, as compared to the OTC world that this chapter has summarized.

Customers of futures and other listed derivatives negotiate a set of initial form documents, and then they access electronic trading platforms that have developed over time. These platforms included a wide range of software applications and "middleware" systems provided by vendors.

For derivative transactions to be entered in the exchange-traded world, the first step is to enter into a contractual relationship with a clearing firm that, in essence, sponsors access into what today is generally an electronic market (as opposed to the OTC market, which is a face-to-face market with fewer market controls prior to Dodd-Frank).

The firm that sponsors access into the listed derivatives market first develops a risk profile of the trader, firm, or adviser trading on behalf of the firm. Up to this point, there is little or no difference between the OTC and exchange-traded markets, because the party seeking to trade must provide financial information, evidence of trading authority, and so forth, to a counterparty or to either a dealer (in the case of the OTC market), a clearing member, or a futures commission merchant or FCM, (in the case of the exchange-traded derivatives markets). In both cases, the OTC dealer and FCM monitor the counterparty trader's creditworthiness; however, the OTC dealer frequently has less visibility (at least prior to the reforms of 2010) into OTC trading activities. This dynamic was a major problem for regulators before and during the 2008 market crises, as discussed in Chapter 1.

Futures and cleared derivatives customers submit orders to clearing firms using technology that is referred to as Internet-enabled, front-end systems provided by ISVs (independent software vendors) that connect in a standardized manner to electronic platforms with exchanges and other customers and their clearing firms.[2] Once customers place orders in the front-end systems, the orders to buy and sell go into a central-order book maintained by a trading host. As an example, Chicago Board of Trade (CBOT) and Chicago Mercantile Exchange (CME) jointly developed TOPS (Trade Order Processing System), which introduced electronic order entry and routes orders placed with FCMs to a trading floor and ultimately to broker terminals.[3]

Electronic-order processing in the exchange-traded, centrally cleared derivatives markets completely eliminated the need for individual paper orders, and it obviated paper-trade Confirmations that were previously used (and often brought about processing problems) in trading OTC.

To give some perspective to today's electronic trading environment with a brief historical perspective, years ago, before electronic platforms developed for widespread use in the futures markets, orders were written on paper and carried by hand to trading floors, or the pit, and there they were manually keypunched for execution. Electronic processing in the exchange-traded space created automated, time-stamped audit trails. Electronic-order processing brings about automatic transmission of orders to a central clearinghouse, where an algorithm matches trades that are then electronically confirmed to the FCMs or clearing members. One such algorithm is FIFO (first-in, first-out). FIFO means that the first buy or sell order that is received in the system at a more aggressive price will be first filled.[4] As introduced in Chapter 3, and then as discussed in greater detail in Chapter 7, once orders are matched and executed, they are sent for processing to a clearinghouse for processing and booking. Once cleared, data concerning cleared trades is provided to clearing members or FCMs.

The Futures Commission Merchant Agreement

Clearing brokers and FCMs are, as we saw in Chapter 3, brokerage firms that solicit and accept orders from customers to trade futures and, in the post-reform world, other cleared derivatives. The role of the FCM is to accept those orders and transmit them to an electronic exchange for processing. None of this happens unless a FCM agreement is negotiated, finalized, signed, and delivered by a customer and its FCM.

The FCM agreement is part of a larger documentation package that includes account information forms (calling for wiring instructions, registration, and account holder data). The FCM agreement may be called a Master Client Agreement (in the case of JPMorgan forms) or simply a Customer Agreement (in UBS securities forms).

FCM Agreements bring about the authorization of the FCM by its customer to buy and sell for the account of the customer (who may be an individual but is frequently a corporate entity, such as a fund or trustee) futures contracts and options on futures. The FCM agreement generally includes a statement of the law, exchange, and clearinghouse rules that apply to the trading through the FCM by the customer, and requires charges and fees to be paid by the customer.

In ways that are at least somewhat similar to the ISDA Master Agreement, the FCM, like the dealer or other counterparty to the ISDA, requires representations and warranties concerning, among other important credit terms, the customer's authority to enter into the FCM agreement and the customer's understanding of the trades to be handled by the FCM. The FCM Agreement also makes clear the obligation of the customer to satisfy original and variation margin requirements, which are discussed in greater detail in Chapters 4 and 5. Once pledged, the FCM's rights with respect to margin are generally prescribed by law, subject to a customer's ability to vary margin-handling arrangements within the bounds of the law.

Like the ISDA Master Agreement, the FCM Agreement includes obligations to make payments, but included in the language are different categories of fees and charges, including, for example, clearing fees, give-up (give-up arrangements are discussed in Chapters 4 and 5) fees, exchange, and other fees.

The accounts that are established under the terms of the FCM Agreement may be liquidated under certain conditions set out in the agreement, which, unless negotiated properly, may include open-ended termination provisions.

Because the FCM acts largely as an agent in bringing about the execution and settlement of listed derivatives contracts, the FCM Agreement gives the

FCM the right to borrow or buy any property necessary to make delivery of assets needed to complete a futures or other listed derivative.

The Addendum to the FCM Agreement

For derivatives that are subject to a Dodd-Frank clearing mandate—which requires the previously OTC-traded derivatives to be centrally cleared—the legal terms of those derivatives are included in an addendum to the FCM Agreement. The Addendum is designed to cover all derivatives that are required by the SEC or CFTC (or both) under Section 723 of Dodd-Frank to be centrally cleared. A form Addendum for cleared derivatives has been developed by an effort which began in 2010 led by the Futures Industry Association (FIA), of which the author was a part. The FIA is a trade association in the United States composed of FCMs.

The Addendum is intended to address the following issues and questions that FCM agreements do not address, such as:

- **Tax Obligations of the Parties.** Whether and to what extent a party to a cleared derivative needs to be responsible for withholding amounts from payments relating to the trade to satisfy tax law.
- **Termination Provisions.** How cleared derivatives that have not matured (and have been submitted to central clearing) are terminated and offset with respect to other obligations, and how termination amounts are calculated, in the event that a derivative cannot be cleared because either party to the trade or the FCM is out of compliance with position limits or other applicable rules or law.

The addendum is also needed for clearing because, without it, parties to a cleared derivatives trade could take the position that clearinghouse and clearing member rules do not apply to the end user.

Give-Up or Execution Agreement

The third component of the exchange-traded derivatives documentation is the give-up, or execution agreement. In order to understand why this agreement is necessary, it is necessary to read about the manner in which executing brokers provide pricing and begin the process of centrally clearing a trade. This material is the subject of Chapter 3 (which provides an introduction to futures and other cleared derivatives) and the next chapter, Chapter 7 (which discusses each stage in the life cycle of a cleared derivative).

In the event that a centrally cleared derivative, including a futures contract, is entered into with a broker who is not able to clear the derivative via a regulated clearinghouse, which the author will refer to as a clearing member (CM), that trade will have to be transferred to a CM, and the give-up, or execution agreement, accomplishes that task. The next chapter includes a detailed discussion of how a derivative is taken up by a CM and then centrally cleared through a CCP, or a clearinghouse. Just as Confirmations evidenced a derivative in the OTC derivatives market, and problems in Confirmation processing led to electronic, paperless trading, give-ups have evolved from paper- or e-mail-based trading to an electronic execution system called the Electronic Give-Up Agreement System (EGUS).

The FIA began its design of EGUS on October 1, 2006, and the system enables multiple parties to initiate a give-up agreement, whether they are executing or clearing brokers or traders.[5] If a trading party prefers to use it's own form of give-up, EGUS permits the firm to alert other system users that the party is the preferred initiator. The initiating party under EGUS may adjust its form and then submit it to all counterparties simultaneously, who then review the give-up, and agree, comment, or request a change to that agreement. EGUS maintains an electronic queue that enables each party to the trade to view the status of the agreement and view the history of the give-up.

In June 2011, the FIA and ISDA jointly published a form for use by cleared swaps market participants in negotiating give-up, or execution-related arrangements. The template published by the two leading trade associations was a product of a committee comprised of representatives from both the FIA and ISDA, including the author, who was a part of a core group of end user participants in the drafting process, including the drafting process for the cleared derivatives addendum which appends to futures (and options on futures) clearing documentation. As this text went to print, the CFTC is reviewing its proposed rule to preclude the use of tri-party *annexes* to the FIA/ISDA form of execution or give-up agreement on the basis that the use of such annexes (which contemplate the clearing broker signing the agreement as a third party, along with the other 2 parties, the customer and executing broker) would constitute an unreasonable restraint of trade and an anti-competitive burden on trading and clearing.

* * *

Readers with interest in cleared derivatives documentation and rulemaking are urged to follow developments in this area after the publication of this book via www.DerivativesGuide.com.

This chapter provides, in summary form, a description of the legal documentation that was used before Dodd-Frank, and it will continue to be used after derivatives reform (as central clearing mandates in Dodd-Frank will

likely be phased-in, at least with respect to derivatives that are not standardized or are not accepted by central clearing parties for clearing). A glossary
of OTC documentation terminology follows below. The next chapter will
take the reader through each of six phases identified by the author as stages
in the life of a centrally cleared derivative, with the first stage constituting
the execution of legal documentation.

GLOSSARY

Key Schedule Terms	Definitions
Affected Party	This is the party that is at fault when a Termination Event takes place.
Close-Out	The unilateral right to terminate one or more contracts. Implied in this term is the exercise of calculating a Close-Out Amount, which is a defined term in the 2002 ISDA Master Agreement.
Close-Out Amount	This is the amount that represents the cost of replacing or requiring the economic equivalent of transactions under a 2002 ISDA, which more carefully defines this key term (see below). Read the lengthy, helpful definition in Section 14 of the 2002 ISDA Master; you won't find it in the 1992 ISDA Master because it was adopted in the 2002 ISDA Master Agreement. Section references in this glossary are to the ISDA Master Agreement.
Close-out netting	The termination of contracts and the replacement of all the obligations of both parties with a single net amount due from one party to the other. The objective is to arrive at a single amount that represents the exposure to a counterparty. The key issue is the enforceability of this concept. ISDA has commissioned the writing of legal opinions regarding Close-Out netting enforceability in over 30 jurisdictions, worldwide. As a prerequisite for a bank to minimize capital reserves assuming the application of close-out netting, regulators require a jurisdiction-specific legal opinion on enforceability.
Defaulting Party	This is the party that is at fault in the course of an Event of Default. Contrasted with affected party.
Determining Party	This is the party that determines the Close-Out amount.

Early Termination Date	This is the date on which close-out takes place. It's determined in accordance with Section 6(a) or Section 6(b). Take a look at these sections because they illustrate how the substantive rights of the parties differ, depending on whether the event/development giving rise to termination is an event of default or a termination event. Sections 6(a) and 6(b) are very different in many important respects.
Events of Default	Section 5(a) lists these "EoDs": failure to pay, an event that constitutes bankruptcy in Section 5(a)(vii) is one example. Different in many respects from Termination Events.
First Method	This is one (currently obsolete) method used to determine damages under the 1992 ISDA Master. This method must be viewed in light of an election to calculate damages using Market Quotation or Loss. Generally obsolete or discarded in part due to regulatory treatment.
In-the-money	A derivative is in-the-money if it is valued or marked with a positive value so, it is an asset. A key concept; claims for damages are rooted in this term.
Loss	This is a method used in the 1992 version of the ISDA Master Agreement for calculating losses and costs from terminated transactions. Gains from terminated transactions are subtracted from losses.
Market Quotation	This is a method of calculating the replacement value of terminated transactions. Calculation is by reference to quotations from reference-market makers. This is only a concept used in the 1992 version of the ISDA Master Agreement.
Out-of-the-money	A derivative is out-of-the-money if it is valued or marked with a negative value; it is a liability to the party that is in-the-money. Another key damage concept.
Payment netting	In a swap, both parties exchange payments. Rather than each party arranging a separate wire for its respective payment, the ISDA Master Agreement in Section 2(c) permits the netting of payments in the same currency with respect to the same transaction on the same payment date so that the payments are essentially added together and one payment is made by the party whose payment amount is greater than the other party. Contrast with Close-Out Netting, defined earlier.

Second Method	This is the one "live" method used to determine damages under the 1992 ISDA Master (and essentially under the 2002 ISDA Master Agreement). Like the first Method, this method must be viewed in light of an election to calculate damages using either market quotation or loss.
Set-off or Offset Termination Event	A set-off clause is a standard feature in a Schedule. Section 5(b) of the ISDA Master Agreement lists these events, which include the occurrence of an event that makes a transaction illegal, a force majeure event (under the 2002 ISDA Master); a tax event, a credit event upon merge—these are just a few. Think of these events as events that may be beyond the immediate control of the parties (and so perhaps we should look at these in a different way from Events of Default, because the substantive rights of the parties are different with EODs versus Termination Events. There is, and has been, a move away from thinking about termination events or Events of Default as fault-based. Note that termination events also include Additional Termination Events which are events that are tailor-made to fit the credit profiles of the parties to the ISDA and, perhaps, affiliates.
Unpaid amounts	These are the amounts that are owing to one party as of the Early Termination Date. These include amounts for transactions that have not been settled as of the Early Termination Date. For physically-delivered transactions, these are amounts that need to equal the fair market value of "that which was (or would have been) required to be delivered."

NOTES

1. The Investment Company Act of 1940, 15 U.S.C. § 80a-1 et seq.
2. John W. Labuszewski, John E. Nyhoff, Richard Co, and Paul E. Peterson, *The CME Group Risk Management Handbook: Products and Applications* (Hoboken, NJ: John Wiley & Sons, 2010), 37.
3. Chicago Board of Trade, *The Chicago Board of Trade Handbook of Futures and Option* (New York: McGraw Hill, 2006), 43–45.
4. Labuszewski et al., *The CME Group Risk Management Handbook,* 37.
5. "Outlook," *Futures Industry* (November–December 2006): 68–69.

CHAPTER 7

The Life Cycle of a Cleared Derivatives Trade

This chapter includes the anatomy of a cleared derivatives trade, from the execution of legal documentation, as described in Chapter 6, to trade settlement. The author bases the description of the cleared derivatives life cycle on his own experience negotiating derivatives, including futures, coupled with research on the evolving law and rulemaking in the United States.

While this chapter is not intended to be a comprehensive anatomy of a trade, it is hoped that it gives the reader an introductory view of a cleared derivative from start to finish. The reality—and, for this chapter, the challenge—is that the anatomy of cleared derivatives in the United States and throughout the world continues to develop from the time this book went to print to the present date. With this awareness, the author attempted to meet that challenge by taking a snapshot of the cleared derivative process at one point in time, right as this book went to print, surveying the changing legal and technical landscapes, and projecting forward not only with respect to trading practices, but the contours of the market in the future, which will be described later in Chapter 9.

The reader is encouraged to view the evolving details of trade life cycle and market developments as updated from time to time in the author's website for this text, www.DerivativesGuide.com.

There are six phases in the anatomy of a cleared derivatives trade.

STEP ONE: LEGAL DOCUMENTATION

We pick up in Chapter 7 where we left off in the previous chapter: the negotiation, execution, and delivery of appropriate legal documentation.

In the previous chapter, the over-the-counter (OTC) documentation, architecture, and the foundations for cleared derivative trading (e.g., the

211

FCM Agreement, Cleared Derivatives Addendum, and Give-Up or Execution Agreement) were introduced.

The legal documentation is, and must be, tailor-made to fit the product, counterparty, and margin requirements. Accordingly, no one-size-fits-all approach can be taken, and qualified, licensed legal counsel should be retained to protect your rights; numerous issues and intermediate steps need to be considered with qualified counsel, and several but not all are offered here.

Prior to negotiating legal documentation for cleared derivatives, however, it is important to develop, implement, monitor, and continuously evaluate the party's derivative policies and procedures, including its lists of permitted counterparties, clearing members or futures commission merchants (FCMs). With these derivative policies, procedures, and recommendations in place, we next turn to considerations that are involved in executing appropriate legal documentation in the new world of cleared derivatives.

In light of the unique nature of each clearinghouse and its unique set of clearing rules, a single set of standardized documents for all cleared derivatives worldwide has not been completely developed at the time this book went to print by an industry group such as the International Swap and Derivatives Association, Inc. (ISDA). As discussed in the previous chapter, the Futures Industry Association (FIA) began its development of a set of model standardized legal documents for clearing derivatives in the United States and elsewhere. All should consider, as recommended in the Introduction of this text, working with qualified, licensed professionals for developing a customized approach to derivatives along these lines:

- **Inventory Derivatives.** Identify the derivative products and trading strategies. This recommendation is discussed in greater detail in the next chapter.
- **Identify Counterparties.** This entails matching the derivative products and trading strategies (referenced in the previous bullet point) with counterparties, as well as intermediaries such as brokers, dealers, and clearing members (or FCMs) that are needed to execute, clear, and settle the trades.
- **Utilize Business Relationship Managers.** Usually legal documentation cannot be entered into, and negotiations cannot begin, unless a broker's business relationship manager sponsors the process. Once this sponsorship takes place, the broker typically provides the required legal documentation as a part of the onboarding process.
- **Develop Best Practice Documentation.** As discussed in Chapter 7, even if the broker (i.e., the clearing member or FCM) has its own required documentation, developing a best practice set of legal documents that are best suited for your trading is recommended.

■ **Identify Clearing Houses that Are Able to Clear Your Derivatives.** Not all clearinghouses will clear and process the derivatives that are needed to execute a particular centrally-cleared derivatives trading strategy. During the same process that is used to inventory derivatives, select intermediaries (e.g., FCMs) and enter into legal documentation, it is important to select clearinghouses and determine whether the clearinghouse will require specific forms (whether electronic or otherwise) for clearing derivatives. The CME requires, for clearing via Globex, the End User License Agreement, or EULA, for example.

A comprehensive set of legal documents for clearing a trade at one clearinghouse will not necessarily be suitable for clearing at another clearinghouse. The set of legal documents required for trading a derivative that is cleared through the Chicago Mercantile Exchange (CME) will differ from the set of documents necessary for clearing a derivative through the London Clearing House (LCH). For each clearinghouse, clearing member, and customer or client which clears derivatives, an individualized set of documents is contemplated; a single set is illustrated in Figure 7.1 for use with CME as the clearing house. It is highly recommended that the reader review Figure 6.1 and Figure 6.2 and the accompanying discussion.

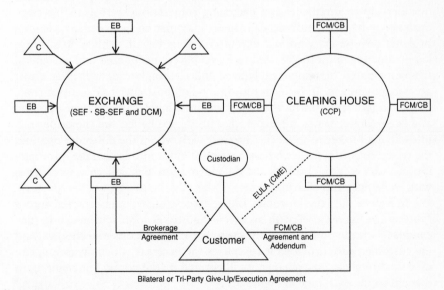

FIGURE 7.1 The Universe of Clearing Relationships and Documentation for CME Clearing

Because the old world of OTC derivatives trading did not include the concept of an "execution facility" such as a swap execution facility (a SEF, security-based stock execution facility, or designated contract market, as such terms were discussed in more detail in Chapter 4 and abbreviated in the circle to the left within Figure 7.1; the use of SEF in this chapter will refer to both swap execution facilities and security-based swap execution facilities), an executing broker (EB in Figure 7.1), a clearing member (FCM/CB), and a clearinghouse (CCP, in Figure 7.1 as detailed in Chapters 3, 4, 6 and later in Chapter 9), the first step in the process is to ensure that the proper legal documentation is in place with respect to each of these entities. The previous chapter introduced each entity and the relationships among them. A more detailed discussion of Figure 7.1 follows next.

While there are six steps within the life cycle of a cleared derivative, the steps, each described in the pages which follow, should be conceptualized within two distinct phases: execution and clearing. Chapter 3 explains the very clear distinction between the execution of a trade and the submission of that trade for clearing. This Chapter and Figure 7.1 as its preview, is described from the vantage point of the customer within the largest triangle in the lower-center of the diagram, with other customers, each represented by "C," aligned around the exchange, the circle to the left within Figure 7.1.

It is contemplated that market participants (e.g., customers, brokers, advisers, and others) may become a member of an SEF directly by meeting membership requirements and becoming subject to SEF rules. Most swap dealers will be SEF members. Customers may turn to swap dealers, clearing brokers, or advisers who will execute on their behalf (if they do so, brokerage documentation will need to be reviewed, negotiated and executed). It is anticipated that some exchanges and clearinghouses will offer direct access to members. In order for an individual customer to execute a trade on an electronic platform, the customer must have trading documentation and license agreements in place both with the exchange and the dealer (i.e. introducing broker or executing broker) with whom the customer executes the trade. Accordingly, each customer must enter into brokerage documentation with executing brokers and documentation (e.g., a license agreement) with exchanges and clearinghouses.

In Figure 7.1, the customer in the largest triangle has entered into a "Brokerage Agreement" with an executing broker to its left, which in turn can place a trade on behalf of the customer if the customer so chooses, and the customer also, provided it completes the necessary documentation, can execute directly at an exchange, as illustrated by the dotted line pointing to the left, to the exchange in Figure 7.1.

Circled around the exchange in Figure 7.1 are other customers (in triangles), which may or may not have direct access to the exchange, as well as other executing brokers, whose buy and sell orders provide market depth, or liquidity, to the exchange. This will be described further in the second phase within the life cycle of a cleared derivative.

The customer may have its own custodian that maintains its assets. Some members of the buy-side have urged the CFTC to permit customer collateral to remain in one or more accounts established and maintained by the customer's custodian, subject to clearinghouse and clearing member rights to recover such margin upon the default of the customer.

To clear via CME, the customer executes an electronic license agreement called an End User License Agreement, or EULA, which gives the customer in Figure 7.1 the right to use CME's electronic Globex platform.

As discussed in the previous chapter, if the customer executes a trade via an exchange and then is required to (or voluntarily) clears that trade, the trade must be taken up by a member of a clearinghouse that will accept that trade for clearing. To bring this about, the customer will need to enter into a clearing agreement which is, as illustrated in Figure 7.1, designated as the futures commission merchant (FCM)/clearing broker (CB) agreement. In Chapter 6, we described industry efforts in the United States to prepare a form addendum for previously cleared OTC derivatives, and that addendum is referred to as the cleared derivatives addendum (but referenced in Figure 7.1 as "the addendum"). Other customers enter into FCM/CB and addendum sets with other clearing brokers connected to the clearinghouse with a line, which symbolizes the members' compliance with clearinghouse rules and applicable law.

The author emphasizes that there are variations to Figure 7.1 with respect to market structure and documentation requirements—it is expected that such structure and requirements will evolve over time. As one variation, the CME ClearPort clearing system allows access by different means: by broker entry (either using a third-party matching interface or the manner illustrated in Figure 7.1, through a clearing broker) or by means of the CME Facilitation Desk which actively interfaces with the buyer and seller to every trade prior to the trade being submitted to the clearinghouse.

Step One is quite important for many reasons, several of which have been discussed here. The most fundamental point to be made is that, without executing the proper documentation with an executing broker, trading will not be "enabled," and the customer cannot pass to the second step of the cleared derivatives life cycle.

STEP TWO: TRADE EXECUTION VIA AN SEF, SB-SEF, OR DCM

The second step in the life cycle of a cleared derivative transaction is trade execution. At the outset, it is important to understand what is meant by the term "execution." When the term execution is used in the context of the post-Dodd-Frank market for U.S. derivatives, the term means the acceptance of offers to buy or sell made through an SEF or other exchange or regulated system.

U.S. regulators have proposed a range of rules to govern trade execution, which, once finalized, may change the trade execution phase (or other phases in this chapter). This part of the chapter builds on the information provided in Chapter 4, in which the author indicated that the SEC will have jurisdiction over single-name credit default swaps (CDS) and equity derivatives (but not most equity options which are generally outside of Dodd-Frank), and the CFTC will have jurisdiction over broad-based index CDS, interest rate derivatives, most currency derivatives, and broad-based equity index derivatives.

Therefore, depending on the derivative (i.e., either a swap or security-based swap), the appropriate regulator mandates, for that product, an SEF (or, in the case of security-based swaps, a security-based SEF) to be used for trade execution. Once mandated, the CFTC (for swaps) and SEC (for security-based swaps) may require, as discussed below, requests for quotes from a minimum number of executing brokers (the CFTC at least initially proposed rules which would require five or more price providers; the SEC did not propose a minimum number of counterparties to a trade).

It may not be that all trades are mandated for clearing and execution on an SEF. According to early rule proposals by the U.S. regulators, if a trade is not mandated for central clearing (and the end user exemption is not available, as discussed in Chapter 4), and no other exemption to the mandate for SEF-based trading applies, the trade must be executed via a regulated market such as an SEF (or security-based SEF).

It is also important at the outset of the Step Two discussion to understand what policy makers intended to accomplish at this step in the cleared derivatives life cycle. In the bilateral OTC derivatives market that existed before Dodd-Frank, price discovery and trade negotiation took place on a private, largely unregulated basis in a manner that permitted customization and flexible trading. However, an opaque, interconnected market fraught with counterparty and systemic risk developed. See Chapter 1, Seven Causes of the 2008 Market Crises.

Much like bond trading before the introduction of TRACE (also discussed in Chapter 1), OTC derivatives trading historically existed in generally an opaque market that was vulnerable to price distortion, the development of disputes over valuation and, ultimately, in 2008, widespread OTC market seizures, at least with respect to certain derivatives and structured products such as collateralized debt obligations.

The events of 2008 precipitated the adoption of the futures model that was the subject of Chapter 3. In futures markets, trading takes place on exchanges that are regulated and far more transparent, at least when compared to the OTC derivative market.

The second step in the life cycle of cleared derivatives is, therefore, a significant departure from the bilateral, more negotiable way in which trades are executed—for a few reasons. First, it is more transparent because, as we discuss in Chapter 9, the trading venue is electronically based and accessible in real time by numerous market participants and, by design, regulators.

Futures exchanges, which policy makers used as models to a great extent for post-reform trading, generally utilize limit order book trading models that match buyers and sellers using computer algorithms. Dodd-Frank requires that all derivatives mandated for central clearing to also be traded on an SEF. According to the CFTC's proposed regulations to govern SEFs, they are to employ a central limit order book model (or CLOB) or a request for quote (RFQ) model, according to rules proposed but not finalized by the time this book went to print.[1]

The CFTC further proposed that a market participant that utilizes an RFQ be required to send its trade request to at least five market participants; the SEC's proposal on the same subject does not require broad communication of trading interest, which some believe would conceivably increase hedging costs.[2]

By comparison, OTC derivatives trading to date has generally taken place by means of voice brokering via telephone, or by means of order book or RFQ trading models that employ electronic communication management technology.

Similar to SEF-based execution in the manner in which two parties to an ISDA (the subject of discussion in the first part of Chapter 6) engage in OTC derivatives trading, single dealer and electronic trading platforms have been the principal means for negotiating derivatives. This mode of negotiation was generally rejected by the mandates imposed by Dodd-Frank, which include mandates to bring about a more transparent market, a deeper market with more dealers offering a greater range of trades, as well as trade pricing. A central objective of organized electronic trading platforms in the post-reform trading environment is therefore pricing competition. By bringing together more market participants via an electronic trading venue, more providers of liquidity are available, thereby reducing many of the market deficiencies described in Chapter 1 and possibly the likelihood of future market seizures.

Lawmakers and regulators in the United States now require regulated trade execution not only for improved transparency and better pricing, but also operational efficiency, (including error prevention mechanisms in the processing of paper trade confirmations, as discussed in the previous chapter).

An additional objective of Dodd-Frank's SEF mandate is to make monitoring and regulating of OTC derivatives by regulators (such as the SEC and CFTC, as well as the other regulators introduced at the outset of Chapter 4) more feasible. Organized platforms are intended to provide the time stamping of trade executions, orders, and expressions of trading interest that give regulators visibility to detect market manipulation and other market abuses.

While the objectives of lawmakers in requiring electronic platforms like SEFs are clear, less clear in the post Dodd-Frank environment (at the time this book went to print) is what exactly the SEFs must do, and whether, in reality, SEFs will perform as mandated in Dodd-Frank. This text presumes that there will be multiple SEFs that will eventually bring about a vibrant market that gives its participants a broad range of choices in trade execution, both at a low cost and in a transparent manner compared to OTC trading, or, at least this was the intent of Title VII of Dodd-Frank.

SEFs will be available to a wide range of qualified market participants with rules for access that are objectively set and applied in practice. Dodd-Frank requires SEFs to comply with certain enumerated Core Principle introduced in Chapter 4, and these platforms will be subject to regulation also as described in Chapters 4 and 5. SEFs will be expected to provide connectivity to swap data repositories (SDRs), which are also described in greater detail in Chapter 4 and later in this chapter.

The reader, perhaps at this point, wonders why this discussion does not describe in sharp detail what exactly an SEF is and how it operates. This is a function of the drafters of Dodd-Frank providing such a broad (and vague) mandate for SEF-based trading. According to the text of Dodd-Frank, Title VII, an SEF is the following:

> [A] *trading system or platform in which multiple participants have the ability to execute or trade by accepting bids or offers made by multiple participants in the facility or system through any means of interstate commerce, including any facility that facilitates the execution of swaps between persons; and is not a designated contract market.*[3]

The takeaway is that Dodd-Frank does not rigidly mandate a single execution facility that merely allows one party to buy and one party to sell. Instead, Dodd-Frank establishes a framework for regulation in order to fine-tune three distinctly different functions: trading, trade processing, and execution. By trading it appears that SEFs are intended to facilitate the "interaction of multiple bids or multiple offers."[4] This is to take place, in practice, by a computer algorithm. Execution is, as the term implies, the acceptance of bids or offers, and trade processing is the electronic communication of proposed, accepted, and confirmed derivative trades.[5]

The Precursors to SEFs

The earliest entrants into the SEF market were Bloomberg L.P. (Bloomberg) and Javelin Capital Markets (Javelin). Both registered for clearance to operate as SEFs for certain categories of derivatives in early 2011. Javelin, the later of the two entrants, executed its first cleared interest rate swap through International Derivatives Clearing Group, LLC (IDCG), on a pilot basis, in 2010.[6]

Bloomberg publishes analytics and data as this book went to print on five million financial instruments and is a leading financial media outlet,[7] and has, for at least 13 years, operated its Bond Trader System, an RFQ system for government securities. Bloomberg positioned that system (along with Bloomberg's Fixed Income Trading Platform, or FIT) as a precursor to the SEF in the post Dodd-Frank market. FIT, which is Bloomberg's electronic trade execution facility, is the foundation for the Bloomberg SEF. Prior to its SEF becoming operational, on March 30, 2011, Bloomberg executives disclosed that J.P. Morgan utilized FIT to electronically execute and clear interest rate swaps and credit default swaps (CDS).[8]

CDS dealers have ticketed trades on Bloomberg using its VCON, or CDXT technology, which supports new trades, unwinds, and assignments of trades.[9] VCON and Bloomberg's CDXT technology (referred to here simply as "VCON") provides the derivatives market one example of how dealers electronically recap certain CDS, including single-name- and index-based CDS. It is important to clarify that Bloomberg's FIT and VCON are not SEFs and were not proposed by Bloomberg to be SEFs, but in fact use technology in a way that may be similar to an SEF approved by the CFTC (as of the date on which this book went to print, no SEF had been approved by the CFTC).

Entering a Trade in an SEF

A new trade entered into an SEF will be entered in much the same way as the trade is submitted for processing in pre-SEF Bloomberg technologies such as VCON and FIT:

- After a dealer and its client negotiate the terms of a CDS, Bloomberg's VCON platform, which may possess trade-processing characteristics similar to other SEF platforms, enables the dealer to enter counterparty information into the platform.

- Counterparty information entered into the VCON platform includes the dealer's client name, contact information, buy or sell direction of the client, and information relating to a prime broker if such a broker exists and assists with the trade for the client.
- If the trade is mandated for central clearing, the VCON platform interfaces with clearinghouses and includes additional fields for additional information, including the name of the clearinghouse, the clearinghouse identifier, and, if the dealer is the member of the clearinghouse and self-clears, then the dealer's name is also entered into VCON. While VCON defaults to the dealer as the member that self-clears the trade, other clearing members may be designated.
- Entry of derivative information. The next step in using the VCON platform is the entry of the key terms of the derivative trade (e.g., ticker/reference entity symbol, currency, trade date, effective date, maturity of trade, and whether restructuring is agreed upon as a credit event, and information about the coupon (a pull-down menu is available for standard CDS such as the SNAC 100 or 500).
- Calculations. The dealer inputs the spread, upfront percentage, and collateral details.
- Proposed trade is communicated to dealer's client for execution.

An SEF enters a trade initiated by a customer or adviser who uses technology that is similar to the FIT (Fixed Income Trading) Bloomberg technology (which, as of the date this book went to print, is still contemplated to be used for trades that are not mandated for execution at an SEF or security-based SEF). The FIT platform has dropdown menus for various markets within which derivatives trade. Dealers code-up, or join, platforms such as FIT before the regulators have approved SEFs (this is likely because dealers view their participation in SEF-based markets as inevitable).

As with FIT, it is expected that Bloomberg will reference a table listing the types of underliers, or securities and the trades that are subject to the mandatory SEF requirement. For interest rate swaps which are already traded via existing Bloomberg technology, the platform shows, with respect to credit default swaps and interest rate swaps, multiple dealers (illustrating a deep pool of market liquidity). Multiple pricing types are also displayed in different colors in the FIT platform:

- Firm (designated by magenta; traders can click and trade these and the dealer on the other side of the trade will accept the trade all or nearly all of the time).
- Executable and enabled (designated by blue).
- Indicative pricing (orange).

The customer can click on a dealer's price and a single dealer's order ticket will be generated; Bloomberg technology enables that ticket to be changed to an RFQ or inquiry to that dealer if the customer desires.

The technology enables traders to launch an RFQ to up to five dealers (whether or not required by the CFTC by final rule). Traders may ask their broker to "price up" a trade by sending an inquiry ticket and then, in return, electronically, the customer will get a set period of time (for example, three or five seconds) to accept the broker's offered price for the trade.

The trade ticket is automatically populated with standard terms and by clicking "submit," Bloomberg technology users submit the trade to the dealer (also at this stage, in Step Two, the customer may indicate whether the trade is to be cleared and if so, which clearinghouse will be utilized for clearing; designation of a clearing member is not necessary or required at this stage).

The next phase in the life cycle of the post Dodd-Frank derivatives trade is the use of a trade matching utility that enables both sides to the trade to communicate and confirm acceptance before the trade is readied for clearing by a clearing member.

STEP THREE: ALLEGING AND AFFIRMING A TRADE; REPORTING IN REAL TIME

The final step in the execution phase, before we clear the trade, is the electronic generation of a trade ticket, and the alleging and affirmation of the trade to confirm trade details. Once this has taken place, it can be said that the trade is "executed."

After the pricing of a trade is determined and initial trade processing begins to move forward towards settlement, it is contemplated that real-time reporting of a legally-binding trade will take place. Reporting takes place at two stages in the cleared derivatives life cycle: first, upon execution, and later, in the clearing stage.[10]

In the pre-SEF electronic market, parties on sides of the same trade use Bloomberg VCON, MarkitWire, FEC, or some other utility (also referred to as middleware or an affirmation platform) to do the following:

1. **Allege the Trade.** The dealer or executing broker in our prior example regarding the Bloomberg VCON or CDXT platform proposes, or alleges the terms of the trade matched (via the SEFs matching process.
2. **Affirm the Trade.** The client of the executing broker receives the broker's alleged trade and either affirms the trade or rejects it as deficient (i.e.,

one or more of the alleged trade details are incorrect or do not reflect the trade matched via the SEF).

3. **Assign the Trade to a Clearing Member.** If affirmed, the client (as a counterparty to the executing broker) then assigns a clearing member to clear the affirmed/matched trade.

As the final stages of execution, the dealer finishes populating the trade details and VCON communicates to the client's Bloomberg terminal, and the client receives, a pop-up notice that includes those trade details, and a very short period of time to elect to proceed with the trade.

At that point, the client can press the [CALC] button on the pop-up notice to view the underlying to the CDS trade and then, after confirming the other CDS trade details, the client can press the button marked [AFFIRM] to positively acknowledge or affirm the trade. In accomplishing these steps, a cleared derivative has been electronically confirmed between the two parties, and a legally-enforceable executed trade results.

In our example regarding the Bloomberg VCON-based platform, both the dealer and its client (or, alternatively, the executing broker and its counterparty) may monitor their trade by means of the VCON platform. In the Bloomberg system, a matched and affirmed trade is moved to the Matched/Affirmed Trades panel.

Once that occurs, the CDS trade will be designated for clearing at, for example, CME's ClearPort Clearing Service, and the trade may then be allocated.

VCON and other services enable the parties to the trade to monitor in real time both sides at the allocation stage, and the status of the trade or trades throughout the life of the trade cycle.[11]

STEP FOUR: THE FCM TAKE-UP

In the fourth phase of the life cycle of a cleared derivatives trade, once a cleared derivative has been negotiated and its details successfully alleged and affirmed, then a member of a clearinghouse is assigned, the trade is executed and then the trade is given up to that member (if the executing broker or its affiliate is not also a member of the clearinghouse where the trade is to be cleared).

If the clearing member is not the end user/customer's counterparty to the trade executed via the SEF, then a clearing member must take up the trade executed between the end user/customer and executing broker. That process is, as discussed in the previous chapter, evidenced in an agreement referred to as a give-up (or execution) agreement. In a three-way give-up agreement, the three parties to the agreement are the end user/customer (the client in the CDS example previously discussed), the counterparty to the client in the trade executed via the SEF, and the clearing member/FCM of the end user/customer.

The industry, as represented in significant part by the FIA, undertook a lengthy process from 2010 to 2011 to complete a model standardized legal documentation for cleared U.S. derivatives (a summary of that effort is provided in Chapter 6). The FIA effort, in which the author of this text participated, saw the evolution of the give-up agreement from a trilateral agreement to a bilateral agreement between the executing broker and the counterparty to the trade executed via the SEF (and then a bilateral agreement with trilateral annexes). While a detailed discussion concerning that evolution is outside the scope of this chapter, the upshot of a trilateral arrangement is that it entitles a clearing member (FCM or clearing member) or the executing broker to have recourse for losses sustained if a trade does not clear and has to be terminated. The end user/customer would have recourse against the clearing member under the FCM Agreement (discussed in Chapter 6).

At this stage in the life cycle of a cleared derivatives trade, the FCM/clearing member undertakes a credit check of the end user/customer to ensure that applicable positions limits are not exceeded. The FCM/clearing member may also determine if the end user/customer is sufficiently creditworthy before the FCM/clearing member takes up the trade from the executing broker and end user/customer.

If the FCM/clearing member wishes to proceed to clear the trade, it submits the trade to the central clearinghouse where the FCM/clearing member is admitted as a member. (A discussion of the process whereby a clearing member or FCM becomes a member of a clearinghouse is provided in Chapter 3).

STEP FIVE: TRADE IS CENTRALLY CLEARED

After the clearing member ensures that its customer is in full compliance with applicable position limits (discussed in Chapter 4), and conducts other checks, and other legal and contractual requirements are satisfied, the trade is submitted to the clearinghouse by means of an electronic platform, such as MarkitSERV or other electronic interface, and a notification is provided by the clearinghouse (which may or may not accept the trade for clearing).

Along with providing the status of alleged trades and whether trades are affirmed, services like MarkitSERV enable the end user/customer, the executing broker, and the derivatives clearing member/FCM to monitor, in real time, the status of each trade, at each step in the life cycle of cleared derivative trades.[12]

A Clearinghouse May Reject a Trade

There are instances where a clearinghouse will reject a trade. CME states in its rules dealing with OTC derivative clearing that it will only accept a derivative for clearing if the trade is within the bounds set by the CME, which imposes these and other requirements, namely, that the trade:

- Satisfies the contract specifications.
- Is submitted by an authorized clearing member which is in compliance with clearing rules.
- Does not cause the clearing member's position limits to be exceeded.[13]

CME will reject a trade, for example, if it:

- Conflicts with information received by CME by another service.
- Is incomplete or erroneous or appears to be a result of a technology error or other problem.
- Is required to be terminated by a regulatory authority.[14]

Clearinghouses may also amend or revoke position limits for clearing members, and may refuse to clear a trade if the clearinghouse determines that the clearing member is in breach of clearinghouse rules.[15]

In the event that a clearinghouse accepts a trade for clearing, the clearinghouse calls for initial margin as a pre-condition to accepting a trade. Chapter 3 provides a more detailed discussion of the process whereby a trade is margined.

Initial margin and variation margin requirements originate from the clearinghouse but are guided and directed by applicable law. A third form of margin, excess margin, is in some cases required by the clearing member from the end user/customer under clearing member house rules.

Trades Are Margined

In the event that a clearinghouse declines to clear a trade, the clearinghouse notifies the clearing member that submitted the trade, at which point the trade may be "ported," or submitted through a different clearing member (this may take place if, for example, the initial clearing member is out of compliance with clearinghouse rules causing the clearinghouse to reject the trade).

If the trade cannot be ported or transferred to a different clearing member in that instance, and if the trade must then be terminated, losses then are to be calculated (while Chapter 6 provides a basic outline of the relevant legal documentation, it cannot and should not be deemed to be legal advice; qualified and licensed counsel should in this instance be sought, as such counsel should be retained throughout the life cycle of cleared trades).

STEP SIX: THE TRADE IS REPORTED FOR THE SECOND TIME

As described in greater detail in Chapter 4, cleared derivative trades are to be reported and monitored, and open trades are to be settled by means of offsetting remaining amounts due under the terms of the trade as executed via the SEF against posted amounts of initial and variation margin (i.e., accounts which include, for example, one account holding posted margin for the end user/customer, and the other for the counterparty to the end user/customer in the trade executed via the SEF).

Reporting obligations in centrally-cleared trades are as follows:

- Upon trade execution, **SEFs** are to make available public price information, trading volume, and other information prescribed by the CFTC (security-based SEFs are to publicly report as required by the SEC).
- **Swap dealers** and **major swap participants** (and security-based swap dealers and major security-based swap participants) are to report on items specified by regulators (the SEC and CFTC or applicable prudential regulators) and maintain daily trading records (see Chapter 4).

* * *

The foregoing 6 steps described in this chapter are meant to provide an early outline of the important phases in the execution and clearing of a derivative in the derivatives market that exists or in some cases *will* exist in the United States *after* the implementation of Dodd-Frank. As the life cycle and regulatory requirements along the way will change over time in a very dynamic regulatory environment, the reader is encouraged to visit www.DerivativesGuide.com.

NOTES

1. Core Principles and Other Requirements for Swap Execution Facilities, CFTC, *Federal Register*, January 7, 2011.
2. Securities and Exchange Commission Release No. 34 638925, at CFR Parts 240, 242, and 249.
3. Dodd-Frank Section 721.
4. Ibid.
5. See Dodd-Frank Section 733.
6. "Javelin Swap Execution Facility Names Hisler and Koppenheffer as CDS and IRS Heads," www.thejavelin.com, February 22, 2011.
7. Ben MacDonald letter of April 4, 2011, to secretary Elizabeth Murphy, Securities and Exchange Commission.
8. Ivy Schmerken, "JP Morgan Executes and Clears CDS and IRS Trades via Bloomberg Professional," *Wall Street Technology*, March 30, 2011.
9. Bloomberg, *CDXT <GO> User Guide: The Fastest Way to Ticket CDS Trades on Bloomberg*, www.cmegroup.com/trading/cds/files/Bloomberg-VCON-CDXT-CME-CDS-User-Guide.pdf.
10. Blackrock, Presentation to the CFTC Technology Advisory Committee (TAC), Dodd-Frank Derivatives Regulation Interconnectivity, March 1, 2011.
11. *Bloomberg CDXT<GO> User Guide*, 7.
12. "Preparing for OTC Derivatives Clearing," MarkitSERV, June 10, 2010, www.markitserv.com/ms-en/media-centre/preparing-for-otc-derivatives-clearing.page.
13. CME Clearing Rules, Section 5.1.3.
14. CME Clearing Rules, Section 5.1.4(a)(b)(d).
15. CME Clearing Rules Sections 5.1.6 and 5.1.4(c)

Three

Trading Before and After Reform

CHAPTER 8

The History of Derivatives and Futures

We study history in a serious way to prevent the recurrence of mistakes. To some, derivatives reform after the 2008 market crises was driven by the *mistaken* belief that derivatives actually caused the crises, and therefore need to be reformed. Derivatives reform in the United States is now both extensive and comprehensive. To many, this is simply a mistake.

To the extent reform is grounded in a belief or philosophy that derivatives are inherently dangerous, then such reform was, is and will be misguided. Derivatives are no more inherently dangerous and destructive than fire. Ok, fires have caused damage! To generations of humans, fire has however been a productive, necessary force of nature. Like fire, the derivative has been used, misused, and the cause of loss since the beginning of time, or at least since early recorded history, as this chapter illustrates.

Early recorded history provides numerous examples of how traders and others in ancient and modern commerce have used and misused derivatives–for thousands of years. Risk is an integral part of commerce, and because derivatives are exceedingly useful in allocating and managing risk, derivatives have been a part of commerce throughout the ages.

Derivatives have also been the subject of regulation. Over the years, as governments imposed restrictions to rein in speculative derivatives, for hundreds of years traders have circumvented those regulations–or attempted to do so. As traders and financial technology sidestepped law and regulation, market excesses led to crises. Market crises involving derivatives have existed for thousands of years and, indeed, like business cycles, occur and reoccur time and again.

The purpose of this chapter is to provide an extensive historical context, presented chronologically in the pages that follow, for understanding current legislative and regulatory initiatives, which make more sense when viewed as one continuous series of events following all that has transpired in ancient and modern commerce.

The historical summary of derivatives provided in this chapter is a product of my numerous visits to the Library of Congress in Washington, DC over the years to supplement previous research and practical experience. It is hoped that when the reader of this chapter learns that people entered into contracts hundreds of years ago to allocate risks of loss arising out of, for example shipwrecks, the reader will see in those contracts similarities with credit default swaps discussed later in the chapter. As risk existed at the beginning of time, so, too, must have derivatives.

The term derivatives found its way into the vernacular of our modern legal system in the U.S. in the early 1980s. Some experts in the historical use of derivatives point to the first use of derivatives in 1982 by the prominent U.S. federal court, the Federal District Court for the Southern District of New York, which published one decision which includes this discussion:

> When exercised, options on physicals lead to the delivery of the physical commodity itself; thus they are "first derivative" instruments but one step removed from the underlying commodity. Options on futures are "second derivative" instruments which give rise only to delivery of a futures contract, a contractual undertaking which can be transferred to third parties to buy or sell a fixed amount and grade of a certain commodity on some specified date.[1]

The word derivatives makes its first appearance in English reported case law in 1995.[2] The second edition of the *Oxford English Dictionary* did not include a definition of "derivatives" for use in commercial contexts, and reported that decisions of courts in the United States first included the term only in the early 1980s.[3] The use of the word derivative, in fact, followed many thousands of years after the earliest uses of the financial instrument, as we shall see. As late as 1993, *The Oxford Dictionary for the Business World* defined derivative to mean a "financial instrument valued according to the expected price movements of an underlying asset, e.g., a commodity, currency" and the dictionary defines derivative market as a "futures or options market derived from a cash market."[4]

As we will soon see, the exchange of promises and allocation of risk in that exchange is sufficient to constitute a derivative in the most technical sense of the word, however, this chapter makes the point that these exchanges and thus derivatives must have existed in the beginning of time, and so did derivative-related losses and so derivatives reform pre-dated Dodd-Frank

THE EARLIEST DERIVATIVE

Many of the derivatives we will read about in the pages that follow, including those that were evidenced by clay tablets thousands of years old, were forward transactions. In this chapter, we describe in much greater detail the derivative known as a forward. For purposes of understanding the earliest derivatives, a brief summary of a forward is provided here.

A forward is, like many other derivatives, a promise for something to take place in the future. Adding more detail, the transaction is a legally enforceable contract calling for the sale of a specific quantity of a commodity at an agreed-upon price with the settlement (delivery) of that commodity occurring at some point in the future. Examples of this were provided in the Introduction.

To further illustrate, we consider a commercial airline company. The company needs fuel. It needs certainty with respect to the price of that fuel, because fuel prices fluctuate. You might enter into a forward with a dealer of derivatives that would manage the risk of the fluctuation in jet fuel prices over time. For a premium, the dealer would sell you a forward, or a promise that, if the price of the fuel exceeds an agreed-upon level, the dealer will pay you a certain amount of money that will compensate you for the amount that you would otherwise pay due to the increase in the price of jet fuel. By entering into this forward, the airline may, in essence, fix its jet fuel expenses by paying a premium for the dealer to assume the risk of an increase in those expenses. In this example, the exchange of a premium takes place now, and the payment by the dealer takes place forward in time.

Instead of forwards relating to jet fuel, the earliest transactions involved barley, and later the subject of derivatives included slaves, soldiers, and, in the earliest instances of utter misuse of these transactions, wives.

Before taking the chronological tour of the historical development of derivatives, a few observations are in order. The survey that follows is intended to touch on only some of the highlights of the development of these financial tools, especially as they relate to current derivatives reform. The reader looking for a comprehensive, historical survey is directed to lengthy, exceptional works that provide exactly that.[5] History is only as accurate as the person who tells it. I am solely responsible for any mistakes in this chapter—and, indeed, in all of this text.

TREES, FORESTS, AND WILDFIRES

Trees, forests, and wildfire destroying forests provide a somewhat helpful analogy to describe not only the destruction of markets, but also the derivatives traded within them.

If a large tree is cut at its foundation, the cross-section will show years and years of growth, with each ring evidencing growth around the ring that developed before it.

Like a massive tree stump and a vast forest of redwoods, derivatives and the markets within which they trade are awesome in terms of size and growth. If we look at just one of the many trees in that forest and examine the rings in a cross-section of it, the earliest years and development of that redwood—and of each derivative—are more easily understood. Rather than experiencing bewilderment when viewing that growth and the sheer, awesome size of the $615 trillion global derivatives market (in 2009), we need to view each tree, or a group of trees within the derivatives forest, and see the development over time.

Taking the analogy of trees a few steps further, the market for derivatives may appear as a vast forest of redwoods, and the most complex derivative, the collateralized debt obligation (CDO), is like a massive redwood that stretches miles into the sky. The CDO is introduced in Chapter 1 and discussed further in Chapter 10.

In order to understand derivatives, futures, and the innovations that led to the current products, it is important to see how adjustments to the products were necessitated over time by forces of geography, national security, economics, the environment, and even the weather. By reading this chapter, as well as Chapters 3 and 10, a greater appreciation of the current law, products and markets will be acquired.

Themes within Derivatives History

Within the historical perspective provided in this chapter, the reader will see a clear, panoramic view of how governments have regulated derivatives and futures over time, the results of that regulation, and the way in which we can bring about the proper use of derivatives today.

There are two primary themes that develop in our survey:

1. Derivatives arose out of the need to manage risks, such as the adverse movement of commodity prices and the opportunity to profit by assuming those risks. These commercial needs have likely existed since the beginning of time.
2. Global regulation of derivatives is developing in a coordinated way for the first time in the history of the world because unregulated risk-taking presents a threat to the now interlocked global economy.

The history of derivatives and of futures within the broader category of derivatives is so vast and generally undocumented that many relatively recent articles point to the late twentieth century as the starting point for these instruments. For example, a 1994 article in *Time*, "How the Game Began," included the statement "The business of derivatives can be traced back to Chicago..."[6] Many financial historians believe that the first derivative, an interest-rate swap, was executed between the World Bank and IBM Corporation in 1981.[7]

Derivatives were used many thousands of years before Chicago became an American city. Pinpointing with absolute precision the first derivative is an impossible task for a number of reasons. History has blind spots. Some periods of time were not recorded or were recorded on records that were subject to conflicting translations, or the historical record includes other gaps due to many factors. Financial historians believe that, although Chinese civilization has one of the longest histories and has enjoyed the earliest technological advances and had the first, most developed economy, historical records of finance in the early years of China are deficient in many respects.[8] Problems in historical records from Europe emerge according to one historian because European authors may have deliberately refused to record financial abuses.[9]

Accordingly, because ancient records from the Far East are not available, the summary that follows relies on early Middle Eastern and Western history.

DID THEY EXIST IN ANTIQUITY?

Buying and selling commodities has taken place for many thousands of years. Commodities, such as grains and livestock, were the subjects of transactions that, if settled today, would be considered forwards or futures contracts. Those who produced commodities frequently entered into arrangements whereby the foodstuffs and other commodities which they expected to bring to market would be purchased ahead of time in order to minimize the risk of adverse fluctuations in commodity pricing and also to get around storage and infrastructure problems which existed at the time.

The history of financial instruments such as derivatives and the markets within which they trade is, first and foremost, a history of the barter system: centuries of exchanges of goods and services needed by one party with those required by another. Over time, the methods and products of that exchange have become increasingly sophisticated but, like the base of a massive redwood tree, the beginnings are quite simple, and understanding it is important to developing an appreciation for the way financial products are traded and regulated today.

OTC AND EXCHANGE DERIVATIVES

Two markets for derivatives developed from the beginning of time to the present day: the over-the-counter (OTC) market and a market represented more formally by an exchange. We discuss these markets in depth in

Chapters 3 and 10. The concern of a producer, such as a farmer, to obtain remuneration now for what the farmer will produce in the future gave rise to a derivative that is today referred to as a forward. Although forward purchases between individuals outside any formal market are simply referred to as forwards, standardized forward arrangements that take the form of contracts that are exchanged on a market are called futures. In the pages that follow, we will rather easily see that products that today are referred to as commodity futures, in fact, existed for hundreds of years or even many centuries, and were traded by means of forwards over time.

The market for forward contracts included numerous buyers and sellers who entered into a very straightforward arrangement, calling for one to buy and the other to sell. The agreement between them also called for delivery of the subject of the bargain at some point in the future. The agreement bound the seller to deliver and the buyer to tender the consideration, or money, in exchange for delivery. Generally, no money changed hands at the point of contract. There was little more to it than that.

In the earliest days of these contracts, every feature of the arrangement was separately negotiated; there were no standardized contracts (which are the hallmark of a futures contract and futures market today). In the ancient forward market, just as is the case today, nearly every term was customized, including the price, quantity, and quality of the goods that are the subject of the forward.

The forward market, compared to today's futures market, involved so much more in the way of transaction costs, from the start to the finish of the contract. A buyer had to locate a seller, and once they found each other, each term was negotiated. Markets existed at fairs, wharfs, and churches in large cities, but not throughout the countryside. Parties to a trade were typically not subject to market rules or conventions.

As the forward market became more organized, the market gradually evolved into today's futures exchange, with traders entering into contracts with standardized terms and trading conventions. Over time, formal, organized exchanges developed, but now we are getting ahead of ourselves.

BACK TO BIBLICAL TIMES

Our starting point, controversial to some perhaps, is the Old Testament book of Genesis, where, unbeknownst to Jacob, he enters into arguably the first recorded derivative, an option to marry. Some view this arrangement as a forward. The key differences are described in Chapter 10. Also significant is that Jacob's transaction, whatever we call it today, later is subject to the first breach of a derivative and settlement of that breach—it's all in Genesis.

To understand that first forward, a short summary would be helpful. In Genesis 29, within the Old Testament of the Bible, we find Old Testament stalwart Jacob as he takes a journey to the land of the people of the east, where he comes upon a well covered with a stone. Sheep tended by Rachel are nearby. Jacob removes the stone to enable Rachel's sheep to drink water.

Rachel and Jacob discover that they are cousins and Jacob is invited to stay with Rachel's father, Laban. Laban was the father of two daughters, Rachel, and Leah, the elder of the two. Over time, after Jacob demonstrates his work ethic and worthiness, Jacob and Laban discuss wages for Jacob's labor. Jacob, who by this time has fallen in love with Rachel, proposes to work for Laban for seven years in return for the right to marry Rachel. Laban apparently agrees, and an option for Jacob to have the hand of Rachel in marriage was executed.

Laban and Jacob's arrangement is therefore the world's first physically settled, European option executed OTC. The trade date for this derivative is around 1700 B.C. and the settlement date is seven years after the trade date.

Seven years pass, a short time for Jacob, as "they seemed unto him but a few days, for the love he had to her."[10] On the date of settlement of the first, earliest recorded derivative in written history, Laban holds a celebratory feast and later in the evening arranges for Jacob to wed not Rachel, as originally arranged, but Leah, concealed by a veil. Breach!

The morning after, Jacob approaches Laban. "What is this thou has done to me? Did not I serve with thee for Rachel? Wherefore then thou hast beguiled me?"[11] Laban's reply brings into question the legality of the option written by Laban and held by Jacob seven years ago. Laban tells Jacob that a father's giving the hand of a second-born to marriage is not "so done in our country" and so now that Jacob has married one daughter, Laban persuades Jacob to work another seven years for another, Rachel. Following the first option, physical settlement, default, and subsequent option for Jacob to marry Rachel after seven more years of labor, the Old Testament tells us that in the end, that Jacob's arrangements resulted in two wives and 12 sons thought to be the patriarchs of the 12 tribes of Israel.

Ancient scripture includes other descriptions of derivatives and risk management. The earliest civilizations were agrarian societies and risk, of course, certainly did exist and, just as they are today, derivatives were tools to manage, or hedge that risk. Commentators point to the Old Testament and early hedging by an Egyptian pharaoh:

The Egyptian Pharaoh was concerned over a dream he had in which seven healthy cows were consumed by seven sickly cows, and seven healthy ears of corn were consumed by seven sickly ears. The Pharaoh called upon Joseph to interpret the dream. Joseph explained that the dream indicated seven years of plenty, to be followed by seven years of famine. The financially astute Pharaoh, wanting to hedge the risk of famine, proceeded to buy and store huge quantities of corn, allowing Egypt to prosper during the years of famine.[12]

Although the details are not precise, traders in the Biblical era used derivatives as we know them today, in ways that resemble the Malawi derivative described in the Introduction.

The New Stone Age

The earliest use of derivatives by the inhabitants of Mesopotamia were generally driven by the need to secure a food supply and obtain slave labor, according to historians.[13] Ancient records evidence agreements for the future delivery of rights to people and commodities. Historians found that around 2800 B.C., the Sumerians, a southern Mesopotamian people that lived in present-day Iraq, developed a form of writing based on linear cuneiform script.[14]

The contracts were evidenced in triangular, wedge-shaped script, called cuneiform, thought to be used by trained scribes documenting domestic and international transactions that likely involved market participants in what is now referred to as the Middle East, but also included Crete, Cyprus, and the Aegean islands.[15] Western antiquities expert Christopher Walker indicates that the vast majority—approximately 85 percent—of early clay tablets document economic transactions involving income and expenditures of ancient temples in a location today which is modern Iraq. Commodities, domestic animals, and cloth are the subjects of those transactions.[16]

Christopher Walker, Assistant Keeper within the Department of Western Antiquities of the British Museum, translated the earliest barley contract and the first bearer bond for the delivery of slaves in the future.

Translation of an Early Barley Forward, circa 1700 B.C.

Three kurru of barley, in the seah-meausre of Shamash, the meshequ measure.

In storage, Anum-pisha and Namran-sharur, the sons of Sinid-dianam have received from the naditu-priestess Iltani, the Kin's daughter.

At harvest time they will return the seah-meausre of Shamash, the mesheque measure, to the storage container from which they took it. Before Belshunu son of Shamash-bani. Before Ibni-Marduk son of Saniqpi-Shamash.

Month Ulul, 19th day, year in which King Abieshuh completed a statute of Entemena as god.[17]

Translation of a Forward to Purchase Rights to Slaves, circa 1700 B.C.

2042/3 qu of oil in the measure of Shamash, to the value of 1/3 mina 2/3 shekels of silver, as the price of healthy slaves from Gutium, Warad-Marduk son of Ibni-Marduk has received from Utul-Ishar the troop-commander on the authority of Lu-Ishurra son of Ili-usati.

Within one month he shall bring healthy slaves from Gutium. If he does not bring them within one month, Lu-Ishkurra son of Ili-usati will repay 1/3 mina 2/3 shekels of silver to the bearer of this tablet. Before Ilshu-ibni son of Sineribam.

Before Iluna son of Ipqusha. Before Belshunu son of Ilshubani. Before Ipqatum son of Taribum. Month Ab, 6th day, year in which King Ammisaduqa, the faithful obedient Shepard of Shamash and Marduk, etc.[18]

These records suggest the existence of a market of forward transactions calling for the delivery of commodities and slaves.

Questions Surrounding Early Derivatives

The details of this market and the manner in which transactions were executed are unclear and questions vastly outnumber answers. Why were derivatives used, and were these transactions entered into verbally? Where did the negotiations take place? Between whom? Who wrote the 30-sign cuneiform script on clay? Were all transactions reduced to a written form? How were these transactions settled and when was currency first used in settlement? Although many of the important details of early derivative transactions are beyond the scope of this appendix and the book, some features of these early transactions bear mentioning.

In Edward J. Swan's excellent historical work, *Building the Global Market: A 4000 Year History of Derivatives,* ancient Mesopotamian society comprised, in part, an organized agrarian economy in which grain and other commodities were frequently needed, traded, and served an important function as a way to make the people physically secure from invasion.[19]

Over time, bartering for exchange, which was common some 4,000 years ago, eventually gave way to transactions that were settled by means of metal which today we refer to as coinage, or currency. In a brief history of the foreign exchange market, Shani Shamah wrote of the first usage of coinage and the first foreign exchange markets:

> *Early Greek coins were almost universally accepted in the then known world; in fact, many Athenian designs were frequently mimicked, proving the coinage's popularity in design as well as acceptability. Cowries (shells) were viewed as money in 1200 B.C. The first metal money and coins appeared in China in 1000 B.C. The coins were made of base metals, often containing holes so that they could be put together like a chain. The first paper bank notes appeared in China in 800 AD and, as a result, currency exchange started between some countries.*[20]

As city-states developed and grew, the inhabitants of these political entities grew in number to the point where their need for grain and other commodities outstripped their ability to control the area that produced the commodities. Neighboring areas were beyond their control, and the disputes and wars that developed there jeopardized the city-state's ability to secure trade of commodities. Weather patterns were similarly beyond their control.

As a result of these realities, Mesopotamian people developed forms of trade that included forward contracts that would make the grain supply and the timing of deliveries more certain notwithstanding these risks and realities.

One type of forward contract which developed during this time was the grain loan agreement, which included all the classic characteristics of a forward. For a price to be paid at the time which the agreement is struck, a seller agreed to deliver a commodity such as grain at some point in the future. The price would be denominated in a shipment of a certain amount of grain or silver. The grain loan would be entered into before the planting of grain, and delivery would take place after harvest, "at the threshing floor."[21] In the early and even prehistoric periods of the history of the world, this was the setting for the first derivatives.

In the years leading up to the Roman empire and thereafter, there is evidence supporting the conclusion that commodities exchanged on the spot, rather than at some point in the future. Private grain sales in Lower Egypt generally took place after harvest during the months of September and January. This suggests that spot contracts predominated. If farmers sold their grain under forward contracts, then three-quarters of the sales would not have been consummated in the months immediately after harvest, as records indicated.[22]

By approximately 200 B.C., the law of sales existed in Rome, and that law enforced a contract for the sale of property that comes into the possession of the seller in the future.[23] A futures contract thus came within the law of sales in the Roman empire.

Whereas the legal systems that preceded the Roman laws in the Mediterranean and Middle Eastern regions required, at different points in history, formalities such as a writing, witnesses, and formal acts to bring about an enforceable contract, Roman law did away with the need for a deed, witnesses, and formal acts.[24]

THE DARK AGES AND MEDIEVAL EUROPE

The Dark Ages seized the development of finance, according to historians. During this period, which began after the fall of the Roman empire in AD 476, coinage and treasures were hoarded or buried for safekeeping, and this period of time saw the widespread disruption of trade and the wholesale deterioration of the social contract.[25]

Around AD 476, which historians tell us was the year in which the Roman empire fell, international trade continued to grow along with the Arabian empire during the expansion of Islam. Islamic tenets however disapproved of commercial profit and interest; derivative trades in the Arab empire were disapproved by legal and religious scholars.[26] The Qur'an includes prohibitions against usury and gambling. These developments coalesced to slow the evolution and use of derivatives in the Middle East, where, according to archeological records, they originated.

Over time, the derivatives trade migrated north to Italy and the markets in the rest of Europe.[27]

These developments did not altogether prevent the use of derivatives in the Middle East. Derivatives appear to have been used consistently throughout the ages in many regions to address the need for certainty in agreement and delivery of goods at some point in the future.

Not everything fell with the fall of Rome. The Church of Rome, which had its own canon law which was based on Roman law, continued to govern commerce as an alternative to Germany's secular law.[28] Among the many by-products of the Crusades was the opening of commerce in the markets of the East to large-scale European business.[29]

Trade of goods and future deliveries of international trade became necessary in fifth-century B.C. Greece:

> By the fifth century B.C., sea-borne international trade was a crucial part of the commercial life of Greece. Some accommodations were made to promote trade in goods for future delivery, but the laws governing this type of commerce were strict. In Athens, speculative

loans at high rates of interest to finance contracts for future delivery of some vital commodities were permitted. These were commonly called "bottomry" loans. For example, loans on badly needed imported grain were permitted. The lender was permitted to loan the costs of the importation of grain at annual rates of between 10 and 48 percent, depending on the length and consequence risk of the sea voyage required. If the grain was lost during the voyage, the borrower owed nothing. If the voyage was successful, the lender received principal and interest.[30]

The sixth and seventh centuries saw the reentry of coinage, and reemergence of Christianity into England, a development that resembled the original entry of coinage into economies some 600 years earlier.[31]

Church power to regulate commerce increased over time. The Church regulated commodity trading by imposing a range of punishments including excommunication and the resulting loss of the right to receive the Church's sacraments and a Christian burial. Because many believed in the influence of spiritual power in commodity trading around this time, excommunication was a serious punishment.[32]

THE MUSLIM EMPIRE

The expansion of the Muslim empire in the seventh and eighth centuries brought about a complex and sophisticated economy and society which included arrangements for the future delivery of goods.[33] However, as Muslim expansion strengthened, derivatives fell out of favor.

In the seventh and eighth centuries, a new force appeared: the Arab empire of the followers of Mohammed. They overran much of the Middle East, North Africa, and parts of Europe and imposed their own code of Islamic laws. A striking aspect of this law was its distrust of commercial profit, particularly transactions that earned interest on capital. Most derivative contracts fell foul of these prohibitions and gradually disappeared from the reported commercial life of the Middle East.[34]

The Muslim empire distrusted Christians and organized trading in markets. Therefore, trade by Christians in the regions within the Arab empire was curtailed, and marketplaces for traveling merchants were regulated in a way that was unprecedented. Derivatives were generally disapproved in Muslim societies due to the prohibition of usury within the Qur'an, and

Muslim expansion in the heart of economies and trade routes then in existence is beyond dispute:

> *For the Christianised lands of the former Roman Empire, Arab expansion was a political, religious, and commercial disaster. The Mediterranean Sea, which had been the highway of European/ Middle-Eastern commerce for almost 3,000 years, was in the hands of an enemy of the European kingdoms and the Byzantine empire. By the mid-eighth century, the observation of the Medieval Arab historian, Ibn Khaldun that the Christians could "no longer float a plank in it" was painfully close to being true.*[35]

In Byzantine commerce, traveling merchants within the Muslim empire were required to lodge and trade only in certain areas called Mitata.[36] Mitata were not established to facilitate trading, but instead were enforcement and monitoring tools:

> *Mitata were not set up for the convenience of traders. They allowed Byzantine officials to segregate and keep an eye on foreign merchants whom they regarded (with some justification) as vulgar, violent, or crooked. Merchants in these quarters were subject (until the end of the twelfth century) to Byzantine law and (until 1082) only allowed to stay for maximum periods of time (depending on nationality) of three to six months.*[37]

DEVELOPMENT AND EARLY USE OF THE BILL OF TRADE OR EXCHANGE

During this period, the bill of trade developed. It was one of the most widespread transactions for speculation. The development of the bill of trade arose out of the increasingly international nature of commerce and along with it came the infusion of different currencies into trade.

Entering the eleventh century, long-distance trade became the norm in many cases, and, as a result, many different types of coins issued from emperors, kings, and townships, and a new cottage industry of moneychangers developed.[38] For the merchant who was buying and selling in different jurisdictions spanning continents, it was important to change currency in one place to the currency in the market in which the merchant needed to purchase goods.

If a merchant in Venice needed to buy goods that existed in Genoa, where the merchant must pay for the goods in local currency, a bill of exchange is needed. The transaction entailed an advance of money on credit in Venice and a promise to repay that advance in another location, Genoa, in a different currency, such as this one:

> *Genoa, 31 January [1182]*
>
> *Witness: Coenna of Luca, Girardo Encina, Giovanni Corrigia.*
>
> *I, Alcherio, banker, have received from you, Martina Corrigia, a number of deniers for which I promise to pay, personally or through my Messenger to you or your accredited messenger, 9 [pounds] s. 13¹/₂ Pavese before the next feast on S Andrew [30 November]. Otherwise I promise to pay you, making the stipulation, the penalty of the double, etc.*
>
> *Done in Genoa, in front of the house of Barucio, in the bank of Alcherio, the last day of January.*[39]

By the twelfth century, several merchant cities in Italy had banking, exchange, and trade facilities. The practice of merchants meeting at fairs to conduct business gave way to more frequent, and then daily gatherings, where doing business through designated brokers was required.[40]

During this time, international trade in the Mediterranean witnessed the use of different forms of currency, which further necessitated the development of foreign exchange transactions. Contracts for exchange increased as trade expanded. Forwards continued to be traded during this period. For example, English monasteries entered into forwards with foreign merchants to sell commodities, such as wool, for as many as twenty years in advance.[41]

Early Beginnings of Exchanges

As we move into the twelfth and thirteenth centuries, the early beginnings of modern exchanges and the profession of brokers began to take form. In twelfth-century France, banks subcontracted debt servicing to individuals who also traded bank debt. These subcontractors could be referred to as the first brokers in France, who inserted themselves in the middle of lenders and borrowers, and buyers and sellers in a variety of contents, such as this one:

> *In November 1275, the following contract was made.*
>
> *"[A] deed executed in London in November 1275, by which the abbey of Darnhall [Chesire] sells to Giles de Ayre, agent for John Wermond of Cambrai, 12 sacks of good wool of the best crop*

[colliette] of Hereford, at nine marks a sack ... The wool is to be ... as good as the best crop of Dore [Abbey Dore in Hereford] ... Giles has paid 80 marks in earnest [en arres] and will pay the rest on delivery. ... The convent shall convey the wool to London at their own risks and deliver it to Giles before 1 August 1276, under penalty of £20 to be paid in aid of the Holy Land for every day's delay."

This contract is interesting in that that it involves a "broker," Giles de Ayre, acting as middleman between the seller (the abbey of Darnhall) and the buyer (John Wermond of Cambrai). At about this time, it became common to use English brokers as middlemen between the abbeys producing wool and the foreign wool buyers. These brokerage relations often arose as part of reciprocal futures contracts, whereby English middlemen contracted with Italian merchants to supply wool from ecclesiastical estates and, in return, Italian merchants made contracts to supply spices and other goods for which the English brokers would find buyers in England.[42]

After Bruges became the principal market for English wool, trade began to generally grow in Bruges in mid-thirteenth century.[43] Some stories suggest that the origins of the term "bourse" came from the Latin "bursa," meaning "a bag" because, in thirteenth-century Bruges, the sign of a purse (or perhaps three purses), was hung on the front of the house where merchants met.[44]

Historians write that by the end of the thirteenth century, a code that made illegal certain acts of derivatives brokers was established and records exist showing the adjudication of disputes and award of monetary damages.[45] The following brokerage activities were declared indictable offenses:

- Forestalling (intercepting and buying goods on the way to market).
- Engrossing (buying commodities in bulk for resale later).
- Regrating (buying goods in one part of the market and reselling them in another; a practice which, according to one commentator writing in 1765, was "highly criminal at common law").[46]

Spot Trades Were Enforceable, Forwards Were Not

Perhaps the most important development in the law during this period in Europe has to do with the timing of obligations in a commercial contract. There were periods in which a simultaneous exchange of goods for payment was the only type of contract that was enforceable by the law. Early Germanic tribal law and Greek law did not permit ownership and possession of property to occur at different times. The simple cash sale (as opposed to a transaction that included an early agreement and later settlement forward in time) was not only the norm but the only legal transaction structure.[47] Accordingly, contracts that did not call for immediate delivery of property were not enforceable. The public policy behind this must have been to reduce disputes, fraud, and litigation.

The law and custom of on-the-spot trading presented a difficult challenge to derivatives, including forwards, which contemplate one or more series of payments or deliveries at some point in the future after the initial agreement is struck.

Trade and finance exploded in the era spanning from 1485 to 1640 due, in large part, to the discovery by the Europeans of the New World, the West Indies, North and South America, as well as Africa, Southeast Asia then Australia and New Zealand.[48] However, arguably the most important development during this era was the decline of the Church as a central part of in trading.

AFTER THE PROTESTANT REFORMATION

In the fifteenth and sixteenth centuries, European trade in continental and international markets continued to grow. During these centuries, and especially near the end of the sixteenth century, the decline of the Church as a major player in derivatives and commodities markets and trades took place.[49]

The seventeenth century is regarded as the first century of secular trading in Europe since the fall of Rome.[50] Trading centers moved from Burges in the thirteenth century to Antwerp and Amsterdam and then to London over time. England began its world commercial dominance with several key initiatives. To raise money and expand its kingdom, the crown in England issued charters for exploration and the opening of new markets. In the course of doing this, England protected trade routes and built economic hegemony by, among other things, establishing the Royal Exchange.

To London merchants in the mid-sixteenth century, a rebellion in 1566 in the trading center at Antwerp necessitated a more secure international forum within which to trade. On June 6, 1566, Sir Thomas Gresham, the grandson of a prominent Tudor merchant, laid the first stone for the Royal Exchange at a site in Cornhill; the architect modeled the exchange after the bourse of Antwerp.

Executory Contracts Acknowledged

Gresham's Exchange was operational in late 1567, and by that time the law included provisions for the regulation of brokers, and also enforced executory contracts.

> [T]*he actual conferral of tangible benefit was no longer essential to make an executory contract enforceable. In the case of Gower v. Capper, the [English] Court said, "a promise against a promise is sufficient ground for an action."*[51]

Brokers were permitted to do business as long as each posted 100 pounds as a performance guaranty, took an oath not to sell the goods of others "in his own name," and refrained from usurious transactions and transactions between two "non-Londoners."[52]

By the eighteenth century, the early European derivative markets saw their first market—and derivative crises, in the form of the South Sea Bubble and tulip crashes in seventeenth-century Holland, which will be described in detail in later in this chapter.

Early Credit Default Swap Structures

The precursors to modern credit derivatives, such as credit default swaps, came in the form of speculation on shipwrecks and insurance provided by insurers for travel on the high seas:

> *English insurance underwriters in the 1700s often sold insurance on ships to individuals who did not own the vessels or their cargo. The practice was said to create an incentive to buy protection and then seek to destroy the insured property. It should come as no surprise that seaworthy ships began sinking. In 1746, the English Parliament enacted the Statute of George II, which recognized that "a mischievous kind of gaming or wagering" had caused "great numbers of ships, with their cargoes, [to] have . . . been fraudulently lost and destroyed." The statute established that protection for shipping risks not supported by an interest in the underlying vessel would be "null and void to all intents and purposes." For a time, however, it remained legal to buy insurance on another person's life in England. It took another 28 years and a new king, King George III, before Parliament banned insuring a life without an insurable interest.*[53]

The Beginnings of Modern Derivative Trading

Derivatives and futures were traded first in London, then overseas as the English empire expanded. In North America after the American revolution, British regulation of commerce including derivatives was replaced by the regulations of each state, which generally followed English common law.[54] For example, in New York, any sale of securities in which the seller did not have possession at the time of sale was void, but interestingly short sales involving certain commodities were legal.[55]

Early futures trading in the North American colonies before the revolution was driven by a vibrant international commodities market for wheat, peas, port, beef, fish, and tobacco.[56] Dutch New Amsterdam in the seventeenth century, present-day New York City, exported 60,000 bushels of wheat, and a century later, commodity exports grew to 160,000 pounds sterling.[57]

North American Exchanges

The late seventeenth and early eighteenth centuries saw the opening of the first organized exchanges on the continent of North America, and the first exchange opened around 1691 on Wall Street.[58] Later, in 1727, the Meal Market, a grain exchange, also opened in a location that today is known as lower Manhattan.[59] Local government mandated that grain, corn, and meal be traded only on the Meal Exchange.[60]

In the early eighteenth century, the 13 British colonies that would become the core of the United States were subject to the same laws governing commerce and derivatives that existed in the United Kingdom and in other British colonies.[61]

Futures contracts during the eighteenth century were referred to as time bargains.[62] These arrangements were part of everyday commerce in London.[63] Intellectual support for futures trading was provided by Adam Smith in his discussion "Concerning the Corn Trade" in *The Wealth of Nations*.[64] Smith wrote that futures trading in commodities—in particular, corn—was a justifiable undertaking even if futures trading resulted in "extraordinary profit." According to Smith, whose commentary next brings to mind the modern Malawi weather derivative detailed in the Introduction of this book:

> *The unlimited, unrestrained freedom of the corn trade, as it is the only effectual preventative of the miseries of a famine, so it is the best palliative of the inconveniences of a dearth; for the inconveniences of a real scarcity cannot be remedied, they can only be palliated.*

*No trade deserves more the full protection of the law, and no trade
requires it so much, because no trade is so much exposed to popular
odium. . . .*

*It is in years of scarcity . . . when prices are high, that the corn mer-
chant expects to make his principal profit. He is generally in contract with some farmers to furnish him for a certain number of years
with a certain quantity of corn at a certain price. This contract price
is settled according to what is supposed to be the moderate and
reasonable, that is, the ordinary or average price. . . . In years of
scarcity, therefore, the corn merchant buys a great part of his corn
for the ordinary price, and sells it for a much higher price. That
this extraordinary profit, however, is no more than sufficient to put
his trade upon a fair level with other trades, and to compensate the
many losses which he sustains upon other occasions, both from the
perishable nature of the commodity itself, and from the frequent
and unforeseen fluctuations of its price, seems evident enough. . . .*[65]

The Royal Exchange solidified its standing as a major market in derivatives both in London, when it was built, and in a similitude of the exchange
that was erected in present day New York, in 1752. Swan writes that the
Royal Exchange on the New World of the Atlantic Ocean was an exchange
for "puts," "refusals," "bargains for time," and other futures contracts.[66]

Financial instruments developed to accommodate international trade
because commerce in the eighteenth century required international shipping
and futures payments for goods to be delivered at later points in time. One
such instrument, a bill of exchange, came into use. A bill of exchange is a
written order by one party, the drawer, to another party, the drawee, to
pay money to a designated payee. A bill of exchange is a derivative because
its value is derived from the performance at a future time of one party, the
drawer, to the other party, the drawee.

These instruments are quite simply the predecessors to checks used today
and drawn on business and personal bank accounts, which are payable on
demand. Prior to the use of currency, bills of exchange, in fact, served as
currency in early commerce. In early New Amsterdam, a seventeenth-century
bill of exchange read this way:

14 July

Worthy, right deservet Mr. Luyhas Arents, Greeting:

*Whereas I am authorized by the late Shipper [first name illegible]
Deught, as well as by letters of Cornelius van Delvendrip, notary at*

the Hague, to address myself to you, so I make bold to request you hereby to pay, eight days after sign of my bill of exchange dated 19 [sic.] July 1662, to Shipper Jan Jansen Bestevaar or his order, on my account, the sum of 50 guilders current money in cash I shall thankfully satisfy you. These then serving for advice, if I should not come to speak personally to you before this is handed to you, as I am about to sail in the Ship Arent. Was signed TOBIAS FECKE.[67]

After the revolution and at the turn of the nineteenth century, the domestic and international commodities trade in America experienced a boom. By 1802, the United States was the largest supplier of cotton to England.[68]

Another derivative that developed early in the nineteenth century, in connection with international shipping, was the prepaid forward. A prepaid forward, as described in greater detail in Chapter 10, is an agreement whereby one party commits to sell to another party, the buyer, a certain quantity of goods at a price determined initially at the time of contract. This is a forward. The forward becomes a prepaid forward when a portion of the purchase price is prepaid up-front, at the initial moment of the bargain.

Sold by sample to prospective buyers, the cotton trade was accomplished by means of prepaid forward contracts:

The importer was usually expected to advance half the value o the goods as soon as he received the invoice from the exporter...But in general most exporters expected prompt payment or even an advance before the goods were sold, especially if they were acting for a planter.[69]

The validity of forwards and futures contracts in the mid-nineteenth century depended on the intent of the parties. On the one hand, contracts that arose out of the parties' purely speculative intent were deemed an illegal wager, and on the other, futures contracts in which the parties honest intent was to bring about the future delivery of goods at an agreed upon price were of full legal effect and thus were enforceable, as Justice Matthews of the U.S. Supreme Court wrote:

[A] contract for the sale of goods to be delivered at a future day is valid...when the parties really intend and agree that the goods are to be delivered by the seller and the price to be paid by the buyer; and, if under guise of such a contract, the real intent be merely to speculate in the rise and fall of prices, and the goods are not to be delivered, but one party is to pay to the other the difference between

*the contract price and the market price of the goods at the date fixed
for executing the contract, then the whole transaction constitutes
nothing more than a wager, and is null and void.*[70]

Contracts for Differences (CDFs) and Early S&Ls

In England, futures contracts for differences (still, with these, no physical
delivery was contemplated) were also not enforceable at law, and therefore
void.[71] Eventually, British law in both statutes and cases interpreting statutes
over time permitted contracts for differences, along with contracts for future
delivery of commodities.[72]

Following the development of British building societies a century earlier,
American thrifts, known as building and loans (B&Ls), helped the working
class save for the future purchase of homes.[73] These B&Ls, the precursors
to savings and loans (S&Ls), first emerged in 1831 in a few Midwestern
states in America. S&Ls and the thrift industry thrived in the decades that
followed the Second World War, until the United States basically bailed out
the thrift industry prior to the subprime housing bust in 2007 and 2008.

Nineteenth-Century German Bank Failures

In late-nineteenth-century Germany, a series of bank failures were caused
by futures speculation on exchanges.[74] The German Exchange Act of 1896
banned on-exchange contracts that called for future delivery of grain out
of concern that these transactions were abused by insider traders and short
sellers, with price manipulation along the way. These developments led to
the enactment of the Exchange Act in Germany.[75]

The results following the enactment of the Exchange Act in Germany
are instructive for reform efforts today. Just as the Gaming Act of 1845
in England resulted in derivatives continuing to be enforced and performed
outside the formal legal system, traders in Germany continued to trade
futures notwithstanding the German Exchange Act prohibition on futures.
The German Exchange Act experience, therefore, was among the earliest
illustration that where new law is not properly implemented, the new law
will fail.[76]

AN EARLY SIGHTING OF THE TERM
COMMODITY POOLS

In England, until 1986, the regulation of futures, commodities, and commodity pools was not comprehensive in nature. In the 1930s, share-pushing

salesmen persuaded parts of the unsophisticated public to make investments in commodity pools, according to a report published by the Bodkin Committee on investment fraud:

> *We refer to the somewhat numerous examples of circulars distributed in large numbers to the public, in which they are invited to participate in so-called "pools." The advertisers in the case of commodity pools are firms or limited companies in no way connected with any of the recognized markets in commodities or metals.... The concerns engaged in this class of enterprise invite the public to participate in a pool which is being formed "to complete the financing of a shipment" of a certain commodity.... Business of this character should, in our opinion, be regulated.*[77]

The Bodkin Committee findings became the basis of the Prevention of Frauds (Investment) Act of 1939, which imposed licensure and registration requirements for persons who solicited share sales. The act also prohibited cold calling.[78]

TEN WISE MEN

World War II contributed to the delay in the implementation of the Prevention of Frauds Act of 1939 until 1954.[79] In 1958 the Act was consolidated, and it remained as the only significant regulation of futures and investment in the United Kingdom until 1986.[80]

> *After the collapse of commodity firms and scandals at Lloyds of London before 1982, English professor L. C. B. Gower, a leading authority in investments and investment regulation, published a paper entitled "Review of Investor Protection: A Discussion Document," which, after concluding that the UK lacked a comprehensive, well-coordinated system of regulation, Professor Gower found that the UK has sacrificed effective regulatory oversight in favor of market efficiency:*
>
> *So far as these markets are concerned, self-regulation reigns supreme to an even greater extent than in the case of The Stock Exchange or Lloyd's. The only semblance of governmental or other outside control that resulting from the surveillance of the Bank of England [footnote omitted] surveillance which it now exercises without any specific statutory backing.... The present weakness as I see it, is*

that the self-regulation of the Exchanges and the surveillance of the Bank of England are directed towards the efficient running of the markets and the protection of the members in their dealings inter se on the Exchanges, and not towards the protection of investors the ultimate clients on whose behalf they are dealing.[81]

The Governor of the Bank of England appointed an advisory group called the Ten Wise Men following Professor Gower's published statements.[82] A white paper followed, outlining new comprehensive legislation for the regulation of investments in the United Kingdom. This led to the Financial Services Act of 1986 (FSA), which was enacted on November 7, 1986.[83]

The English FSA

English financial historian Edward Swan characterizes the FSA as a "reasonably liberal policy toward futures transactions."[84] Section 63 of the FSA repeals the invalidation of naked short sales, stock forwards, and futures that call for the future delivery of stock that was not owned at the time of contract.[85] Previous restrictions on contracts for future delivery that were overturned by the FSA may have caused trading revenues that would otherwise have been captured by English markets to be diverted to markets outside the United Kingdom, according to Swan:

Therefore, at the time it made its regulatory distinctions, both in Sir John Barnard's Act and in the previous Bill against stock jobbing, the government was aware of the role of commodity futures contracts in securing future supplies of vital natural resources. Restrictions on allowing English merchants to deal on such terms may well have prompted Baltic merchants to seek other markets among England's enemies.[86]

The Great Tulip Crash

In seventeenth century Europe a tulip options and futures market existed.[87] Tulips were introduced to the Dutch in 1593 from the Ottoman Empire.[88]

In seventeenth-century Europe, tulips were widely sought after at the time, and they became the subject of one of the earliest international market crises in futures and options. The tulip crash developed in this way:

After a time, the tulips contracted a non-fatal virus known as mosaic, which didn't kill the tulip population but altered them causing "flames" of color to appear upon the petals. The color patterns came in a wide variety, increasing the rarity of an already unique flower. Thus, tulips, which were already selling at a premium, began to rise in price according to how their virus alterations were valued, or desired. Everyone began to deal in bulbs, essentially speculating on the tulip market, which was believed to have no limits.

The true bulb buyers (the garden centers of the past) began to fill up inventories for the growing season, depleting the supply further and increasing scarcity and demand. Soon, prices were rising so fast and high that people were trading their land, life savings, and anything else they could liquidate to get more tulip bulbs. Many Dutch persisted in believing they would sell their hoard to hapless and unenlightened foreigners, thereby reaping enormous profits. Somehow, the originally overpriced tulips enjoyed a twenty-fold increase in value—in one month![89]

By 1636, established markets existed for spot sales as well as future sales of tulips and tulip bulbs.[90] Participants in the market sold or traded tulips or tulip bulbs for speculative purposes. In one case, it was reported that a buyer offered to sell 12 acres of land for one of two existing *Sempe-Augustus* bulbs.[91]

As is the case with all economic bubbles before they bust, insanity prevailed. From the period 1635 to 1637 in Amsterdam, an unregulated futures and options market thrived during a time when bankruptcies doubled.[92] With the price of tulips and tulip bulbs skyrocketing, the market saw both speculative on-the-spot transactions and futures contracts, as well as options on futures contracts:

Tulip bulbs were being sold from one party to another—many times over—before it was ultimately delivered. Payment for bulbs were not due until they were actually dug from the ground in the summertime. This was termed by the Dutch as windhandel, *or "wind trade." By the time the Dutch government began to regulate the tulip market the speculation had become too great.*

By February 1637, the tulip market had abruptly collapsed in Holland. On April 27, 1637, the Dutch government canceled all tulip futures contracts. It was decreed that futures in tulips could no longer be traded as an investment, but only as an actual product in the marketplace. Holders of option contracts walked away and the value of tulips crashed.[93]

The South Sea Bubble

From tulips, we next turn to the high seas. In the beginning of the eighteenth century, the British Empire ruled international trade. During this time, private enterprises were incorporated; in 1711, the South Sea Company was established. This company entered into a pact with the British government to acquire exclusive rights to trade in the South Seas in exchange for assuming and consolidating the national debt incurred by the British government in connection with the War of Spanish Succession (1701 to 1714).[94] The South Sea Company thereby acquired a monopoly of all trade to the Spanish Colonies in South America in exchange for assuming 10 million pounds of British debt.[95]

A speculative bubble involving the share prices of the South Sea Company, and other new ventures, developed:

> *In January of 1720, South Sea Company stock was trading at a modest £128. In an effort to stir up popular interest in the company's stock, the directors circulated false claims of success and fanciful tales of South Sea riches. The share price rose to £175 in February. Interest in the company was furthered along in March when the government endorsed a proposal from the company to assume yet more of the national debt in exchange for shares of South Sea Company stock. The South Sea Company's proposal was chosen over that of its chief competitor, the Bank of England. With investor confidence mounting, the share price climbed to approximately £330 by the end of March.*

> *The South Sea Bubble was not an isolated bubble event in 1720. As the South Sea Bubble was developing, a general interest in joint-stock investment opportunities was also picking up pace. By the middle of 1720, sometimes known as the "Bubble Year," the market was flooded with a remarkable range of new ventures, each creating smaller bubbles as the speculative frenzy mounted. South Sea Company stock benefited from the investor mania and by May it was at £550.*

> *The Bubble Act was passed in June, requiring all joint-stock companies to receive a royal charter. The legislation had been introduced by the South Sea Company, presumably as a means of controlling competition in the burgeoning market. The South Sea Company received its charter, perceived as a vote of confidence in the company, and by the end of June its share price had spiked to a peak of £1050.*

As with other bubbles that developed hundreds of years later, including the speculative dot-com bubble in early twenty-first century America, the South Sea Bubble burst. "The hoped-for Spanish [trade] concessions never materialized and the stock of the South Sea Company crashed in September 1720."[96]

A Committee of Secrecy established by the British Parliament initiated a formal investigation into the bursting of the South Sea Bubble and the use of options and forward contracts to purchase South Sea Company stock. The committee found widespread use of contracts which were entered into at one point in time for the purchase of South Sea Company shares that would, at some point later, be delivered to the buyer under the contract.[97] The prevalent use of these contracts, which today we recognize as forwards, was not the only disturbing aspect of the speculation relating to the South Sea crash.

The investigation revealed that options to buy South Sea Company stock were given at no cost to influential nobles and British government officials, such as the Chancellor of the Exchequer, John Aislabie, who stood to gain upon the appreciation of South Sea Company stock at no cost.[98] The investigation also revealed the practice of stock jobbing, bargains for time, and related practices which today are similar to the delivery of equity under call options, forwards, and futures contracts.

The Committee of Secrecy investigating the South Sea Company and the resulting free fall of its company stock concluded that the call options and delivery of South Sea Company stock under forward contracts were derivatives that were essentially borrowed from similar trading strategies that traders used in Amsterdam and other Continental markets.[99] The Committee concluded in its regulatory review after the South Sea Company equity collapse:

> Now, the Dutch and other foreigners having so large an interest in our public funds, has given rise to the buying and selling of them for time by which it is to be understood, the making of contracts for buying and selling against any certain period of time; so that the transfer; at the public offices is not made at the time of making the contract; but at the time stipulated in the contract for transferring it; and this has produced modern STOCK JOBBING, as I shall presently have occasion to shew. Nothing can be more unjust or inequitable that the original design of these contracts nor nothing more infamous than the abuse that has been, and still is, made of it.[100]

The British Parliament held a series of hearings and its members sponsored bills to prohibit call and forward contracts referred to at the time as bargains in time and stock jobbing.[101]

The premise underlying legislation to outlaw these derivatives was that these instruments were the source of market manipulation. The concept of shorting a security, that is, borrowing the security from someone and immediately selling after the borrow, with a promise to repay it later, was similarly the subject of Parliamentary scorn during debate there in 1733.[102] Sir John Barnard sponsored a bill that, once enacted in 1734, became Sir John Barnard's Act. He proclaimed in parliamentary debate:

> *The many bad consequences of stock jobbing are, I believe, well known; and that it is high time to put an end to that infamous practice.... It is a lottery, or rather a gaming-house, publicly set up in the middle of the City of London, by which the heads of our merchants and tradesmen are turned from getting a livelihood or an estate, by the honest means of industry and frugality; and are enticed to become gamesters by the hopes of getting an estate at once. It is, Sir, not only a lottery but a lottery of the very worst sort; because it is always in the power of the principal managers to bestow the benefit—tickets, as they have in mind. It is but lately since, by the arts and practices of stock jobbing, the East India stock was run up to 200£ percent and in a little time after it tumbled down again below 150£ several millions again were lost and won in a single job, and many poor men were undone; so barefaced were some men, at the time, in the infamous practice of stock jobbing, that, after that stock began to fall, they sold it cheaper for time than for ready money; which no man would have done, unless he had been made acquainted with the secret which came afterwards to be unfolded, but was then known to a very few.*
>
> *This, Sir, is a domestic Evil, an Evil which, tho' fatal in its Consequences, yet does not perhaps immediately draw any money out of the nation; but there is a foreign Evil attending the game of stock jobbing[.].*[103]

Early British Exchange Markets

British derivatives and futures markets continued largely unabated in the eighteenth century. Although stock jobbing, or the practice of entering into contracts for the future delivery of stock, was outlawed by the Sir John Barnard Act of 1734, less formal markets for stock jobbing continued in a way that is similar to the modern over-the-counter or OTC derivatives market, while more accepted commodity sales and futures contracts were effectuated in the Royal Exchange.

> *[In 1734] England's commodity trade was conducted in the august surroundings of the Second Royal Exchange...whereas the*

less respectable share trade, banished from the Royal Exchange, was carried on in the shady precincts of Exchange Alley and nearby coffee houses by marginal brokers and much despised stock job-bers. Therefore, it does not seem surprising that the group deprived of the convenience and addition of trade provided by futures con-tracts were the unpopular stock dealers rather than solid commodity merchants. Despite the passion that the stock jobbing aroused, the government's attempts to prevent it had small success. Dealers in the Alley generally ignored Sir John Barnard's Act and continued to trade in derivative contracts for future stock delivery.[104]

In the early to middle parts of the nineteenth century, the decisions of the courts and acts of Parliament in Britain, which were influential legal precedent in the United States, created an entirely inconsistent stream of prohibitions on derivatives and future delivery of stock. A court's decision to enforce a forward contract to deliver stock at some point in the future would later be deemed invalid by a subsequent law prohibiting such contracts.

In 1826 for example, a forward or futures contract would be stricken down in England under the following rationale, stated in the decision in *Bryan v. Lewis*:

> *I have always thought, and shall continue to think, until I am told by the House of Lords that I am wrong, that if a man sells goods to be delivered on a future day, and neither has the goods at the time, nor has entered into any prior contract to buy them, nor has any reasonable expectation of receiving them by consignment, but means to go into the market and to buy the goods which he has contracted to deliver, he cannot maintain an action upon such a contract. Such a contract amounts, on the part of the vendor, to a wager on the price of the commodity, and is attended with the most mischievous consequences.*[105]

Bryan v. Lewis stands for the proposition that the law did not recognize the value of a promise to perform the delivery of goods at some point in the future based on an earlier promise—and exchange of consideration in connection with that promise. This decision, in *Bryan v. Lewis*, only afforded legal enforceability to an exchange of goods *on the spot*. Historians referred to *Bryan v. Lewis* as a "disappointingly misanthropic view and detrimental to the development of derivatives markets."[106]

In 1836, the case of *Wells v. Potter* overturned *Bryan v. Lewis*. In *Wells*, a broker filed a lawsuit to recover debts that the broker incurred in connection with arranging options to purchase, at some time in the future, Spanish or Portuguese bonds.[107] The defense in *Wells v. Potter* was that the broker's claim was unenforceable because arranging the options without possessing the bonds was illegal under English law, specifically the Stock Jobbing Act, which we now know as the Sir John Barnard Act.[108]

In the court's rejection of that defense, the court found a way to side for the plaintiff, the broker, and still be consistent with the Sir John Barnard Act's prohibition against stock jobbing.

> *The Court unanimously decided in favour of the plaintiff. Tindal CJ said: "[I]t appears that foreign securities are not within the statute." Bosanquet [Justice] said, in distinguishing Bryan v. Lewis is adverse to the plaintiff, inasmuch as it is to be inferred from the opinion that a contract such as this is void at common law. Where it is said there, however, is to be considered merely as dictum.*[109]

The courts in England first struck down as invalid, then a decade later enforced the validity of futures contracts until the enactment of the Gaming Act of 1845. Just as the *Wells* decision in 1836 appeared to lay a foundation for the enforcement of forwards and futures (at least for the delivery of securities), the Gaming Act of 1845 invalidated contracts for future delivery, "in which parties did not intend to deliver any goods, but simply to pay 'differences.'"[110] The Gaming Act was a statute whose supporting rationale was grounded in legislators' intent to "protect the public, high and low, against improper gambling."[111]

Looking back at the nineteenth century derivatives and securities futures markets after the enactment of the Gaming Act in 1845, two conclusions can be drawn. First, derivatives were not enforced by the courts if the parties to the derivatives never intended to bring about physical delivery of the subject of the derivative, such as a stock, bond, or commodity.[112] Those contracts (in which the parties never intended to settle a derivative by one party physically tendering stock or other security) were invalidated by the courts as illegal, speculative gambles.[113]

The second development in mid-nineteenth-century derivatives, arising out of judicial decisions and the Gaming Act of 1845, was the continued use of futures contracts *notwithstanding the inability of the parties to futures contracts to obtain orders of enforcement by the courts.* Instead, contracts continued to be formed, and were performed without resort to the legal system, but out of a concern by many in the market to maintain a proper *reputation*; peer pressure facilitated the earlier market.

> *Traders were forced to rely on peer pressure and the customs of the markets, such as the Royal Exchange, in enforcing the performance of their contracts. Undoubtedly, this was a powerful incentive. It would be hard for anyone to do business at the Royal Exchange once it was learned that he did not perform his bargains.*[114]

The Gaming Act had a negative effect on the development of derivatives as financial instruments that could be enforced by courts until the passage in Britain of the Financial Securities Act of 1986. This 1986 act included an exemption to section 18 of the Gaming Act for "any contract entered into by either or each party by way of business."[115]

THE MODERN ERA BEGINS IN THE STATES IN 1848

The modern era of futures began in the United States in 1848 with the establishment of the Chicago Board of Trade. As detailed in Chapter 3, the Chicago Board of Trade enabled farmers and other market participants to enter into forwards on an exchange (and thus futures contracts, as opposed to forwards, which are derivatives in the OTC market) to hedge against pricing contingent on macroeconomic factors.

The late nineteenth century and early parts of the twentieth century in the United States saw a disbursed collection of exchanges, in addition to the Chicago Board of Trade:

> *In May 1884, the New York Produce Exchange took possession of new premises. By 1911, it was trading in meat, wheat, corn, rye, oats, barley and other grains, flour, meal, hops, hay, straw, seeds, port, lard, tallow, greases, cotton-seed oil, animal and vegetable oils, naval stores, butter and cheese, in quantities from single packages to entire cargoes.*[116]

The legal and economic relationships which were formed in futures trading in the early years of the Chicago Board of Trade continue to be formed today, although the process of creating those relationships is faster, more efficient, and international in nature, as we will see in the next chapter. Today the Chicago Board of Trade is joined by over a dozen other major international futures exchanges, all providing an effective forum for trading futures contracts around the clock.

As regional exchanges and clearinghouses sprouted in the United States in the mid- to late-nineteenth century, the OTC derivatives market did not thrive due, in large part, to key decisions handed down by the courts in the United States.

Futures markets were encouraged in the United States in part because contracts traded on those markets involved an identifiable interest in a commodity, such as grain. For cases in which the litigants established that neither party to contracts has such an interest, the courts refused to uphold such contracts. For example, an 1884 U.S. Supreme Court decision—worth

mentioning again here—found that a contract in which the parties speculated whether goods would be delivered in the future was not enforceable:

> [I]f, *under guise of such a contract, the real intent be merely to*
> *speculate in the rise or fall of prices, and the goods are not to be*
> *delivered, but one party is to pay the other the difference between*
> *the contract price and the market price of the goods at the date fixed*
> *for executing the contract, then the whole transaction constitutes*
> *nothing more than a wager, and is null and void.*[117]

The distinction between the intent to physically settle a trade with the
delivery of a commodity, such as corn or gold, became an important factor
in determining whether the CFTC today retains jurisdiction of a transaction,
as discussed in the analysis of the new U.S. law of derivatives in Chapter 4.

EARLY-TWENTIETH-CENTURY AMERICA

At the turn of the twentieth century in the United States, the agrarian economy and dependence on the elements such as weather, along with infrastructure and storage facilities, necessitated the use of forward contracts by
farmers and others to protect against price fluctuations in commodities.[118]
Before the development of organized exchanges, these transactions
(e.g., forwards) were informally entered into by farmers and merchant
counterparties.

During this time, the markets within which forward transactions were
traded were fragmented because of different regulatory requirements by the
various states. Each state regulated derivatives (or what courts and legislators
deemed as wagers) on its own. For example, in 1901, Massachusetts enacted
laws prohibiting wagering contracts in stocks or commodities in which no
actual purchase was intended.[119] Entering into a futures contract in North
Carolina was against a law enacted four years later there, and in Alabama
and Arkansas (as well as several other states enacting prohibitions for the
first time, or amending earlier prohibitions), at least some forwards were
similarly prohibited.[120] Wisconsin passed this law:

> *Whereby sentence is provided of not more than ten years or less than*
> *one year in the state prison for any...person holding property or*
> *money in any manner in a trust capacity...who shall buy, sell, deal*
> *or traffic in any goods, stocks, grains, etc., by making or requiring*
> *any deposit, payment, or pledge of any margin or money to cover*
> *future fluctuation in the price of such articles.*[121]

1907 BANKERS PANIC

Swan writes that this era of separate state laws was the result of the development and aftermath of the Panic of 1907 in the United States, also known as the 1907 Bankers' Panic. This event included a 50 percent free fall of the New York Stock Exchange and ensuing runs on banks and trust companies, as well as widespread recession and panic attributable to runs on banks and widespread loss of investor confidence.[122]

> Commodity trading (specifically, a scheme to corner the market in the United Copper Company) was at the heart of the Panic of 1907.[123] Historians focusing on the Panic of 1907 have identified common themes in both the market crises of 2008 and the panic just over a century ago, including the failure of market intermediaries and sources of short-term liquidity. "Financial events of 2008 among New York City intermediaries are eerily similar to those...of 1907," wrote Ellis W. Tallman and Jon R. Moen in January 2011.[124]

Futures speculation was largely viewed as gambling in a way that was contrary to religious and other views that predominated at the time,[125] just as the derivatives entered into at the height of the 2008 crises by prominent hedge fund managers including John Paulson were viewed as bets and gambling.[126]

Three significant developments relating to derivatives arose from the Panic of 1907:

- A body of common law from precedent handed down by the United States Supreme Court that legitimized certain futures transactions with certain attributes.
- The 1913 passage of the Federal Reserve Act that established the Federal Reserve as the central bank of the United States.
- Generally, widespread reform sentiment.

As for the first development, Swan writes that U.S. Supreme Court decisions were necessary not only due to a void in federal regulation, but also because of confusion created by the interpretation of certain state laws that, in some cases, included put and call options within the statutory prohibition of gambling.[127] Swan wrote:

> By this time, the many state regulations, the lack of overall federal regulation and the continuing boom in futures trading of a vast range of commodities caused a great deal of legal confusion and contradiction. Many of these were left to resolution by both the

*state and federal courts. "The confusion is demonstrated by the fact
that the Courts of Illinois, of all places, consistently included certain
kinds of 'option' contracts, within prohibition of state gambling
laws." However, after the turn of the century, the U.S. Supreme
Court began to make decisions showing recognition that futures
speculation was a legitimate part of commerce.*[128]

The U.S. Supreme Court in *U.S. Board of Trade of Chicago v. Christie
Grain & Stock Co.*[129] changed the test of a whether a futures contract
is valid from the intent of the parties—to whether the contract was made
for a "serious business purpose."[130] Thus, an early important distinction
between OTC and exchange-traded derivatives came out of U.S. common
law (as opposed to statutory or regulatory law) with its origins in the Panic
of 1907.

The Panic of 1907 also created widespread reform sentiment that resulted in not only new law at the state level, but also the beginnings of
federal law to safeguard the U.S. economy and futures trading within it, and
a development and revamp of the financial infrastructure, which lacked adequate clearing facilities, according to several who studied the 1907 market
crises in depth.[131]

This reform sentiment led to the enactment of the Cotton Futures Act,
some nine years after the Panic of 1907.[132] Rather than prohibit cotton
futures speculation, as agricultural interests had hoped, the act made futures contracts prohibitively expensive unless those contracts satisfied the
requirements of the act, which barred verbal contracts and imposed a tax
as a penalty for nonconformance with the act.[133] Importantly, the act required contracts to reference prices in certain circumstances to five spot
markets designated by the Secretary of Agriculture. The Act also excluded
certain contracts, such as forwards, by providing exemptions to the new
law. Cotton became the only commodity so regulated until grain futures
were similarly regulated with a tax per bushel.[134]

World War I brought about in the United States the first coordinated
effort to sell securities to retail investors in the form of the Liberty Loan
program of 1917.

Exchanges prior to the Great Depression had an intensely speculative
aura that contributed to federal regulation of futures, but did not effectively
reign in abuses in this trade that led to Great Depression fallout:

*But many were opposed to the exchanges' intense speculative na-
ture. For instance, in 1921, a United States Senator commented
that the Chicago Board of Trade was so much of a "gambling hell"
that "Monte Carlo or the Casino at Havana are not to be compared to it." Public outcry against the perceived speculative abuses*

of both the exchanges and futures activity that was off-exchange, such as bucket shops, led Congress to enact the Futures Trading Act ("FTA") in 1921. The FTA sought to halt price manipulation and bucketing by levying a prohibitive tax on any grain futures that were off-exchange and therefore not under the supervision of the Secretary of Agriculture as a "contract market."[135]

Grain Futures Act

The first attempt by Congress to discourage or at least rein-in OTC off-exchange derivatives failed the following year. In 1922, the U.S. Supreme Court held the Futures Trading Act of 1921 as an unconstitutional exercise of the federal taxing power.[136] In response to that Court's 1922 decision in *Hill v. Wallace*, Congress enacted the Grain Futures Act of 1922, which eliminated the earlier law's tax on grain but laid the foundation for subsequent regulation of derivatives in general, and futures in particular.

The U.S. Congress passed the Grain Futures Act of 1922, which imposed licensure requirements on exchanges and mandated that futures trading must occur only on licensed exchanges. In light of the Supreme Court's *Hill* decision the year before, which interpreted the Constitutional power to tax to not include the power to tax OTC transactions, Congress in 1922 relied on the Commerce clause within the U.S. Constitution. Farmers opposed the Grain Futures Act, which was subject to another challenge on constitutional grounds as well.

Farmers had an innate distrust of futures markets and the price discovery functions that those markets, some of which of course were in distant cities, provided. According to testimony before the U.S. House of Representatives' Agriculture Committee, "the man who managed or sold or owned those immense wheat fields has not as much to say with the regard to the price of the wheat than some young fellow who stands howling around the Chicago wheat pit could actually sell in a day."[137]

The 1922 law was again challenged with a claim that it was unconstitutional, but the United States Supreme Court upheld the Grain Futures Act the following year.[138]

Accordingly, future sales of grain in the United States were only permissible if consummated on an exchange designated by the Department of Agriculture after the enactment of the Grain Futures Act. Exchanges were threatened by the revocation of licenses in the event that fraud and market manipulation took place in the course of trading by members on exchanges.

The Grain Futures Act also prohibited members of an exchange from issuing false or misleading information about crop conditions and the use of corners, or monopolies, to control commodity pricing.[139]

Just as in England, so, too, in Germany traders entered into transactions in which the actual physical delivery of goods was not contemplated. In time, only some members of Congress sought to pass legislation in the United States, too, that prohibited trades that did not physically settle, equating those trades with gambling:

> The Grain Futures Act of 1921–22 passed by large House ma-
> jorities with most of the opposition coming from the East. This
> legislation did not satisfy the more committed opponents of futures
> markets, who equated futures trading with gambling and had sought
> to ban or to tax futures transactions if the parties to the transaction
> did not expect delivery. These opponents urged far more stringent
> regulation of futures markets. They were unsuccessful because a
> substantial majority of senators believed the 1922 legislation had
> adequately dealt with the manipulation issue and were opposed to
> restricting the hedging functions of futures markets.[140]

The Great Depression

In 1929, nearly 10,000 banks failed in the United States,[141] commodity prices experienced a devastating collapse[142] and core foundations of the economy were shattered. Roughly half of all mortgages were delinquent.[143] This was the greatest and most widespread economic devastation of a purely economic nature to visit a country in the history of the world. Although the frequent and widespread seizures in the 2008 to 2009 housing markets in the United States were also historic, the housing market in the early 1930s actually experienced unprecedented desolation that has not been matched by any economic crisis since that time:

> It was January 1934. The Great Depression was five years old—but
> still had another five years to run. The carnage was horrific: From
> 1929 to 1934, U.S. personal income plunged 44%, real output
> nosedived 30%, and the unemployment rate soared to 25% of the
> American labor force. With the nation's economic landscape laid to
> waste, it should be no surprise that home foreclosures were soaring,
> too: Residential real-estate foreclosures doubled between 1926 and
> 1929—before the Great Depression actually began. According to a
> new study by the Federal Reserve Bank of St. Louis, the foreclo-
> sure rate jumped from 3.6 per 1,000 mortgages in 1926 to 13.3 in
> 1933. In that year, in fact, 1,000 home mortgages were being fore-
> closed each day. By Jan. 1, 1934, as many as half of all residential

mortgages were delinquent, putting them at risk of foreclosure. Clearly something had to be done, elected officials believed. In an attempt to slow that surge, 27 states changed key laws in a way that created a temporary moratorium on foreclosures. Still other state and municipal governments passed permanent measures that made it tough for aggrieved lenders to foreclose on properties whose mortgages were delinquent.[144]

President Franklin Delano Roosevelt wrote that "[u]nregulated speculation in securities and in commodities was one of the most important contributing factors in the artificial and unwarranted 'boom' which had so much to do with the terrible conditions of the years following 1929."[145]

On July 9, 1932, the Dow Jones Industrial Average closed at 41.63 after a fall of 91 percent compared to its level three years earlier. "Total trading volume that day was a meager 235,000 shares. 'Brother Can You Spare a Dime' was one of the top songs of the year."[146]

Though equities and bonds were the principal instruments that drove the markets, complex investment structures also existed. Investors in pools of mortgages did exist, and during the Great Depression the mortgage pools were serviced by cash.

Banks had become so illiquid, and depositors so terrified of losing their money, that checkwriting ground to a halt. Most transactions that did occur were carried out in cash. Alexander Dana Noyes, financial columnist at the New York Times, *had invested in a pool of residential mortgages. He was repeatedly accosted by the ringing of his doorbell; those home owners who could still keep their mortgages current came to Mr. Noyes to service their debts with payments of cold hard cash.*[147]

Investors everywhere winced with the pain of recognition of the patter of comedian Eddie Cantor, who sneered about what his broker told him, which was "to buy this stock for your old age. It worked wonderfully. Within a week I was an old man!"[148]

The early 1930s saw dramatic lawmaking and regulatory action as a result of these bank failures and the Great Depression, with President Franklin D. Roosevelt moving Congress to enact and send to the White House for passage a new massive body of law regulating finance in general, and derivatives and futures in particular, as we detailed in Chapter 1.

Among these statutory initiations, one commodity law and two securities laws enacted by Congress arose from the Great Depression: the

Commodity Exchange Act of 1936, the Securities and Exchange Act of 1934,[149] which created the U.S. Securities and Exchange Commission (an independent agency of the United States charged with the primary responsibility of enforcing federal securities laws and regulating the securities industry), and the Securities Act of 1933, which principally requires registration of securities unless an exemption applies.

The regulatory reach of the SEC under federal laws enacted in 1933 and 1934 only extended to those transactions and assets that came within the definition of securities within the Securities Act of 1933. This meant that the SEC lacked jurisdiction to require the registration and disclosure of OTC derivatives and futures contracts, all of which were not included in that definition.

Modern derivative providers grew out of another important post—Great Depression law enacted in 1933 called the Glass-Steagall Act of 1933.[150] This law sought to address the public concern that bank depositor money should not support a bank's securities business. The Act required U.S. banks to choose one or the other but not both business lines, thereby bringing about the separation of securities operations from commercial banking and giving rise to Morgan Stanley from J.P. Morgan & Company.[151] The repeal of Glass-Steagall over five decades later and the merging of commercial banks and proprietary trading including derivatives was a factor in the Great Recession of 2008.

With respect to futures regulation, until the Great Depression and the enactment of the Commodity Exchange Act of 1936, there existed a complicated patchwork of state, federal, and court-prescribed common law.[152] This legal environment was unsettled and chaotic and of course was driven by public opposition to futures trading. At least one U.S. Supreme Court decision found that grain futures executed on organized exchanges were illegal and void as gambling under state law.[153]

The Great Depression, overproduction of grain, and the resulting drop in grain prices resulted in U.S. legislation and the establishment of the Federal Farm Board to remedy those developments.[154] In 1930, the Grain Stabilization Corporation boosted wheat prices by buying wheat with government funds, much like Mortgage backed securities were purchased after 2008, but this created the perception in the grain market that there existed an artificially created surplus pool of grain, resulting in a further decline of prices.

The economic ruin caused by the Great Depression was so deep and widespread, and the federal law that followed was so comprehensive, that OTC derivatives and exchange-traded futures were not singled out for regulation in a meaningful way, in contrast to what we saw in Chapter 4. For futures regulation to take hold, it took yet another collapse in the commodities market, in 1935.

The Beginnings of U.S. Futures Law

> *It should be our national policy to restrict, as far as possible, the use of these [futures] exchanges for purely speculative operations.*
> —President Franklin D. Roosevelt, Message
> to Congress, February 9, 1934

In 1934, President Roosevelt introduced into the U.S. Congress the Commodity Exchange Act of 1936, or the CEA, the acronym that is used for this historic act even today.[155] The CEA is, as amended to date, the primary foundation for the regulation of the futures markets in the United States. The CEA essentially replaced the Grain Futures Act (changing all references to grains to commodities) and extended federal regulation of certain enumerated commodities including cotton, rice, mill feeds, butter, eggs, Irish potatoes and grains.[156]

With the collapse of the price of cotton in 1935 and continuing public opposition to trading in commodities (and the accompanying perception that the Grain Futures Act did not result in proper regulation of speculation in the markets), Congress passed and President Franklin D. Roosevelt signed into law the Commodity Exchange Act of 1936.[157]

In 1936, the Commodity Exchange Act replaced the Grain Futures Act of 1922, and it increased the federal government's regulatory powers over futures trading, as we discussed at length in Chapter 3.[158]

The CEA has these primary features:

- The coverage of the statute was expanded beyond grain to a range of agricultural (although, significantly, not mineral) commodities.
- An antifraud provision (Section 4b) was incorporated, which forbade any member of a futures exchange ("contract market") from defrauding anyone in a futures contract transaction.
- The establishment of a Commodity Exchange Commission, consisting of the Secretary of Agriculture, the Secretary of Commerce, and the Attorney General, which is authorized to set permissible limits on the amount of speculative trading on futures contracts.
- Futures commission merchants and floor brokers were required to be registered with the Commodity Exchange Commission.
- Futures commission merchants (FCMs) were required to "segregate customer funds by holding them in trust in separate accounts."[159]

In addition to the foregoing, a key concept put into motion by the CEA is the use of a central exchange. The CEA requires that all futures be traded on an exchange which is regulated by the Commission so that sunlight can be cast on the process whereby futures contracts are priced as well as other aspects of futures trading.[160]

As a result of the CEA, futures contracts were priced on exchanges and cleared through clearinghouses either owned by the exchanges or affiliated in some way with exchanges. A more detailed discussion of exchanges and clearinghouses is provided in Chapter 3.

The CEA is the single greatest act of the twentieth century U.S. derivatives legislation for two reasons: it provided the foundation for the reform of the OTC derivatives market as embodied in the Dodd-Frank Wall Street Reform and Consumer Protection Act which followed the 2008 market crises, and it also subjected futures trading to a broad regime of legal requirements and enforcement mechanisms. To summarize, for the first time in the history of the world, CEA created:

- A regulated exchange that performs a price discovery function in a transparent manner.
- A clearing concept whereby trades are to be cleared via a central clearinghouse with rules that require that members have the financial wherewithal to assure contract performance and a guaranty of performance by the clearinghouse.
- Margining of trades.
- Prohibitions against manipulation and fraud.
- Self-regulation mechanisms that are imposed on exchanges.
- Supervision of exchanges and clearinghouses.
- Consumer protection rules.
- Regulation of intermediaries.
- A disclosure mechanism to bring about transparency for the public.
- The position limit concept to prevent excessive speculation.
- Enforcement mechanisms, fines, and penalties for violations.[161]

The CEA remained intact and generally survived challenges until 1974, which was, in many respects, a watershed year in the history of futures law in the United States, as discussed in the pages that follow.[162]

Futures Trading Halted

Suspension of trading of futures contracts and the imposition of price controls on a number of commodities resulted from the United States' involvement in World War II.[163] Markets in cotton and wool continued to exist, and the Commodity Exchange Commission monitored these markets carefully.[164] "Following [World War II], futures trading was gradually restored to normal. There was some disruption and calls from politicians to further restrict speculation caused by the Korean War. There were also investigations of price manipulations of egg and rye futures prices."[165]

S&Ls AND MORTGAGE FINANCE FUNCTIONS WELL BEFORE ABUSES

United States regulation of residential mortgage finance comes in waves. After a crisis, the regulation of mortgage finance generally results in agencies created, laws passed, and interpretative rules promulgated. Once a crisis in the mortgage finance market in the United States subsides and new laws take effect, order appears to be restored, for a time.

This was the experience of the residential mortgage finance market in the United States after the Great Depression, and before the S&L crisis in the mid-1980s and mid-1990s. To review, in the middle of the 10-year Great Depression in the United States, as many as half of all residential mortgages were delinquent and at risk of bank foreclosure.[166] These failures led to, among other things, the establishment of two entities that played important roles in the 2008 market crises.

THE CREATION OF FANNIE AND FREDDIE

The Great Depression, which brought about foreclosures during parts of the 10-year depression at a rate of 1,000 per day,[167] led to historic federal reforms that included the creation of new agencies—the Federal Home Loan Bank System, Homeowners Loan Corporation, Fannie Mae, the Federal Housing Administration, and the Federal Deposit Insurance Corporation—all of which were intended to create more stable national banking and housing systems.

A period of stability followed and continued into the second half of the twentieth century in the United States. After World War II, until the late 1970s, the system worked. The savings and loan industry was effectively regulated by the federal government, with a mission to take people's deposits and then provide loans for the purpose of helping people to buy homes. Federal agencies and programs insured those loans, mortgage discounts were provided through the FHA and Veterans Administration, and a secondary mortgage market developed to guarantee a steady flow of capital. Savings and Loans (S&Ls) were required to make 30-year fixed loans, and there was a steady increase in home ownership and few foreclosures.[168]

Over time, S&Ls expanded the financial services offered to customers to include checking accounts in the late 1970s, consumer and commercial loans in the 1980s, and later commercial real estate loans. With the passage of the Garn-St. Germain Depository Institutions Act in 1982, S&Ls expanded, in 1982 and again in 1984, the ability to hold commercial real estate. As of January 1, 1984, S&Ls, which were originally designed of course to make residential real estate loans, were then authorized to make commercial, corporate, business, and even agricultural loans.[169]

DISCO, DEALERS, SWAPS, AND REDLINING IN THE 1970s

Swaps developed from the evolution of international finance. Following the collapse of the Bretton Woods Agreement, exchange rates became extremely volatile in the early 1970s and created an environment that fostered innovation designed to hedge foreign exchange exposures.[170] Events in the sphere of international relations eliminated in various respects a "fixed" payment environment and fostered innovation including growth in derivatives.

> *In 1971, the United States freed the gold price; then the Arabs embargoed oil. If bondholders still harbored any illusion of stability, the bankruptcy of Penn Central Railroad, which was widely owned by blue-chip accounts, wrecked the illusion forever. Bond investors, most of them knee-deep in losses, were no longer comfortable standing pat. Gradually, governments around the globe were forced to drop their restrictions on interest rates and on currencies. The world of fixed relationships was dead. Soybeans suddenly seemed quaint; money was the hot commodity now. Futures exchanges devised new contracts in financial goods such as Treasury bills and bonds and Japanese yen, and everywhere there were new instruments, new options, new bonds to trade, just when professional portfolio managers were waking up and wanting to trade them. By the end of 1970, firms such as Salomon [Brothers] were slicing and dicing bonds in ways ... never dreamed of, blending mortgages together, for instance, and distilling them into bite-sized, easily chewable securities.[171]*

In this environment, and as countries imposed protectionist measures to make the acquisition of foreign currency more difficult for foreign market participants, the modern swap market grew out of a structure referred to as parallel, and substantially similar, back-to-back loans.[172]

The Back-to-Back Loan as the Precursor to Swaps

As a precursor to foreign exchange swaps and other swaps within the derivatives family, multinational financial firms and organizations developed and used the back-to-back loan. In this structure a U.S. company seeking British capital enters into an agreement with a British company which needs U.S. dollars. The British company obtains from a domestic bank in the U.K. the capital sought by the U.S. company and tenders the British capital to the U.S. bank in exchange for dollars, thereby circumventing fees and taxes imposed on foreign exchange transactions involving foreigners.

According to John F. Marshall and Kenneth R. Kapner, before 1979, derivatives included futures, listed options, forwards, OTC options and hybrid securities. 1979 marked the start date of swaps markets.[173] The family of financial transactions known today as derivatives expanded to include the swap transaction in the mid- to late twentieth century. A swap is merely an exchange of promises that is more fully developed in its terms than the exchanges that occurred prior to the twentieth century:

> *A swap is a contractual agreement evidenced by a single document in which two parties, called counterparties, agree to make periodic payments to each other. Contained in the swap agreement is a specification of the currencies to be exchanged (which may or may not be the same), the rate of interest applicable to each (which may be fixed or floating), the timetable by which the payments are to be made, and any other provisions bearing on the relationship between the parties.*[174]

These contractual arrangements were initially cumbersome in the early 1970s because the capital and currency requirements of the contracting parties were frequently not the same. The risk of nonperformance by one party overseas also created challenges. "The other problem associated with back-to-back and parallel loans—finding a party with matching requirements—was sold through the intervention of swap brokers and market makers who saw the potential of this new financing technique."[175] The market needed a third party to match bargaining parties and step in between their contracts to enable the market to function. Dealers, such as large international banks, became those third-party matchmakers.

In the late 1970s, market participants began to trade the first currency swaps on a global scale. After the 1970s, the OTC derivatives market began its historic climb to become the greatest market in modern finance, starting in 1981 with negligible transaction volume to hundreds of millions and billions thereafter.

By the beginning of the 1980s, the foundations for explosive growth in derivatives were laid; as one commentator put it, "[t]he 1970s brought disco, President Jimmy Carter, and innovation in derivatives."[176] In the 1970s, investors could hedge against future interest-rate increases or adverse changes in foreign currency; parties bargained for the right to the purchase of currencies at specific rates and quantities in the future.[177]

Residential Mortgage Initiatives: Redlining

In the mid-1970s, the civil rights movement brought to light the practice of racial discrimination in the residential housing market in general and redlining in particular. This led to the passage of the Community Reinvestment Act in the United States. This act is important because it instilled in U.S. presidential administrations from 2000 to 2008 the need to increase home ownership, especially within low-income populations, which traditionally could not access credit for home ownership. This emphasis coincided with two unrelated developments that fostered subprime consumer lending:

1. Federal law that removed caps on interest rates (the Depository Institutions and Monetary Control Act).
2. The gradual elimination from the 1980s to the mid-1990s of conservative residential lending by savings and loans, in favor of generally the expansion of savings and loan risk taking, mismanagement, and fraud.

These developments created an environment for subprime lending, which, when coupled with securitization in the absence of federal regulation, as discussed in Chapter 1, and then the housing bust in the United States, led to the Market Crises of 2008 and resulting reforms.

The Watershed Year of 1974

With the rapid development in the twentieth century of derivatives, swaps and futures contracts beyond physical and agricultural commodity-based futures to include futures contracts on currencies, stock indices, and other financial instruments, the U.S. Congress saw the need for a federal agency with more power and an authorizing statute with greater reach and effect.

By passing the Commodity Futures Trading Commission Act of 1974, the U.S. Congress dramatically amended the CEA to bring about a far more comprehensive body of regulations covering futures contracts.

In 1981, empowered by the Commodity Futures Trading Commission Act of 1974, the Commission that resulted from this Act subsequently created the National Futures Association (NFA), which, as an industry association, helps the Commission enforce industry standards, law and regulation. Futures industry professionals are licensed and registered by the NFA and are subject to compliance to Commission rules as executed by the NFA.

The NFA has the power to bar a member from trading due to unethical or fraudulent conduct, but the Commission initiates more serious proceedings.

Commodity Futures Trading Commission

The Commodity Futures Trading Commission Act of 1974 established the Commodity Futures Trading Commission (CFTC), and armed that agency with powers greater than those of the Commodity Exchange Authority. Whereas the CEA only authorized the regulation by the Commodity Exchange Commission of certain agricultural commodities enumerated in the CEA, the 1974 Act granted the CFTC exclusive jurisdiction over futures trading in all commodities.[178]

The year 1974 is important to the OTC derivatives market in the United States because, as discussed in Chapter 3, it marked the date of the first clear mandate that these derivatives and swaps are not subject to CFTC regulation, so long as they are entered into on a regulated market. The Commodity Futures Trading Commission Act of 1974 included an important set of provisions that are referred to today as the Treasury Amendment, which stated:

> *Nothing in this chapter [the CEA] shall be deemed to govern or in any way be applicable to transactions in foreign currency, security warrants, security right, resale's or installment loan contracts, repurchase options, government securities, or mortgages and mortgage purchase commitments, unless such transactions involve the sale thereof for future delivery conducted on a board of trade.*[179]

This gave the U.S. Department of Treasury assurance that the large, OTC foreign exchange and other segments of the OTC market would be excluded from CFTC regulation, so long as the trades within the U.S. market satisfy certain requirements such as the mandate that such trades be carried out only between sophisticated investors, or, as stated elsewhere in the law, eligible contract participants (ECPs):

> *Excluded derivative transactions... [n]othing in this chapter... governs or applies to an agreement, contract, or transaction in an excluded commodity if (A) the agreement, contract, or transaction is entered into only between persons that are eligible contract participants at the time at which the persons enter into the agreement, contract or participant; and (B) the agreement, contract, or transaction is not executed or traded on a trading facility.*[180]

U.S. REGULATORS FORMALLY RECOGNIZE SWAPS

By the end of the 1970s, the international OTC derivatives market was born, and swaps began to trade among sophisticated market participants.

The CFTC defined a swap as "an agreement between two parties to exchange a series of cash flows measured by different interest rates, exchange rates, or prices with payments calculated by reference to a principal base (notional amount)."[181]

The term "swap" is critically important for reasons discussed in Chapter 4. The reader is directed to that chapter, as the meaning of this key term changed dramatically on July 21, 2010, in connection with the passage and enactment into law of the Dodd-Frank Wall Street Reform and Consumer Protection Act.

Turf Battles by U.S. Regulators over Derivatives

Starting in 1974 and throughout the 1980s and 1990s, the reach of regulators such as the CFTC into the swaps market was hotly contested, and the banking industry basically sought a regulatory pass to generally conduct derivatives outside of the regulation of the CFTC.

> *With regard to swap transactions, in 1989 the CFTC backed off from its view that it had jurisdictional authority over commodity swaps, and issued a policy statement that provided a safe harbor for most swaps from CFTC jurisdiction. The Commission ruled, however, that '[s]wap transactions eligible for safe harbor treatment may not be marketed to the public.' The banking industry, dissatisfied with the CFTC's Swap Policy Statement lobbied Washington for a bill that would exclude swaps from the CEA. The banking industry's lobbying efforts ultimately resulted in an exemption and not an exclusion. The Futures Trading Practices Act, effective October 1992, amended the CEA to authorize the CFTC to grant exemptions from essentially all of the CEA's provisions. In January 1993, the CFTC exercised its new authority, exempting certain types of swaps from most of the requirements of the CEA, including the exchange-trading requirement, but not from the antifraud and manipulation provisions of the CEA, in what has now become known as the Swaps Exemption. The exemption, however, is limited to very sophisticated participants.[182]*

As for the Securities and Exchange Commission, that U.S. regulator generally refrained from regulating derivatives with a few important exceptions.

The reach of the SEC generally extended to derivatives only to the extent that they come within the definition of securities but not restricted securities. For example, Amendments to the Securities Act of 1933 included specific exclusions from that act for "nonsecurity based swap agreements" and prohibitions that bar SEC regulations from requiring market participants to register any security-based swap agreement.[183]

Swaps Excluded from U.S. Regulation

The CFTC affirmed the 1974 Treasury Amendment exclusion of swaps and certain other derivatives from the reach of the CFTC by issuing a statutory interpretation in 1985. The CFTC stated in that interpretation that the Treasury amendment was limited to transactions between "sophisticated and informed institutions" and not retail investors and the general public.[184]

THE BIRTH OF THE OTC MARKET

The year 1989 was important in the development of derivatives because it marked the second time in which the CFTC made it clear that privately negotiated, off-exchange instruments (like those that were the subject of the Treasury Amendment in 1974), namely, swaps, were outside of the reach of the CEA and therefore the jurisdiction of the CFTC, provided that those swaps are privately-negotiated.

> [Swaps outside of the jurisdiction of the CFTC are those that are the product of] [t]ailoring ... through private negotiations between parties and may involve not only financial terms but issues such as representations, covenants, events of default, term to maturity, and any requirement for the posting of collateral or other credit enhancement. Such tailoring and counterparty credit assessment distinguish swap transactions from exchange transactions where the contract terms are standardized and the counterparty is unknown.[185]

Accordingly, the CEA did not, as of 1989, apply to swaps that are not marketed to the public but instead are privately "negotiated by the parties as to their material terms, based on individualized credit determinations and documented by the parties in an agreement or series of agreements that [are] not fully standardized."[186]

Banks and other market participants that entered into swaps did not know what to think about the 1989 Policy Statement issued by the CFTC and claimed that the statement created legal uncertainty.

THE EVOLUTION OF OPTIONS MARKETS

Historians generally know little about nineteenth-century options, except that the derivative and the market in which it traded was basically corrupt.[187] In the early 1900s, trade groups called the Put and Call Brokers and the Dealers Association created an early options market.[188] Members of these groups basically acted as matchmakers. If someone waned to hold an option, a trade-group member tracked down a seller of the option willing to write it. If the matchmaker failed to locate a seller for the buyer, the matchmaker's firm would, under certain conditions, write the option itself. This is one example of an early broker (one who matches a buyer and seller) and a dealer (one who takes a position in the transaction.)[189]

This early OTC options market while viable had many shortcomings. It was not a liquid market in which options could be freely transferred. Holders of options were unable to get out of their positions by selling their options before they expired; options were held until they matured (i.e., were exercised or expired).[190] Like the OTC market today, buyers of options had to grapple with counterparty risk; if the seller defaulted by, for example, leaving town before performance, the holder of the option of course experienced a loss.

Then the Chicago Board of Trade in 1973, the world's largest exchange for commodity futures, organized the Chicago Board of Options Exchange (CBOE), an exchange exclusively for trading options on stocks.[191] Call option trading began on April 26, 1973, and the first puts were added four years later.[192] Like exchanges for futures, the CBOE created a central marketplace for options by standardizing terms and conditions, thereby adding liquidity. The CBOE also added a clearinghouse that guaranteed to the buyer of an option that the seller would perform its contractual obligations under the option.[193] Options trading grew rapidly until an event that seemed at the time to bring down the entire system: the crash of 1987, which, while critically important is but mentioned in passing here, due to the focus of this text.

After the crash of 1987, many individual investors who previously used options fled from that market, and it was 10 years before the options market recovered to its pre-1987 level.[194] By 2004, total option-trading volume for the first time exceeded one billion.[195] Then, as trading listed options continued to improve and gain traction within the investment community, this market saw a new competitor emerge: the OTC market, where market participants could customize trades to fit individualized risk mitigation or speculative needs.

Over time, exchanges for standardized derivatives such as options began to lose market share to a growing OTC derivatives market as Don M. Chance and Robert Brooks wrote in 2007:

> *Soon thereafter, firms began to create other types of over-the-counter contracts...and, as expected, options began to be used as well [in the OTC market]. Because of the large minimum size of each transaction and the credit risk, however, the general public is unable to participate in this new, revised over-the-counter market. The growth in this institutional over-the-counter market has placed severe pressures on the options exchanges. By the early 1990s the exchanges were trying to become more innovative to win back institutional trade and to stimulate the public's interest in options. These trends, however, should not suggest that options are failing in popularity; in fact they are more popular then ever with corporations and financial institutions, but the growth is concentrated in the over-the-counter market.*[196]

Today put and call options are among the only derivatives that trade in the two markets within this trade: the OTC and exchange-traded markets.

The OTC market grew steadily because of many factors described in Chapter 1, and a few should be summarized here. Government approval was not necessary for OTC derivatives to develop and gain traction and popularity in the OTC market. As a result, options began in the 1980s and 1990s to be traded OTC and the basis of options comprised a wide range of assets (or, in industry parlance, underlyers) such as foreign and domestic stock indices currencies, equities, and commodities.

THE FUTURES TRADING AND PRACTICES ACT AND THE 1993 SWAPS EXEMPTION

Uncertainty in the market as to which derivative is "legal" and where derivatives can legally be traded was one of the factors that led to the passage by Congress in 1992 of the Futures Trading Practices Act (FTPA), which amended the CEA to create an exemption from the CEA's mandatory exchange and central clearing mandate and a "swap agreement" that is "not part of a fungible class of agreements that are standardized as to material economic terms..."[197] Swap transactions that have fixed terms that are not subject to private negotiation do not come within the exclusion from the CEA that was codified by the FTPA in 1992.[198]

Swaps with individualized terms were not to be traded on exchanges (this was not the practice in any event; individualized swaps were not exchange traded or cleared). Regardless of whether they were intended, the FTPA provided statutory authority for bilateral swap negotiation outside the purview of the CEA and beyond the jurisdiction of the CFTC.

Around the time that the CFTC expressly withdrew from the regulation of private swaps, the market in OTC swaps began a growth spurt not only in terms of market size but also in trade complexity, to become, by 2009, a $615 trillion in national global market, the largest financial market of its kind in the history of the world.

For the beginnings of the organization of the formidable OTC market, we look to the early 1980s.

ISDA

In the early 1980s, derivatives were something of a novel transaction in modern finance. Derivatives were evidenced by contracts that banks developed on an individual basis for frequently their interest-rate-swap customers. If a company wanted an interest rate swap, it would turn to a bank for that contract, but that contract would differ in many important respects from a contract for a very similar transaction offered by another bank. Banks received varying fees and substantial spreads for arranging and documenting the earliest derivatives in the OTC market in the 1980s: interest- rate swaps and derivatives based on foreign currency (FX).[199] As more and more of these trades took place, individual banks developed their own standard forms to evidence these transactions, which were sought by other banks, large corporations, and governmental entities.[200]

The early interest rate and FX derivatives were evidenced by their own standard form agreements, which were structured as master agreements.[201] Once dealers entered into interest-rate swaps with end users, such as large corporations, the dealers would in turn trade their interest-rate exposure to other banks, but substantial time and effort were expended to harmonize each dealer's own form of master agreement trade-by-trade.[202] The negotiation experience was described this way:

> *Each swap dealer's standard contract, including the definitions of the terms used in the contract, was unique. The result was that swaps with ostensibly identical terms were different depending on the individual who had negotiated the swap and the dealer from which they came. . . . Market participants fought about everything, not because their position was necessarily, or even arguably, more correct, but, invariably, because their position was more familiar. Few of the instructing institutions understood their forms well enough to take a*

view on what could or could not be changed. Their representatives were sent out with instructions to resist change for fear of undoing the magic of the documentation. As a result, what lawyers like to call the battle of the forms quickly developed.[203]

Around 1984 a group of dealers informally began efforts to organize a trade group to streamline swaps.[204] Salomon Brothers contacted 10 other financial-services firms and assembled the firms to discuss the standardization of derivatives documentation for swaps entered into OTC.[205]

In the first half of 1985, the International Swap Dealers Association (later changing the organizational name to International Swaps and Derivatives Association, Inc.) formally organized and established a code of standard terms for interest-rate swaps.[206] ISDA published its first code of swaps, *The Code of Standard Wording, Assumptions and Provisions for Swaps, 1985 Edition,* which addressed the cash flows of interest-rate swaps and amounts payable on the early termination of swaps.[207]

ISDA expanded its 1985 code in subsequent years and, leading up to the release of the most recent version as of the date of the publication of this text, the 2002 ISDA Master Agreement. We discussed previously in this text improvements made and market factors that drove the sets of standardized forms published by ISDA for OTC swap market participants.

Other efforts to standardize derivative documentation followed. The British Bankers Association offered standardized interest-rate swap documentation under the title "British Bankers Association Interest Rate Swaps," affectionately called "B-Bears."[208] In the years that followed, the British Bankers Association and ISDA codes and documentation were subsequently amended to form standard documentation that continues to be used throughout the OTC derivatives market.

Between 1985 and 1987, interest-rate and currency swaps were the primary focus of ISDA. In 1987, ISDA published the 1987 Interest Rate and Currency Exchange Agreement, which served as a boilerplate agreement between parties whose derivatives entailed multicurrency, cross-border transactions.[209]

Since the 1980s, ISDA pioneered efforts to minimize the cost of OTC derivatives trading and counterparty risk by developing standardized agreements such as two versions of the ISDA Master Agreement (discussed in detail earlier), by bringing about the issuance of legal opinions on the enforceability of netting and collateral arrangements and by promoting sound risk-management practices.

As ISDA-supported derivatives trades expanded in scope beyond interest-rate swaps, the trade organization subsequently changed its name to the International Swaps and Derivatives Association, Inc.

THE 1987 CRASH AND 1990s CRISES

The markets crashed on October 19, 1987. In the years leading up to that crash, equity markets posted strong gains, steadily increasing in volume and value from mid-1982 to mid-1987.[210] The financial markets increasingly saw the execution of program-trading investment strategies in which computers executed substantial volumes of equities under certain conditions.[211]

Investment strategies leading up to the crash also included the use of portfolio insurance, which is designed to limit the losses investors face in a declining market by incorporating models that decreased equity exposure in falling markets.

A week before the crash on October 19, the *Wall Street Journal* published an article citing concerns that in a falling stock market, portfolio insurance could "snowball in to a stunning rout for stocks,"[212] and, generally speaking, that is exactly what happened the following week, as reported in the *Journal* on October 20:

> *The day posed an unprecedented test for the nation's financial futures markets. Many traders long have wondered how index futures and options would function if stocks were in a free fall, and yesterday these new markets clearly hit their limits. First, stock-index futures speeded stock price declines, nearly quintupling previous record one-day drops. Then, as buyers fled the market in alarm, trading nearly dried up, temporarily preventing the markets from functioning as a hedging mechanism—their principal reason for existence. The situation was "unique in the history of the futures markets," said Thomas Russo, a New York futures and securities lawyer. "This is a day we will long remember." Within seconds of the open, S&P 500 stock-index futures prices sank 18 points—surpassing the nerve-racking record declines scored in an entire day on Friday. Salomon Brothers Inc. began unloading contracts at an unheard-of rate of 1,000 at a time, dumping more than $600 million in Stock-index futures in the first hour of trading alone, one pit trader estimated.... With no limits on futures prices and regulators in disagreement over the advisability of a trading halt, there was nothing to stop the 80-point free fall of the S&P 500 that ensued.[213]*

The October 1987 crash constituted a shock to the U.S. financial system. The crash demonstrated to regulators and market participants alike that information overload, impairment of market functions, and relatively new devices and investment strategies, such as program trading, can all work together to bring about a massive free fall in the equities and futures markets.

One of the significant outgrowths of the October 1987 crash was the first test in crisis management of the Federal Reserve Board, which encouraged large market participants, in particular banks providing liquidity at the time to brokers and dealers, to work cooperatively to handle a crisis.[214] The Federal Reserve would do the same in major market crises that would follow in 2008, 21 years after the October 1987 crash, as we discussed in the foundational analysis in Chapter 3.

The Savings and Loan Crisis

In the same era, from 1986 to 1995, due primarily to unsound real estate lending and mismanagement by S&Ls, the United States experienced an S&L crisis that resulted in one-half of all S&Ls failing; the number of federally-insured S&Ls declined from 3,234 to 1,645 according to the Federal Deposit Insurance Corporation.

The following is a detailed summary of the major causes for this crisis according to the United States League of Savings[215]:

- Lack of net worth for many institutions as they entered the 1980s, and a wholly inadequate net-worth regulation.
- Decline in the effectiveness of Regulation Q in preserving the spread between the cost of money and the rate of return on assets, basically stemming from inflation and the accompanying increase in market interest rates.
- Absence of an ability to vary the return on assets with increases in the rate of interest required for deposits.
- Increased competition on the deposit-gathering and mortgage-origination sides of the business, with a sudden burst of new technology making possible a whole new way of conducting financial institutions generally and the mortgage business specifically.
- A rapid increase in the investment powers of associations with passage of the Depository Institutions Deregulation and Monetary Control Act, (also known as the Garn-St. Germain Act), and, more important, through state legislative enactments in a number of important and rapidly growing states. These introduced new risks and speculative opportunities that were difficult to administer. In many instances, management lacked the ability or experience to evaluate them or to administer large volumes of nonresidential construction loans.
- Elimination of regulations initially designed to prevent lending excesses and minimize failures. Regulatory relaxation permitted lending, directly

and through participations, in distant loan markets on the promise of high returns. Lenders, however, were not familiar with these distant markets. It also permitted associations to participate extensively in speculative construction activities with builders and developers who had little or no financial stake in the projects.

- Fraud and insider transaction abuses were the principal cause for some 20 percent of savings and loan failures for the past three years and a greater percentage of the dollar losses borne by the FSLIC.
- A new type and generation of opportunistic savings and loan executives and owners—some of whom operated in a fraudulent manner—whose takeover of many institutions was facilitated by a change in FSLIC rules, which reduced the minimum number of stockholders of an insured association from 400 to one.
- Dereliction of duty on the part of the board of directors of some savings associations. This permitted management to make uncontrolled use of some new operating authority, while directors failed to control expenses and prohibit obvious conflict of interest situations.
- A virtual end of inflation in the American economy, together with overbuilding in multifamily, condominium-type residences and in commercial real estate in many cities. In addition, real estate values collapsed in the energy states of Texas, Louisiana, and Oklahoma, which was, in large part, due to falling oil prices and weakness that occurred in the mining and agricultural sectors of the economy.
- Pressures felt by the management of many associations to restore networth ratios. Anxious to improve earnings, they departed from their traditional lending practices into credits and markets involving higher risks, with which they had little experience.
- The lack of appropriate, accurate, and effective evaluations of the S&L business by public accounting firms, security analysts, and the financial community.
- Organizational structures and supervisory laws, adequate for policing and controlling the business in the protected environment of the 1960s and 1970s, resulted in fatal delays and indecision in the examination/supervision process in the 1980s.
- Federal and state examination and supervisory staffs were insufficient in number, experience, or ability to deal with the new world of savings and loan operations.
- The inability or unwillingness of the now defunct Federal Home Loan Bank Board and its legal and supervisory staff to deal with problem institutions in a timely manner. Many institutions, which ultimately closed with big losses, were known problem cases for a year or more. Often, it appeared, political considerations delayed necessary supervisory action.

The foregoing summary of the causes of the S&L crisis is important because many of these causes were similar to those that the author has identified in Chapter 1 as direct, coalescing causes of the 2008 market crises.

The Birth of Subprime Residential Mortgage Lending

After the S&L crisis, the subprime mortgage real estate crisis began to take root in the early 1990s.

Subprime lending is a form of financing of consumer and residential loans at high interest rates to individuals whose credit profile suggests a high risk of default. Subprime borrowers are middle-class or low-income families who, for a variety of reasons, obtain loan proceeds at interest rates that are higher than those offered on conventional loans.

Subprime lending in the residential mortgage sector thrived during a period of time in which mortgage origination and securitization, which are described in Chapter 1, were not subject to stringent federal or state regulation. In the mid-1990s, subprime lending was not as attractive to lenders as it was a decade later, before the collapse of the U.S. housing market. In the decade that preceded the market crisis of 2008, mortgage products that were attractive to subprime borrowers, including loans with adjustable rates, coupled with lax regulation, fueled massive unrestrained subprime lending.

> To cover their risk, [subprime] lenders charge [subprime] borrowers higher-than-conventional interest rates. Or they make "adjustable rate" loans, which offer low initial interest rates that jump sharply after a few years. Only a decade ago, sub-prime loans were rare. But starting in the mid-1990s, subprime lending began surging; these loans comprised 8.6 percent of all mortgages in 2001, soaring to 20.1 percent by 2006. Since 2004, more than 90 percent of the sub-prime mortgages came with exploding adjustable rates. With interest rates low, housing prices on a steady risk and practically no government regulation, mortgage finance companies devised high-interest, high-fee schemes to entice families to take out loans that traditional savings banks would not make. Many of the lenders were legitimate operations providing a market for credit-risky people. But there also were huge corporations, such as Household Finance, that sought extraordinary profits through unsavory means, called predatory loans. Not subject to government regulation, they bent the rules, lowering normal banking standards. Mortgage bankers, the street hustlers of the lending world, often used mail solicitations and ads that shouted, "Bad Credit? No Problem!" "Zero Percent

*Down Payment!" to find people who were closed out of home
ownership, or home owners who could be talked into refinanc-
ing... the sub-prime lenders didn't hold on to these loans. Instead,
they sold them—and the risk—to investment banks and investors
who considered these high interest rate, sub-prime loans a gold-
mine. By 2007, the sub-prime business had become a $1.5 trillion
global market for investors seeking high return.*[216]

Derivatives and Futures after 1994

In 1994, people began to predict in an eerily accurate way the market crisis of
2008. In congressional testimony in 1994, following his study of derivatives
markets, comptroller general Charles A. Bowsher testified:

*The sudden failure or abrupt withdrawal from trading of... large
U.S. dealers could cause liquidity problems in the markets and
could also pose risks to others, including federally insured banks
and the financial system as a whole.... In some cases intervention
has and could result in a financial bailout paid for or guaranteed
by taxpayers.*[217]

Also in 1994, John Lindholm, writing in the *Columbia Business Law
Review*, stated:

*The size of the derivatives market, coupled with the fact that ap-
proximately seven financial institutions account for nearly all of the
exposure of American banks, leads some regulators to fear a ripple
effect. Under this scenario, a major bank or banks might accumu-
late losses, default on payments, and set off an interbank financial
crisis affecting the entire market.*[218]

The shocking aspect of this is not that the market crisis of 2008 was
almost perfectly predicted over a decade earlier, in 1994, but in 1994, the
market continued to see major, high profile, front-page articles of severe
failures in which derivatives played at least a role. For context that helps
explain this complacency, a brief step back and review of the derivatives
market in the 1990s may be helpful.

One former Morgan Stanley derivatives trader wrote that, by the mid-
1990s, derivatives became the largest market in the world and caused significant damage just 15 years after the beginnings of their widespread use in
the early 1980s:

*Derivatives have become the largest market in the world. The size of
the derivatives market, estimated at $55 trillion in 1996, is double*

the value of all U.S. stocks and more than ten times the entire U.S. national debt. Meanwhile, derivatives losses continue to multiply. Of course, plenty of firms made money on derivatives, including Morgan Stanley, and the firm's derivatives group is thriving, even as derivatives purchasers lick their wounds. Some clients tired of having their faces ripped off or being blown up, and business declined briefly in 1995 and 1996.[219]

In 1993 other banks joined Morgan Stanley, a leading derivatives provider in the United States, as derivatives revenues expanded, as did the geographical reach of the U.S.-based banks:

In the early 1990s, when the derivatives business became more competitive in the United States, [derivatives] salesmen looked abroad for victims, especially in Latin America and the Far and Middle East. Senior management ventured abroad on business trips they called "safaris" hunting large derivatives deals they called "elephants." These managers described prospective sales in terms of hunting down big game, and their derivatives safaris often contemplated real hunting trips.[220]

Massive Losses in the Mid-1990s

The bankruptcy filing by Southern California's Orange County in 1994 constituted the largest municipal default in the history of the United States.[221]

In 1994, the same year that Orange County, California, became bankrupt after a $1.7 billion loss, and losses were experienced by two sophisticated, publicly traded companies, credit derivatives were born.

In June 1994, a group of J.P. Morgan bankers at the retreat devised a means by which credit risk—the risk of default on an underlying loan—could be passed off to another party or essentially insured by payment of a premium under the terms of a credit-default swap (CDS).

Originally designed to insure against the default on corporate loans prior to 1994, credit derivatives were innovated and CDSs were applied in the secondary residential mortgage market and this innovation, while excellent in principle but unregulated in practice, played a major role in the market crisis of 2008.

In 1994, high-profile litigation and losses involving derivatives continued to steal headlines. Procter & Gamble and Gibson Greetings, sustained $102 million and $23 million in losses, respectively. Around this time, the U.S. General Accounting Office (GAO) issued a report that concluded that the market structure and derivatives within the OTC market could present major systemic risks to the financial system as a whole.[222]

The GAO Report focused on the absence of federal regulation of dealers and the lack of minimum capital requirements on those dealers in a manner that is generally required of banks. In light of this absence of federal regulation over derivatives, the GAO Report urged greater oversight of derivatives activities by the Securities and Exchange Commission (SEC), more expansive disclosure requirements to explain derivatives and their risk to investors, and mark-to-market accounting for derivatives and other financial instruments. Looking back, this admonition resulted in very little federal action to prevent future derivative-related losses.

The mid-1990s continued to witness massive derivative losses on various continents throughout the world. Old line, and established Baring's Bank became bankrupt after a $1.3 billion loss in 1995. In the Far East, Sumitomo, one of the first Japanese *keiretsu* powers of interlocked financial networks, suffered $2.6 billion in losses in 1996. The government of Belgium lost $12 billion in 1997, and the National Westminster Bank lost $143 million in 1997.[223] Concern mounted. For example, in 1997, a decade before the most recent financial crises, the Chairman of the CFTC, Brooksey Born, expressed concern about the potential risks that unregulated derivatives posed to the overall economy. Effective, concerted regulatory action was absent.

In 1998, as we discussed in Chapter 3, the use of derivatives and subsequent failure of the hedge fund Long-Term Capital Management (LTCM) triggered a Federal Reserve-led rescue that prevented the destabilization of American and possibly international markets. Still, no comprehensive regulatory action to rein in the use of derivatives resulted.

The decade after October 1987 witnessed severe credit and market deterioration in several financial sectors, caused by the Russian credit crisis and fallout from the September 1998 failure of LTCM with its 2 Nobel Prize winners and veteran investment managers.

Long-Term Capital Management earned for its investors returns of more than 40 percent each year and did so using arbitrage strategies and thousands of derivative contracts,[224] as described here:

> This one obscure arbitrage fund had amassed an amazing $100 billion in assets, virtually all of it borrowed—borrowed that is, from the bankers [assembled at the offices of the New York Federal Reserve for purposes of establishing a fund to bail out LTCM]. As monstrous as this indebtedness was, it was by no means the worst of Long-Term's problems. The fund had entered into thousands of derivative contracts, which had endlessly intertwined it with every bank on Wall Street. These contracts, essentially side bets on market

*prices, covered an astronomical sum—more than $1 trillion worth
of exposure. If Long-Term defaulted, all of the banks in the room
would be left holding one side of a contract for which the other
side no longer existed. In other words, they would be exposed to
tremendous—and untenable—risks. Undoubtedly, there would be
a frenzy as every bank rushed to escape its now one-sided obligations and tried to sell its collateral from Long-Term.... Officials
had wondered what would happen if one big link in the chain
should fail.*[225]

The 1998, failure of LTCM, a very large market participant, the Federal Reserve's soliciting the participation of other, remaining market participants, as well as other federal efforts to manage market crises would repeat
itself not once, but at least three times a decade later in 2008, when, in a
single year, Bear Stearns, Lehman Brothers, and AIG (as well as other financial services firms such as Washington Mutual) failed, threatening much of
the entire global financial system.

In 1998, the CFTC released statistics that showed that the OTC derivatives market has grown—and continues to grow—by leaps and bounds.
These remarkable statistics cited by the CFTC indicate that the regulators
were aware of segments within the OTC market which appeared to be dou-
bling at least annually.

*Use of OTC derivatives has grown at very substantial rates over
the past few years. According to the most recent market survey by
[ISDA], the notional value of new transactions reported by ISDA
embers in interest-rate swaps, currency swaps, and interest-rate options during the first half of 1997 increased 46% over the previous six-month period. The notional value of outstanding contracts
in these instruments was $28.733 trillion, up 12.9% from year-
end 1996, 62.2% from year-end 1995, and 154.2% from year-end
1994. ISDA's 1996 market survey noted that there were 633,316
outstanding contracts in these instruments as of year-end 1996,
up 47% from year-end 1995, which in turn represented a 40.7%
increase over year-end 1994[.]*[226]

THE COMMODITY FUTURES MODERNIZATION ACT OF 2000

With this growth and the losses in the 1990s in mind, on December 21,
2000, the Commodity Futures Modernization Act (CFMA) was signed
into law, severely restricting the CFTC's and the SEC's ability to regulate

OTC derivatives[227] and bringing about sweeping changes to the way derivatives traded.

An important theme that weaves through the provisions of CFMA is the liberalization of derivatives and futures regulation to free-up the most sophisticated derivatives (including futures) market participants, such as large banks, in order to permit them to compete with their non-U.S. counterparts. Another key theme embodied in CFMA was that regulation by the CFTC would not be evenly applied across the board, but instead would depend on the sophistication of the party trading the product and the market within which it traded.

Other key features of the CFMA, which constitutes the most comprehensible reworking of derivatives (and futures) in the United States prior to Dodd- Frank, included:

- The establishment of core principles and standards to permit clearing-houses and exchanges in futures to satisfy regulatory mandates.
- Clarifying and making more certain the legality of privately-negotiated swaps, provided that certain conditions were satisfied.[228]

The CFMA also directed the CFTC to recognize and regulate differently the distinctly separate functions of an exchange and a clearinghouse (described in detail in Chapter 3, a critical foundation for understanding new derivatives law in Chapter 4). The CFMA requires the CFTC to mandate derivatives clearing organizations (DCOs, described in Chapters 3 and 10) abide by a set of core principles which are important for identifying and managing risks associated with clearing, the settlement process of listed derivatives and futures.[229]

ENRON LOOPHOLE

In Chapter 1, we identified the financing tools and finance culture, and specifically special-purpose entities (SPE) as a root of the 2008 market crises. The use of these entities coupled with lax federal regulation caused the 2008 market crises.

One important factor, already discussed in passing in this chapter which resulted in lax federal regulation in the derivatives area was the passage of the Commodity Futures Modernization Act of 2000 (CFMA). The first provision of the CFMA to receive regulatory attention and extensive media coverage was the "Enron Loophole," which was a reference to Section 2 of the CFMA (in particular, subparts (h) and (g) of Section 2 of the CFMA).

That Section created an exemption which remained until the 2008 passage of the Omnibus Farm Bill (which imposed CFTC regulations applicable to fully-regulated exchanges on electronic trading facilities, but not Enron Online, which was one of hundreds of Enron schemes to trade among Enron affiliates). The Enron Loophole exempted certain energy derivatives from regulation by the chief U.S. derivatives (futures) regulator, the CFTC. The loophole has been closed.

THE FIRST DECADE OF THE TWENTY-FIRST CENTURY

Important developments in the first decade of the twenty-first century in derivatives and futures are outlined here, and their roles in the 2008 market crises are described in greater detail in Chapters 1 and 2 earlier in this text:

- The relaxation of the federal regulation of swaps and other derivatives (and before that, the deregulation of banking).
- The availability of credit, coupled with the extensive, unregulated use of mortgage securitization.
- The extensive use of credit derivatives in connection with securitization, and the exclusion of credit derivatives from an effective regulatory regime. (Credit derivatives were excluded, by Title I of the CFMA, from CFTC regulation).
- The failure, generally, of federal regulators to monitor and prevent the 2008 market crises.

It was this last point that the Financial Crises Inquiry Commission (whose role after the 2008 market crises is part of the subject of Chapter 1) addressed as a critical factor behind the crises. As correctly stated in its 545-page report:

> We conclude [that] the government was ill prepared for the crises, and its inconsistent response added to the uncertainty and panic in the financial markets.... As our report shows, key policy-makers...who were best positioned to watch over our markets were ill prepared for the events of 2007 and 2008...They were hampered because they did not have a clear grasp of the financial system they were charged with overseeing, particularly as it had evolved in the years leading up to the crises.[230]

*   *   *

The history of derivatives teaches that these financial instruments have likely been in existence since the beginning of time in some form, and governments have, since periods of antiquity, attempted to regulate speculation following numerous financial crises or upheavals along the way throughout our history. In several of those crises, derivatives played a role. The take-away is not that derivatives are instruments that are inherently problematic or by their very nature lead to investment losses but, instead, that if these financial products and the markets within which they trade are understood and properly monitored and regulated, market crises based on the misuse of tools of finance may be limited. In the next chapter, we continue the historical survey by looking at derivative market structure—before and after the Dodd-Frank reforms.

NOTES

1. Am. Stock Exchange v. Commodity Futures Trading Commission, 528 F.Supp. 1145 (SDNY 1982), quoted in Edward J. Swan, *Building the Global Market: A 4000 Year History of Derivatives* (New York: Kluwer Law International, 2000), 5. (Hereinafter "Swan, *Building the Global Market*.")
2. Swan, *Building the Global Market*, 6.
3. Ibid., 6.
4. Ibid., 7.
5. See, e.g., Swan, *Building the Global Market*, 31; David Courtney, *From Forums to Futures* (New York: Credit Lyonnais Rouse, 1991); J. A. Findlay, *The Baltic Exchange* (London: Witherley, 1927); S. W. Dowling, *The Exchanges of London* (London: Butterworths, 1929).
6. Swan, *Building the Global Market*, 4, n. 15.
7. See Paul C. Harding, *Mastering the ISDA Master Agreements* (1992 and 2002), 3rd ed. (Upper Saddle River, NJ: Prentice Hall, 2010), 9.
8. "Chinese civilization has enjoyed the longest history and has, at least until the present century, directly involved far more people than another. Yet for a number of reasons it is very largely ignored by Western writers, partially from a contagious ignorance, but mainly because our modern Western civilization has been largely derived from Roman and Greek sources which in turn learned much from Mesopotamia and Egypt but nothing directly from China itself; from which with a very few notable exceptions, the West was cut off until the geographical discoveries of the sixteenth and later centuries." Glen Davies, *A History of Money: From Ancient Times to Present Day* (Cardiff, Wales: University of Wales Press 1994), 54.
9. One historian suggests that ecclesiastic writers in the Middle Ages may have turned a blind eye to practices in the foreign-exchange market that violated the law in order not to disturb the business of foreign exchange. "It is very easy to point out inconsistencies between the writing of various scholastic writers, and indeed between writing of the same writer, or to criticize them for their inability to realize or admit openly that anything short of a complete ban on exchange transactions was bound to leave wide loopholes through which the

anti-usury law could be evaded with impunity. To understand the attitude of ecclesiastic writers, we must bear in mind the conflicting considerations of trying to safeguard the defenseless from exploitation and ruin by usurers and, at the same time, abstaining from blocking necessary and essential Foreign Exchange Business. All but the most rigid dogmatists felt impelled to try to reconcile these requirements by turning a blind eye towards the true character of some practices." Paul Einzig, *The History of Foreign Exchange* (London: Macmillan, 1962), 89–90.

10. Holy Bible, Genesis 29 verse 20 (Authorized King James version with explanatory notes and cross-references to the standard works of the Church of Jesus Christ of Latter-Day Saints, 44).

11. Ibid.

12. Joseph L. Motes III, "A Primer on the Trade and Regulation of Derivative Instruments," *St. Mary's University Literary Review* 49: 579, 599, n. 95 (1995–1996), citing Kenneth A. Froot, et al., "A Framework for Risk Management" *Harvard Business Review,* 92 (November–December 1994).

13. See, e.g., Swan, *Building the Global Market*, p. 36.

14. Ibid., 31.

15. Ibid., 35.

16. Ibid., 31.

17. Swan, *Building The Global Market: A 4000 Year History of Derivatives*, 28 (Figure 2.1).

18. Swan, *Building The Global Market: A 4000 Year History of Derivatives*, 29 (Figure 2.2).

19. Ibid., 36.

20. Shani Shamah, *A Foreign Exchange Primer* (Hoboken, NJ: John Wiley & Sons, 2006), 7–8.

21. Swan, *Building the Global Market*, 36.

22. Richard Duncan-Jones, *Structure and Scale in the Roman Economy* (Cambridge, England: Cambridge University Press, New York, 1990), 148–149, cited in Swan, *Building the Global Market*, 76.

23. Swan, *Building the Global Market*, 77.

24. A key contribution of Roman law to the development of derivative contracts was the recognition of consensual contracts (*nudo consensu*). These could be entered into without the formal requirements of earlier Roman law. Nothing more than consent was required. No executed document or deed, no list of witnesses, no formal acts, no specific words, and no delivery of any commodity or its price were required. A pure sale of promises entered into by agreement of the parties was all that was needed. This represents a Roman liberalization of derivative contracts beyond the formalities of Middle-Eastern commerce, and, indeed even beyond the liberality of modern derivative commerce in the United Kingdom and the United States where the doctrine of consideration might prove an impediment to such a consensual agreement. A description of these consensual contracts is found in sections 135–138 of the third book of *The Institutes of Gaius*. Cited in Swan, *Building the Global Market*, 78.

25. Davies, *A History of Money*, 116.

26. Swan, *Building the Global Market*, 95.
27. Ibid., 85.
28. Ibid.
29. Ibid., 111.
30. Ibid., 61.
31. Davies, *A History of Money*, 118–119. ("Since Christianity and coinage had disappeared from England together it seemed highly appropriate and unsurprising that it became widely accepted that they also returned together ... the influence of Christian missionaries in persuading Nordic rules to issue their own coined moneys is indisputable.").
32. Eileen Power, *The Wool Trade in English Medieval History* (Oxford: Oxford University Press, 1941), 52, cited in Swan, *Building the Global Market*, 110–111.
33. Swan, *Building the Global Market*, 95.
34. Ibid., 83.
35. Ibid., 95–96.
36. Ibid., 99–100.
37. Ibid., 100.
38. Ibid., 103.
39. Ibid., 103–104.
40. Ibid., 102.
41. Anna Stolley Persky, "Do the Math: The Role of Derivatives in Fiscal Fallout," *Washington Lawyer* (June 2010): 24.
42. Swan, *Building a Global Market*, 119–120.
43. Swan, *Building a Global Market*, 115.
44. Ibid.
45. Ibid., 119–120.
46. Sir Edward Coke, *Third Part of the Institutes of the Laws of England*, 4th ed. (London, Crooke, Leake, 1669), 178–180, cited in Swan, *Building the Global Market*, 37–38; also (with respect to "Regrating," citing Stephen Browne, *The Laws Against Ingrossing, Forestalling, Regrating and Monolising* (London: W. Griffin, 1765), 1–2.
47. Douglas M. MacDowell, *The Law in Classical Athens* (London: Thames & Hudson, 1978), 138, cited in Swan, *Building the Global Market*, 60.
48. Davies, *A History of Money*, 41.
49. Swan, *Building the Global Market*, 139.
50. Ibid., 157.
51. Ibid., 154–155.
52. Ibid., 155–156.
53. "CFTC Chair Gary Gensler Addresses Markit OTC Derivatives Markets Conference," *Wall Street Journal* blogs, March 9, 2010. Available at http://blogs.wsj.com/marketbeat/2010/03/09/cftc-chair-gary-gensler-address-to-markit-otc-derivatives-markets-conference/.
54. Swan, *Building the Global Market*, 213.
55. Ibid., 214.
56. Ibid., 190.

57. Ibid., 190–191.
58. E. R. Carhart, "The New York Produce Exchange," *American Produce Exchange Markets, The Annals of the American Academy of Political and Social Science* (Philadelphia: American Academy of Political and Social Science: 1991), quoted in Swan, *Building the Global Market*, 191.
59. Swan, *Building the Global Market*, 191.
60. Ibid., 191.
61. Ibid., 190–191.
62. Ibid., 190.
63. Ibid.
64. Adam Smith, *The Wealth of Nations*, vol. 2 (London: David Campbell, 1991), 23–42.
65. Swan, *Building the Global Market*, 189–190 (emphasis added).
66. Ibid., 191.
67. Herbert Alan Johnson, *The Law Merchant and Negotiable Instruments in Colonia New York 1664 to 1730* (Chicago: Loyola University Press, 1963), cited in Swan, *Building the Global Market*, 192.
68. Swan, *Building the Global Market*, 214.
69. Michael M. Edwards, *The Growth of the British Cotton Trade: 1780–1815* (Manchester: Manchester University Press, 1967), 110, cited in Swan, *Building the Global Market*, 214.
70. *Irwin v. Willar*, 110 U.S. 499, 508–09 (1884), cited in. Swan, *Building the Global Market*, 219. See also Swan, *Building the Global Market*, 220 n. 133.
71. Swan, *Building the Global Market*, 222.
72. Ibid., 223.
73. "Savings and Loan Industry, U.S.," *EH.Net Encyclopedia,* edited by Robert Whaples. June 10, 2003, http://eh.net/encyclopedia/article/mason.savings.loan.industry.us.
74. Swan, *Building the Global Market*, 224.
75. Ibid., 224–225.
76. "Legislation Affecting Commodity and Stock Exchanges," *Harvard Law Review*, 45 (1932): 912–925, 925 n. 60. "However the [German Exchange Act] was not a success, did not prevent small speculators from continuing to lose money in futures, and was blamed for the deterioration of the German markets. 'Future dealings in grain and stocks were not in fact abolished, but the brokers reverted to more primitive exchange mechanisms in order to evade the law. And such dealings as were carried on were of doubtful legal validity. As a result of this situation the markets in grain and stocks were greatly narrowed, fluctuations were of greater extent, business was driven to foreign exchanges, and commercial ethics were demoralized.' . . . Consequently, the [German] Exchange Act was partially repealed in 1908." Cited in Swan, *Building the Global Market*, 224–225.
77. "Share-Pushing: Report of the Departmental Committee Appointed by the Board of Trade, 1936–1937, Cmnd. 5539 (London: HMSO, 1937): 14–15, cited in Swan, *Building the Global Market*, 225–226.
78. Swan, *Building the Global Market*, 226.

79. Ibid., 227.
80. Ibid.
81. Ibid., 228.
82. Ibid., 230.
83. Ibid.
84. Ibid., 232.
85. Ibid., 212, 232.
86. Ibid., 232.
87. Vanessa Cross, "Dutch Tulipmania in 17th Century Holland." www.suite101 .com/content/dutch-tulipmania-in-17th-century-holland-a209292.
88. Andrew Beattie, "Market Crashes: The Tulip and Bulb Craze," Investopedia, at www.investopedia.com/features/crashes/crashes2.asp.
89. Ibid.
90. Charles Mackay, "Tulip mania," in *Extraordinary Popular Delusions and the Madness of Crowds*, Chapter 3 (London: Richard Bentley, 1841), cited in "Tulip mania," Wikipedia, http://en.wikipedia.org/wiki/tulip_mania.
91. Ibid.
92. Cross, "Dutch Tulipmania."
93. Ibid.
94. "South Sea Bubble Short History," www.library.hbs.edu/hc/ssb/history_print .html.
95. "South Sea Bubble Short History; see also Andrew Beattie, "Market Crashes: The South Sea Bubble," www.investopedia.com/features/crashes/crashes3.asp.
96. Swan, *Building A Global Market*, 182.
97. Ibid., 183–184.
98. Ibid., 182.
99. Ibid., 183.
100. Ibid., 183–184.
101. Ibid., 185.
102. Ibid., 185–186.
103. *The History and Proceedings of the House of Commons from the Restoration to the Present Time* (London: Rich and Chandler, 1742), vol. 7, 379–385, cited in Swan, *Building the Global Market*, 185–186.
104. R. B. Fergusson, "Commercial Expectations and the Guarantee of the Law: Sales Transactions in Mid-Nineteenth Century England," in G. R. Rubin and David Sugarman (eds.), *Law, Economy and Society, 1750–1914* (London: Abingdon, 1984), and other sources. Cited in Swan, *Building the Global Market,* 187–189.
105. Ry & Moody KB (1826), 386, cited in Swan, *Building the Global Market,* 207–208.
106. Ibid., 208.
107. Ibid., 209.
108. Ibid.
109. 2 Bing (NC) 722 (1836), cited in Swan, *Building the Global Market,* 209. English law prohibited stock jobbing applied to the future delivery of stock, but not the future delivery of commodities such as cotton.

110. 8 & 9 Vict c. 109, cited by Swan, *Building the Global Market,* 211.
111. *Hansard, Parliamentary Debates* (3rd Series) Vol. 82 (London: Cornelius Buck, 1845) 794, cited in Swan, *Building the Global Market,* 211, n. 85.
112. Swan, *Building the Global Market,* 212–213.
113. Ibid.
114. Ibid., 212.
115. Ibid., n. 89.
116. E. R. Carhart, "The New York Produce Exchange," *American Produce Exchange Markets, The Annals of the American Academy of Political and Social Science,* 38 (2) 533 (Philadelphia: American Academy of Political and Social Science, Sept. 1911), cited by Swan, *Building the Global Market,* 223.
117. *Irwin v. Williar,* 110 U.S. 499 (1884), referenced in Persky, "Do the Math," 24.
118. Carolyn H. Jackson, "Have You Hedged Today? The Inevitable Advent of Consumer Derivatives," *Fordham Law Review,* 67 (1998–1999): 3205, 3218.
119. Swan, *Building the Global Market,* 243.
120. Ibid.
121. Ibid., 244
122. Yale M. Braunstein, "The Role of Informational Failures in the Financial Meltdown," 2009, www.google.com/search?client=safari&rls=en&q=Yale+Braunstein,+the+role+of+informational+failures+in+the+financial+meltdown,+2009&ie=UTF-8&oe=UTF-8.
123. Robert F. Bruner and Sean D. Carr, *The Panic of 1907: Lessons Learned from the Market's Perfect Storm* (Hoboken, NJ: John Wiley & Sons, 2007), 38–40.
124. See, e.g., Ellis W. Tallman and Jon R. Moen, "The Transmission of the Financial Crisis in 1907: An Empirical Investigation," Past, Present and Policy, 4th International Conference; "The Sub-prime Crisis and How it Changed the Past," Graduate Institute, Geneva, February 3–4, 2011, 8.
125. Swan, *Building the Global Market,* 246.
126. Gregory Zuckerman, "Trader Made Billions on Subprime," *Wall Street Journal* (January 15, 2008), in Michael Lewis, ed., *Panic! The Story of Modern Financial Insanity* (New York: W. W. Norton & Co., 2009), 362–64.
127. Swan, *Building the Global Market,* 248.
128. *Jamieson v. Wallace,* 167 Ills. 388; *Walker v. Johnson,* 59 Ills. App. 448; and *Lamson v. West,* 201 Ills. App. 251.; R. B. Westerfield, "Middlemen in English Business 1660–1760," *Transactions of the Connecticut Academy of Arts and Sciences,* 19 (May 1916): 93, 244. All cited in Swan, *Building the Global Market,* 248.
129. 198 U.S. 236 (1905).
130. Swan, *Building the Global Market,* 249. The implication made by Justice Holmes of the Supreme Court in Christie was that futures contracts that were made on a board of trade, were to be regarded as serious in business purpose, regardless of the parties' intent in making the contract.
131. Ellis W. Tallman and Jon R. Moen, "The Transmission of the Financial Crisis in 1907: An Empirical Investigation," Past, Present and Policy, 4th International Conference, "The Sub-prime Crisis and How it Changed the Past,"

Graduate Institute, Geneva, February 3–4, 2011. "... we believe that the transmission of the Banking Panic of 1907 to the financial market more generally, and the rest of the country (and the rest of the world) was not the result of only the trust company runs. Despite the initial distress on the stock market, the panic had only minor effects on the interior of the United States or on international markets until the New York Clearing House imposed a suspension of convertibility of deposits into currency on October 26," 3.

132. 39 Stat. 476 (1916), 26 U.S.C. Sections 731-752 (1926).
133. Swan, *Building the Global Market*, 249.
134. Ibid., 249–251.
135. Jackson, "Have You Hedged Today?"
136. *Hill v. Wallace*, 259 U.S. 44 (1922), cited in Swan, *Building the Global Market*, 251.
137. Jonathan I. Levy, "Contemplating Delivery: Futures Trading and the Problem of Commodity Exchange in the United States, 1875–1905," *American Historical Review* 307 (2006), citing "Fictitious Dealings in Agricultural Products: House Committee on Agriculture Hearing Reports" (1892); see also B. Peter Pashigian, "The Political Economy of Futures Market Regulation," *Journal of Business* 59, no. 2, pt. 2 (1986): 157. The focal point of opposition to futures trading were the grain farmers in the Great Plains.
138. *Board of Trade v. Olsen*, 262 U.S. 1 (1923).
139. B. Peter Pashigian, "The Political Economy of Futures Market Regulation."
140. Ibid.
141. "How the Fed Works," *Time* (December 28, 2009–January 4, 2010): 73.
142. Thomas A. Tormey, "A Derivatives Dilemma: The Treasury Amendment Controversy and the Regulatory Status of Foreign Currency Options," *Fordham Law Review* 65 (1997): 2313, 2325–2326.
143. Michael Lewis, *The Big Short: Inside the Doomsday Machine* (New York: W. W. Norton & Co., 2010), 55.
144. William Patalon III, "Study of Great Depression Shows Postponed Foreclosures and Spikes in Mortgage Rates," November 6, 2008, www.contrarianprofits.com/articles/study-of-great-depression-shows-postponed-foreclosures-and-spikes-in-mortgage-rates/7969.
145. Franklin Delano Roosevelt letter to the House Committee on Interstate and Foreign Commerce (Mar. 26, 1934), quoted in the November 24, 2009, seminar presentation at K&L Gates LLP by former CFTC head Walter Lukken, available at www.klgates.com/newsstand/Detail.aspx?publication=6047.
146. Jason Zweig, "What History Tells Us About the Market," *Wall Street Journal*, October 11–12, 2008.
147. Ibid.
148. Ibid.
149. 15 U.S.C. Section 78d.
150. Frank Partnoy, *F.I.A.S.C.O.: Blood in the Water on Wall Street* (New York: W. W. Norton & Co., 2009), 43
151. Ibid.
152. Swan, *Building the Global Market*, 252–253.

153. Ibid., 251; Jonathan Lurie, "Commodities Exchanges as Self-Regulating Organizations in the Late Nineteenth Century: Some Perimeters in the History of American Administrative Law," *Rutgers Law Review* 28 (1975): 1127.

154. Swan, *Building the Global Market*, 254.

155. 7 U.S.C. Section 1, et seq.

156. Commodity Futures Trading Commission, "Futures Regulation Before the Creation of the CFTC," available at www.cftc.gov/About/Historyofthe CFTC/history_precftc.html.

157. Swan, *Building the Global Market*, 254–255.

158. See also U.S. House of Representatives Report No. 421, 74th Congress, Accompanying the Commodity Exchange Act, March 18, 1935.

159. Swan, *Building the Global Market*, 255.

160. CEA, 7 U.S.C. Section 6(a) (2009). Violation of the exchange requirement is a felony, and the CEA authorizes the imposition of substantial fines. CEA, 7 U.S.C. Section 13(b)(2009).

161. Phillip McBride Johnson and Thomas Lee Hazen, *Derivatives Regulation* (New York: Aspen, 2004), Section 1.18.

162. Tormey, "A Derivatives Dilemma," 2313, 2326.

163. Swan, *Building the Global Market*, 255.

164. Ibid., 256.

165. Ibid., 255–256.

166. Patalon III, "Study of Great Depression."

167. Ibid.

168. John Atlas and Peter Dreier, "The Conservative Origins of the Sub-Prime Lending Crisis," *The American Prospect*, December 18, 2007. Available at http://prospect.org/cs/articles?article=the_conservative_origins_of_the_subprime_mortgage_crisis.

169. Ibid.

170. John F. Marshall and Kenneth R. Kapner, *Understanding Swaps* (New York: John Wiley & Sons, 1993), 4.

171. Roger Lowenstein, *When Genius Failed: The Rise and Fall of Long-Term Capital Management* (New York: Random House, 2000), 8.

172. Marshall and. Kapner, *Understanding Swaps,* 3.

173. Ibid., 1.

174. Ibid., 3.

175. Ibid., 5.

176. Persky, "Do the Math," 25.

177. Ibid.

178. CFTC, "Futures Regulation Before the Creation of the CFTC."

179. Jackson, "Have You Hedged Today?" 3205, 3220, quoting, in n. 152, 7 U.S.C. Section 2(ii).

180. 7 U.S.C.A. Section 2 (d)(1)(2009).

181. 54 Federal Register 30694 (July 21, 1989).

182. Jackson, "Have You Hedged Today?" 3205, 3221.

183. *Securities Act of 1933* (New York: Aspen Publishers, 2008), Section 2A.

184. Joanne T. Medero, "The Great Treasury Amendment Debate," *Futures Industry* (March 1997): 19.
185. 54 Fed.Reg. 30694 (July 21, 1989).
186. Ibid.
187. Don M. Chance and Robert Brooks, *An Introduction to Derivatives and Risk Management* (Mason, OH: South-Western, Cengage Learning, 2007), 23.
188. Ibid.
189. Ibid.
190. Ibid.
191. Ibid.
192. Ibid.
193. Ibid.
194. Ibid.
195. Ibid.
196. Chance and Brooks, *An Introduction to Derivatives and Risk Management*, 23–24.
197. Pub. L. No. 102-546.
198. See 58 Fed.Reg. 5587 (January 22, 1993).
199. Sean M. Flanagan, "The Rise of a Trade Association: Group Interactions Within the International Swaps and Derivatives Association," *Harvard Law Review* 6 (2001): 211, 234.
200. Ibid., 211, 234–235.
201. Ibid., 211, 235.
202. Ibid.
203. Jeffrey B. Golden, "Setting Standards in the Evolution of Swap Documentation," *International Financial Law Review* 13 (May 1994): 18, cited in Flanagan, "The Rise of a Trade Association," 211, 235.
204. Marshall and Kapner, *Understanding Swaps*, 195.
205. Flanagan, "The Rise of a Trade Association," 211, 235 (2001).
206. Marshall and Kapner, *Understanding Swaps*, 21, 195.
207. Ibid.
208. Ibid.
209. Francesca Taylor, *Mastering Derivatives Markets* (Upper Saddle River, NJ: Pearson Education, 2007), 341.
210. Mark Carlson, *A Brief History of the 1987 Stock Market Crash with a Discussion of the Federal Reserve Response*, Finance and Economics Discussion Series, Divisions of Research & Statistics and Monetary Affairs (Washington, DC: Federal Reserve Board, 2007), 3.
211. Ibid.
212. B. Garcia, "An Appraisal: Portfolio Insurance Could Fuel Stocks' Fall, Critics Say," *Wall Street Journal* (October 12, 1987): 43, cited in Carlson, *A Brief History*, 4.
213. Scott McMurray and Robert L. Rose, "The Crash of '87: Chicago's 'Shadow Markets' Led Free Fall in a Plunge that Began Right at Opening," *Wall Street Journal* (October 20, 1987), quoted in Michael Lewis, *Panic: The Story of Modern Financial Insanity* (New York: W. W. Norton & Co., 2009), 20–21.

214. Carlson, *A Brief History*, 22.
215. Atlas and Drier, "The Conservative Origins of the Sub-Prime Lending Crisis."
216. Atlas and Drier, "The Conservative Origins of the Sub-Prime Lending Crisis."
217. Andrew Ross Sorkin, *Too Big to Fail* (New York: Viking, 2009), 5.
218. John A. Lindholm, "Financial Innovation and Derivatives Regulation—Minimizing Swap Credit Risk under Title V of the Futures Trading Practices Act of 1992, 1994," *Columbia Business Law Review* (1994): 73, cited in Motes III, "A Primer," 579, 581 n. 8.
219. Frank Partnoy, *F.I.A.S.C.O.*, 15.
220. Ibid.
221. Mark Baldassare, *When Government Fails: The Orange County Bankruptcy* (Berkeley and Los Angeles, CA: University of California Press, 1998), 2–3.
222. Ibid.
223. Philip McBride Johnson, *Derivatives: A Manager's Guide to the World's Most Powerful Financial Instruments* (New York: McGraw Hill, 1999), p. ix.
224. Lowenstein, *When Genius Failed*, xix.
225. Ibid.
226. 63 Fed.Reg. 26114 (May 12, 1998).
227. Persky, "Do the Math," 27, quoting Lynn A Stout, Paul Hastings Professor of Corporate and Securities Law, UCLA School of Law.
228. Robert W. Kolb and James A. Overdahl. *Futures, Options, and Swaps* (Malden, MA: Blackwell Publishing, 2007), 39–40.
229. Kolb and Overdahl, *Futures*, 41.
230. Financial Crisis Inquiry Commission, *The Financial Crises Inquiry Report* (New York: PublicAffairs, 2011), xxi.

CHAPTER 9

Market Structure Before and After 2010

This chapter is intended to serve as a primer on derivative markets, clearinghouses, and data repositories.

To provide the reader with a historical panoramic view of the markets, we start with ancient market structures and briefly describe practices that are thousands of years old, according to historical records and documentation retrieved by the author at the Library of Congress in Washington, DC. After three short, sweeping paragraphs which describe four centuries of market practice, the reader is then given a tour of the transformation of older markets into modern markets (and the continued transformation of those markets following the 2008 market crises. The reader is encouraged to review the differences between exchanges and clearinghouses discussed in Chapter 3 and view new market developments as updated from time to time in the author's website for this text, www.DerivativesGuide.com.

ANCIENT COMMODITY MARKETS

Temples served as the first exchanges and clearinghouses, according to the earliest recorded Sumerian history, circa 3000 B.C.[1]

Temples in ancient times were storehouses for commodities, banks for loans, and depositories for documents and valuables. The chief banker was the Sun God, acting through temple priests and priestesses.[2] Banks continued to exist after 625 B.C.[3]; the earliest forms of deposit were not coins or minerals, but grain first, then crops, fruit, then a system of warehouse banking developed in 320 B.C.[4]

Historians indicate that exchanges eventually relocated from places of worship to medieval fairs by the twelfth century.[5] At that time, however, transactions for immediate delivery appear to have predominated, and futures and forward trading generally began around the thirteenth century.[6] As infrastructure improved and modern cities developed, fairs were replaced with market centers,[7] though many of the markets were held outdoors, then indoors, including the predecessor to the American Stock Exchange, whose curbstone brokers conducted their last outdoor session on June 23, 1921.[8]

EARLIEST MODERN EXCHANGES

We cannot jump to the twentieth century without discussing, as previewed in Chapter 3, the Osaka Rice Exchange. Historians point to the Osaka Rice Exchange in the mid-seventeenth century as the first commodities exchange in modern history.[9] Chapter 3 discusses in greater detail that exchange and the rice tickets which formed the basis of trading there. Fast-forward all the way to the turn of the nineteenth century, during which time the great city of Chicago developed developed. The reader should be aware that supply and demand imbalances there, including the glut of commodities at harvest coupled with inadequate storage and infrastructure problems, contributed to the need for an organized marketplace in which thousands of participants conducted business using a range of derivatives (first over-the-counter or OTC, then on organized exchanges) such as forward contracts, first for corn, then wheat.[10]

In 1848, 82 merchants gathered above a flour store in downtown Chicago to form the Chicago Board of Trade (CBOT), a central exchange for commodities.[11]

Standardized contracts and a system of margining, or collateralizing trades, were introduced when grain trading was formalized with standard contracts at CBOT in 1865.[12] Grain merchants agreed on months for delivery; for example, March was the most logical choice for grain delivery because the end of winter brought about an improvement in avenues of transportation.[13]

New exchanges formed and commodities were traded in cotton, eggs, coffee and then financial futures, as colorfully described in Emily Lambert's recent excellent text, *The Futures: The Rise of the Speculator and the Origins of the World's Biggest Markets*.

Floor brokers working on behalf of individual traders, or companies, would receive orders and, like an auctioneer opening an auction, yell out the order, find a buyer for its selling customer (or vice versa) and then write the trade details on an order sheet and literally toss it on the trading floor, where a runner would pick up the order sheets and deliver them to a clearing firm and ultimately, a clearinghouse, which would match trades "like socks, making sure every buyer and seller was part of a pair."[14]

THE GREAT DEPRESSION AND BUCKET SHOPS

With futures markets located in major metropolitan cities—as opposed to the countryside, where many commodities were grown—the farming community became increasingly distrustful of futures pricing: the process by which their crops from hard labor were valued and then sold. This distrust, coupled with the adverse effects of widespread speculation in securities as well as in commodities leading up to the Great Depression, contributed to federal regulation of futures in the United States. One type of trading venue which also led to early reform was the bucket shop.

In President Roosevelt's letter to the U.S. Congress Committee on Interstate and Foreign Commerce on March 26, 1934, the President identified a primary cause of the epic financial devastation in the U.S. following 1929:

> *Unregulated speculation in securities and in commodities was one of the most important contributing factors in the artificial and unwarranted "boom" which had so much to do with the terrible conditions of the years following 1929.*[15]

Much of the abusive trading in the twentieth century took place in bucket shops. A bucket shop, an illegitimate market structure, provided a venue for pure speculation in forward contracts and futures. Rather than a market where a seller enters into a contract with a buyer, and goods are, as we expect, exchanged a bucket shop constituted a different kind of market structure where customers merely speculate on movements in commodity prices. Customers formed a view on either upward or downward price momentum and entered into a contract with the bucket shop, instead of a partner on a floor where trading in commodities took place. In a bucket shop, the order is merely *booked* and no actual trading occurs. The problem with bucket shops is that unless they maintained an equilibrium between buyers and sellers taking opposite views, the bucket shop fails, and the owners fail to settle their customer accounts then fled.[16] States imposed bucket shop or gaming laws and brought about felony convictions for those who violated them, and arrangements that bucket shop patrons entered into in contravention of those laws were null and legally void.

In response to efforts to curb derivatives activities by means of bucket shop laws, courts have held that where a valid business purpose exists, state gaming and bucket shop laws cannot be used to invalidate a derivative transactions. The U.S. Fourth Circuit Court of Appeals, for example, ruled in *Salomon Forex Inc. v. Tauber* that a trader whose refusal to pay amounts owed on 68 Swiss franc and Australian dollar FX forward and option transactions cannot base that refusal on New York and Virginia gaming laws. The court in *Salomon* found that the transactions were made for a valid business purpose.[17] So early efforts to invalidate derivatives based on old gaming and bucket shop laws failed, and derivatives in early U.S. markets were upheld.

Bucket shops began to take market share from legitimate exchanges. Losses from defunct bucket shops resulted. This became a major market problem and federal regulators in the U.S. began to officially approve certain regulated markets, leading to a phenomenon known as the contract market monopoly. This term, "contract market monopoly" has been used over the years to refer to the monopoly that, for much of the twentieth century, was enjoyed by organized commodities markets that were designated as a contract market under the Commodity Exchange Act. All contracts for the sale of a commodity for future delivery, to be lawful, had to be executed on a market designated by early U.S. futures regulators as a properly organized, regulated, "designated contract market."[18] The Commodity Exchange Act prohibits commodity futures trading via any market or venue, including of course bucket shops, other than a contract market.

OPEN OUTCRY AND PITS GIVE WAY
TO THE MACHINES

Apart from bucket shops, many of the venues, or exchanges, which we have considered in the trading of derivatives up to the nineteenth and twentieth centuries fall into the open outcry futures exchanges. These evolved into electronic exchanges such as the CME Globex electronic trading platform.[19]

To review, before the introduction of electronic trading of futures and options on futures, and prior to the first interest rate swap in 1981, buyers and sellers of standardized derivatives conducted business on trading floors within pits designated for certain markets of commodities. In 1998, open outcry trading accounted for nearly all, or 95 percent of U.S. futures trading volume, but eight years later, open-outcry trading fell to one-half, with electronic trading making up the rest.[20]

Electronic trading most dramatically changed market structure in several important respects. Trading electronically enables the global market to function in all time zones and without geographical bounds. In summary, this is how electronic trading works. After gaining access to electronic platforms, customers, advisors, and others enter orders in electronic "front ends" to an electronic trading host maintaining a central order book. The central order book and computer algorithms (which give weight to factors such as the time received, price, and other factors) determine the priority of orders and acceptance. Prior to a trade being matched, a customer has a limited period of time for canceling or revising an order before the trade is locked. Confirmations of matched trades are electronically generated, affirmed, routed to the customer, and then to the clearinghouse.

Electronic trading systems today are regulated in the United States according to the products that are traded, the parties who trade them, and the manner in which they trade on the systems. With thousands of years of trading now behind us, we next take an equally fast, sweeping tour through late twentieth century trading and regulation following the 2008 market crises.

In 1971, significant changes in derivatives took place when foreign exchange rates were allowed to float freely without government intervention. This provided an impetus for the development of new futures contracts and creative currency arrangements—and parallel loans.

In 1972, the Chicago Mercantile Exchange created futures contracts on currencies. These futures were the first contracts that were not based on physical commodities.[21] Seven years later, stock index futures came to the futures market. Futures markets had already become highly organized and functioned in ways which were similar to exchanges for equity trading (somewhat similar to stock exchanges in major markets such as London, New York, and Tokyo, futures exchanges limit trading to specified futures contracts; members trade on stock and futures exchanges for either themselves or others, as brokers).[22] There are however, when we compare futures and stock markets, more differences than similarities. Unlike purchasers of equity interests, buyers of futures do not acquire an ownership interest with respect to the underlying assets *until and unless delivery occurs* (and this occurs infrequently, as traders use market liquidity to sell positions before delivery in a process, this is referred to as "offsetting").[23]

Another difference at the settlement stage is noteworthy. Both the futures and stock exchanges require clearing. In the futures market, the clearinghouse actually takes the other side of each transaction that is cleared, becoming the seller to every buyer and the buyer to every seller. The clearing that takes place in a stock market does not entail a clearinghouse that steps into the middle of the trade, as is the case in the clearing of futures contracts. The reader is directed to Chapter 3. Clearinghouses do not guaranty performance in the purchase and sale of stock. In the clearing of futures contracts, delivery and payment are guaranteed by the clearinghouse.

Margin is therefore a critical component in futures clearing given this critical difference. In order to ensure that a clearinghouse can guarantee payment and delivery, the clearinghouse must value open futures trades continuously, mark the contract to market at the end of each day and thereby enable the clearinghouse to solicit collateral, as margin, to offset movements in price within the market in which the futures contract is traded. A customer whose contract has moved in her or his favor will be credited, and another customer's account will be debited to account for the movement in price. To enable that process to work, the customer is required to keep maintenance margin (which in 2008 was approximately 75 percent of the initial margin)[24] and additional margin is called if the level of maintenance margin falls below the set maintenance margin level.[25] Members of clearinghouses may, under their own internal rules, impose additional margin, based on the credit profile of the futures customer. At maturity, or final settlement of the futures contract, the clearinghouse assures that the aggregate cash receipt of the seller and the net cash payment by the buyer are identical[26] to the price specified in the contract. The daily mark-to-market practice of futures trading alters only the timing of these cash flows, and at all times the clearinghouse has equally balanced short and long positions.[27]

As the law governing OTC derivatives continues to develop, exchanges, or electronic trading platforms (SEFs, or swap execution facilities, as introduced in Chapter 4) will emerge and they continue to evolve.

Prior to Dodd-Frank, there were primarily two trading platforms in the United States: designated contract markets (DCMs) and national securities exchanges (NSEs).

A DCM, also referred to as a board of trade, is an exchange that operates under the regulatory regime established by the Commodity Futures Trading Commission (CFTC), the regulator that, under Section 5 of the Commodity Exchange Act (CEA) and as discussed in Chapter 3, is responsible for administering the regulatory mandates of the CEA.

An NSE is an exchange for securities regulated by the Securities and Exchange Commission (SEC), which is charged with the responsibility of implementing the regulatory mandates of the Securities Exchange Act of 1934 (Exchange Act). Section 6 of the Exchange Act requires NSEs to register with the SEC.

The market participants in the exchange-traded, cleared derivatives (i.e., futures) space included futures commission merchants (FCMs), introducing brokers (IBs, executing brokers or EBs), commodity pool operators (CPOs), commodity trading advisors (CTAs), associated persons (APs) and, as already discussed in Chapter 3, floor brokers and floor traders.

An important part of the designation of an individual or entity is the requirement to register with and become subject to the regulatory regime of the CFTC. Because FCMs and EBs play a role in the execution and clearing of a trade, a brief description of each is necessary. An FCM is an entity or individual that, generally, solicits or accepts orders to buy or sell futures contracts and accepts assets including cash for such activities. Registration with the CFTC is required.

An executing broker solicits or accepts orders to buy or sell, but in contrast to an FCM, does not accept money for those services, and registration is required unless certain exemptions apply.

To this point we have discussed the futures market structure, its key component parts, a few of the key participants and its evolution over many centuries. For the balance of this chapter we turn our attention to the important aspects of new derivatives market structure in the United States.

REFORM OF U.S. MARKET STRUCTURE

As a result of the enactment of new derivatives law which we refer in Chapter 4 as Dodd-Frank, 2 new trading platforms are mandated in the United States, one for swaps and the other for security-based swaps. Both of these terms are discussed in detail in Chapter 4.

There are 4 important attributes of the new market structure for derivatives in the United States. Just as the futures market at the turn of the twentieth century drew regulatory attention due to bucket shops and the rampant speculation that preceded the Great Depression, the OTC derivatives market failures in 2007 to 2008, whose causes and effects are summarized in the Introduction and Chapter 1, led to *massive* reform efforts that fundamentally and forever re-shaped OTC derivatives trading at least in the U.S. and other large markets. There are four new attributes of[28] the new market structure:

- Trading of swaps on designated contract markets (DCMs).
- Swap execution facilities and security-based swap execution facilities (both are referred to in this chapter as SEFs).
- Clearinghouses for swaps.
- Swap data repositories (SDRs).

SEFs, clearinghouses, and SDRs are new features, when compared to the manner in which derivatives traded OTC since 1981, when the first swap between the World Bank and IBM took place.[29]

Dodd-Frank mandates that all derivatives be executed via either an SEF (regulated by the CFTC) or a security-based SEF (regulated by the SEC). SEFs, swap execution facilities, and security-based SEFs must, under the first reform mandates, provide multiple participants with the ability to execute or trade swaps in an organized and fully-regulated way, which, prior to Dodd-Frank, was nonexistent, at least in the OTC derivatives market. Using interstate commerce, it is contemplated that many market participants will accept bids and offers through SEFs and security-based SEFs. Though swaps may be executed through designated contract markets and security-based swaps may be executed via national securities exchanges, this chapter focuses on trade executions on SEFs because SEFs are an entirely new creation of Dodd-Frank and, as such, have generated many questions, the vast majority of which were unanswered when this text went to print. The goal of this Chapter is to introduce the reader to this new market venue and describe how policymakers sought to move all OTC trading to a regulated exchange, or a "SEF" or "SB-SEF" (a security-based swap execution facility), and then in certain required circumstances, settlement via a clearinghouse as described in Chapter 3, with reporting mandates along the way.

The most important feature of derivatives reform in the post Dodd-Frank derivatives trading market in the U.S. is the direction given to U.S. regulators, namely the SEC and CFTC, to mandate the central clearing of certain derivatives previously traded OTC.

While not all derivatives in the OTC market will be subject to the clearing mandate, the United States, as a member of the G-20, committed to the conversion of much of the OTC market to a centrally cleared market by the end of 2012. This was a very ambitious commitment. All derivative trades that are mandated for central clearing must also be executed via an exchange, that is, swap execution facility or SEF or other regulated venue. All OTC trades are to be collateralized in accordance with regulatory mandates, and all OTC trades and centrally cleared trades are to be reported to a swap data repository. All of this is, post 2010, new.

To review, the CEA requires that trading in futures must take place in a regulated contract market. A contract market is understood as a board of trade or other exchange that is designated as such by the CFTC.[30] Accordingly, a board of trade seeks a CFTC designation as a contract market if it sponsors futures contracts or options on commodity futures, and the CEA requires contract markets to abide by core principles.[31] Designated contract markets are self-regulatory organizations that are subject to CFTC oversight; securities exchanges are subject to SEC oversight, although the extent of CFTC and SEC oversight differs in many respects.[32] Regulators are charged with the responsibility of taking the OTC derivatives market and regulating it in a similar way.

If the CFTC or SEC mandates under Dodd-Frank that a derivative, or category of derivatives, are to be centrally cleared, then, unless the exchange or clearinghouse refuses to clear the derivative or an exception applies (as discussed in Chapter 4, which describes the end user exception to the clearing requirement), it is *illegal* for that trade to be executed bilaterally, as it had previously been executed in the OTC market. When a category of derivatives or a derivative becomes subject to the clearing mandate, those entering into that derivative must begin the trading life cycle by using the appropriate facility, also as described in Chapter 4, which describes the provisions in Dodd-Frank on trading venues such as SEFs.

SEFs are designed in Dodd-Frank to facilitate price discovery in a transparent manner. Clearinghouses are intended to bring about post-execution trading activities, including settlement.

DERIVATIVE CLEARING ORGANIZATIONS (DCOs)

All derivatives mandated for clearing must be executed on SEFs or DCMs, and then cleared by means of Derivative Clearing Organizations, or DCOs. A clearinghouse that clears swaps must register as a DCO with the CFTC, which proposed on December 15, 2010, a comprehensive set of principle-based rules that would govern DCOs. These proposed rules would enable the CFTC to have in place an early warning system that would alert the Commission of a significant decrease in the financial resources of the DCOs as well as the source of that decrease, or other adverse development that could interfere with the clearing of derivatives by DCOs. This early warning system was absent prior to 2011 in OTC markets, as discussed in Chapter 1.

These proposed rules are designed to implement 16 core principles[33] with which a DCO must comply in order to be registered and to maintain registration as a DCO under the Commodity Exchange Act (the CEA), as amended by Section 725(c) of the Dodd-Frank Act.[34] These are the principles.

> *Applicants are to exercise "reasonable discretion" in satisfying principle-based registration requirements by demonstrating that the applicant: (i) has sufficient financial means to fulfill clearing obligations; (ii) shall establish appropriate membership requirements for clearing members; (iii) has the ability to manage risks associated with clearing; (iv) has the ability to complete settlements on a timely basis; (v) can ensure the safety of member and participant funds; (vi) has rules and procedures to handle member and participant defaults; (vii) can monitor compliance with rules as well as enforce rule infractions and discipline members for those infractions; (viii) has established and can activate emergency measures in case of disasters; (ix) can interface with by reporting to the CFTC to enable the regulator to monitor and provide oversight with respect to the applicant's clearing activities; (x) retains records of clearing activities for at least five years after the creation of the record; (xi) can assure access to information to the public; and (xii) does not adopt a rule that would have an anti-competitive result, or otherwise impose an "anticompetitive burden" on trading. The foregoing principles were set forth in the CEA prior to the enactment of the Dodd-Frank Act.*

After the enactment of Dodd-Frank, the CFTC proposed four distinct categories of obligations that DCOs would have in relation to maintaining their status as registered DCOs:

1. Reporting.
2. Recordkeeping.
3. Public information.
4. Information sharing.[35]

DCOs that clear swaps are to provide information concerning these swaps, pursuant to CFTC requests. DCOs that clear security-based swaps are to provide requested information to the SEC, upon its request.

Reporting

Dodd-Frank amends the CEA to bring about transparency to the heretofore opaque OTC derivatives market through elaborate reporting requirements at 2 separate junctures in the trading and clearing process:

- **Reporting at execution.** Real-time reporting is required as soon as technologically possible after trade execution, no matter if the swap is subject to a central clearing mandate or remains OTC.
- **Reporting at clearing.** Reporting is also mandated at the settlement or clearing stage. Regulators are also empowered by Dodd-Frank to obtain reports from swap data repositories, which are introduced, next.

SWAP DATA REPOSITORY

Dodd-Frank introduces a new entity into the post 2010 market structure, the swap data repository, which accepts data, confirms data acceptance to the parties, maintains that data pursuant to regulatory requirements, monitors and analyzes the data, and is subject to rulemaking and regulatory action with respect to reported data.

Along with requiring the retention of documentation, Dodd-Frank requires that swaps and security-based swaps be reported to a registered trade repository. Every six months, the CFTC and the SEC are required to issue a written report to the public regarding the trading and clearing in the major categories of security-based swaps or swaps, and the market participants and developments in new products, on an aggregate basis.

Swap dealers are obligated to report uncleared swaps. For trades that do not involve a swap dealer, major swap participants in the trade are obligated to report; otherwise, the parties are to determine which party reports, so with this we next briefly introduce market participants.[36]

MARKET PARTICIPANTS IN THE OTC DERIVATIVES TRADE

No discussion of markets would be complete without at least an introduction to the participants in the market. This chapter then concludes with an outline of the other individuals who perform critical functions in every functioning market, the regulators. OTC derivatives markets are comprised of two counterparties, frequently referred to in trade parlance as dealers on the one hand, and "end users" or funds on the other.

The two broad classifications of persons who trade are hedgers and speculators. Hedgers include financial institutions that manage or deal in interest-rate-sensitive instruments, foreign currencies or stock portfolios, and commercial market participants, such as farmers and manufacturers, that market or process commodities. Hedging is a protective procedure designed to effectively lock-in prices (or otherwise manage risk) that would otherwise change due to an adverse movement in the price of the underlying commodity.

Market participants in the OTC trade are not to be confused with market participants in the listed, exchange-traded and centrally cleared derivatives, futures, and options-on-futures markets, but the reality is that in both the exchange-traded and OTC derivative markets, many common denominators exist, as illustrated in the pages that follow.

Traders that Speculate or Hedge

Futures markets and OTC markets both enable the hedging party to shift the risk of price fluctuations. The typical objective of the hedging party is to protect the profit that he or she expects to earn from farming, merchandizing, processing operations, or investing.

The speculator is, in effect, the risk bearer (or insurer) who assumes the risks that the hedging party seeks to manage or avoid. Speculators rarely make or take delivery of the underlying commodity; rather, they attempt to close out their positions prior to the delivery date. Because the speculator may take either a long or short position in commodities, it is possible for him or her to make profits or incur losses regardless of whether prices go up or down. Without a speculator there is no hedging.

Those That Face Both Hedgers and Speculators: Dealers

A dealer makes a market in a swap or other derivative. A dealer will not keep the risk that it undertakes in a trade, but instead will act effectively as an intermediary between two parties—a buyer and a seller, for example—and collect a profit along the way. Large dealers are major participants in the OTC market in financial commodities. For a more detailed analysis of the financial services firms that come within the definition of swap dealer and security-based swap dealer in Dodd-Frank, the reader is directed to Chapter 4. As for the economic drivers for dealers and the evolution of the dealer role, the following summary is useful:

> *Dealers/traders typically profit in the derivatives market from speculation/arbitrage activities, from fees and spreads earned by creatively structuring transactions, or simply by acting as intermediaries. Originally, dealers/traders acted as intermediaries only. Quickly, this involvement changed to an active portfolio participation; in addition to facilitating a transaction, a dealer/trader prices the transactions and becomes the counterparty on one side of the transaction. Generally, the dealer/trader's strategy is to cove (lay-off to others) the risk exposure of a net portfolio risk using cash market or other derivative positions. By operating as the market makers for derivatives, dealers/traders add liquidity and competitive pricing to the market place.[37]*

Chapter 4 describes two new categories of market participants, swap dealers and major swap participants, which are referred to in this part of the text as swap entities, and, as the most active players in the U.S. derivatives industry, these entities are the subject of extensive rule making and a helpful schematic and accompanying discussion are provided in Chapter 4 to enable the reader to determine whether a derivatives market participant is a "major swap" or "major security-based swap" participant.[38]

Those That Regulate Hedgers, Speculators, and Dealers

The swap entity rules that the CFTC proposed are designed to implement a few of the pillars supporting the new derivatives market in the United States, as envisioned by Congress when it passed Dodd-Frank:[39]

- Registration of swaps entities as the first step toward comprehensive regulatory oversight.
- Requiring swaps entities to implement effective risk management systems.
- Requiring compliance with business conduct requirements.
- Designation of a chief compliance officer and requiring the officer to carry out a range of regulatory mandates.

In the United States, Dodd-Frank constituted an historic reset of the regulation of derivatives and futures. While Chapter 4 brings this historic legislation into sharper focus, providing extensive detail available up to when this book when to print, the following is a summary, in outline format, of the regulators and their jurisdiction over the reformed U.S. derivatives market:

- **CFTC** (Commodity Futures Trading Commission). U.S. Congress gave the CFTC jurisdiction over these financial products:
  - Futures.
  - Options on futures.
  - Swaps, as defined by Dodd-Frank (see Chapter 4), including:
    - Options on, and other derivatives with underliers other than securities and narrow-based indices.
    - Futures, options, and swaps on commodities.
    - Certain credit-default swaps and "mixed swaps."
- **SEC** (Securities and Exchange Commission). U.S. Congress gave the SEC jurisdiction over securities, which includes:
  - Stocks.
  - Bonds.
  - Options on shares, bonds, and narrow-based indices (see Chapter 4).
  - Certain credit-default swaps and "mixed swaps."
  - The regulators also have anti-fraud jurisdiction over the foregoing and other financial products.
- **Banking Regulators** (e.g., Federal Reserve and Department of Treasury). U.S. Congress gave banking regulators jurisdiction over banking products that, under Dodd-Frank, are derivatives.
- **State Regulatory Authorities.** State authorities retain jurisdiction over financial products to the extent federal regulators do not have jurisdiction.

Having completed a very summary review in Parts One and Two of this text of the futures and derivatives markets, both before and after the historic reform of these markets commenced in 2010, the final part is dedicated to help the reader with less experience in derivatives understand these important financial tools and how they continue to be regulated.

NOTES

1. Sidney Homer and Richard Sylla, *A History of Interest Rates* (Hoboken, NJ: John Wiley & Sons, 2005), 25.
2. Ibid., 27.
3. Ibid., 27.

4. Alyn Davies, *A History of Money* (Cardiff: University of Wales Press, 1994), 49, 51.
5. Chicago Board of Trade *The Chicago Board of Trade Handbook of Futures and Options* (New York: McGraw-Hill, 2006), 97–98.
6. Ibid.
7. Ibid., 98–99.
8. Robert Sobel, *AMEX: A History of the American Stock Exchange, 1921–1971* (New York: Weybright and Talley, 2000), 1.
9. A. G. Malliaris, *Futures Markets*, (Brookfield, VT: Elgar Reference Collection, 1997), xxv.
10. Emily Lambert, *The Futures: The Rise of the Speculator and the Origins of the World's Biggest Markets* (New York: Basic Books, 2011); *Chicago Board of Trade Handbook of Futures and Options*, 100–102.
11. *Chicago Board of Trade Handbook of Futures and Options*, 102.
12. Ibid., 102.
13. Ibid., 104.
14. Lambert, *The Futures*, 20–21.
15. Walter Lukken, "Fun with Derivatives Regulation." Presentation, K&L Gates Trading Conference, November 24, 2009.
16. Philip McBride Johnson and Thomas Lee Mazen, *Derivatives Regulation* (New York: Aspen, 2004), 355 n. 2.
17. *Salomon Forex Inc. v. Tauber*, 795 F.Supp 768 (E.D. Va 1992) aff'd 8 F.3d 966 (4th Cir. 1993).
18. Johnson and Mazen, *Derivatives Regulation*, 50, 53. The contract market monopoly: "Until the year 2000, it was generally understood (although the Act was less than crystal clear prior to 1983) that all domestic "contracts of sale of a commodity for future delivery" had to be executed on an organized commodities market that was 'designated' as 'contract market' under the Commodity Exchange Act.... The scope of the CFTC's original contract market monopoly was also placed in doubt as a result of court decisions.").
19. *See* www.cmegroup.com/globex/introduction.
20. Robert W. Kolb and James A. Overdahl, *Futures, Options, and Swaps* (Malden, MA: Blackwell, 2007), 48.
21. Frank K. Reilly, *Investment Analysis and Portfolio Management* (New York: Harcourt Brace, 19, 94), 813.
22. Ibid., 814.
23. Ibid.
24. See, e.g., "Maintenance Margin is usually approximately 75% of initial margin," Margin Requirements, Heritage West Futures Brokers (2008), http://www.heritagewestfutures.com/margin-requirements.html.
25. Ibid.
26. Ibid.
27. Ibid.
28. The reader is to keep in mind that the words security-based precede those SEFs and SDRs that handle purchases, sales, and data reporting relating to security-based swaps, which are discussed in Chapter 8.

29. Mary S. Schaeffer and Mary S. Ludwig, *Understanding Interest Rate Swaps* (New York: McGraw-Hill Professional, 1993), 13.

30. Johnson and Mazen, *Derivatives Regulation*, 150–151.

31. Ibid., 150–151.

32. Ibid., 152–153.

33. To be registered and to maintain status as a DCO, an applicant must comply with the core principles set forth in the CEA, as amended by the Dodd-Frank Act. See 7 USCa-1 Section 7a-1(b). The Dodd-Frank Act added additional principles relating to the avoidance of conflicts of interest, internal governance, the composition of the DCO's governing board and the handling of legal risk.

34. See 75 Fed. Reg. 63732 (Release No. 34-63346) (Oct. 18, 2010) (proposing regulations to implement Core Principle P (Conflicts of Interest); 75 Fed. Reg. 63113 (Release No. 34-63346) (Oct. 14, 2010) (proposing regulations to implement Core Principle B (Financial Resources). The CFTC also is proposing regulations to implement Core Principles A (Compliance), H (Rule Enforcement), N (Antitrust Considerations), and R (Legal Risk) and expects to issue two additional notices of proposed rulemaking to implement DCO core principles.

35. Information Management Requirements for Derivatives Clearing Organizations, 75 Fed. Reg. 78185 (December 15, 2010).

36. See 76 Fed. Reg. 76604 (December 8, 2010).

37. KPMG, *Solving the Mystery of Derivatives* (Washington, DC: KPMG Peat Marwick, 1994), 38–39 (1994).

38. See, e.g., 75 Fed. Reg. 71379 (November 23, 2010).

39. See Dodd-Frank Wall Street Reform and Consumer Protection Act, Public Law III—203,124 Stat. 1376 (2010).

Four

Continuing Education

As the name implies, a derivative is, on the most basic level, nothing more than a contract whose value derives from some other asset, such as a bond, a stock or a quantity of gold. The key to derivatives is that those who buy and sell them are each making a bet on the future value of that asset. Derivatives provide a way for investors either to protect themselves—for example, against a possible negative future price swing—or to make high-stake bets on price swings for what might be huge payoffs. At the heart of the business is a dance with time.

—Gillian Tett, *Fool's Gold*

CHAPTER 10

Survey of Derivatives

This chapter is designed to assist the reader who is less familiar with derivatives and the basic structure, use, and regulation of these financial products. Chapters 4 and 10 are to be read in tandem; Chapter 4 discusses the importance of the characterization of OTC derivatives as swaps (regulated in the United States by the Commodity Futures Trading Commission [CFTC]), or security-based swaps (regulated by the U.S. Securities and Exchange Commission) or other category of derivatives.

This chapter is a primer on the principal categories of derivatives and, as each is discussed and many are illustrated, the author will identify each derivative as a swap or security-based swap, according to information available in the earliest phases of rulemaking in the United States. This will help enable readers to determine whether they are major swap participants or major security-based swap participants, swap dealers, or security-based swap dealers, and so forth. These labels have important regulatory connotations, as described in Chapter 4.

However, a cautionary statement is appropriate at the outset: as this book goes to print, many of the important categories and definitions in the new law of derivatives in the United States are not in final form, so statements made in this chapter (e.g., statements labeling a derivative as a swap or security-based swap) may not be accurate, and the reader is encouraged to follow regulatory and other developments on the website for this book, www.DerivativesGuide.com.

This chapter also helps explain why derivatives are not merely bets, but serve important functions in our society. Gillian Tett stated in her excellent work on the development of the credit derivatives market in the United States, *Fool's Gold* (and her statement warrants repeating):

> As the name implies, a derivative is, on the most basic level, nothing more than a contract whose value derives from some other asset, such as a bond, a stock, or a quantity of gold.... Derivatives provide a way for investors either to protect themselves—for example,

against a possible negative future price swing—or to make high-stake bets on price swings for what might be huge payoffs. At the heart of the business is a dance with time.[1]

Before we dive into derivatives, a quick step back to look at markets is necessary; a brief review is important for purposes of drawing the distinction between derivative and non-derivative markets, and over-the-counter (OTC) and exchange-traded derivative markets. The global financial markets today fall into two very distinct categories: cash markets and synthetic markets. The cash markets are traditional markets that we are most familiar with today. In cash markets, as the name implies, assets and rights are sold for cash or cash equivalents. In the early agrarian economies, early market participants first traded, or bartered, then they eventually sold what was harvested and coinage or other cash forms were used in the sale. Cash markets, of course, continue to exist today and there are many.

Synthetic markets are markets in which buyers and sellers enter agreements to buy and sell something in the future for a price that is subject to an agreement. However, the buyer and seller frequently do not exchange anything of value (aside from their promise which has at least legal value) when they have a "meeting of the minds." Instead, they look into the future and take different positions on an asset and risks associated with that asset. The insurance market falls within the category of synthetic markets, for example, as do the markets for derivatives.

The synthetic market actually began at least as early as 3,500 B.C., as we saw in Chapter 8, and today it is, by far, the largest market in the world in uncompressed notional values, with hundreds of billions in aggregate (notional) value.

Derivatives (a term which, as discussed in the Introduction, encompasses both OTC derivatives and derivatives traded by means of an organized exchange), and futures, which, for review, are a standardized type of derivative that is traded on an exchange and settled through a clearinghouse, are agreements between a future buyer and future seller. Their agreement includes just a few specifics: price, the asset which is to be exchanged or which is the subject of the trade (this is called an underlier), which may be a physical commodity such as corn or natural gas, and a future date when the transaction will take place. Reduced to their most basic components, these are the common elements in every derivative:

- Buyer and seller.
- A synthetic market.
- Underlier.
- Future price.
- A future date for exchange.[2]

OVERVIEW OF THE STRATEGIES AND TRADE STRUCTURE

Within the synthetic markets, derivatives are traded either by means of an organized exchange or privately, in what is referred to in industry parlance as the over-the-counter (OTC) market, which the previous chapter explored.

As we survey products that are traded either in the OTC or on exchanges, some basic derivative strategies will also be introduced, such as how to:

- Enter into contracts giving third parties the right to buy portfolio securities for a fixed price at a future date (e.g., writing call options).
- Enter into contracts giving third parties the right to sell securities to the traders for a fixed price at a future date (e.g., writing put options).
- Buy the right to purchase securities from third parties (call options) or the right to sell securities to third parties (put options) for a fixed price at a future date.

The structure of many—if not most—derivatives discussed in this chapter will have common features illustrated by Figure 10.1.

All derivatives begin with one party facing another, as illustrated in Figure 10.1. Either or both of the parties may be acting as an agent for one or more additional parties. The terms "Party A" and "Party B" are part of

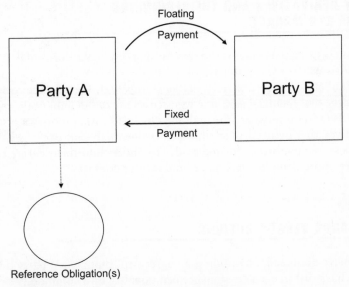

FIGURE 10.1 Common Features of Derivatives

OTC derivative parlance; end users are frequently, but not exclusively, in the Party B position in OTC derivative documentation, and financial derivative dealers are commonly Party A's.

Many derivatives contemplate one party undertaking a covenant to tender a payment periodically, in a fixed amount (or an amount based on an index), in exchange for the other party assuming the risk to pay a variable amount based on, for example, the diminution of value of an underlying asset (in the case of a credit-default swap, or CDS, described in this chapter) or perhaps an increase or decline in an index level. The variable payment is frequently called the floating payment (and the party obligated to make the payment is frequently referred to as the floating amount payor) and is represented in Figure 10.1 by the curved arrow pointing to Party B, suggesting that Party B pays a fixed amount, or fee, for the assumption of a risk of variable payment by Party A. Because the derivative is a financial instrument that derives its value from something else, that value, in Figure 10.1, will relate to some contingency concerning "reference obligations," which may include a basket of securities or other assets, an index, or a single security, such as a bond.

Figure 10.1 and the lines within it are meant to help less experienced readers understand the component parts of the basic derivative structures which are described in this chapter.

EARLY DERIVATIVES AND THE BEGINNINGS OF THE OTC MARKET

Archeologists help us understand that the first physical records of derivatives were forwards for the purchase of grain; their discoveries in the modern-day Middle East were described earlier in this text. Because the forward is among the first financial instruments discovered, and in light of the fact that forwards (and options) are the building blocks for other more sophisticated derivatives that evolved over time in the twentieth and early twenty-first centuries, it is important for the reader to understand them before turning to other, more complex derivatives and futures contacts.

FORWARDS VERSUS OPTIONS

As we have discussed, an option is an agreement that gives a party the right to purchase or force a sale of a specified quantity of a commodity or other asset at a set price, at some point in the future. As we discussed in Chapter 4, depending on the underlier, or reference obligation, forwards and options will be either swaps, security-based swaps or securities.

A forward contract is an agreement that requires one party to purchase or sell a specified quantity of an asset to another party at a specified date in the future, at a set price. An option on the purchase of a single security, if that security is a restricted security (such as a municipal security) will likely fall within the security-based swap and if the underlying security is not a restricted security (as defined in federal securities law), then the option will be a security (not a security-based swap).

Forwards are designed to hedge or speculate with respect to price fluctuations. As an OTC derivative that developed over time without an organized market, forwards are customized to fit the needs of the two parties to the forward. A standardized forward is a futures contract that is traded on an exchange and settled, or cleared by means of a clearinghouse. If the forward calls for the purchase of emissions credits, then the forward is a swap and will be governed by the CFTC.

The price for the asset that is subject to a forward contract may be paid up-front (a prepaid forward), or paid at the settlement of the derivative. As with other derivatives that are traded OTC, there is substantial customization in the forward market; terms for forwards include various amounts and maturities, and are subject to individual negotiation by the parties to the trade.

Forwards are settled privately. Due to the customization of the forward product, each party to the forward generally needs to settle or "close out" the forward with each other. Forwards are not fungible products as compared to futures contracts, which, because of their standardized terms, may be closed out or offset with an opposing position. Generally, there is no direct means of offsetting or closing out a forward contract by taking an offsetting position as one would a futures contract on an exchange. If a trader desires to close out a forward contract position, the trader generally will establish an opposite position in the contract, but will settle and recognize the profit or loss on both positions simultaneously on the delivery date.

So, unlike the futures contract market in which a trader who has offset positions will recognize profit or loss immediately, in the forward market, a trader with a position that has been offset at a profit will generally not receive such profit until the delivery date, and likewise a trader with a position that has been offset at a loss will generally not have to pay money until the delivery date.

In recent years, however, the terms of forward contracts have become more standardized, and in some instances, such contracts now provide a right of offset or cash settlement as an alternative to making or taking delivery of the underlying commodity.

As discussed in Chapters 3 and 4, global financial services regulation is having the effect of standardizing derivatives that have frequently traded OTC, such as forwards or credit default swaps. This standardization, coupled with regulatory initiatives, is gradually having the effect of converting the derivatives market into a market that more closely resembles the futures market.

OPTION BASICS

In this part of the chapter, we will unpack the component parts of one of the more important derivatives: the option. Along with forwards, the derivative that parties most frequently used from the earliest periods in antiquity was the option, so we first turn to the option and, because of its widespread use both on and off exchanges, we will dedicate a more lengthy discussion in this chapter on options and option strategies.

Nearly all the most complicated derivatives include a series of options. However, the option itself is an extremely straightforward and elegant instrument which is widely used today and has been for thousands of years.

An option is an agreement between two parties that gives one party the right to purchase or force a sale of a specified quantity of an asset (e.g., shares of stock) or commodity at a set price, at some point in the future. One party to the option is a holder, owner, or buyer of the option. This party has the right to exercise the option. The other party writes the option and sells it to the holder, who owns the option.

An option entitles its holder to exercise, for a price (a premium), the right to purchase an asset (in the case of a call option) or the right to sell an asset (a put option). The party to the option that has the right to exercise the option is said to be long the option. The other party is referred to in industry parlance as the writer (or seller) of the option, and just as the holder or buyer is said to be long the option, the writer or seller is short the option.

An option includes these component parts:

- An agreement between the writer and holder of the option.
- A premium that the buyer, or holder pays for the right to buy or sell upon exercise of the option.
- The asset on which the option is based (the underlying security or underlier).

- The strike price, which is the price at which the holder (or buyer) may exercise the option to buy (in the case of a call option) or sell (in the case of a put) the underlying asset.
- The period of time (or expiration date) in which the option may be exercised. The pricing and value of options are based on the foregoing, however pricing and valuation are outside of the scope of this text.

Two Option Categories: Calls and Puts

Now that we have described the component parts of an option, the next step is to describe two fundamental option strategies that are frequently used in both the OTC and listed options industries.

Call Options   We are most familiar with call options. The management of a company is frequently compensated with call options, which gives the holder the right to purchase a security from the writer (seller) of the call option at a specified price at or until a specified date.

Writing (selling) a call option obligates the seller to sell the underlying security to a purchaser at a specified price if the purchaser decides to exercise the option, unless that decision is made automatically. The seller receives a premium when it writes a call option.

A call option is covered if the seller simultaneously holds an equivalent position in the security underlying the option. So, whereas a holder of a call option obtains the right to buy, the holder pays a premium for the right to purchase a security or other asset from the writer at a specified price (until a specified date).

An investor who should consider buying a call option based on equity shares is one who believes that a particular stock may be undervalued and will appreciate over time, and one who wants to profit from that appreciation. The option is a favorable strategy for the investor who anticipates a rise in value of the particular stock but does not want to commit her or his entire capital to purchase the shares. In this way, equity call options give that investor leverage by enabling the investor to dedicate a limited capital outlay to get into a position without having to commit capital to purchase the shares.

Although the investor stands to lose the premium payment, the profit potential for the long call is unlimited as the underlying stock continues to rise, so long as the option has not already expired prior to execution. Even if the value of the underlier falls dramatically, the call option buyer's risk is limited to the total premium paid for the option. The holder of a call breaks even at the point at which the underlying stock price is equal to the call's strike price, plus the premium paid for the option. As with any long option, an increase in volatility has a positive financial effect on the long-call strategy (while decreasing volatility has a negative effect). Time decay has a negative effect.[3]

Put Options   Puts should never be confused with calls, which we have already discussed. Holders of call options get the right to buy. Holders of put options get the right to sell. A put option is the right to take an asset, such as a security, out of an inventory and sell, or put, it onto the lap of the other party, which pays a negotiated price for the security. A put gives the right to sell a security to the writer (seller) of the put option at a specified price until a specified date. Writing (selling) a put option obligates the writer to acquire the underlying security from a purchaser at a specified price if the purchaser decides to exercise the option. The writer receives a premium when it writes a put option. When a put option is purchased, the buyer pays a premium to the writer for the right (but not the obligation) to sell a security (or other asset) to the writer for a specified price, frequently at any time, until a certain date. Upon exercise of the put option, the writer of the put is obligated to buy, and the holder of the put is obligated to sell upon exercise of the option.

OPTIONS PRICING

As with any other derivative, the value of an option will fluctuate depending on the value of the asset underlying the option. The price that a buyer pays for the option, which we have referred to as the premium, is made up of two component parts: intrinsic value and time value. These are two concepts that will be introduced here in a summary fashion, as derivatives pricing and valuation, while important, are generally beyond the scope of this text.

Intrinsic Value

When traders say, "it's five dollars in-the-money" or "that derivative is out-of-the-money," they are referring to the intrinsic value. Intrinsic value is a way of describing the worth of the option at any given time in relation to the rights purchased at the point of contract by the parties. If a senior manager of a technology company (in this text, we'll refer to that company as "Tech Co.") holds call options to purchase Tech Co. stock after the introduction into the market of a popular handheld device by Tech Co., that manager will likely be holding an option that is in-the-money, which is to say, the price that the manager must pay to acquire Tech Co. stock will likely be *lower* than the price the manager would have to otherwise pay in the market for the same stock.

To further illustrate using the Tech Co. manager's call option as our example, if the strike price in the call option as our example was set at $250, and Tech Co. shares have appreciated to $325 in the market, then the manager would pay $250 for each share, a price that is lower than the $325 that the manager would have to pay for the stock (in the market in the absence of that call option). The manager's option, then, is said to be in-the-money because the strike price is less ($75 less) than the market value of the underlying stock. In trade parlance, the Tech Co. call option is 75 points in-the-money. The manager, if he or she is able to exercise the option (typically there are timing restrictions on option awards as a part of compensation in the employment context), could exercise the Tech Co. call option by paying the strike price, acquire the shares, and then resell them for $75 of profit. Options may also be sold.

If a trader holds a put option on Tech Co. stock and the value of the stock has fallen below the strike price, the put is in-the-money to the extent of the difference between the strike and the market prices. If a holder of a Tech Co. put holds an option with a strike price of $250, and Tech Co. shares fall below $250 to $225, the put is 25 points in-the-money.

If an option is in-the-money, it has intrinsic value. There is no intrinsic value to an option if it's out-of-the-money. Incidentally, an option whose premium and strike price are the same is said to be at-the-money.

Thus, whatever an option is, whether it be in-the-money or out-of-the-money, that value is called intrinsic value, and it makes up one-half of the premium.

The other half is referred to as time value.

Time Value

Subtract the intrinsic value from the premium, and the balance that remains is referred to as time value. Time value reflects the time that remains before the option expires worthless. Option premiums will generally be greater with longer periods of time that remain before the option expires.

Closing an Option

The following discussion illustrates the basics concerning writing and holding options; options are typically written and held in tandem with decisions concerning the asset that underlies the option. If the market price of the underlying security rises or otherwise is above the exercise price, the put option will expire (worthless) and the put option holder's loss will be the value of the paid premium, and the writer's gain will be limited to the premium received. On the other hand, if the market price of the underlying security or asset declines, or is otherwise below the exercise price, the writer may elect to close the position or take delivery of the security at the exercise price. In that event, the writer's return will be the premium received from the put option minus the cost of closing the position or, if it chooses to take delivery of the security, the premium received from the put option minus the amount by which the market price of the security is below the exercise price.

BASIC OPTION STRATEGIES

As generally discussed in the preceding pages, a call option written by a trader on a security gives the holder the right to buy the underlying security at a stated exercise price; a put option gives the holder the right to sell the underlying security at a stated exercise price. In the case of options on indexes, the options are usually cash settled, based on the difference between the strike price and the value of the index.

Writers of options receive a premium for writing a put or call option, which results in a profit to the writer in the event the option expires unexercised (or is closed out at a profit). The amount of the premium will reflect, among other things, the relationship of the market price and volatility of the underlying security or securities index to the exercise price of the option, the remaining term of the option, supply and demand, and interest rates. However, by writing a call option on a security, the writer limits its opportunity to profit from any increase in the market value of the underlying security above the exercise price of the option. By writing a put option on a security, the writer assumes the risk that it may be required to purchase the underlying security for an exercise price higher than its then-current market value, resulting in a potential capital loss unless the security subsequently appreciates in value. In the case of options on an index, as for the party that writes a call, any profit by that party (with respect to portfolio securities expected to correlate with the index) will be limited by an increase in the index above the exercise price of the option. If a fund writes a put on an index, the fund may be required to make a cash settlement greater than the premium received (if the index declines).

If the writer of an option wishes to terminate its obligation in a listed options setting, it may effect a closing purchase transaction. This transaction is accomplished, in the case of exchange-traded options, by buying an option of the same series as the option previously written. The effect of the purchase is that the clearing house will cancel the writer's position. Timing is key; closing purchase transactions are not something which can be done at any time. The writer of an option may not effect a closing purchase transaction after it has been notified of the exercise of an option. In the same way, an investor who is the holder of an option may liquidate its position by effecting a closing sale transaction. This transaction is accomplished by selling an option of the same series as the option previously purchased. No guarantee exists that assures either party to an option that either the writer or holder will be able to affect a closing purchase or a closing sale transaction at any particular time. Also, OTC options may be closed out only with the other party to the option transaction, as there is no common exchange and standardized derivative to close out (contrary to listed and centrally-cleared derivatives).

Although many strategies are unique to the product, the common denominators for many strategies are:

- Using derivatives as a substitute for direct investment in securities or other assets.
- Using swaps or other derivatives with underliers that include an index, a single security, or a basket of securities to gain investment exposures (e.g., by selling protection under a credit default swap).
- Using currency derivatives (including currency forwards, futures contracts, swap contracts, and options) to gain exposure to a given currency.
- Buying credit default protection; using derivatives in an attempt to hedge or reduce its investment exposures. (For example, an investor may use credit-default swaps to take an active short position with respect to the likelihood of default by an issuer, whose debt is the "underlier" of the CDS.)
- Using currency derivatives in an attempt to hedge or reduce some aspect of the currency exposure in its portfolio. (For these purposes, an investor may use an instrument denominated in a different currency that the investor believes is highly correlated with the relevant currency.)
- Using derivatives in an attempt to adjust elements of its investment exposures to various securities, sectors, markets, and currencies (without actually having to sell existing investments or make new direct investments. For instance, the investor may attempt to alter the interest rate exposure of debt instruments by employing interest rate swaps. Such a strategy is designed to maintain the investor's exposure to the credit of an issuer through the debt instrument but adjust the investor's interest-rate exposure through the swap. With these swaps, the investor and its counterparties exchange interest rate exposure, such as fixed against variable rates and shorter duration against longer duration rates.)
- Using currency derivatives in an attempt to adjust currency exposure or seeking currency exposure that is different (in some cases, significantly different) from the currency exposure represented by its portfolio investments.

EXCHANGE-TRADED OPTIONS

Standardized options that trade on an exchange and are centrally cleared are treated as securities (not security-based swaps, unless the underlying securities are restricted securities) and regulated by the SEC.

The way these securities are described is as follows: the name of the underlying security appears first when referencing an option, then the month in which the option expires, then the strike price, type of option, and premium, in this way: Long 1 [Company name] May 300 Call 30. We will unpack this further.

In listed (as opposed to OTC) trade parlance, the security underlying the option comes first in the name of the option. The number of shares of the listed option is generally a round lot, or 100 shares. In OTC options, the two parties negotiate the number of shares; in listed derivatives trading, the derivatives are "cookie-cutter" or more standardized.

Exchange-traded options expire on a fixed date; the month in which the expiration takes place follows the name of the issuer of the underlying security. Holders of listed options have the right to exercise the options by a fixed expiration date, and if the date passes without exercise, the option expires, worthless. The date of expiration with listed options is fixed by the exchange on which the option trades.

The exercise price, or strike price, is next in the name of the option. This is the price at which the buyer buys the stock in the case of an equity call option (or sells the stock in the case of a put, as described). The holder of a call option locks in the price at the strike price, or the price at which the holder can purchase the underlying security (and this is a good thing in the event that the value of the underlier increases over time). As review, the holder of a put option has the right to sell a security at the strike price to the writer of the option. OTC options will have negotiated strike prices; with listed options, the strike price is fixed (and usually is set in five-dollar increments).

After the name of the issuer of the stock that forms the basis of the option, the expiration month, and exercise price, the next feature of the option that is referred to is the type of option: a put or a call. Puts and calls are covered above.

The final detail that rounds out the full name of the option is the premium. The premium is the current market value of the option. Premiums are referred to as "points", so if a premium to purchase the option is three dollars, the value of the option contract is three points. The buyer of the option pays this amount to the seller, or writer, in exchange for the rights that are conveyed under the option to the buyer. The premium of the option will rise as the value of the underlying security rises, and likewise the option premium will fall with the falling value of the underlier.

In the case of listed, or exchange-traded options, the premium is typically the only part of the option that is not standardized. Market forces determine the value of the premium. A number of variables combine together to create the value of the premium: the underlying stock's value, the market within which the issuer operates, distributions on the underlying stock, such as dividends, the period of time which remains before the option expires and can no longer be exercised, and a comparison of the strike price (the price at which the option is exercised after the premium is paid) with the price of the underlying stock.

SWAPS FOLLOW OPTIONS IN THE EVOLUTION OF DERIVATIVES

After the development of the OTC derivatives forwards and options, the next derivative to evolve into use was the swap. Swaps are contracts between two parties wherein each exchanges a stream of payments computed by reference to a hypothetical (or notional, the opposite of actual) amount, and the price of the asset that is the subject of the swap. This asset is referred to from time to time in derivative nomenclature as "the reference obligation." Many swaps are traded off-exchange in the OTC market, although recently, as a result of regulatory changes, certain swaps are now being traded in electronic trading facilities and cleared through clearing organizations.

Swaps are usually entered into on a net basis using payment netting, that is, the two payment streams are netted out in a single cash settlement on the payment date (or dates) specified in the agreement, with one party receiving, or paying, as the case may be, only the net amount of multiple payments. Swaps do not generally involve the delivery of underlying assets or principal, although, in the case of foreign currency swaps, they frequently do. Accordingly, the risk of loss with respect to swaps is generally limited to the net amount of payments that the party is contractually obligated to make during the life of the swap. In some swap transactions, one or both parties to the swap may require collateral to support, or assure, the fulfillment of payment obligations. If the counterparty defaults, the risk of loss consists of the net amount of payments which the party is contractually entitled to receive, less any collateral deposits entrusted to the nondefaulting party.

There are various types of swaps, such as, for example, total return swaps (TRSs), credit default swaps (CDSs) and interest rate swaps (IRSs). Swaps generally exist in categories of OTC derivatives such as credit derivatives and equity derivatives. Credit derivatives derive their value from the creditworthiness of an underlying obligor, which is referred to as the reference obligor in derivatives parlance. Equity derivatives are, as the name implies, based on the performance of an issuer's equity shares, or a group of issuers' equity shares, whether in the form of a basket of equities or an index. We will consider each category in turn.

CREDIT DERIVATIVES

Credit derivatives are attractive because they can synthetically replicate a short or long position in corporate (or other, for example government) bonds or loans, such as commercial loans issued by a bank or other issuer. Like other derivatives, there is generally no limit to the utility of credit derivatives.

In the years prior to the 2008 market crises, credit derivatives grew with leaps and bounds. The International Swaps and Derivatives Association, Inc., or ISDA, announced that in the one-year period between 2006 and 2007, the growth rate for credit derivatives was an astounding 75 percent.[4]

With a credit derivative, one party is seeking to sever from its overall exposure the risk of a default (or other credit-related event, such as a bankruptcy) of one or more borrowers. That is basically the role of a credit derivative: one party seeks to separate credit risk from other risks such as market risk, legal documentation risk, and so forth.

Since credit risk is at the heart of a credit derivative, it is important to proceed with at least a basic understanding of credit risk. All debt instruments reward one party—typically the lender only—for taking the risk that the other party will default. That reward is packed into the interest rate that a borrower pays the lender. The interest rate that accompanies a loan is comprised of several components: the lender's cost of funding, risk of inflation, and the credit profile of the borrower, including its assets, assets that may serve as collateral, third party obligations, borrowing history, and so forth.

Credit risk accompanies any loan from any lender. Credit derivatives are frequently structured on corporate or sovereign debt; in recent years, they have been increasingly controversial when they are structured on the debt of governments or divisions of governments such as counties, or financial services firms.

Credit Default Swaps

Next to the collateralized debt obligation, or CDO, which is described in Chapter 1 and illustrated in Figure 10.2, the derivative with singular notoriety from the market crises of 2008 is the CDS.

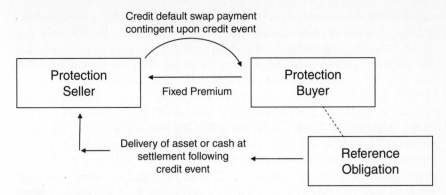

FIGURE 10.2   Credit Default Swap

It is generally accepted that CDSs were invented in the early 1990s, although the CDS structure may have existed before 1990. CDSs are bilateral contracts, like any other swap, as illustrated in Figure 10.2.

This derivative is best understood by comparing it to an insurance policy (although a CDS is not insurance in the ordinary sense of the word, because in a CDS, no person is required to own the underlying asset, bond, numerous securities, or an index on which the derivative is based; accordingly, there is no "insurable interest" in a CDS).

In Figure 10.2, the party needing protection is referred to in OTC derivatives parlance as the "protection buyer," and trade confirmations frequently state in headings the name of the party which buy's protection (a concept described in this chapter in greater detail), along with the party that sells it. As with Figure 10.1 near the beginning of this chapter, the buyer and seller of protection enter into a swap where streams of payments may be exchanged under certain conditions (negotiated by the two parties to the trade). Just as an insured would under an insurance contract, the protection buyer pays a fee, or fixed premium, to the protection seller, typically on a quarterly basis. In exchange for that fee, the protection seller agrees to provide compensation upon the occurrence of a credit event relating to the subject of the derivative (the reference obligation, a bond or loan, for example), as described below.

The structure of a CDS is quite straightforward: the buyer of credit default insurance pays a premium in exchange for a payment by the other party to the CDS, the protection seller, upon the occurrence of a contingency specified in the CDS (i.e., a "Credit Event," such as, for example, events relating to the underlying debt or collection of debts, such as the default or restructuring of the debt, the bankruptcy of the reference obligor that issued the debt on which the CDS is based). If the CDS references sovereign debt, a credit default may be a moratorium on debt servicing by the sovereign, in which case, if a moratorium is one of the credit events with respect to which the protection buyer pays a premium for protection, the protection seller makes a negotiated contingent payment to the protection buyer.

Credit derivatives in general, and CDSs in particular, allow a financial services company or a bank, to lay off the credit risk of a loan to another party, without the bank's borrower knowing about the CDS, and allow the bank to keep extending credit to its borrower when, initially, it may not have wanted to (or was permitted by regulators to) extend a loan of a certain amount to the borrower. CDSs allow financial institutions (and other parties, but primarily financial institutions such as banks) the ability to dispose (or acquire) credit risk. The CDS isolates certain specific risks relating to loans (or to the underlying lender).

CDSs have become so popular that indexes of CDS products have developed, and the cost of obtaining protection for certain financial institutions is an accepted indicia of those institutions' financial health.

To summarize, the buyer and seller of protection enter into a bargain whereby if a certain credit event takes place during the term of the CDS, the seller of protection, like an insurer under an insurance contract, is obligated to make a payout.

So as review, in a CDS, like other swaps, the transaction calls for an exchange: the buyer of the CDS pays the seller a periodic stream of payments over the term of the CDS much (like an insured pays an insurer under an insurance contract). The protection buyer makes this stream of payments, referred to in the documentation as the fixed amount, in return for a contingent payment. The reason that we refer to this as a contingent payment is that the protection seller's obligation to pay is conditioned upon the occurrence of a specified credit event (e.g., failure to pay, bankruptcy, moratorium on sovereign debt, or restructuring of debt) and the satisfaction of certain notice requirements. Upon the occurrence of a credit event, such as the default of the underlying loan (or loans) or the bankruptcy of the debtor, the underlying reference obligation is typically traditional debt in the form of a bond. This swap is analogous to insurance but, because neither party generally owns the assets that underlie the CDs, there is no insurable interest and, therefore, a CDS is not insurance in the customary sense.

To make sure the reader sees the fundamental economics of the CDS trade, the buyer of protection through the CDS enters into this derivative for purposes of transferring credit risk, hedging its exposure or its concentration in certain areas of exposure. On the other hand, parties that sell protection through the CDS do so to earn a fixed payment by assuming the credit risk. Protection sellers also are drawn to CDSs due to limited access elsewhere to credits. CDSs are attractive to protection sellers and protection buyers because the swaps may be customized at various levels: the maturities, cash flows, and the underlying credits may range from short-term durations to midrange and longer terms, and the underliers may be traditional bank loans, aircraft leases, or equipment leases to corporate bonds or sovereign debt.

A credit event generally (and not exclusively) means a bankruptcy, failure to pay, or obligation acceleration. If a credit event occurs, the seller typically must pay the contingent payment to the buyer, which is typically the par value (or full notional value less recovery rate) of the reference obligation. The contingent payment may be a cash settlement or physical delivery of the reference obligation in return for payment of the face amount of the obligation.

The payment that the must be made by the protection seller upon the occurrence of a credit event is generally meant to compensate the protection buyer for the decrease in value of the underlying obligation. The diminution of value is generally determined by auctions or other means to determine what a buyer would pay for the bond (after the credit event).

As further review, 2 parties sometimes may enter into a CDS without either owning the underlying debt that is referenced in the CDS paperwork or trade confirmation. CDSs in which one party owns the underlying debt or loans are common. One party, the protection seller, takes a long view with respect to the underlying loan, believing that the obligor of the loan will continue to timely pay its creditor until maturity. Five-year maturities for CDSs are common. The other party, the protection buyer, is said to take a short view, and enters into the CDS with the view that the underlying obligor may likely or will default, or the specified credit event will take place. The protection buyer may simply want to buy, as the name implies, protection against a credit event. The reference obligation need not be the debt of either party to the CDS.

Protection buyers, especially those whose CDS is based on distressed debt, will pay an upfront, independent amount or upfront margin that is, as Chapter 3 describes in greater detail, designed to give the protection seller security against default by the buyer. Aside from this payment, the protection buyer need not pay a commission, and the buyer typically does not have to enter into the market and pay for the underlying, referenced credit.

Before the occurrence of a credit event, the protection buyer makes payments to the protection seller (these are represented by the straight line in Figure 10.2). These payments may vary. The protection buyer's payment obligations may reset quarterly based on the cost of insurance. The buyer's payment obligation may even be a one-time obligation, up front, just like an option holder's premium payment.

The CDS protection seller (like the writer of an option) may never have to make a payment to the protection buyer (as is the case with insurance contracts); if the parties negotiate up-front for the protection seller to pay the protection buyer after the occurrence of a credit event, and the specified credit event never takes place, the protection seller is contractually and legally entitled to receive all protection-buyer payments without making a single payment to the protection buyer.

After the occurrence of a credit event that is specified in the CDS, the protection buyer no longer needs to pay the premiums called for in the CDS documentation, which is discussed next. On the date of the credit event, referred to as the "event-determination date," the protection buyer's fixed amounts cease to accrue and are no longer payable to the protection seller. The protection buyer delivers a notice to the protection seller of the credit event; the notice typically needs to satisfy certain criteria (e.g., in the notice, the protection buyer may need to attach or reference a *Wall Street Journal* article that evidences the occurrence of the credit event).

Although the parties usually settle the CDS by means of a cash payment, the seller of protection may also buy the underlying obligation, or, in CDS parlance, the "deliverable obligation," from the protection buyer, at par, and, in doing so, makes the protection buyer whole after the occurrence of a credit event (which would otherwise cause the value of the underlying debt to decline significantly).

If the CDS is, under the CDS documentation, required to be physically settled (the norm today is cash settlement, which will be discussed next), then, after a credit event, the protection buyer will select a certain predetermined principal amount of bond or bonds specified in the CDS documentation, and the deliverable obligations are tendered to the protection seller (as illustrated by the arrow to the left of the reference obligation in Figure 10.2), in exchange for cash to the protection buyer. The protection seller will then own the bond(s), whose value have, in all likelihood, diminished following the credit event, and the protection seller will hold cash that represents the value of the deliverable obligations.

Most CDSs are settled via cash settlement. The cash settlement amount that is generally negotiated is determined by means of a calculation agent designated in the CDS documentation (i.e., the trade confirmation). This amount is generally the previously agreed on notional amount (i.e., the amount that both parties agreed on as the overall value of the loans or credit referenced in the CDS) multiplied by the higher of zero or 100 percent minus the final price of the underlying loans after the credit event, as determined by dealer quotes.

If the CDS has as its reference obligation a single security, or a narrowly based index, it is likely that the regulators in the United States will deem that derivative a security-based swap. This is regulated by the SEC. A CDS on a basket of securities or an index such as the S&P 500 are swaps regulated by the CFTC.

CDSs, prior to reform, were entirely negotiated, traded, and settled OTC. Both parties typically utilized forms published by the ISDA, which are summarized in greater detail earlier in this text. These forms included either the 1992 or 2002 ISDA Master Agreement, as modified to the credit profiles and needs of each party by a Schedule. Many, if not all, parties to CDSs seek collateral from their counterparties; the ISDA form that the association published for purposes of negotiating collateral is the Credit Support Annex or CSA.

The ISDA Master Agreement, Schedule, and CSA do not complete the CDS (and other OTC derivative) documentation. These are foundational documents that provide a fulsome structure of rights and obligations for all the OTC derivatives that the 2 parties trade with each other, over the course of their OTC derivatives trading relationship. In certain cases, where timing is critically important, the parties may temporarily forgo the ISDA Master Agreement (sometimes referred to as the ISDA) and the ancillary documentation, and instead negotiate a long-form confirmation that may take as many as 20 to 30 pages to evidence a CDS. This form of confirmation will be entered into by the parties, who generally, in doing so, have insufficient time to "negotiate an ISDA," and intend at some later point to more fully document their rights and obligations through an ISDA Master Agreement. If the parties to a CDS execute an ISDA, they next negotiate the economics, maturity, credit events, and settlement details of their CDS, and these key CDS terms are included in the trade Confirmation.

Negative-Basis CDSs

Negative-basis CDSs are swaps which are generally between banks seeking capital relief (in the position of protection buyers) and companies that insure debts—that is, monoline insurers, which generally establish special purpose vehicles as the CDS protection sellers. In the CDS, the protection buyer has acquired an asset, or acquires a loan, then buys protection against the decline of that asset from a monoline insurer. The characterization of the CDS as a swap or security-based swap will depend on the asset or index on which the trade is based, as discussed in the preceding pages.

Once a bank obtains credit protection in the form of a CDS from a monoline, that bank generally is able to free up the capital that regulations would have required to be set aside for the loan. From a regulatory capital perspective, the credit risk that the bank assumes when making the loan is shed to the protection seller under the CDS that references the loan.

Protection buyers and sellers to negative-basis CDS may modify the type of payment that the protection seller is obligated to pay upon the occurrence of certain credit events. This payment, referred to as a modified cash settlement, requires the protection seller to pay only the shortfall in the scheduled payments that arise upon the occurrence of a specified credit event.

CREDIT-LINKED NOTES AND OTHER SECURITIES

Like protection sellers in a CDS, buyers of credit-linked notes seek to take on the credit risk that underlies the note. Whereas CDS protection sellers are generally financial institutions, hedge funds, or banks, issuers of credit-linked securities are limited-purpose trusts or other special-purpose vehicles which, in turn, invest in a derivative or basket of derivatives, such as CDSs, interest rate swaps, and other securities, in order to provide exposure to certain fixed income markets. As this text went to print, the regulators did not finalize rules concerning the characterization of credit-linked notes and structured products (which likely will be deemed securities under the regulatory jurisdiction of the SEC), or the definition of "swap," for that matter.

As another illustration of the utility of this derivative, an investor may invest in credit-linked securities as a cash-management tool in order to gain exposure to a certain market and to remain fully invested when more traditional income-producing securities are not available. Like an investment in a debt security, investments in credit-linked securities represent the right to receive periodic income payments (in the form of distributions) and payment of principal at the end of the term of the security. However, depending on the manner in which the credit-linked product is structured, these payments may be conditioned on or linked to the issuer's receipt of payments from (and the issuer's potential obligations to) the counterparties to the derivative and other securities in which the issuer invests.

TOTAL RETURN SWAPS

Total return swaps are among the author's list of preferred derivatives; they are both elegant and useful structures. TRSs are contracts in which one party, the total return payer, agrees to make payments of the (total) return from a designated underlying asset or assets, which may include security, baskets of securities or securities indices, during the specified period, in return for receiving payments equal to a fixed or floating rate of interest

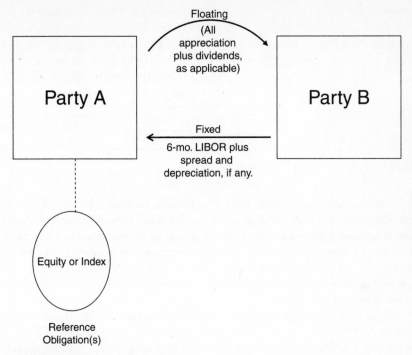

FIGURE 10.3 Total Return-Swap

and, typically, a LIBOR-based "spread" (or the total return from the other designated underlying assets). The structure is brought into sharper focus in Figure 10.3.

The underlying assets may or may not be owned by a party to the TRS. TRSs handled by the author in 2011 contemplated the total return payor establishing a special purpose entity that owned, for example, a portfolio of bank loans or other loans throughout the term of the derivative.

TRSs are generally credit derivatives and depending on the underlier, they may be either a swap (regulated by the CFTC) or a security-based swap (regulated by the SEC); if a party to the TRS is the total return receiver, then the *credit* risk for the underlying asset is transferred in exchange for its receipt of the return on that asset (in that case it's a credit derivative). The total return receiver, in exchange for the appreciation on the underlying asset, pays to the total return payer a fee for the instrument and assumes the obligation to pay any depreciation of the underlying asset or assets. If a party is the total return payer, it hedges the economic risk of the underlying asset, and receives a fixed fee from the total return swap receiver. However, the

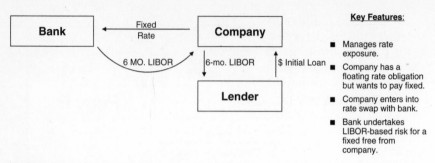

FIGURE 10.4   Interest Rate Swap

TRS structu is also frequently used in equity derivatives, which replicate the ownership of an equity or other security. Because of the passage of U.S. tax law concerning the handling of dividends in a TRS and other structures, the author highly recommends that the reader consult qualified tax counsel along with qualified derivatives counsel for a range of determinations that will affect the performance of the TRS and drive the tax and other obligations of the parties to the trade.

Figure 10.3 includes the basic features of swaps first illustrated in Figure 10.1, with the exception that the total return receiver in a TRS also bears the risk that the reference obligation(s) will depreciate in value, and basic TRS transactions require the total return receiver to make a payment to the TRS payor to account for that depreciation in value.

INTEREST RATE SWAPS

Interest rate swaps, which are generally characterized as swaps within the regulation of the CFTC, involve the exchange by one party to the swap with another party of interest payments, such as an exchange of floating-rate payments for fixed-rate payments with respect to a notional amount of principal. Figure 10.4 provides an illustration of this classic derivative.

In an interest rate swap, as illustrated and described in Figure 10.4, one party to the swap (usually a swap dealer) commits to perform a floating interest rate payment obligation (on a loan, such as a commercial real estate loan, with respect to which the other party to the swap is the obligor or debtor) in exchange for the other party to the swap paying a fixed payment to the party that makes the floating payment. The party who wants to get out of an underlying floating payment, that is, a payment that is based on an index that changes over time, is expecting the fixed payment to be lower than the floating rate.

Both parties to the swap described in the preceding paragraph negotiate the manner in which the fixed and the floating payments are calculated. One party, typically the dealer, is the calculation agent who, during the term of the swap, actually makes the calculations and requests the payments made based on the calculations.

Whereas a forward or futures contract would include a calculation of a single payment based on an index at a time in the future, and typically require that payment to be made at a later date, a swap such as an interest rate swap contemplates a series of calculations for the floating rate and requires the exchange of the payment based on that rate, typically netted against the fixed payment so that one party makes one payment on a specified payment date.

Related to interest rate swaps are caps, floors, and collars. Investors may use interest rate caps, floors, and collars for similar purposes as interest rate futures contracts and related options. Interest rate caps, floors, and collars are similar to interest-rate swap contracts because the payment obligations are measured by changes in interest rates as applied to a notional amount and because they are individually negotiated with a specific counterparty. These will be "swaps" regulated by the CFTC.

The purchase of an interest rate cap entitles the purchaser, to the extent that a specific index exceeds a specified interest rate, to receive payments of interest on a notional principal amount from the party selling the interest rate cap.

The purchase of an interest rate floor entitles the purchaser, to the extent that a specified index falls below specified interest rates, to receive payments of interest on a notional principal amount from the party selling the interest rate floor.

The purchase of an interest rate collar entitles the purchaser, to the extent that a specified index exceeds or falls below two specified interest rates, to receive payments of interest on a notional principal amount from the party selling the interest rate collar.

Investors use interest rate caps, floors, and collars for some of the same purposes as those for which they use futures and options, and these interest rate products present similar risks and opportunities as those associated with futures and related options. These swaps, if entered into within the United States in 2010, are done in the OTC market. However, under the reforms discussed in Chapter 4, regulations will likely require that many interest rate and other swaps be centrally cleared by central clearinghouses, over time. This process would require swap end users to enter into clearing documentation and post initial and mark-to-market-based margin (determined by central clearinghouses and discussed in Chapters 3 and 4).

Step 1: Portfolio Manager (PM) wants to take a view with respect to any equity.

> (Portfolio may for a variety of reasons be unable to obtain the shares of the equity [including, for example, timing issues, etc.]).

Step 2: PM identifies a swap provider and outlines the economics of the trade.

Step 3: Trade details are exchanged and approved, with the swap dealer providing a trade confirmation.

Swap Structure:

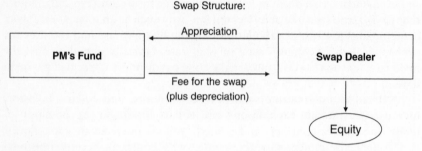

FIGURE 10.5   Equity Swap Structure and Steps in Basic Trading

EQUITY SWAPS

Equity swaps involve an agreement by two parties to exchange returns calculated with respect to a notional amount of an equity index (e.g., the S&P 500 Index), a basket of equity securities, or individual equity security, and their structure is illustrated in Figure 10.5.

Equity swaps provide an effective illustration of why derivatives are a powerful, widely-accepted investment and risk management tool. If a portfolio manager is unable, for whatever reason, to secure an investment in an equity by a purchase in the cash market, or if an investor is unable to obtain exactly the right exposure to a market, industry, or issuer, an equity derivative, as an OTC instrument, is an effective tool for synthetically replicating an investment in the traditional cash market.

An equity swap replicates the cash flows that may be received from a stock or other equity investment.[5]

> *It is sometimes useful to think of the equity swap as replicating the cash flows that the equity return receiver would have experienced if it could have borrowed an amount equal to the notional amount in the debt market and invested it into the equity. The equity return payer is in the position it would have been if it had shorted the equity and invested the proceeds in floating rate debt.[6]*

The three basic steps to entering into an equity swap are illustrated in Figure 10.5, and the documentation for this swap, is discussed earlier in this book.

CURRENCY DERIVATIVES

Foreign currency exchange rates may fluctuate significantly over short periods of time, and these fluctuations frequently result in adjustments to asset pricing and values, salaries, and a host of other economic changes. This is a very complex area that is fraught with risk that necessitates currency derivatives, many of which are swaps regulated by the CFTC (although the U.S. Department of the Treasury proposed in 2011 that certain foreign exchange forwards and foreign exchange swaps be excluded from the definition of swap).

Exchange rates are generally determined by domestic and international economic and political developments, the forces of supply and demand in the foreign-exchange markets, the relative merits of investments in different countries, actual or perceived changes in interest rates, and a variety of other complex factors. Currency exchange rates can also be affected unpredictably by intervention (or the failure to intervene) by United States or foreign governments or central banks, or by currency controls or political developments in the United States or abroad. These and other currencies in which investors' assets are denominated may be devalued against the U.S. dollar, resulting in a loss.

Forward foreign currency contracts are contracts between two parties to purchase and sell a specific quantity of a particular currency at a specified price, with delivery and settlement to take place on a future date that is agreed on by the parties to the contracts. Currency futures contracts are contracts to buy or sell a standard quantity of a particular currency at a specified future date and price. Options on currency futures contracts give their owner the right, but not the obligation, to buy (in the case of a call option) or sell (in the case of a put option) a specified currency futures contract at a fixed price during a specified period. Options on currencies give their owner the right, but not the obligation, to buy (in the case of a call option) or sell (in the case of a put option) a specified quantity of a particular currency at a fixed price during a specified period. An investor may also purchase forward foreign-exchange contracts in conjunction with U.S. dollar-denominated securities in order to create a synthetic foreign-currency-denominated security, which approximates desired risk and return characteristics where the nonsynthetic securities either are not available in foreign markets or possess undesirable characteristics.

Investors that are permitted to invest in securities denominated in foreign currencies may buy or sell foreign currencies or deal in forward foreign-currency contracts, currency futures contracts and related options, and options on currencies. These investors may use such currency instruments for hedging, investment, or currency risk management. Currency risk management may include taking active currency positions relative to both the securities portfolio of the investor and the investor's performance benchmark.

A currency swap is an agreement to exchange cash flows based on the notional difference among two or more currencies (and this swap operates in a way which is similar to an interest rate swap). A currency swap involves the exchange by a party and its counterparts of the cash flows on a notional amount of two or more currencies based on the relative value differential among them, such as exchanging a right to receive a payment in foreign currency for the right to receive U.S. dollars. Currency swap agreements may be entered into on a net basis, or may involve the delivery of the entire principal value of one designated currency in exchange for the entire principal value of another designated currency. In such cases, the entire principal value of a currency swap is subject to the risk that the counterparty will default on its contractual delivery obligations.

Options are used both in the OTC and exchange environments, as discussed in preceding pages. There are also a number of listed options on the futures contracts on the leading futures exchanges, which will be discussed later in this Chapter. These contracts offer investors and risk mitigators an additional set of financial vehicles to use in managing exposure to the cash and commodities markets.

In addition to futures contracts and options on the futures contracts, there is also an active OTC market in derivatives tied to a wide range of commodities (such as natural gas). Unlike most of the exchange-traded futures contracts or exchange-traded options on the futures contracts, each party to such a contract bears the credit risk that the other party may not be able to perform its obligations under its contract.

PROPERTY DERIVATIVES

Now that we have discussed the structure for TRSs, or total return swaps, we turn to property derivatives, which are frequently structured in ways which are similar to TRSs, with an index as the reference obligation (or "underlier"). Property derivatives with broad-based indices as the reference obligation will likely be swaps under the jurisdiction of the CFTC.

As illustrated in Figure 10.6, the 2 parties to this swap base their agreement on a benchmark (which is a commercial property index), or the cash flows of a real estate asset such as a whole loan or subordinated debt.

At inception, two parties to a property swap structure as a TRS agree to exchange the (total) return of an asset, in exchange for a fixed or floating amount, plus any appreciation or depreciation with respect to that asset. An investor who has a large real estate portfolio may therefore reduce its exposure by entering into a property derivative structured as a TRS in order to receive a payment that hedges risks associated with that portfolio.

In a TRS based on an index, as illustrated in Figure 10.6, there are 2 legs, or payments, exchanged by the parties: the total return leg, paid by the return payer, is typically the published values of an index and the floating rate leg, which is paid by the return receiver, is typically negotiated by the parties to be LIBOR plus a spread, constituting the equivalent of the anticipated return of the applicable index (similar to an equity swap). The 2 legs are netted against each other, producing one payment by 1 of the parties to the TRS.

For the return receiver (also referred to as the buyer), the TRS constitutes the economic equivalent of borrowing the notional amount (which, unlike actual money borrowed, may be set at any amount agreed upon by the

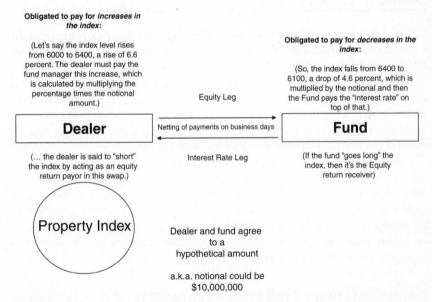

FIGURE 10.6 Property Derivative Structured as a TRS with an Index as the Underlier

parties to the swap) at LIBOR plus the spread (which is determined by the notional amount, the underlying index or asset, and the maturity of the swap). The return receiver synthetically owns the underlying asset (or index) and is said to go long with respect to that asset. Conversely, the party that is the return payer is said to short the underlying asset by bargaining to pay the return in exchange for the appreciation or depreciation of the asset. Thus, a return receiver in an index TRS is said to short the index (or other asset) with the view that the index (or asset) will underperform.

In most TRS transactions, the frequency and impact of a default by 1 of the parties is greatly curtailed because the risk upon early termination is limited to the movement in the underlying index or cash flows relative to the notional amount of the swap, and this amount is set by the parties at the outset of the swap. Because there is no transfer of property, the fees and expenses typically associated with real estate transfers are significantly reduced or eliminated. Additionally, the use of a financial intermediary (e.g., a dealer with a superior credit rating) as counterparty to all transactions further reduces credit risk and expense.

Property derivatives are traded, as this text went to print, OTC, as opposed to trading on an exchange. These are swaps regulated by the CFTC.

COMMODITY DERIVATIVES

Commodity-based OTC derivatives, which are generally governed by the CFTC as swaps, contain either generic or highly customized terms and conditions (and are available to a range of participants). Many of these OTC contracts are cash-settled forwards for the future delivery of natural gas or petroleum-based fuels, and other commodities. Others take the form of swaps in which the two parties exchange cash flows based on predetermined formulas tied to the natural gas spot price, forward natural gas price, or natural gas or other commodity futures contract price.

These transactions frequently entail risks which are also managed by derivatives. To protect itself from the credit risk that arises in connection with such contracts, a market participant may enter into agreements with each counterparty which provides for the netting of its overall exposure to its counterparty. Parties to derivatives may require that the counterparty be highly rated and provide collateral or other credit support to address exposure to counterparty risks.

Options on Forward Contracts or Commodities

An option on a forward contract or commodity gives the buyer of the option the right, but not the obligation, to take a position at a specified price in the underlying forward contract or commodity. However, similar to forward contracts, options on forward contracts or on commodities are individually negotiated contracts between counterparties and are typically traded in the OTC market. Therefore, options on forward contracts and physical commodities possess many of the same characteristics of forward contracts with respect to offsetting positions and credit risk that were described earlier. These are regulated by the CFTC.

ENERGY SWAPS

An important category within commodity derivatives is energy swaps. Energy derivatives, which are generally swaps regulated by the CFTC (however, care must be taken with respect to how these trades are settled), are traded in both the OTC and exchange-traded markets. In this part of the Chapter, oil swaps, which are among the most widely used derivatives in the market, are briefly examined. Oil options, which incorporate many of the concepts discussed in the preceding pages, are also widely used.

Simply put, an oil swap in the OTC market is an agreement between two parties to exchange, over the course of the derivative's life, cash flows that are calculated with reference to an agreed-upon oil index and are typically reset at certain intervals. The basic features of this swap are illustrated in Figure 10.7.

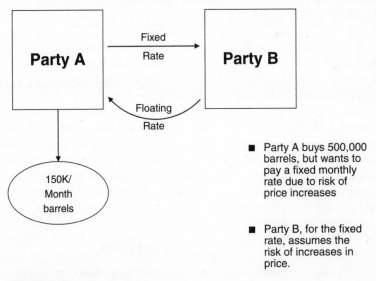

FIGURE 10.7 Energy Swaps

In this figure, Party B may be a large oil company and its counterparty, Party A, could be another company in the oil industry, perhaps a refiner. As is often the case in our modern economy, the refiner is concerned about the rise in oil prices, so with this price risk it enters into a one-year swap. The swap is structured to match perfectly the underlying transaction, in this case, the purchase of 500,000 barrels of oil. In trade parlance, the refiner "pays fixed, receives floating."

The payments made during the life of the swap by Party B will be calculated with reference to an agreed-upon price quoted in the industry (e.g., an index). One party generates a trade confirmation that sets forth the various terms, the other party reviews and accepts the confirmation, and the 2 then will generally have a binding, enforceable swap.

On each date specified in the swap confirmation, U.S. dollar payment obligations will be netted so that if, for example, on a payment date the average monthly rate is 1 dollar and 80 cents greater than the fixed price per barrel set by the parties at trade execution, then the oil company has a payment obligation that is the product of 500,000 multiplied by 1.80, and the oil company pays that resulting amount, U.S.$900,000, to Party A, which uses that amount to offset the price increase in oil. The risk of additional costs incurred due to increases in the price of oil has thereby been hedged.

STRUCTURED PRODUCTS, SECURITIZATION, CDOs, AND CDOs SQUARED

In Chapter 1, we considered the misuse of securitization as a cause of the 2008 market crises and in doing so, we explained the securitization process. That process basically entails the conversion of regular payment streams into securities, thus the term "securitization."

Figure 10.8 is a basic illustration of two securitized products, the collateralized debt obligation, CDO, and the CDO^2. The reader is referred to Chapter 1 for a step-by-step discussion of how payments made by obligors (in Figure 10.8, represented by mortgagors' homes) eventually are cycled through the structure to bond holders towards the right-hand side of Figure 10.8.

Structured notes are derivatives for which the amount of principal repayment and interest payments is based on the movement of one or more factors. These factors may include, but are not limited to, currency exchange rates, interest rates (such as the prime lending rate or LIBOR), referenced bonds, stock indices, individual stocks or baskets of stocks, or one or more

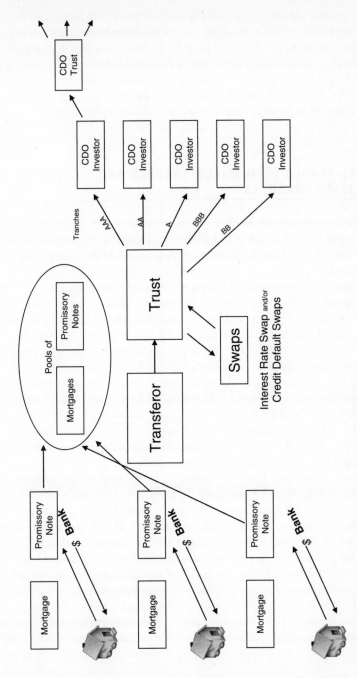

FIGURE 10.8 Collateralized Debt Obligation and CDO²

debt instruments (or combinations thereof). Some of these factors may or may not correlate to the total rate of return on one or more underlying instruments (referenced in such notes). In some cases, the impact of the movements of these factors may increase or decrease by means of multipliers.

As of the date on which this text went to print, the characterization of structured products has not been the subject of final rulemaking.

EXCHANGE-TRADED DERIVATIVES: FUTURES AND OTHER LISTED PRODUCTS

As discussed at length in Chapter 3, futures (which are neither swaps nor security-based swaps but are within their own category of financial products regulated by the CFTC) are financial arrangements that naturally evolved from forwards.

A futures contract, much like a forward, is a binding agreement to buy or sell an asset, usually a financial instrument or commodity at some point later in the future. However, unlike a forward, a futures contract is subject to an organized, orderly, standardized, and systemic trading process that affects every aspect of the trade, from pricing to settlement. The price for the purchase (later in time) is discovered through futures trading on an exchange, which is subject to daily settlement and margining procedures. These contracts are standardized according to certain specifications of the asset as well (as the delivery date, time, and location). Futures were and continue to be heavily regulated in the United States; they are not considered swaps, but are squarely within the jurisdiction of the CFTC, as are options on futures and foreign exchange futures.

Whereas a forward may be entered into by parties for purposes of buying and selling at any later point in time any asset and any amount, grade, or quantity of that asset, a futures contract is by necessity more standardized in terms of the grade or quality of the asset, the quantity, and when the asset is to be settled (or, in futures parlance, "delivered"). The pricing for the contact is determined by the offers to purchase and sell the futures contract on an established exchange, which sets the terms of the contract (e.g., the grade, quantity, and delivery date for settlement).

The traditional futures contract is an agreement between a seller and a buyer which the seller (called a short) will deliver to the buyer (called a long), at a price agreed to when the contract is first entered, and the buyer will accept and pay for a specified quantity and grade of an identified commodity in the future. As described in the history of derivatives and futures in this text, forwards and then futures developed first in the agricultural sector and expanded into other industries, such as energy, and then into the financial services industry. Today, futures contracts are traded on a wide variety of agricultural, financial, and other commodities, including agricultural products, bonds, stock indices, interest rates, currencies, energy, and metals.

ADDITIONAL RESOURCES

This book is intended to provide an early step to develop an understanding of derivatives and the evolving law which governs them, and the markets in which they trade. No single text can possibly set out to achieve the goal of capturing all information that is necessary for a reader to master, let alone become familiar with, derivatives.

It is highly recommended that the reader consult a range of professionals (including legal, tax, and accounting professionals) with in-depth and lengthy experience with derivatives when addressing derivatives, structured products, and other complex instruments of finance. As discussed in the Introduction, in order for a meaningful dialogue to take place with these professionals, at least some familiarity with derivatives and futures is necessary, and this book is intended to help position the reader to take an early step toward acquiring an understanding of what these instruments are, and how they have begun to be subject to new law and regulation.

The new law and regulation of derivatives continue to evolve at a rapid pace in many markets throughout the world on a weekly, or even daily, basis so, as the reader must not and cannot expect this book to be a guide that captures new developments after publication, the reader is encouraged to follow these developments, as well as new law and regulation, by means of online resources such as the resources which follow.

There are a number of resources that the reader may find very helpful, and this chapter provides references to online resources, which include references to glossaries of some of the terms used throughout the book and in the industry (although the reader cannot rely on the precision or legal validity of the words defined in those glossaries).

ONLINE RESOURCES

- The author's website: www.DerivativesGuide.com
- Derivatives and Futures Education
  - www2.isda.org
  - www.futuresindustry.org
  - www.cftc.gov/ConsumerProtection/EducationCenter/CFTCGlossary/ glossary_d.html
  - https://www.theice.com/education.jhtml
- Listed Options Education
  - www.cboe.com/LearnCenter/
  - www.cboe.com/LearnCenter/courses.aspx
- Implementation of Dodd-Frank
  - www.sec.gov/spotlight/dodd-frank/dfactivity-upcoming.shtml#11-10
  - www.cftc.gov/LawRegulation/DoddFrankAct/index.htm
- Investor Education Websites
  - www.sec.gov/investor/links.shtml

GLOSSARIES

www.cmegroup.com/education/glossary.html

www.liffe.com/help/glossary/l.htm

www.optionseducation.org/help/glossary/default.jsp

NOTES

1. Gillian Tett, *Fool's Gold* (New York: Free Press, 2009), 9 (emphasis in original).
2. Michael Durbin, *All About Derivatives* (New York: McGraw-Hill, 2010), 1.
3. CBOE Call Option Strategies, www.cboe.com/Strategies/EquityOptions/Buy ingCalls/Part1.aspx.
4. "ISDA Mid-Year 2007 Market Survey: Credit Derivatives at $45.46 trillion," The International Swaps and Derivatives Association, Inc., News Release, September 26, 2007.
5. See Anthony C. Gooch and Linda B. Klein, *Documentation for Derivatives: Annotated Sample Agreements and Confirmations for Swaps and Other Over-the-Counter Transaction* (London: Euromoney Books, 2002), 717.
6. Ibid.

About the Author

Gordon F. Peery is a derivatives and futures lawyer and a partner of K&L Gates, LLP, a global law firm of nearly 2,000 lawyers.

As a senior associate practicing with a leading Washington, DC law firm in 2001, Gordon assisted clients in televised hearings held in the U.S. Congress involving structured finance and derivatives provided by banks to Enron Corp. Since that time, he has negotiated several hundred derivative trade confirmations, schedules, and Credit Support Annexes to the International Swaps and Derivatives Association (ISDA) Master Agreements and futures agreements. In 2010, Gordon provided counsel to the staff of members of the U.S. Congress regarding derivatives reform in the United States. Since then, he has been actively involved in the monitoring of the law of derivatives and has researched, written, and submitted requests to alter proposed regulations to the Commodity Futures Trading Commission (CFTC) and to the U.S. Treasury. In April 2011, he was invited by officials of the government of Canada and practitioners in Canada to speak on derivatives reform in the United States and assist with the consolidation of Canadian law and regulations on derivatives. His observations have been sought by regulators in Southeast Asia and he has subsequently taught courses on derivatives reform in Hong Kong, Brunei and elsewhere in the Far East. As Gordon previously lived in Japan and focused his undergraduate studies on that country, China, Southeast Asia, and the Far East, he continues to avidly watch the development of the law and practice in alternative finance in these areas.

In December 2011, Gordon worked with clients to bring about changes following the failure of MF Global. As a part of that work he met with the Chairman and Commissioners of the CFTC. Gordon currently acts for influential participants in the derivatives market in the shaping of new documentation for central clearing of derivatives. Included among his clients are individual investors, municipalities, hedge funds, mutual funds, fund complexes, boards of directors of funds, global money managers, charitable organizations, pensions and trusts, as well as analysts and large traders whom Gordon represented before the U.S. Treasury, CFTC, Securities and Exchange Commission (SEC), and Congress.

Gordon has authored and co-authored several dozen publications and has spoken at seminars in various leading markets throughout the world on numerous subjects relating to futures, the derivatives trade and international policy. He is an active member of and contributor to the International Swaps and Derivatives Association (ISDA) and the Futures Industry Association (FIA). The Peery family resides in Orange County, California, and the Washington, DC, area.

Index

Schlesinger, Arthur M., Jr., 72
SDRs. *See* Swap data repositories (SDRs)
Securities:
   credit-linked, 335–336
   mortgage-backed (*see* Mortgage-backed
      securities)
Securities Act of 1933, 136, 140, 265
Securities and Exchange Act of 1934, 185,
   264
Securities and Exchange Commission (SEC):
   creation of, 264–265
   derivative regulation authority, 148
   derivative regulation review, 146–147
   mixed swaps and, 142
   new derivatives regulation, 61
   security-based swap regulation, 141–142
   SPEs and, 30
Securities Exchange Act of 1934, 136, 140,
   163, 304
Securitization, private-label residential
   mortgage-backed, 45–47
Security-based swaps (SBSs):
   major swap participants, 64, 155,
      162–163
   SEC regulation of, 133, 141–142
SEFs. *See* Swap execution facilities (SEFs)
Senate. *See* U.S. Senate
Settlement, daily, 110–112
Shad/Johnson Accord Index Act, 98
Shadow banking system:
   capital requirements, derivatives and, 38–39
   generally, 34–35
   REITs as banks, 35–38
Smith, Adam, 246–247
South Sea Company, 253–255
Sparks, Daniel, 68
Special-purpose entities (SPEs), 287
Special purpose vehicles (SPVs), 25
SPEs and. *See* Special-purpose entities (SPEs)
SPVs. *See* Special purpose vehicles (SPVs)
Stable value contracts, 145
Statutory law of derivatives. *See* U.S.
   derivatives rulemaking
Structured products, accounting practices
   and, 49–51
Subprime residential mortgage lending, 271,
   282–283
Survey of derivatives:
   CDOs and CDOs squared, 345–347
   commodity derivatives, 343–344
   credit derivatives, 329–335

credit-linked notes/securities, 335–336
currency derivatives, 340–342
early derivatives/OTC market beginnings,
   320
energy swaps, 344–345
equity swaps, 339–340
exchange-traded derivatives, 347–348
exchange-traded options, 327–328
forwards vs. options, 320–322
generally, 317–318, 348–349
interest rate swaps, 337–339
option basics, 322–324
options pricing, 324–326
option strategies, basic, 326–327
overview, strategies/trade structure,
   319–320
property derivatives, 342–343
structured products/securitization,
   345–347
swaps follow options, 329
total return swaps, 336–337
Swan, Edward J., 237, 247, 251, 260–261
Swap(s):
   abusive, 159
   banking products and, 145–146, 176
   centrally cleared, 115
   CFTC regulation of, 138, 139–140
   credit default (*see* Credit default swaps
      (CDSs))
   energy, 344–345
   equity, 339–340
   exclusions from term, 140
   following options, 329
   formally recognized, U.S., 273–274
   interest rate, 337–339
   mixed, SEC/CFTC jurisdiction, 142
   security-based (*see* Security-based swaps
      (SBSs))
   statutory laws, 73–75
   Title VII overview of, 137–138
   total return, 336–337
Swap data repositories (SDRs), 151, 158,
   305
Swap execution facilities (SEFs), 171–172,
   305–307

Taxpayers, Title VII:
   Dealers (*see* Dealers/major participants,
      obligations)
   generally, 163–164
   major swap participants, 155, 162–163